Savely Dudakov

The History of a Myth
Essays on Russian Literature of XIX–XX century

Edited by Nina Stavisky and Michael Golubovsky
Translated from Russian by Anna Tucker

Boston ♦ 2021

Savely Dudakov

The History of a Myth
Essays on Russian Literature of XIX–XX century

Edited by Nina Stavisky and Michael Golubovsky
Translated from Russian by Anna Tucker

Copyright © 2021 by Estate of S. Dudakov

All rights reserved. No part of this book may be reproduced, stored in a retrieval system, or transmitted by any means, electronic, mechanical, photocopying, recording, or otherwise, without written permission from the copyright holder(s), except for the brief passages quoted for review.

ISBN 978-1-950319435
Library of Congress Control Number 2021935768

Book Design by M·Graphics © 2021
Cover Design by Larisa Studinskaya © 2021

Published by M·Graphics | Boston, MA
 www.mgraphics-books.com
 info@mgraphics-books.com
  mgraphics.books@gmail.com

Printed in the U.S.A.

Contents

EFIM ETKIND: *In Place of Foreword* 1

PREFACE
SEMYON REZNIK: *A Forgery of the Tsarist Secret Police
  from the Perspective of the Twenty-First Century* 3

INTRODUCTION 15
  Anti-Judaic Literature in Old Rus' 17
  *The Penetration of Freemasonry into Russia and
    Anti-Masonic Literature of the Eighteenth Century* 26
  The Pale of Settlement 34

CHAPTER 1
THE WAR OF 1812 AND DENUNCIATION "OF ALL RUSSIA"
  Poles and Jews 41
  The Blood Libel and Ritual Accusations 50
  Russian Freemasonry and Sectarianism 55

CHAPTER 2
THE GREAT SECRET OF FREEMASONS
  The Jewish Question and Russian Literature 65
  F. V. Bulgarin's Novel "Ivan Vyzhigin" 71
  The Real Vyzhigin (J. E. Przecławski) 78
  The Provocateur's Catechism 85
  Acta Proconsularia 92

CHAPTER 3
ZEALOTS
  Pan-Germanism and Pan-Slavism 96
  I. A. Brafman's "Kahal Book" 104
  Satan's Elixir 108
  Gog and Magog (B. M. Markevich and V. V. Krestovsky) ... 117
  "The Yid is Coming" 127

Chapter 4
Enemies of the Human Race
Agent Provocateur (S.K. Efron-Litvin) 134
The Transfiguration of Satan 141
The "Satanic Affair" (S.A. Nilus) 149
"A Concentrated Universal Force" 154
Apostle of Heresy 166

Chapter 5
Twentieth-Century Satanists
Spiders (E.A. Shabelskaya) 173
Between Two Wars 186
Occultist Executioners 194

Chapter 6
The Soviet Version of Anti-Semitism
Reanimation 200
Chronic Totalitarianism 204

Conclusion 230

Addendum
The Protocols of the Elders of Zion (short overview) 233
The Evil Storyteller (N.P. Wagner) 246

Notes and Literature 265

Bibliography 315

Principal Works of S. Dudakov 333

Index 336

In the early XX century a fake document titled *The Protocols of the Elders of Zion* rose from the depths of the Russian secret police. This falsification was spread by the White emigres and greatly affected Hitler's ideas and the Nazi practices. Although European sources, which are included in the body of the fake and which date back to the XIX century, had been found, it remained unclear why *The Protocols* surfaced in Russia of all places.

In this book an Israeli historian and culturologist Savely Dudakov (1939–2017) conducts a detailed research of this issue. He was the first to dig out the branches of Russian religious, anti-Judaic, and anti-Masonic literature and a wide range of pulp fiction of the mid- and late-XIX century from under the boulders of time.

He brought to light the main mythologems of the fake in the form of a "Judeo-Masonic conspiracy theory." Dudakov's work provides a long list of publications, many of which are included into historical literature and scholarship for the first time.

The propaganda of *The Protocols* ideas lives on as anti-Semitism, "fight against Zionism," and Islamic fundamentalism. This makes *The History of a Myth* a work of current interest.

IN PLACE OF A FOREWORD

EFIM ETKIND
Honorary Professor of Paris Nanterre University

(From review of the first Russian edition, Moscow 1993)

Savely Dudakov's work presents a wide-ranging research dedicated to the history of social thought and literature in Russia in the XIX and XX centuries. The subject chosen by the author had never been researched by historians as a whole, although separate essays on certain time periods do exist. However, there had been no generalized picture of the development of the anti-Judaic thinking, therefore this work is a great achievement of S. Dudakov.

The four volumes of *L'histoire de l'antisémitisme* by Leon Poliakov is a purely historical work and as such cannot compete with the research of S. Dudakov. Besides, Dudakov gives brief but deep and accurate characterizations of a number of interesting authors. Among them are J. Przecławski — the pages dedicated to him are brilliant, N. Y. Danilevsky, Y. Brafman, B. M. Markevich, Vs. Krestovsky, S. K. Efron-Litvin, S. A. Nilus et al. Every one of these authors deserves a serious study, despite the vulgarity and ridiculousness of their ideas and theories. S. Dudakov, as a rule, can present the views alien to him with surprising calm, balance, and logic.

The reader shall learn that each of the above-mentioned authors is a villain, with pogroms and prison camps on his conscience as a result of a seemingly abstract discourse, the reader shall learn it from an austere historical narration, because the author does not impose his emotions on the reader and does not allow himself either sarcasm or derogatory phrases. Some of these authors we barely remember, or know of them only from doubtful sources. For example, Boleslav Markevich has been completely forgotten as an anti-Judaic novelist. *The Concise Literary Encyclopedia* (1967) informs us that he had reported the activists of the liberation movement, cruelly bullied Saltykov-Shchedrin, the *narodniks* and Turgenev, and wrote anti-nihilistic novels with aristocratic monarchists as protagonists.

We know that the word "Jew" was unofficially banned in Brezhnev's time. However, the entry for Markevich seems almost comical: it means that Markevich cannot be labeled as anti-Semitist.

But this was his main trait! Markevich is known in Russian literary history due to the fact that A. K. Tolstoy counted him as his closest friend and wrote many highly meaningful letters to him. S. Dudakov notes quite fairly that A. K. Tolstoy disapproved of his friend's racism.

The traditions of the XIX century, however, were such that irreconcilable ideological opponents could remain friends and respect and even love one another.

S. Dudakov analyses the views of Russian authors very well, and even wisely, and does not agree with the common opinion of their treatment of Jews. His study of A. S. Pushkin's poem *A Black Shawl* is convincing as well as his analysis of N. V. Gogol's *Taras Bulba*.

PREFACE

A Forgery of the Tsarist Secret Police from the Perspective of Twenty-First Century

Semyon Reznik
Washington

The book "Anti-Semitic Literature of the XIX–XX centuries and *The Protocols of the Elders of Zion*" occupies the central spot in the significant and very substantive literary legacy of the Israeli historian, writer, and scholar of literature Savely Dudakov (1939–2017). It is based on the material of his Grand PhD thesis that Dudakov had defended at the University of Jerusalem.

The book was first published in Moscow in 1993 by the publishing house "Nauka." This miracle happened mostly thanks to the efforts of Savely's close friend, D. A. Chernyakhovsky. A renowned Moscow psychiatrist and a man of vast knowledge and various interests, Chernyakhovsky had many friends and acquaintances, some of them leading scientists and scholars. He collected several reviews of Savely Dudakov's manuscript from most respectable and influential scholars, among them a well-known linguist and culturologist, a corresponding member of the Russian Academy of Sciences (and later an academician) S. S. Averintsev. The reviews were such that the leading publisher of the Academy of Sciences could not reject the manuscript. The book saw light as generally edited by D. A. Chernyakhovsky, but not under the author's title. The title was *The History of a Myth* and the subtitle was *Essays on Russian Literature of the Nineteenth and Twentieth Centuries.* A short editor's abstract on the flipside of the title page said:

"The author of the book being offered to the reader, a famous Israeli scholar Savely Dudakov, has analysed consistently and in detail the specifics of the development of literature and of social and political thought in Russia in the second half of the nineteenth and early twentieth century. He pays special attention to mass popular fiction of the time, such as the works by forgotten authors of the 'second rank' — Vs. Krestovsky, B. Markevich, S. Efron, N. Wagner, et al."

So, what is the book about?

As I was informed by a close friend of Savely Dudakov, Professor Mikhail Golubovsky, the back of the cover had another abstract that said that *The Protocols of the Elders of Zion* was a fake forged by the Tsar's secret police. Not much of a surprise there, but before the book was published, Chernyakhovsky was ordered to replace the cover, lest the printed copies be destroyed. The situation was saved by an artist who suggested a truly Solomonic solution: to remove the abstract. This was done. "For two days the members of the historical editing team and even some of their family members were wiping the unfortunate abstract off five thousand copies with cotton balls soaked in acetone!" (S. Dudakov. In: *Sketches of Love and Hate*. M. 2003).

Remember that this happened in the post-Soviet times, during Eltsin's presidency. Censorship had long been eliminated and freedom of speech and *glasnost* had reached their peak. Nevertheless, the leading publisher of the Academy of Sciences that ventured to print this book, was preparing it for printing frightened by its own audacity.

Why? What were the publishers afraid of?

The answer to this question may be the book itself. It researches the underlying processes that formed an important part of Russia's social consciousness and spirituality, the things that Russian "patriots" are so proud of. But Dudakov sets a mirror in front of their eyes...

The book analyses in detail the facts that prepared and made possible the arrival of *The Protocols of the Elders of Zion*, the main anti-Semitic fraud of the XX century that a renowned American researcher Norman Cohn called "a blessing for genocide."

It is widely believed that *The Protocols of the Elders of Zion* were first published by Sergei Nilus as an addendum to the second edition of his book *The Great within the Small* that came out in 1905. The same year *The Protocols* were published by Georgy Butmi. The title of his book is very simple and expressive: *The Enemies of the Human Race. The protocols of the Elders of Zion* are framed here by a large preface and conclusion by the author. The text of *The Protocols* differs stylistically, but not essentially, from that of Nilus.

However, the very first publication of *The Protocols*, under a no less expressive title "The Jewish Program for Conquering the World," took place two years previously in ten issues of the newspaper "Znamya" (23 August — 7 September, 1903). The owner and chief editor of the paper was Pavel Alexandrovich Krushevan (1860–1909), one of the leading ideologists of the Black Hundred and the inspirer of the bloody Kishinev pogrom that shook the world in April of the same year, 1903. It was not easy for him to publish *The Protocols*, since strict censorship rules were still in action and it prohibited "setting of certain groups of the population against others." Krushevan managed to gain an audience with the all-powerful Minister of Internal Affairs von Plehve, and received his permission to circumvent the censorship committee. The comparison of the newspaper text with the two book texts shows that Krushevan, most likely, received the manuscript from Butmi rather than Nilus.

Creation of *The Protocols* is still shrouded in many layers of mystery. The original text of the forgery was in French, but that manuscript has not survived. Stylistic differences between the text of Krushevan/Butmi and that of Nilus lead us to believe that two independent Russian translations existed. The client was P. I. Rachkovsky, the head of the foreign department of Russian Security and a seasoned provocateur. The executors were two well-known journalists and secret agents of the same Security, M. Golovinsky and I. Manasevich-Manuilov.

Works on the origins of *The Protocols* mention other candidates for this role. One of them is Elias von Cyon, a man who lived two lives: that of an outstanding physiologist and reputable opinion journalist and that of a scandalous international adventurist who became a personal enemy of the Minister of Finance S. Yu. Witte. The persistent idea of *The Protocols,* that of Say the almighty gold that "Elders of Zion" use to corrupt and enslave the *goyim*, is illustrated by such details that there can be no doubt that those were shots fired at Witte and his financial policy, which was aimed at strengthening the ruble and backing it by gold.

According to one theory, an illegal pamphlet against Witte was confiscated from von Cyon, in which was described a "Jewish conspiracy" to enslave the world with the help of gold and corrupting the masses with liberal rhetoric on brotherhood, equality, human rights, etc. This hypothesis is based on the fact that von Cyon did not shun forgeries and hoaxes, and some ideas of *The Protocols* echoed his early pamphlets. If so, Rachkovsky and his cronies had to perfect von

Cyon's draft in the way that turned the Russian Minister of Finance into "Elders of Zion."[1]

In his other book, *Sketches of Love and Hate* (M. 2003, pp. 262–282) Savely Dudakov analyses in detail the arguments for and against von Cyon's participation in the creation of *The Protocols of the Elders of Zion* and leans towards a legal formula of "released but remains under strong suspicion."

There is still no final answer to the question of who fabricated *The Protocols*. It is still unclear what part the above mentioned or any other unknown persons played in it. This is, as well, the conclusion of the author of the most recent detailed study of the origins of *The Protocols*, the French culturologist Pierre-Andre Taguieff (*Les Protocoles des sages de Sion. Faux et usages d'un faux/ "Protokoly sionskikh mudretsov: falshivka i yeyo ispolzovaniye*. Gesharim/Bridging Cultures. 2011). One thing is beyond doubt: the first publishers of *The Protocols* and those who set it on the road to life were Krushevan, Butmi, and Nilus.

Whereas Nilus was a religious man who lived as a hermit and spent time visiting monasteries and socializing with elders, Holy Fools, miracle workers and other "God's people," Butmi was a man earthly and politically active. In a short time, he published a series of booklets called "Denunciation speeches" which he solemnly dedicated to the Union of the Russian People. In this series appeared the book *Enemies of the Human Race* with *The Protocols of the Elders of Zion* at its center. In two years, he republished this book at least four times.[2] This does not go well with the opinion that in pre-Revolution Russia *The Protocols* were not in demand and were even banned by the government.[3]

However, around 1908 Butmi's name disappeared from every source and *The Protocols* in his edition were never printed again, while Nilus re-printed his book in 1911 and 1917.

Nilus's book was a favorite of the Empress Alexandra Fyodorovna. She brought it with her in her exile and never parted with it until the very night of the royal family's execution in Yekaterinburg on July 16, 1918.

---

[1] Norman Kohn. *Warrant for Genocide. The myth of Jewish world-conspiracy and the Protocols of the Elders of Zion.* Harper & Row Publishers, NY and Evanston, 1967, P. 106

[2] G. Butmi. *Oblichitelniye Rechi. Vragi Roda Chelovecheskogo. Posvyashchayetsya Soyuzu Russkogo Naroda.* Fourth Edition, revised and amended. S.-Pb., 1907.

[3] First expressed in the book: *Yu. Delevsky. Protokoly Sionskikh Mudretsov (Istoriya Odnogo Podloga).* With Foreword by A. V. Kartashov, "Epokha," Berlin, 1923.

After the Bolshevik revolt, the Black Hundred propaganda insisted that what had been planned by "the elders of Zion" finally happened in Russia. The Black Hundred-leaning ideologists greatly influenced the propaganda machine of the White movement. Nilus's version of *The Protocols* began spreading. The two hundred thousand victims of Jewish pogroms during the Civil War were the result of the first stage of "the protocols" orgy.

After the defeat of the White movement *The Protocols* were taken to the West and were used to explain the Russian turmoil. Shortly, they were translated into the main European languages and caused significant excitement. In the United States, the automobile king Henry Ford (1863–1947), in 1920, sponsored publication of half a million copies of *The Protocols*. After that, they were reprinted in the newspaper he patronized, and later these articles were compiled into a book *The International Jew* that was published under Ford's name.[4]

The Protocols influenced not only extreme anti-Semitists or naive simpletons. Having read the book, Winston Churchill said that now he understood what had happened in Russia and who was directing the Bolshevik bosses. The London newspaper *The Times* seriously wrote that, having won WWI, Great Britain avoided German domination but could be facing a more frightening threat of enslavement by Jews.[5]

However, this enchantment did not last. In August of 1921, in Constantinople, another correspondent of *The Times,* Philip Graves, met a Russian refugee, a former landowner, who during the Civil War had served the leadership of Denikin's army and searched for the proof of the authenticity of *The Protocols*. During his research, he came across a rare book by the French opinion journalist Maurice Joly published in 1864, *The Dialogue in Hell Between Machiavelli and Montesquieu*. This was sharp satire aimed at the hypocritical regime of Napoleon III who had camouflaged his despotism with liberal rhetoric.

In *the Dialogue*, the secret thoughts of Louis Napoleon are voiced by Machiavelli and the liberal views — by Montesquieu. The Florentian

---

[4] Many social organizations of the USA, including the Presidents of the USA Woodrow Wilson and Theodore Roosevelt, signed petitions against Ford's anti-Semitic campaign. The journalist Herman Bernstein and the banker A. Shapiro sued Ford for libel and moral damage to the Jewish diaspora of the USA. Savely Dudakov specifically mentions that in 1927 Ford had to pay reparations to Bernstein, to apologize to all the Jews of the country in the name of L. Marshall, and to announce the confiscation and ban on future publication of the book "The International Jew." — *(Note by the Editors)*.

[5] *The Times*, May 5, 1920, quoted from: Norman Kohn, mentioned work, Pp. 71, 152–153.

wins, for he once discovered the secret of any autocracy: to hold and strengthen his despotic power, the Ruler must not say what he really thinks but that which is expected of him at the moment; he must give promises freely, yet break them as easily, if necessary; otherwise, he is ruined.

Graves was astounded to see that *The Protocols of the Elders of Zion* was an overhaul of Maurice Joly's pamphlet. Self-denouncing speeches put by Joly in the mouth of Machiavelli (Louis Napoleon) were turned into cunning schemes of "the elders of Zion." Philip Graves told about this in three issues of *The Times*.[6]

A little earlier, in the USA, a small book by renowned journalist and translator Herman Bernstein (1876–1935) *History of a Lie* was published. In this book, Bernstein showed that the main ideas of *The Protocols* were borrowed from the fictional novel *Biarritz* by Sir John Retcliffe (a.k.a. Hermann Goedsche (1815–1878)). In the novel, there is a chapter that describes a meeting in the night at the Jewish cemetery in Prague where a rabbi rises from the grave to share with his co-believers the secret plan for conquering the world.[7] As Savely Dudakov points out, this excerpt called "The Jewish Cemetery in Prague and the Council of the Representatives of the Twelve Tribes of Israel" was published in Russian back in 1872. Therefore, *The Protocols of the Elders of Zion* are double plagiarism: the text by Maurice Joly is combined with the phantasmagory by Goedsche/Retcliffe.

However, only very naive people could think that the discovery of the truth about this forgery would stop people from being interested in it. *The Protocols* were utilized by Adolf Hitler and his party, at first tiny and comical. With its strengthening in Germany and the appearance of similar parties in other countries, the influence of *The Protocols* was once more on the rise. They were reprinted over and over not only in Germany, but also in France, Italy, Poland, Switzerland, and other countries.

In 1934, in Bern, the origin of *The Protocols* became the subject of a court hearing. One of the testimonies was given by a famous Russian political emigration activist, the unmasker of secret agents of the Tsarist security, and later a staunch enemy of Bolshevism, Vladimir Burtsev. After the process he wrote and published a book, in which he not only demonstrated the false nature of *The Protocols*, but also

---

[6] *The Times*, August 16–18, 1921, quoted from Norman Kohn, mentioned work, P. 72.
[7] Ref: Herman Bernstein. *The Truth About "The Protocols of Zion." A Complete Exposure*. Introduction by Norman Cohn. KTAV, N.Y., 1971.

revealed the details of the forgery. The book's title clearly speaks for its content: "*The Protocols of the Elders of Zion* is a proven forgery. (Rachkovsky forged *The Protocols of the Elders of Zion* and Hitler made them globally famous)."[8] It could not be clearer.

Alas, to the adherents of *The Protocols* authenticity, any unmasking of the forgery was water off a duck's back. "I once again thoroughly studied the "Zion Protocols." Today I talked to the Fuehrer about them. He agrees with me that the "Zion Protocols" can be considered absolutely authentic," Josef Goebbels wrote in his journal on Thursday, May 13, 1943.

The Protocols are 115 years old and their obvious falseness has been known for nearly a hundred years, and yet this weapon of mass destruction kept crushing human lives after its denunciation as well as before. Today, they are still published and quoted, and continue to require fresh sacrifices.

Anti-Semitism is an international phenomenon, which is proven by the history of creation and spread of *The Protocols*. The virus of hatred for the "minor people" crosses seas and oceans, deserts and mountains, as well as national, ethnic, and language borders. This is one side of the coin. The flip side is that in order to cultivate and multiply the "protocol" virus a well-prepared nutrient medium is necessary. In the absence of a nutrient medium the virus cannot multiply enough to cause an epidemic.

Savely Dudakov's primary attention is focused on hundreds of years of preparing this medium in Russia and it becoming more and more concentrated and sharp smelling. Although the subtitle sets the boundaries at the XIX–XX centuries, the book encompasses almost a thousand years, from the Baptism of Rus' to the later Soviet era. The main method of Savely Dudakov is uncovering the secondary layer of the great Russian literature.

We all know the creations of Pushkin, Lermontov, Turgenev, Tolstoy, Dostoyevsky, Chekhov, Bunin, Bulgakov, and other authors of the front rank: this is a part of our common spiritual experience as well as that of any educated person. But these are just the tops. At the time when these great writers lived and created, works by other authors were widely published. Some of those were successful and influenced the shaping of the moods and minds of the Russian society as a whole.

If we remember the name of Faddei Bulgarin, it is the name of a snitch and a bastard who poisoned the life of the great Pushkin.

---

[8] Oreste Zeluk Editeur; Paris; 1938.

However, in Pushkin's time Bulgarin was a well-known publisher, opinion journalist, and writer. His novel *Ivan Vyzhygin* was very popular and actively influenced the reading public. A significant place in it is taken by a narration about Jewish way of life. "Only through swindlery, robbery, and cheating could Jews become wealthy, and, despised and persecuted, they became the masters of Westland": this is the sum total of the ideological content of Bulgarin's novel according to Savely Dudakov.

He researched biographies and creations by such authors as Josef Przecławski, B. M. Markevich, Vs. S. Krestovsky, the author of the slandering *Book of Qahal* A. Brafman, another convert and renegade S. K. Efron, G. Bostunich, and the great adventurist E. A. Shabelskaya.

The book mentions other long-forgotten fiction and opinion writers that sowed in the masses the seeds of heavy prejudice, malice, and hatred.

Savely Dudakov's book shows how, under the brisk quills of these writers, the ancient religious intolerance of Hebrews gradually, consistently, and, I would say, relentlessly turned "enemies of Christ" into enemies of Russia and of the entire human race; how your garden variety disdain towards clever, semi-destitute ragpickers mixed with fierce envy of successful "Rothschilds" turned into the schizophrenic idea of a Yiddo-Masonic conspiracy against thrones and altars; and how it culminated in *The Protocols of the Elders of Zion*.

The notion of "anti-Semitism" itself was first introduced by a German opinion writer, Wilhelm Marr, in 1879, in his book *The Way to Victory of Germanism over Judaism*. The term became widely used not only in Germany, but also in France, Spain, and other European countries. This was explained by the fact that the traditional religious intolerance of Jews, i.e., *Judeophobia*, had by then become ineffective, since the social mindset of both Christians and Jews became more secular.

Jews were allowed into high society gatherings and professional organizations; their participation in cultural activity, journalism, and social life had significantly increased. Those who continued to hate Jews for "crucifying Christ" and "drinking the blood of Christian infants," etc., were looked at as fools mired in backwood medieval prejudice. The hatred of Jews demanded a weightier, modern, and "scientific" basis. It was found in racial theories according to which human races are divided into those of higher and lower value. The lower ones, doomed to pitiful surviving, were all "colored" peoples: black, yellow, and red...

These lower races also included "Semites," meaning the descendants of Shem, the oldest son of Noah the forefather. Most of them were Arabs that populated the countries of the Middle East; they could be despised and discriminated against mostly long-distance.

However, their "first cousins," Jews, lived nearby; and, since to hate them as *infidels* became outdated, the term "anti-Semitism" provided the opportunity to treat them as worthless *aliens*. Besides, it did not allow Jews to avoid persecution by converting to Christianity; if you were *genetically* low, it was forever.

Russia was special in the fact that anti-Semitism here did not replace religious intolerance but added to it. It is known that the mass pogroms of the 1880s and of the early XX century often happened in the name of God. Pogrom mobs would advance on Jewish quarters armed not only with pitchforks and crowbars, but also with gonfalons, religious chanting, and priests' blessing.

The religious component of *The Protocols of the Elders of Zion* is particularly deeply studied in Savely Dudakov's book.

If asked what the most specific feature of this book is, I would say it is overflowing with knowledge. It contains and conceptualizes vast literary and historic material that has been thoroughly studied and digested by the author.

This book is a powerful remedy for illusions. It is greatly necessary for the Jews who strive to understand the fate of their people in Russia. But it is no less necessary for Russia. For Jews, this narration is a terrible, cruel, bloody past that cannot be fixed, but must and can be understood and overcome. It is even more important for Russia itself to understand and overcome this past, for this is tightly connected with its future. Russia will not become a truly free and prosperous country, until it sorts out, soberly and objectively, the dark side of its "spirituality." Judeophobia that culminated in *The Protocols of the Elders of Zion* has for centuries intoxicated and continues to intoxicate the social consciousness of a great country. Only by getting rid of this intoxication and by cutting these bonds, Russia will be able to truly liberate itself and "join humanity" (Chaadayev). I know of no other book that would demonstrate this as conclusively and convincingly as this book by Savely Dudakov.

In memory of Professor Shmuel Ettinger

INTRODUCTION

Despite many facts proven by modern scholarship of borrowings from Western European sources such as des Mousseaux, Joly, Drumont, Goedsche et al. and of outright plagiarism (about 40% of the text according to P. N. Milyukov), [1] the historical and literary reasons for *The Protocols of the Elders of Zion*'s appearance on the Russian soil *still remain* unexamined.

The wide popularity of this "classic" work of S. A. Nilus in the modern, especially Arabic, world and the reanimation of ideas of "police" authorship in the so-called anti-Zionist works of Soviet authors determine the specific goals and tasks of this research dedicated to one of the most modern theories of misanthropy.

The political mythology of the modern anti-Semites can be divided into two incongruent historical and literary traditions that flow in different directions. On one hand, Nilus's plagiarism is presented as original because the birth and growth of the Judeo-Masonic conspiracy myth in the literary creations of the Russian "patriots" since the end of the XVIII century has been completely ignored. On the other hand, drawing the reader's attention to the Western European roots of *The Protocols* allows for them to be declared something of a generally recognized doctrine that does not require any additional proof of the existence of such Jewish conspiracy against the rest of the world.

Therefore, understanding the Russian nature and origins of *The Protocols of the Elders of Zion* presents a most important problem in the history of anti-Semitic ideas.

That is why the author offers us neither yet another list of references to new results of dating back *The Protocol's* publication nor a collection of abstracts and quotes that would allow us to determine who *The Protocol's* author was, but an original concept of *messiano-fictitious* development of anti-Semitic ideas in Russia, which, unlike the pasquinades and lampoons of the European writers of the XIX century, culminated in the work of S. A. Nilus's that won the minds and hearts at the era of totalitarianism and genocides.

Due to multiple instances of uncovering the forgery of *The Protocols* by Russian critics (P. Milyukov, V. Burtsev, [2] Yu. Delevsky [3] et al) as well is in Rollin's [4] work and a fundamental research by N. Konn, [5] the "police" origins of *The Protocols* are beyond any doubt. However, since anti-Semitic ideas in Russia have not been researched enough and the Russian anti-Semitic pulp fiction of the second half of the XIX century and the first quarter of the XX century (B. Markevich, Vs. Krestovsky, N. Wagner et al) has been largely forgotten, the problem of the creation of *The Protocols* has been researched quite randomly and in anti-historical fashion.

As a result, the principles of adhering to historical truth in literary research were abandoned. At the same time, it is well known that Shakespeare's borrowing from Danish and Italian sources does not make his plays either Danish or Italian. That is why the scholars of Shakespeare quite naturally looked for answers in the history of *English* literature and not in the foreign sources.

The situation is very similar when it comes to the Russian origins of *The Protocols*. The answer here should be sought not with John Retcliff or Maurice Joly, but in the memoirs of O. Przecławski and novels of Vs. Krestovsky. The geo-political ideals of pan-Germanism and pan-Slavism were *the consequence* of real historic events focused first on the confrontation between Russia and France and later Russia and Germany in the *mid*-XIX century that by the end of the century were transformed into a confrontation between the Orthodox "Messiah-chosen" Russia and the Jesuit Catholic — Masonic Republican — Jewish Capitalist Europe.

The triumphant expansion to Europe of the strictly Russian interpretation of the Judeo-Masonic conspiracy theory was a direct consequence of the Bolshevik revolution, which inherited the Messianic geo-political role of Russia (by then the USSR), and that could not but lead to a new confrontation between the *prison for its people* and Europe.

Thus, the methodological basis for this research is comprised of its *concept*, its scholarly *analysis* with *the aid* from historic-fictional material that is not widely known even to specialists, the study of *historical and literary logical sequence* of the work by the forgotten authors of the previous century, and *a sketch of the creative works* of the modern Soviet authors, whose names and works cannot be listed in full in a research of this size.

The author pays special attention to the historiographic analysis of the works that contain, to a different degree, the definitions of the im-

INTRODUCTION

perial treatment of Jews in Russian as well as of the Judeo-Masonic conspiracy theory.

Supported by the works of L. Polyakov, [6] the author presents the Russian origins of *The Protocols* as a crucial part of the development of Judeophobic ideas and connects the literary heritage of the authors of delations and denunciations as well as the appearance of these ideas in pulp fiction, with certain characteristics of the specific historic-political situation.

It should be noted that the research of this problem was built on the chronological description of facts and phenomena, which, naturally, influenced the stages of this work and chapters of the research:

1. Socio-political thought of the late XVII — early XIX century and the origins of the Judeo-Masonic conspiracy theory in Russia.
2. Pulp fiction styling of anti-Semitic ideas in the Russian literature of the second half of the XIX century.
3. "Documentary truth" and "factography" of testimonies in a physiological sketch of 1870–90s.
4. The revolutionary tendencies in Russia and "protective" literature.
5. *The Protocols of the Elders of Zion* in modern totalitarian societies.

Of course, an essay on the anti-Semitic literature of the XI–XV centuries, as well as a description of masonic literature at the time of the rise of the Russian Empire, form a necessary and logical introduction to the topic. The socio-ideological analysis of the creative works of the Soviet anti-Semitic authors logically summarizes the development of the myth of a world-wide Jewish conspiracy.

ANTI-JUDAIC LITERATURE IN OLD RUS'

Anti-Judaic polemic literature (polemic in a religious, not an ethnic sense) appeared in Russia immediately after the spread of Christianity. The import of the old Bulgarian and Greek (Byzantian) literary samples contributed to the fast development of copycat and compilation genres, that led finally to chronicles and later to apologetic collections.

The Byzantian type of Christianization of Russia was supposed to generate in Russian scholars the desire to justify the "grace" of enlightenment.

At the same time, unlike in the era of early Christianity in the Western and Eastern Roman Empire, where the apologetics of the new teaching had to face a strongest resistance of the enforcers of the "law" (let us remind you that the first Christian propagandists came from Judaic circles), Russia not only was unfamiliar with Judaic tradition, but had a very vague idea of Hebrews themselves. [7]

That was the reason for the appearance of abstract anti-Judaic ideas in the Old Russian literature: Jews were neither threatening proselytism (forbidden in their circles), nor too great a presence (the Jewish settlement in Kiev in the early XII century was small in numbers and, consequently, not a competition). [8] So the Kiev pogrom of 1113 and the following "Princes ruling" during the reign of Vladimir Monomakh to banish Jews from the Kyivan Rus' should be considered first and foremost a *Christian* (religious) act and not economic and political (xenophobic) one: "For if the Lord loved you and your Law, you would not be scattered in the strange lands. Do you also expect to be accepted by us?" [9]

Chronicles in Old Rus' undoubtedly were born due to familiarization with foreign examples. Thus, talking about Yaroslav Vladimirovich, who loved reading books "at night and in the day," the chronist noted that the Prince "gathered many scribes to translate from Greek to Slavic. And they translated many books..." [10]

A special place among "the many books" was taken by *The Chronicle* by John Malalas (Ἰωαννμζ Μαλαλαζ) and *The Chronicle of George Hamartolos* (Χρονικον τον Γεωργιου Ἁμαρτωλον), which consisted of a small introduction and four chapters.

Malalas' *Chronicle* was consequently recognized as pagan, hence its later title *The Hellenic Chronographia*.

However, its first chapter turned out to be a sort of an introduction to the ancient Russian list of the XIII century that is known under the title *The Archive Chronographia*. It is possible that the editor of *The Archive Chronographia*, pursuing his anti-Judaic goals and putting a "Hellenic" history next to Joseph Flavius's *The Judea War*, knew the opinion of the editor of the so-called *Hellenic and Roman Chronicle*, for whom pre-Christian history was "a whore-like tangle of words."

Things were different with the chronicle of George Monachos "Hamartolos," which to large extent became an example for Russian chroniclers compiling the history of their motherland. Combining in its narration different layers: historical accounts of events, philosophical and theological contemplations, episodes of monastic life and assorted "testimonies" (evidence of orthodoxy) of Christian faith, *The Chronicle of Hamartolos* became the "main source of chronicles."

INTRODUCTION

The many tales of miracles in *The Chronicle* were built along a traditional plot scheme. Typically, an equality sign was set between pagans and Hebrews, and consequently the "savior" from troubles (illness, danger, catastrophe) was always a true believer, meaning a Christian who performed a miracle and so converted the "stray" ones to his faith.

Frequent in *The Chronicle* are arguments about faith, in which the winner is a Christian who performs a "commonplace miracle." Thus, for example, in the tale of Bishop Sylvester it says that Zambry the Hebrew wishes to prove the might of his God and says His name in the ear of a bull that was "held by many men, tied up all over, fierce and very large" and the bull immediately "bucked and inhaled sharply, with his eyes bulging, expired."

Silvester, in the presence of the Caesar, tells the Hebrews that the bull's death is not proof of the might of the Hebrew God, because "the name of the Devil killed the bull" and with the name of Christ the dead bull will come back to life and he "raising his hands to the heavens and praying with tears in his eyes... says: 'I call Your name in front of all people, Christ...'" The bull immediately comes back to life and the Hebrews promptly ask to be baptized. That was "the great joy" that was given them, for great is the "God of Christians." [11]

In another story, a "Yid," a glass blower, upon learning that his son "with Christian children went to church and ate of the bread," "cast him into a burning glass furnace." However, aware of her fanatic husband's "madness towards the youth," the boy's mother enters the furnace and leads out the youth alive and unharmed, for "a wife... come and quell the fire..." The king sentences the glass blower to death not only for the abuse of his son, but for the refusal of the fanatic Hebrew to accept Christianity. [12]

It is not difficult to notice that such tales were meant to confirm the final victory of Christianity over the children of "the slave law," meaning Hebrews.

This is what *The Chronicle of Hamartolos* was about. That is why the arrival to Rus' from Byzantium of "many books" that were created in the era of the *early spread* of Christianity in the pagan world provoked in Russian neophytes an interest not only to the Biblical history of Jews, but also to the history of the fall of Israel and the destruction of its statehood.

And the negative attitude towards everything "Hebrew" (Old Testament) was the point of departure.

V. M. Istrin noted: "The polemic against the Jewish teachings had to have taken place in Old Rus'.

"Of course, Jews were not much inclined to spread their teachings; however, the Khazar Khagan in the VIII century accepted Judaism and, according to a chronicler, the Khazar Hebrews sent their emissaries to Prince Vladimir with suggestions to convert to their faith.

"Whether any of Greek anti-Judaic treatises were translated into Slavic in the ancient times (XI and XII centuries), remains currently unknown. In the old Russian literature, there existed one such treatise, namely *Dialogue of Grégence de Safar with the Jew Erban* that is attached to his *Life*...

"Aside from this *Dialogue*, in the old Russian literature there was another treatise *Teaching of Jacob* containing a discussion between Jacob, a baptized Jew, with other Jews, also baptized, but forcibly, and therefore doubting the truth of the Christian faith. The discussion took place in Carthage in the VII century, during the reign of Heraclius.

"It is not known when this document was translated. Finally, among the manuscripts there exists a collection of speeches by John Chrysostom against Jews, known under the title of *Margarite*, but the time and place of the first appearance of this collection remains unknown." [13]

We shall note that before 1113 *The Primary Chronicle* had already been compiled that included *The Tale of the Baptism of Rus'*, [14] and scribes knew *The Word* of the first Mitropolite Hilarion (*Sermon on Law and Grace*). [15]

Moreover, the first crusades which ended in 1099 with the "liberation" of Jerusalem from Muslims (but not Jews), helped, apparently, to spread the theory of the final "rejection of Yids."

Only in this context of historical events and of the old Russian writings that have reached us we can explain not only the pogrom in Kyiv, but the appearance of anti-Judaic literature in the provinces far away from the Jewish diaspora.

It is not accidental that after 1113, namely after *banishing* the Jews from the Kyivan Rus', who "together with others began to migrate to the Rostov-Suzdal' lands, and while describing the funeral of Andrei Bogolyubsky (1175) the chronicler also mentions the Jews" [16], the first actually anti-Judaic tales appear — *Explanatory Palea* and *Archival (or Judaic) Chronograph* (XIII century).

V. M. Istrin, noting that the compiler of *Explanatory Palea* demonstrated "vast literary knowledge and a great skill in using it for his particular goal," firmly believed (despite the fact that "we do not have any documental proof of that") that the reason for the creation of *Explanatory Palea* was the "spiritual and religious excitement in the Jewish circles" (for example, awaiting the Messiah), which could have transferred to Christians: "With foreign merchants sneaked into Rus' Jews from Germany... We cannot deny the possibility of a sect starting among the Jews, which could get inspiration also from the desire to restore the previous might and from hope of coming of the Messiah...

"This mood Jews could display in their relations with the Russian people... In the bookish people this mood could not help but provoke resistance, which expressed itself in compiling special writings of obvious anti-Judaic character." [17] Therefore, *the reason* for the appearance of anti-Judaic literature in Russia was, in the opinion of the scholar, "the spiritual and religious excitement" *of the Jews themselves.*

However, the genesis of apocrypha, it seems, is a testimony to something different: "The first beginnings of many apocryphal tales are founded in the ancient Hebrew legends, which appeared in the ancient times and first passed from one generation to the next by word of mouth and later were collected into various Hebrew books; from the Hebrew books and legends the apocryphal tales moved to Christian books and mostly into the writings of Ancient Greece and Byzantium; from the Byzantium they spread to all the countries of Europe..."

"While explaining... the Biblical stories the compiler of *Palea* concentrates on the points which match his main goal of showing that the Old Testament was a model for the New Testament and of condemning the Hebrews who did not believe in Jesus Christ: this is the main idea to which all of the explanations and arguments in *Palea* lead. That is why it is quite fairly called *Explanatory Palaea on a Hebrew*... Along with these explanations there are constant addresses to the Yid, often with sharp scolding and blame-laying... Studying different copies of *Palea* we find... that all the addresses to the Yid... are found only in *Revelation of Abraham*, *The Testament of the 12 Patriarchs* and in *The Ladder of Divine Ascent* (the most ancient *Byzantian* sources — S.D.); and they are completely absent in other apocrypha. Based on that we can assume that all apocrypha were included into *Palea* at a later time by the scribes." [18] Therefore, any reference to some eschatological moods of the Jews in XII–XIII centuries that inspired the anti-Judaic pathos of *Palea,* which is based, after all, on Byzantian and Greek sources, has no justification.

The Judeo-Christian struggle, contrary to the opinion of V. M. Istrin, had to do not as much with the "demands of life that appeared, obviously, under new circumstances," [19] as with the realization of their own history and their place in it, because only if God's grace upon "rejection of Judaism" was accepted by St. Vladimir, it should be believed that being "chosen by God" became an *attribute* of the Orthodox church: "The apocrypha perfectly suited the main goal of *Palea* — to show the transforming sense of the Old Testament events; the larger part of them stemmed from the idea that the Old Testament was a model for the New Testament and consist of comparing Old Testament events to those in the New Testament...

"Much more suited to the main goal of *Palea* is *The Testament of the 12 Patriarchs*... *The Testament* is put in *Palea* after the story of Jacob's birth... Addresses to the Yid and notes on the prophetic meaning in the words of the patriarchs are inserted not into all parts of *Testaments* as one may expect based on the character of *Palea,* but only into four: Reuben, Simeon, Levi, and Joseph; however, these addresses and notes are fairly large, skillfully composed and can hardly belong to a simple copyist of *Palea*. It is very probable that *Testaments* are included into *Palea* by its Slavonic translator and editor (a Bulgarian scribe — *S.D.*), if not by its compiler (a Byzantian author — *S.D.*)." [20, 21]

With this circumstance was also connected the struggle for canonization of "the Baptist of Russia" as a saint that became especially pronounced in the late '30s of the XI century "after establishing in 1037 the Russian metropolia when the Greek Mitropolite arrived to Kyiv and with him, of course, the entire Greek clergy." [22]

That is why any attempts of the "cursed Yids" to keep the true faith according to the Old Testament *were,* from the point of view of an ancient Russian scribe, not only anti-Christian, but *anti-Russian.*

At the same time, the shadow of the Mongol invasion looming over Rus', and the significant state division and disunity were the realities of life that should have been compared to the Biblical story of the once mighty and "God chosen" people.

In any case, the anti-Judaic pathos of *Explanatory Palea* stimulated the consolidation of the Russian nation based on Christianity whose victory over the "cursed" proved not only the advantages of the new faith, but established in the new "God chosen" people continuity of the symbols and prophecies. Apparently, these considerations brought to life "somewhere in Lithuania" [23] the *Archival* (or *Judaic*) *Chronograph,* and following it, a small compilation known as *The Words of the Holy Prophets* with "traces of Western Russian language."

One of the phenomena of the anti-Judaism of the Christian literature was based on substitution of meaning of the Ancient Hebrew "בן אדם" — "νιος ανθρωπου" — "Son of Man" ("what is a man that you are mindful of him, the son of man that you care for him?"— Psalm 8:5) and

INTRODUCTION

"χριστου" — "the anointed one" that equals "the savior" ("shall be cut off — משיח — Messiah" — Daniel 9:26) by the New Testament ones, with definitions of a Gospel kind.

That is why the Old Testament presented multiple "proofs" of the true nature of the New Testament, for in *The Pentateuch* (תורה), *Prophets* (נביאים), and *Writings* (כתובים) multiple mentions of the notions "son of man" and "Messiah" allowed Christian ideologists to insist on the "original" nature of the Gospel image." [24, 25]

The coexistence of expectations of "coming of the Messiah," *different in meanings* among Jews and Christians, could not but lead to the opposition of the Jewish *māšîaḥ* and the Christian *Messiah*. The apocalyptic image of a "false prophet" that perishes with the "crimson beast" was transformed with time into the image of the Anti-Christ.

The dual idea of "Christ/Anti-Christ," as the eternal opposition of Good and Evil, one way or another facilitated the outcome in which in the early Christian literary teachings the "false prophet," the Hebrew *māšîaḥ*, was opposed to the true (naturally, Christian) Savior. [26]

Such opposition of the Christian Savior to the Jewish "anti-Christ" was first mentioned in *The Selection of the XIII Century* and defined, in the end, the opposition of the "former" God-chosen people: "Israel did not know me" — to the true believers in Him ("and we learned about His future").

That is why the logical conclusion of this opposition could only have been an indictment. "For pagans and His enemies shall kiss his hand, and His enemies are Jews." [27]

The further history of Russian literature was closely connected to the early anti-Judaic texts, since it was them that served as the foundation for the fight against the "Yids" and provided examples for ideological battles of dissenters with the proponents of the church reforms. [28]

In the process of historical development, the center of the Russian statehood moved from Kiev to Moscow. The rise of the new "mother" of Russian cities demanded, in its turn, an ideological justification.

The well-known phrase "Moscow is the third Rome" mentioned in the letters of the hegumen of the Yelizarov Convent in Pskov, Philotheus, to the Grand Prince Vasili III (XV century) was not enough; it was necessary to prove the ties of the Orthodox Moscow to the "chosen people" and establish the transition of God's Grace onto the Russian people.

This difficult task was accomplished in Russia not without assistance from the Little Russians, enlightened and educated in Jesuit colleges, who created a new myth based on the idea that "Mosoch or Meshech, the sixth son of Japeth, grandson of Noah, is the father and progenitor of all the peoples of Moscow, Russia, Poland, Volhynia, Czechia, Masovia, Bulgaria, Serbia, Croatia and all who speak the Slavonic language, that Moses mentions Mosoch, the forefather of the Moscow people, and Titus Flavius Josephus in *Antiquities says,* that not from the river or from the city of Moscow the Moscow people got their name, but the river and the city received their name from the Moscow people, and that name is Mosoch... all ancient historians Jewish, Chaldean, Greek and Roman and new call Mosoch, the forefather of Moscow and the areas of that name, in many places constantly and clearly understand that the third brother of Lech and Czech, Rus is a true descendant of Mosoch from Japeth..." [29]

The author of this myth of the XVI century was Maciej Stryjkowski. Later, in the XVII century, a student of the Kiev Theological Academy and a deacon of the Kholopiy monastery on the Mologa Timofey Kamenevich-Rvovsky added to the "history":

"Come thee, Mosoch the sixth son of Japeth, our lord and first prince, to the great land of Scythians and this Land of ours so named, to the place of this settlement of Moscow, in which land we now live..."

"This river back then being without a name from the beginning, he Prince Mosoch upon his arrival and settlement beautiful and beloved he Prince Mosoch renamed after his name, himself and his wife the princess beautiful and lovely by the name of Kva.

"And so, by combining together their names, our prince Mos and his princess Kva the fair place was named...

"This Mosoch Prince of Moscow was our progenitor and the first father not only to the Scyphian, Moscow, Slavonic, and Russian peoples, but also to all our many kin states..." [30]

Timofey also insisted that the second river, Yauza, was named by Mosoch after his children: son Ya and daughter Vuza.

The various legends of Moscow originating from Japeth's son Mosoch were collected by the author of the *Synopsis* Innocent Giesel in 1674 in the first history textbook that survived, due to its popularity, about 30 editions before the mid-XIX century.

Many other pre-revolution publications also contain references to the "family tree" of Moscow and the Moscow people growing from the Hebrew forefathers.

One of the most interesting religious and cultural movements in Russia in the Middle Ages was the "heresy of the Judaizers," the first representatives of which arrived in Rus' with the court of a Lithuanian prince Mikhailo Olelkovich and completely "dissolved" in the Russian environment. The "Judaizers," undoubtedly, were joined by the intellectual elite of the time.

In Moscow, its leader was an outstanding diplomat who had visited Western Europe and a writer (the possible author of the famous *Tale of Dracula*), a dyak Fyodor Vasiliyevich Kuritsyn.

The dyak himself died on the eve of cruel persecution (apparently circa 1500) and his brother, also a dyak, Ivan Vasiliyevich Kuritsyn-Volk was burned at the stake with other heretics in 1503. [31]

The movement of the "Judaizers" was cruelly suppressed, and we can hardly doubt that the cruelty of Dracula, which was stressed by the author of the tale of the Volosh Voevoda and which made his name, a symbol, was inspired by real images of that barbaric era.

However, despite the persecution, the heresy of the "Judaizers" did not disappear: almost three centuries later it was found in Voronezh, Tambov, Orel, Kursk and other provinces of Central Russia.

Moreover, the "Judaizers" of the early XIX century insisted on the hereditary connection with the "Judaizers" of the time of Ivan III (which was noted by the researchers of the heresy).

For example, N. N. Golitsyn considered the heresy an echo of the past times of Skhariya "legends of whom had been hiding somewhere among the people." [32]

The fight against the "Judaizers" found its reflection primarily in the prohibition of "unuseful" books, among which were many of the ancient Russian writings of XIII–XIV centuries.

It is not accidental that Ivan the Terrible in his message to the Hundred Chapter Synod called for protection of the purity of Christian teaching from "the murderous wolf and from various intrigues of the enemy" and demanded the Synod's rulings against reading and distribution of books "disgusting to God," "heretical" and "renounced." [33]

This "guardian" function was supposed to be realized also by the grand undertaking that was initiated by Macarius, the Archbishop of Novgorod in the late '20s of the XVI century: the compiling of *The Great Menaion Reader*. Almost simultaneously with Macarius's work appeared the so-called *Illustrated Chronicle of Ivan the Terrible* that included Flavius Josephus's *The Judea War* and *The Explanatory Palea*, which happened to include one of the editions of *Solomon and Kitovras*.

We can state that various collections and chronographs of the XVI–XVII included those writings from the old Russian anti-Judaic literature which later were more than once used against the "Judaizers" and then re-interpreted in the anti-Masonic and anti-Judaic literature.

Therefore, the so-called "Gospel" anti-Judaism (meaning religious "rejection of the Yid") under the circumstances of the bitter fight of the Russian orthodoxy with the heresy of the Judaizers turned to be that fertile ground in which "ideological anti-Judaism," brought into being by the appearance of foreigners in the political life of the society, could appear. [34]

Moreover, the presence in the Russian writings of the Middle Ages of samples of anti-Judaic polemic greatly helped the "continuity" of the ideas of the "people rejected by God," which always found its use in the times of revolutionary reforms and reorganization.

THE PENETRATION OF FREEMASONRY INTO RUSSIA AND ANTI-MASONIC LITERATURE OF THE EIGHTEENTH CENTURY

In the history of the Russian culture, as a researcher noted in the early XX century, there is no more difficult and complicated problem than the one of the origins and spreading of Freemasonry in Russia. [35]

In Russia, Freemasonry appeared almost right after it got formed into "correct shapes" in the West and one of the first lodges was founded in London (1717). Let us remind you that in the late XVII — early XVIII century, invited by Alexei Mikhailovich and Peter I, a huge wave of foreigners flooded Russia. Naturally, the luggage of the "technical human resources" contained not only professional literature, but also books on philosophy, history, and mysticism.

In 1689 the predecessor of the professors Schwarz and Novikov, a German mystic Quirinus Kuhlmann appeared in Moscow. He was born in Breslau to a family of a merchant. He was a devout believer since childhood and, in his own words, was constantly haunted by visions, so Kuhlmann wholly devoted himself to religion. He was educated at the University of Jena at the department of law and continued his studies in Leipzig.

As early as 1674, under the influence of the classical works of Jacob Boehme, he published the book *Neubegeister Boehme,* in which he proved that true knowledge is acquired by a man not through science but as a result of religious self-improvement. Being a herald of the imminent doom of the existing churches and prophesying the coming of a new, true "Jesuit Kingdom" that would replace the sinful "Babylon of the West," Kuhlmann attempted to preach in Holland but was soon banished from Leiden.

INTRODUCTION

It is possible that at the same time he was introduced to the teachings of Sabbatai Zevi. At least, in 1678 he turned up in Constantinople where he intended to convert the local population to Christianity of "his own device" and where he apparently met one of the secret emissaries of the Sabbatean movement Abraham Kunki. [36] His missionary work in Turkey ended relatively well: after a corporal punishment (October, 1678) he was exiled from the Ottoman Empire. While traveling Europe, Kuhlmann met a son of a Moscow colonel, Otto Genin, and then, in late April of 1689, came to Moscow. From then on, the activity of this resident of the German colony became an important factor in the history of the Russian freemasonry.

Kuhlmann's teachings were of a sharply social character and came close to the primitive communism of Anabaptists, because, as he believed, with the establishment of the new order "there would be no tzars, kings, princes, and nobles, and everyone would be equal, all things would be common and nobody would call anything their own..." [37] Kuhlmann, together with his admirer and a like-minded man, a Moscow merchant Conrad Nordermann, was denounced by Pastor Joachim Meinecke and arrested, and under torture both stated that Moscow would incur the wrath of God should they be harmed. Kuhlmann's works and the theosophical books of Boehme were examined by the experts Pastors Meinecke and Wagecir and the Jesuits Tikhonovsky and David. With no interference by the Patriarch of the Orthodox clergy both "heretics" were sentenced to death and burned at the stake on October 4, 1689. Kuhlmann's last words were: "You are just, oh Almighty God, and Your judgements are fair, you know we are dying without fault." [38]

In Russia, execution by burning was rarely implemented. However, despite such a severe punishment, the followers of Kuhlmann still existed among the residents of the German colony for a long time afterward. [39]

Almost immediately after Kuhlmann's death, along with hand-written copies of translations of mystic and hermeticist authors there appeared translations of the writings of "our sainted father Jacob Boehme." [40] One of those (abridged), *The Great Teaching of the Famous and Enlightened by God Ramon Llull,* was compiled by an old believer Andrey Denisov. [41]

An old masonic legend claims that during the reign of Alexey Mikhailovich, the future famous associate of Peter I, General Field Marshal Jacob Bruce (1670–1735) founded the first masonic lodge in Russia. One of the historians of freemasonry published a translation of an obscure German manuscript signed "Carl L..r," in which the following was stated: "Count Bruce... was one of the *Hoher Eingeweihter* of the masons and fruitfully penetrated into the secrets of the masonic order. At the same time, he possessed deep and solid knowledge, which may, possibly, be proven by the writings and notes he left behind and which, in order to escape the curses from the curious eyes, are kept sealed in the Emperor's Academy of Sciences. Bruce also had information about the laws of nature and their spontaneous effects and the calendar compiled by him predicted the weather, or, rather, the natural events of each year for a whole century, and these predictions, apparently, have been coming true as has been witnessed in the last years of the past century by those persons that had a chance to view this calendar... This knowledge of the laws of nature gave Bruce the opportunity to prove to Peter the Great that nature possessed larger powers than was commonly believed; thus, on his deathbed (Bruce died after Peter and not the other way round! — S.D.) Bruce asked Peter the Great, in case the Emperor found his life still useful, to order, after his passing, that his body be rubbed with one of the solutions he had created and, once done, this solution acted such on Bruce's dead body that he began coming to and using his tongue. However, since Peter the Great was satisfied with just that and the rubbing was stopped, naturally, death followed." [42]

Other tales put the founding of the masonic lodge to the later years of the XVII century (to the time of Peter's return from abroad). And one of the anti-masonic (and anti-Peter) legends says that Peter himself was dubbed a freemason by King William III of Orange. [43]

Another influential person who presumably did a lot to facilitate penetration of freemasonry into Russia, was in the opinion of an anti-masonic legend, Franz Lefort (1656–1699). He not only facilitated the European education of the Emperor, but also "pulled" Peter into the masonic lodge, and later, thanks to Lefort, the Emperor founded a masonic Order of St. Andrew with accepted colors for the habits of persons of different ranks. [44] Other versions of the same legend claim that Peter was initiated as a "brother" by Christopher Wren himself, the famous founder of the modern English freemasonry: in the order's lodge in the later years of the XVII century the Master's chair was occupied by Lefort, the Senior Warden was General Patrick Gordon and the Junior Warden was the Tzar himself. [45]

A. N. Pypin believed that only in 1717 Peter I brought from his travels the status of the masonic lodge that he then founded in Kronstadt. [46]

INTRODUCTION

The actions of Peter I were highly valued in masonic lodges and for a long time they performed G. R. Derzhavin's *Song to Peter the Great* in his honor. At the same time, the first documented witness of a masonic lodge in Russia dates to [1731]: that year the Grand Master of the United Grand Lodge of England, Lord Lovell, appointed Captain John Philips as the provincial Grand Lodge "of all Russia." [47]

After ten years this post was given to a talented general, a Scotsman in the service of Russia, James Keith (1696–1758) who later became a Prussian Feldmarschall. [48]

James Keith received his appointment from the hands of his brother John Keith, Earl of Kintore. According to one source, as A. N. Pypin reports, in [1731] he founded the first lodge in Moscow, and another **source says** that it happened in 1732 or 1734 in Petersburg. [49] James Keith was the first to accept Russians into masonic lodges, which earned him the grateful memory of his followers. [50]

The possibility of foreign travel allowed Russians to join masonic lodges abroad: a masonic degree of merchant, shopkeeper, or steward opened doors onto many influential people. It must be said that a special group in masonic lodges was navy men. T. Sokolovskaya lists the members of the masonic lodge *Neptune* in Kronstadt (1781), among whom are the names of the glorious admirals A. G. Sviridov and S. K. Greig as well as the future admiral A. S. Shishkov. [51]

The membership of a masonic lodge often served as a ground for suspicion of treason and espionage. In 1747 the case of Count N. A. Golovin, the first mason among the Russian nobility, led to his arrest on the charges of relations with the Prussian king. He was interrogated in the Secret Office by A. I. Shuvalov, and in the name of the Empress Elizabeth the person on remand was informed that although she "had enough reason to doubt his actions," she "out of her natural kind-heartedness and mercy towards Golovin's youth hoped that he would correct his behavior from then on." [52]

About him belonging to a "freemason order" and about other members of the order, N. A. Golovin testified during the interrogation that he "lived in that order and know that Counts Zakhar and Ivan Chernyshev are in the same order, but other secrets I do not know, only as shown in the printed book about freemasons." [53]

Anti-masonic authors state that one of the first masons in Russia was also Prince A. D. Kantemir, an author and diplomat, who spent most of his life abroad and died in Paris. Antiochus Kantemir was a friend of the prominent masons Voltaire and Montesquieu (whose book *Persian Letters* he translated into Russian). As noted by B. Bashilov,

Kantemir was not only a committed Westernizer but also a "denier of Russia." [54]

In 1750 in Petersburg there existed the lodge "Modesty" and in Riga in the same year the lodge "Northern Star" was founded.

In 1757 M. Olsufyev, likely based on the police investigation by the head of the Secret Office A. I. Shuvalov, composed a report in which he named 35 members of the lodge known to him, and highly praised the actions of the masons: "People of any rank and position, who so wish, the lodge shall accept at various times, through opportunities seeking its fellows above-mentioned with clear proof to testify that this is nothing but the key to friendship and brotherhood, which is forever immortal, and thus grant those who join their society with enlightenment." [55]

According to the testimony of M. Olsufyev, members of masonic lodges were: the three princes Golitsyn, prince S. Meshchersky, R. I. Vorontsov, author A. Sumarokov, historian I. Boltin, the founder of Russian theater Volkov, chamber-page Peterson, officers of guard regiments (Preobrazhensky and Simeonovsky), representatives of the Cadet Corps, musicians and even one *raznochinets* — a shopkeeper Miller. [56]

To the Russian government who was constantly afraid of conspiracies (actually, it itself at that time often came to power as a result of conspiracies), freemasonry could not but seem dangerous. The uneducated Russian commoner who saw in a mason a heretic and an apostate was even more frightened by the new order, with its special rules and incomprehensible secret rites. It is not surprising that in the Russian language at that particular time the word "farmazon" (freemason) appeared and became synonymous to atheism and free thought. [57]

In G. R. Derzhavin's notes there is a notable episode that testifies to the negative attitude of the wide public circles towards freemasons.

When in 1763 Derzhavin decided to travel abroad, he wanted to seek assistance from A. I. Shuvalov. At that time the poet and nobleman lived with his aunt, "a woman naturally clever and pious, but unenlightened and considering the masons who then appeared in Moscow apostates, heretics, blasphemers devoted to Antichrist, of which there circulated unbelievable rumors that they killed their enemies long-distance from several thousand miles and other such nonsense, and that Shuvalov was their head master..." [58]

So, she opposed her nephew's desire.

One of the accusers of freemasons was, most likely, the Archimandrite of the Holy Trinity St. Sergius Lavra Gideon Krinovsky whose sermons preached in the '40s were published. [59]

INTRODUCTION

Of course, the most famous accuser of freemasons was the opponent of Peter's reforms Arsenius (secular name Alexander Matseyevich), who in 1742–1763 headed the Rostov diocese.

He was strict with his subordinates and intolerant of dissent. He opposed the secular government, ignored the rulings of the Spiritual Regulation and promoted the idea of restoration of Patriarchy. For "false and outrageous interpretations of the Holy Scripture" he was tried by the spiritual court in 1763, exiled to a Revel monastery and died in a cell of the Revel prison where he was jailed under the name of Andrei Vrel. [60]

Finally, we should mention the third ideologist of the "anti-masonic opposition," the Bishop of Bryansk and Sevsk Cyril Florinsky (Fliorinsky), a Little Russian like Matseyevich. Although he possessed a number of virtues that brought him well-deserved respect of I. I. Betsky and D. M. Golitsyn, he cruelly persecuted Old Believers, was despotic to his subordinates and argued with secular powers. After multiple reports the Synod removed him from his post and sent him into "retirement" in the Kiev Golden-Domed Monastery.

Naturally, this severe man who also fought prejudice and folk traditions, was an advocate of orthodoxy and a sworn enemy of freemasonry. [61]

Let us note that persecution of freemasons began during the reign of Catherine II, although the Empress was not a persistent or committed opponent of the "free masons" (for example, she supported the Polish freemasons, because in her time they were the conduits for Russian policy). [62]

In 1785–1786 she wrote several comedies denouncing freemasonry: *The Shaman of Siberia, Deceiver,* and *Seduced.* In fact, the main reason for the Empress's anti-Masonic mood was the unbreakable connection between the Russian and the foreign "brothers," and at the time of the French Revolution this connection could not but become "dangerous" for the Russian state. Catherine II paid careful attention to the events in which freemasons played an important part. Her plays became a challenge to all of freemasonry. They, in the words of A. Semeka, became the most well-founded creations of anti-masonic nature in Russian literature. [63]

It is known that the Empress was familiar with two German works that pursued opposite goals: the apologetic book by Gotthold Lessing *Ernst und Falk — Gespräche für Freymaeuere (1778)* and Johann von Goethe's sharply critical comedy *Der Gross-Cophta* (1791). [64]

It seems doubtful that the first polemic treatise aimed against freemasons was written by Catherine in 1758. More probable is something else: *Mystery of an Absurd Society Revealed to the Uninitiated* with the disclaimer "translated from French" appeared in 1780 (the sale of the treatise was announced that year by *The St. Petersburg Vedomosti*). The treatise ridiculed the absurd rituals of freemasons, their extreme mysticism and the "holy of holies" of the society — the sacrament of initiation and the presence of a "mystery." Dividing the Masons into the deceived and the deceivers, Catherine clearly formulated her conclusion: freemasonry existed to cheat the neighbor for the profit of his "masters," who use the naive faith of those around them for the sake of omnipotence and providentiality of the order. These ideas of the treatise formed the basis of her comedies.

On February 4, 1786, the comedy *The Deceiver* was first performed on the palace stage (it had been probably written much earlier). The main character of the play was a charlatan and a swindler Kalifmalkgerston, in whom the audience immediately recognized the famous Cagliostro, who had stayed in St. Petersburg with one of the "fierce" freemasons, I. P. Elagin and who had left the capital on October 1, 1779. The author's thought is surprisingly simple and moralizing: dodgers come to Russia and rob the gullible Russian people. In a letter to Grimm the Empress explained the reasons for her interest in comedy: "Firstly, because it amuses me; secondly, because I would like to revive the national theater, which, in the absence of new plays, has been neglected!" [65]

In the play *Seduced* (written, apparently, in 1785), Catherine created an even sharper and more serious satire on the Russian "brothers." The patronymics characteristic of classicism (Vokitov — Volokitov "procrastinator," Radotov — from the French word *radoteur* "chatterbox," Bragin "moonshiner," Bebetov — reminiscent of the Latin "bibere" (drunkard), Barmotin, Tratov "spender," etc.), a simple plot (a love affair involving the mason's daughter)), accusatory speeches not devoid of wit and realism — this time everything hit the bull's eye. The exposure of charlatans and crooks who came under suspicion of theft could not but sound from the palace as a warning to freemasons and, first of all, to Novikov.

Catherine did not touch on the moral goals of the teachings of "freemasons" (although she was familiar with them), however, seeing intrigues in everything and everywhere emanating either from the Prussian king or from Gatchina, she openly spoke out against philanthropic activity, with a hint at Novikov ("They intend to secretly start

INTRODUCTION

charitable institutions of various kinds, such as schools, hospitals, and the like, and for this they try to attract rich people" [66]), and against "masonic" natural philosophy (" ... he smelts gold, diamonds, composes metals from dew, and who-knows-what from herbs; moreover, he seeks to have meetings with some invisible people, through various pranks and real childishness, at which the intelligent people of centuries past and present laugh ..." [67]), and against immorality ("<he> fell into the abyss ... rose up high ... sat neck -deep in water ... finally got drunk ... unconscious ..." [68]).

The following year, another anti-Masonic play appeared — *The Shaman of Siberia*, perhaps the weakest in this "cycle." At the same time, it was in the last play that the prosecutor's word of the Empress was spoken: the main fault of the Masons is not fraud or ignorance, mysticism or vanity, but the public harm that they cause by creating Masonic lodges and gathering members to crowded meetings.

The Empress's summary resembled an order to her subjects: "If they know for certain that his teaching does not follow the general order, the repercussions will also go to the one who had brought the false teacher ... if not directly, then at least in passing." [69]

Catherine's comedies were a great success. On January 10, 1786 she told Zimmerman: "As far as theater, I have to say that here two Russian comedies appeared: one titled *Deceiver* and another *Seduced*.

The first presents Cagliostro (whom I have not met, nor his wife, although they visited here) in his real person, and the other depicts those he seduced.

Our audience is delighted by these plays, which are indeed amusing. I tell you this so you know how we treat Illuminati." [70]

At Zimmerman's suggestion the plays were translated into German by Arndt (according to A. V. Khrapovitsky, the translator received [300] roubles for the first play).

Later Zimmerman and a friend of Lessing, Nikolai used the images of Catherine's plays and this makes it probable that Goethe was familiar with them. [71]

The crusade against freemasons in Russia ended with trials of N. I. Novikov and A. N. Radishchev.

The history of freemasons in Russia and the experience of anti-Masonic literature, later combined with anti-sectarian studies, became the main sources from which the creators of the "synthetic" myth of "enemies of Russia" derived their "knowledge."

Masonic documents of the XVIII century do not contain any information about the attitude of "freemasons" to Jews. Moreover, the "resolution" of the Jewish question in the programs of Russian freemasons appeared only in the reign of Alexander I. Several general humanistic statements, such as "bear with a Hellen and bear with a Jew" in the spirit of the Gospel, of course, do not paint a picture of the actual state of things.

Undoubtedly, Masonic symbolism and addiction to mysticism by adherents of different lodges contributed to the growth of interest not only in Jewish history and the Hebrew language, but also encouraged familiarization with numerous works of Jewish thinkers on Kabbalah and "hermeticism". However, among the statements of Russian freemasons of the XVIII century there is not one directly related to Jews. [72]

It would seem that, considering such indifference of freemasons to the Jewish question, their ideological connection with the Jews is not only indemonstrable but meaningless. However, in the crucible of Russian reality (not without assistance of home-grown anti-Semites and alchemists) both "earths" (freemasons and Jews) formed a monstrous alloy of the "Judeo-Masonic conspiracy" theory.

THE PALE OF SETTLEMENT

Let us remember that Catherine II had to solve the Jewish question immediately after the successful conspiracy against Peter III.

"On the fifth or sixth day after she took the throne," Catherine wrote in an autobiographical note from the third person perspective, "...she appeared in the Senate... Since in the Senate everything was done according to the schedule, with the exception of emergencies, it so unfortunately happened that at that session the first in line, while they were writing it down, was the bill on permitting Jews to enter Russia. Catherine, under *current circumstances*, had difficulty consenting to that suggestion, which was *unanimously* considered useful, and was rescued from this conundrum by Prince Odoyevsky who rose and told her: "Would Your Majesty, before making her decision, like to see what the Empress Elizabeth wrote in her own hand in the margins of such a bill?"

Catherine ordered the registers to be brought in and found that Elizabeth, with her piousness, had written in the margins: "I wish no profit from the enemies of Jesus Christ."

Not a week had passed since Catherine rose to the throne; she had been raised to it to defend the Orthodox faith; she had to deal with

INTRODUCTION

religious people and with clerics who had not been given back their estates and had no means to support themselves due to this ill-conceived ruling; people's minds, as usual after such a great event, were greatly perturbed: to start her reign with such a measure would not help to calm <the minds> but *to recognize it as harmful* was impossible. Catherine simply addressed the Attorney-General after he had collected the votes and approached her for her verdict, and told him: *"I wish to postpone this matter until later time."* [73]

N. N. Golitsyn and M. F. Shugurov believed that the note contained only, due to the lack of knowledge about Jews, an abstract and humanitarian idea; I. G. Orshansky, J. I. Hessen and S. M. Dubnov pointed at the struggle between the conscience of an *enlightened monarch with good intentions* and the fear of *her pious people and its clerics*. [74]

Indeed, not so long ago many preached from the ambo about "the strengthening of the infidel" and the Synod ruled to banish Armenian churches from Petersburg. [75]

So, "Tartuffe in skirts" who put Russia "on the threshold of Europe," as Pushkin wrote, sensed the necessity of postponing the matter until a later time. This is why she mentioned the *unanimity* of the Senate that permitted Jews into the empire and the actions of Attorney-General A. I. Glebov, who acted in the best interest of the state and realized the political limitations of the decisions of the former Empress. [76]

While answering Denis Diderot's questions on the history of Russia and its political and economic status, which the great encyclopedist compiled in 1773, Catherine had to also clearly state her conception of the Jewish question. Diderot asked: "Jews were banned from entering Russia in 1754 (the philosopher's mistake — *S.D.*) and later that ban was lifted. Are there any Jews? If there are... then on what terms? Are they treated the same as other foreigners? And how many Jews, approximately, are there?" Catherine's response was: "Jews were banished from Russia by the Empress Elizabeth in the beginning of her reign, approximately in 1742. In 1762 there were talks of letting them come back, but, since this suggestion was *made out of place*, the case remained as is; in 1764 Jews were declared merchants and residents of New Russia beyond the Dnieper (Borysthenes). Belorussia is teeming with them: three or four of them have long been living in Petersburg... They are tolerated contrary to the law: people simply pretend that nobody knows they are in the capital. *However, allowing* them into Russia could bring *great harm* to our small merchants, *for these people attract everything to themselves and it could happen that their return would bring more complaints than profit."* [77]

The Empress was of a low opinion about the Russian merchantry and, as noted by one of the researchers, the general educational level of merchants was "almost the same as among peasants: very few of them could read, write or perform calculations with an abacus," [78] and another stated: "Our merchantry as a whole were not nearly ready to turn into businessmen, they held fast to the outdated traditions and did not wish to trade them for any foreign business regulations." [79] Hence, speaking of the danger to Russian merchantry from enterprising and competitive Jews, Catherine replied quite truthfully. (The Jews residing in Petersburg, according to historians' suppositions, were Abraham Peretz, Jehuda-Leib ben Noah "Nevakhovich," Rabbi Nota Schklover and, likely, his son Rebe Berel Schabtai "Berel Notkin" [80]).

Catherine herself used the services of Jewish doctors (she was treated by Mendel Lev, her pharmacist was Samuel Schvenon, etc.) and her banker was Wolf. She also hired Jewish contractors (Abramovich, "David the Yid" [81]), and in 1764 seven Jews from Courland arrived to Petersburg — three merchants, a rabbi with his apprentice, and a shochet with his servant. [82]

Despite the fact that in one of her first orders sent to the Senate Catherine encouraged attracting foreigners, "except Yids," [83] as early as in 1764 she worked a clever plan of relocation of Jews to New Russia. In April of that year Governor-General of Riga received a message from the capital: "Should several merchant people from the New Russia province be recommended by the Custody of Foreigners Office, they shall be permitted to reside in Riga and perform business on the same grounds as merchants from other Russian provinces, according to law. Moreover, when those send forth their assistants, associates, and workmen to New Russia, to reside there, then for their escort and safety, *regardless of the laws and faith,* decent escort and passports shall be given by you. On top of that, should there be three or four men from Mitau who wish to go to Petersburg for carrying out certain requests that the crown has, do give them passports, *without mention of their nationality and questioning them about their law,* and only put their names in the passports; to learn who they are; they have to possess a letter from the merchant Levi Wolf who is present here, and that letter they must show you. Catherine." There was also a notation in German in Catherine's hand: "Should you not comprehend me, it will be through no fault of mine; this letter has been written by the president of the Custody Office himself; keep everything secret." [84]

Naturally, after that representatives of Jewish merchantry appeared in New Russia, and as early as May 2, 1764 David and Leo Bamberger "with mates" signed a contract with the treasury — their guarantor was the Governor-General of New Russia and a freemason himself, A. I. Melgunov. [85]

Since 1775 Jews from Lithuania started moving to Elizabethgrad province [86], and soon after annexation of Belarus (as a result of another partition of Poland) Russia had to decide the fate of another few millions of Jews.

In her conversations with I. M. Dal (the father of the future linguist) Catherine expressed quite "vegetarian" thoughts: "No ethnicity, no matter what it is, should be deprived of citizenship; anyone should be free to receive it..." [87]

However, in real life the Empress acted with caution and often in a clandestine way. Thus, on February 8, 1785 she ordered the Governor-General of Riga and Revel, Count Browne, to populate the posad of Sloka with merchants and tradesmen, not excluding Jews. At the same time, the Empress, beginning with that order, de facto banned the use of the insulting word "Yid" and replaced it with "Jew." [88] In accordance with the Empress's unspoken demand, this became mandatory for all Russian state documents. By the Empress's manifesto on including Belarus into Russia, all its residents, "whichever their ethnicity or rank," were declared Russian nationals and were free to practice their faith and keep their property. Although the legal status of Jews in the Russian Empire at the end of the XVIII century was quite difficult [89], the deliverance from pogroms allowed the Jewish population to restore its numbers. Meanwhile, as early as 1783, despite the resistance from the Poles, Jews participated in elections of village heads and court wardens. Catherine II supported equality in this matter: "Should Jews who register as merchants, by voluntary agreement of community, be elected to any posts according to the Highest Institution, they may not be prevented from assuming such posts and fulfilling their duties." [90]

Catherine II, who did so much for Jews in the first stage of her reign, but *before* the French Revolution (that is, before she defined the Pale of Settlement), was possibly influenced by a favorite of hers, his Highness Prince Gregory Alexandrovich Potemkin (1739–1791), an outstanding political and military figure who was also known for his religious tolerance, unusual for the times (he was friends with the families of Hablitz and Stieglitz [91] and in his retinue there were many baptized and non-baptized Jews, for the most part military suppliers and informants). Paying careful attention to the development of the events in the Ottoman Empire and awaiting its fall, he decided in 1786 to create... an Israeli regiment. [92] This little-known historical fact deserves special attention, since in the literary version it is known from the work of a historian and novelist N. A. Engelhardt (1867–1942), a staff member of Suvorin's reactionist "Novoye Vremya" ("New Times"):

> Now, gentlemen, I invite you to inspect my newly formed Israeli Squadron," said the Bright Lord and walked to the ornamentation depicting a hippodrome of Byzantian kings at the end of the garden. Behind it were vast parade grounds covered in sand, large enough to drill a full regiment.
>
> "What is this Israeli Battalion?" whispered the Bright Lord's retinue.
>
> Nobody knew. But when the battalion suddenly entered the arena, everyone understood without explanation what kind of unit it was.
>
> A unique idea occurred to Potemkin — to form a regiment of Jews and name it the Israeli His Highness Duke Ferdinand of Brunswick's Mounted Regiment, of course, if the duke consented to be a patron of such an unusual military unit. For the time being, only one squadron of the future regiment was presented to the Bright Lord. In lapserdaks, wearing beards and payot as long as their stirrups were short, crouched with fear in their saddles, the Hebrews presented a striking picture. In their almond-shaped eyes was excruciating anxiety and their long cossack pikes held in their bony hands wavered and leaned stupidly, nodding their yellow badges this way and that. However, the battalion commander, a severe German who had worked hard to teach the sons of Israel some horsemanship and military drill, was issuing commands and everything was going according to the regulations. The battalion was especially hilarious attacking. The comical figures with flying peyot and lapserdaks' hems, missing their stirrups and losing slippers and holding their pikes at the ready, made the Greek lady burst out laughing. She was joined by restrained laughter of the other ladies and smiles of the gentlemen. It seemed like the bright Lord wanted exactly that. He halted the drill and thanked the battalion commander.
>
> "No matter, they are getting better in the saddle and with some more training they'll make an excellent troop," Potemkin said seriously.
>
> And he proceeded to elaborate that, when the Ottoman empire would be finally destroyed and Constantinople and the straits were in the Russian hands, then Jerusalem would not be ruled by infidels any longer. Then it would be necessary to move all Jews to Palestine,

INTRODUCTION

because in Europe they were only causing mischief. In their ancestral land they would be revived. In anticipation of that was this future Palestinian force being prepared.

Mr. Zachariah Kleischbotham was absolutely delighted by this project and began spiritedly developing the splendid and humanitarian, as he called it, idea of the Bright Lord. [93]

Despite the "splendid" idea of the Bright Lord, it seems that the comical description of the situation and of the "actors" is biased, since shortly after the events described by N. A. Engelhardt, "in the squares of the rebellious Warsaw" volunteers of Berko Yoselevich's Jewish regiment proved their resilience during the fight against Suvorov's soldiers — all the Jewish volunteers were killed storming Praga, a suburb of the Polish capital. [94]

The Israeli regiment was mentioned by one of the first "zionists" of the XVIII century, Prince Charles Joseph de Ligne (1735–1814) who was a friend of Potemkin and Catherine. He left an interesting memoir about his time in Russia, *Melanges Militaires, Historiques et Littéraires*, in which the chapter "Mémoire sur les Juifs" was dedicated to Russian and Polish Jews. [95] However, the early death of G. A. Potemkin, as well as the French Revolution, prevented forming a Jewish military unit in the Russian army.

It is a paradox that it was precisely Catherine II, who so well understood the right of all the Russian nationals to equal citizenship, who was to establish "the Pale of Settlement" in Russia, which brought so much grief and trouble to Jews.

Maurice Paleologue, the French ambassador in Petrograd during World War I, while noting that "the Jewish question has existed in Russia only from the time of the partition of Poland," stated: "Before that time the Russian government practiced no other policy in regards of Jews but exile and persecution... But... the empress Catherine suddenly established... a strict and repressing regime, of which they have not been rid until this day. The Order of December 23, 1791 narrowed the Pale of Settlement, forbade Jews to practice agriculture and herded them into cities; finally, she introduced the concept that is still active: that anything that is not explicitly allowed to the Jews was forbidden to them. Such an expression of despotism and unfairness, coming from a philosopher empress, a friend of Voltaire, d'Alembert, and Diderot..., is somewhat puzzling."

Catherine II's hatred towards Jews is explained by an indirect yet strong reason.

The empress hated the French Revolution and saw it as a frightening threat to all thrones and a criminal and devilish act. When in 1791 the French *Assemblee nationale constituante* declared the emancipation of Jews and recognized their equal rights, Catherine responded to that with her December 23 Order... Thus, ironically, the noble initiative of the French Revolution evoked in the opposite end of Europe an era of persecution that may have been one of the longest and cruelest of all that the people of Israel had to endure through centuries. [96]

CHAPTER 1

THE WAR OF 1812 AND DENUNCIATION "OF ALL RUSSIA"

POLES AND JEWS

In order to understand the reasons for the appearance of anti-Judaic literature in Russia, it is most important to solve the problem of the relationship between the Jewish population and the original residents of the Kingdom of Poland and Westland, among which the leading role belonged to Catholics and Jesuits.

In the late 1919, a committee was founded to study and publish archive materials concerning charges of ritual murders committed by Jews. The president of the committee was a famous historian S. F. Platonov (1860–1941). The committee included an outstanding historian of the Jewish people S. M. Dubnov (1860–1941), ethnographer and opinion journalist Lev Sternberg (1861–1927), a scholar of Talmud G. Ya. Krasny-Admoni (1881–1970), and Heinrich Sliozberg (1863–1937) who replaced Krasny after he left Russia, archeographer and paleographer V. D. Druzhinin (1859–1937), historian and theologian L. P. Karsavin (1882–1952), and the former head of the Senate archives I. A. Blinov.

Heinrich Sliosberg noticed that until the Beilis case, such accusations were coming from the Polish Catholic circles. Representatives of Orthodoxy had not demonstrated much enthusiasm in regard to those accusations.

For instance, the Holy Synod never commented either on the Saratov case of 1856 or on the Beilis trial, and as for the Metropolitan Filaret, he was always vigorously opposed to such accusations.

It is no coincidence that the experts of the prosecution were most often Catholic priests (for example, in the Beilis trial it was the *Ksiądz*

Pranaitis). As is widely known, the question of the authorship of the anti-Judaic book *Investigations of Murdering by Jews of Christian Infants and Consuming of Their Blood*, which was published in 1844 at the direct order of Nicholas I and the Minister of Internal Affairs Count Perovsky, remained unresolved.

However, the main consultants were also militant Catholics and Polish nationalists: Prince Francis Xavier Drucki-Lubecki (1779–1846), a minister and the state secretary of the Kingdom of Poland I. L. Turkul (1797–1857), an important official of the Ministry of Internal Affairs J. E. Przecławski (1799–1879).

In his memoir J. E. Przecławski specifically stated that Count Perovsky received elucidation of this problem from I. L. Turkul, according to whom in Poland there had been in the past many cases of Jews killing Christian infants. The most memorable trial happened in the late XVIII century in the town of Kalisz where the court ordered: on every anniversary of the crime the town Jews were required to participate in a walk of shame: barefooted, dressed in white shrouds, with rope nooses around their necks they had to circle the cathedral nine times carrying lit candles. Moreover, the author of the memoir pointed out that in the Grodno case of 1816, Jews, against all evidence, were pronounced innocent, for they had claimed that the Poles hated them for remaining loyal to the Russian government. [1]

The committee that was created during the Russian Civil War never published the only volume that had been prepared for publication — the text of acts of the Grodno trial. It was, possibly, in part the fault of S. F. Platonov [2] and I. A. Blinov, a man close to the Minister of Justice Shcheglovitov who had sanctioned the court hearing of the boy Yushchinsky murder charges against M. Beilis. [3]

Apparently, the roots of the Grodno, Velizh and other such cases of the '10s–'20s are hidden in the history of relations between Poles and Jews during the Patriotic War of 1812.

As a result of three partitions of Poland, the entire Belarus and most of Lithuania became part of Russia. These territories before 1843 were included into the Vilen, Grodno, Minsk, Vitebsk and Mogilev provinces. In 1816–1817 their male population was 1,600,000 (2,300,000 in 1834).

The ethnic variety in these provinces was great: Byelorussians, Lithuanians, Ukrainians, Russians, Poles, and, of course, Jews, who made up most of the city population: out of 9,873 residents of Grodno, for example, 8,422 were Jewish (85%). Poles in the Vilna and Vitebsk provinces were a minority (about 10%), however it was them that took

Chapter 1. The War of 1812 and Denunciation "Of All Russia"

almost all official positions in the provincial and *uezd* administrations, courts, schools, and comprised a privileged group of minor and major landowners, lease holders of lands and manors, and, finally, the manor management. [4]

Catherine II, Paul I and Alexander I conducted a careful policy with respect to the Polish nobility, preserving most of their privileges and expanding to them all the rights of the Russian nobility.

The policy of "domesticating" the Polish szlachta helped some of the Polish noblemen to make a successful career in the service of Russia (for example, Prince Adam Czartoryski [5]). Marriages between noble houses of both peoples were not unheard of either (thus, the counts Wielhorski became kin to the princes Gagarin and Count Sollogub married an heiress of an ancient family, one of the Arharovs). Having introduced in the Westland unified provincial administrative units with appropriate provincial institutions and practicing the consistent policy of "the carrot and the stick," the Russian government, nevertheless, had to preserve the old Szlachta law (the Statutes of Lithuania) and the pre-existing Szlachta courts. [6] Naturally, the Polish nobility tried to restore the former state independence of Poland and acted towards it accordingly, with due regard to the international situation of the early XIX century. That is why during the War of 1812, Poles and the Polish-assimilated nobility of Lithuania and Belarus bet on Napoleon and provided him with over 80,000 fighters. Still, the Russian government, even after the successful finale of "the glorious times" (Pushkin) acted as cautiously as in the past and left the governing in the hands of the Polish and Polish-assimilated nobility.

Shimon Ashkenazi in his work *The Kingdom of Poland in 1815–1830* noted that all the officials of provincial administration, the Treasury Chamber, prosecutor's office, including the bailiffs and solicitors, were ethnically Polish. Let us remind you that the civil governor of the Vilna province in 1815–1828 was a Pole, Count Drucki-Lubecki, the vice-governor position was occupied by a Pole Plater-Sieberg, and the same position in the Grodno province was occupied by a Pole Sulistrowski (before him, for a time, the governor of Grodno was Count Drucki-Lubecki). [7]

The Jews that lived in the former Polish territories joined to Russia were indifferent to the Poles' loss of independence. [8] At some point the inability of the Polish government to provide decent living to minorities became one of the reasons for widespread extermination of the Jewish population by the gangs of Khmelnytsky (according to some sources, over 500,000 people).

During the Thirty Years' War and the Great Northern War, Poland became the site of many fights and battles and the first victims of the warring parties were, naturally, Jews. This happened again and again in the XVIII century.

Ukrainians and Byelorussians, during peasants' uprisings, first of all set to exterminating the Jewish population (for instance, Koliyivshchyna). Poles, to save their lives, betrayed their Jewish neighbors to the rebel gangs. Thus, during the defense of Uman from the bands of Gonta and Zhelezniak in 1768, the garrison commander Mladanovitch made a deal with the haidamaka in the hope of saving Poles at the expense of Jews, but this did not help, and over 20,000 Jews and Poles died in the Massacre of Uman. [9]

The actions of the Catholic clergy of Poland that inspired multiple ritual murder charges against Jews facilitated the appearance in 1713 of the book by *Ksiądz* Zhukovsky about the trials, and in 1758 Pikulsky, a monk, published a book aptly titled *The Anger of Yids*.

The wide-spread physical extermination of Jews forced some of the Jewry to convert to Christianity (the number of new converts was especially large among francoists [10]), and among Jews mysticism grew and served as a basis for a new branch of Judaism, namely, Hasidism. [11]

During his Egyptian campaign the French First Consul Napoleon addressed the Jewry with a plea for assistance, promising the African and Asian communities to restore the Temple in Jerusalem, and after that, by the Emperor's "Napoleonic Code" the Jews of France for the first time felt like its equal and full citizens. [12] The utilitarian idea of the constitutional acts aimed at "including Jews into the life of the state" [13] was limited in scope. In the Duchy of Warsaw which had been under the French protectorate until 1812, some anti-Jewish laws were passed that took away from "all practicing Moses's faith" the right to citizenship and the decree of January 29, 1819 made legal for the Jews of Poland trading mandatory military service for a tax of 700,000 zloty per year (this, of course, allowed them to avoid the fate of "cannon fodder" in the following adventures of the Emperor, but gave the Polish Judeophobiacs an excuse to blame Jews for the lack of patriotism. [14]

Alexander I, having ascended to the throne after the assassination of Paul I, introduced a number of liberal reforms. Thus, in 1802 the Jews of Shklov proudly wrote that "the Russian Emperor graced us with his mercy by making us completely equal in rights with other residents and now Jews can take their affairs to court whenever they want where civil courts are available." [15]

Chapter 1. The War of 1812 and Denunciation "Of All Russia"

At the same time the Russian government was concerned by Napoleon's flirting with Jews and in a circular of February 20, 1807 the leaders of the western regions were ordered to keep an eye on Jews' activities, namely, on their probable connections with the Jews of France. However, these concerns were unfounded: the reformatory ideas of Napoleon could not resonate with the Russian Jews. [16]

One of the fiercest anti-Bonapartists was the leader of the Hasids of Belarus, Rebbe Zalman Schneersohn (1747–1812). He made the famous prophecy of the French emperor's death. Moreover, Zalman did his best for the triumph of Russia: qahals and private individuals donated large amounts of money to the Russian government to support the war against Napoleon, and during the "Great Army" invasion, the ailing Zalman Boruchovich, as he was officially addressed by the Russian powers-that-be, was evacuated deeper into the Russian territory.

Immediately after the victorious finale of the Patriotic War, on June 29, 1814 Alexander I ordered to declare to qahals "his gracious favor" for their actions in the time of hardship and promised to issue "a ruling concerning their wishes and requests and in regards to timely improving of their situation." [17]

The future Tzar Nicholas Pavlovich, while on his journey to inspect Belarus after the Patriotic War, put in his journal several criticisms of the Jews, but specifically underlined: "It is surprising that they were perfectly loyal to us in 1812 and even assisted us wherever they could, with a risk to their lives." [18]

Let us remind the reader that the war theater in 1812–1813 was situated in the territories populated by Jews and Feldmarschall M. I. Kutuzov, while serving for two years as the military governor of the Vilna province (1809–1811), knew the situation well. According to A. P. Yermolov, it was a Jew that brought Kutuzov a report from General Wittgenstein containing very important information about the enemy movements. In his notes the Patriotic War hero described an episode when Ataman Platov almost took the emperor Napoleon himself prisoner near the village of Ashmyany thanks to the assistance of a Jew who "led the team through the outlying windmills along an obscure track buried in snow." [19]

Not far from Velizh (near the village of Babinovichi) several Jews took prisoner a French cabinet courier who was carrying an important letter to Napoleon from Paris. The prisoner of war and the messages were sent to Petersburg.

Prince S. G. Volkonsky remembered that episode: "I mention this particular event as a fact of Jews' loyalty to Russia at that time; and true, it was great bravery for cowardly Jews, despite the uncertainty of the events, to perform such a dangerous action — to snatch a courier and bring him to a Russian troop; this was a brave act and deserves to be mentioned; pity I do not recall his name, but I do remember that he was in that place where he lived near Vitebsk as a doctor without a degree (a paramedic — S.D.)." [20]

Another Patriotic War hero, the poet D. V. Davydov, said: "It happened on October 28, 1812 near the village of Lyakhovo where the Russian troops of Figner, Seslavin and Davydov blocked the retreat of Augereau's corps."

Lieutenant Lizogub of the Lithuanian Uhlan regiment spread his uhlans and suddenly attacked the enemy. Denis Davydov saw the following picture: "One of the uhlans was chasing a French jaeger with his saber out. Every time the jaeger would aim at him, he would evade and then resume the chase when the jaeger ran. Noticing this, I shouted to the uhlan: 'Uhlan, shame on you!' He gave no response, turned his horse, waited for the French jaeger to shoot, then pounced on him and cleaved his head. After that he rode up to me and asked: 'Now are you satisfied, Your Honor?' — and at this moment he moaned: a stray bullet hit him in his right leg.

"The strange thing is that the uhlan, who received the Cross of St. George for his heroic actions, could not wear it... He was a Berdichev Jew drafted to the Uhlans. This case proves the opinion that there's no such sort of man that is not prone to ambition and, consequently, not fit for military duty." [21] Let us add that at that time Jews were not supposed to be drafted, so there were very few of them in the active service.

In the magazine "Syn Otechestva" ("Son of the Fatherland," #26, 1816) an essay was published titled "Report of Heroic Action of Ruvin Gummer, Jew, Tradesman of Krinsky Parish of Grodno Province," signed by "An Eager Admirer of Virtuous Heroics."

R. Gummer, living on the lands of a landowner Chapsky during the war, sheltered in the house Lt. Bogachev, a courier with important messages from General Ertell to General Tormasov. Gummer cut one of his daughter's hair to make payot for the lieutenant and delivered him in this disguise to the Russian troops' camp.

When the French learned about the incident, they "with wild ferocity attacked... the family of the honest Jew, burned his house, robbed his property, beat his children and tortured and hanged his faithful, unfortunate wife!"

Chapter 1. The War of 1812 and Denunciation "Of All Russia"

Gummer's heroic actions were confirmed by His Royal Highness Duke of Wuerttemberg. Unfortunately, the article noted, Gummer failed to receive compensation for his financial losses.

The unknown author concluded that Gummer, "this respectable Jew," was not alone but "together with his brothers in faith remained, in secret, unwaveringly loyal to our Fatherland." [22]

The events of the beginning and the end of the Patriotic War are also quite remarkable. On June 13, 1812 the Commander-In-Chief of the Russian forces Barclay de Tolly received a report about the French crossing the Neman and hurried with this news to Vilna where the Emperor Alexander I was at the time.

Barclay de Tolly was greatly surprised to learn that the enemy crossing had been reported to the emperor by Jews on the night of June 12.

Let us remind the reader that long before the invention of telegraph, large European merchant and banking houses in the west regions of Russia (Poland) had their own postal service which was often kept by their Jewish lease holders and innkeepers who were also the mail carriers and received appropriate payment from the bank or the head of the merchant house.

The head of the Moscow Main Staff Archives — the so-called Lefortovo Archives — N. Polikarpov wrote that the Jewish post was ahead of Feld jaeger and couriers by almost 24 hours. [23] Hence, it is not surprising that Jews beat General Baggovut's messenger sent to Barclay de Tolly and passed their message to the mayor of Kovno Bistry and he, in turn, passed it on to the Police Minister Balashov. [24]

At the end of the war the information received by the Jews turned out to be inaccurate: Marshal Oudinot managed to give three zealous Jews the wrong place of the French troops to cross the Berezina and they hurried to pass it on to Admiral Chichagov.

The following is known: Napoleon managed to escape the trap and the three Borisovo Jews were executed by the admiral. However, after an investigation, they were later "posthumously rehabilitated." [25]

The Governor-General of St. Petersburg, a hero of 1812, M. A. Miloradovich, according to M. Lilienthal, stated: "These people are indeed the most loyal servants of the Emperor, we would not have defeated Napoleon without them, and I would not have been decorated with these orders for the War of 1812." [26] Of course, when you compare the actions of the Jewish population to those of the Poles during the Patriotic War, the negative attitude of Poles towards Jews becomes understandable.

A. M. Romanovsky who had no love for "Yids," talked about the events in the town of Chavusy (46 km from Mogilev), where the civilian power was seized and the municipal administration formed of landowners and priests by the Polish population right after the Russian troops retreated; "rejoicing and singing praise and patriotic hymns to Napoleon in the church where the French Eagle was already displayed on the quire," while in the Jews' eyes there were no "joy, nor fear, or sorrow, or despair." The Poles even organized a militia in the town to assist the French and called it "The Guards." [27]

However, after the mob destroyed several Jewish taverns, the neutrality of the Jews disappeared: they began passing important information about troops' movements to the Orthodox residents that remained loyal to Russia (part of the Orthodox clergy headed by Bishop Varlaam betrayed their oath and the Russian Emperor and swore fealty to Napoleon).

Trusting Napoleon to restore the independent Polish state, Poles, devout Catholics, did not react even to the infringement of the rights of the Pope. [28]

Poles were formed into a detachment of the Great Army, and behind the front lines they guarded French communication lines. Moreover, right before the war they successfully sabotaged draft in the Westland (this action was performed by Prince Drucki-Lubecki under the pretense of untrustworthiness of the population [29]).

The leader of the Polish party Adam Czartoryski sensibly left before the war... for Karlsbad for medical treatment, and his father, the president of Sejm of the Duchy of Warsaw, on June 26, 1812 called upon all Poles to leave Russian service. [30]

Nicholas I in his "General Journal of Civil and Industrial Affairs" wrote during his travels of 1816: "In Belorussia the nobility, comprised almost exclusively of rich Poles, never showed loyalty to Russia, and, besides some noblemen from Vitebsk and Mogilev, everyone else swore fealty to Napoleon." [31]

Later the historian N. K. Schilder described the arrival of Russian forces to the Duchy of Warsaw: "In the Duchy of Warsaw nobody, however, met the Russians as liberators. Only Jews in every village in the path of the troops brought out colorful banners with the Emperor's monogram; as the Russians approached, the Jews beat their drums and played their trumpets and timpani." [32]

In Kalisz (a notorious town among Jews) Adam Czartoryski was introduced to the Emperor Alexander I. "The arrival of this passionate adherent of restoration of Poland in the Russian army," the historian noted sarcastically, "served as proof that Poles began to doubt Napoleon's victories and turned to a new sun that was rising in the political heavens of Europe." [33] Most likely, Adam Czartoryski was also present at the reception the Jews held in the Emperor's honor and met with the representatives of the Jewish people Sonnenberg and Dillon, who were the main suppliers for the Russian army. [34]

Admiral A. S. Shishkov, who disliked Jews, stated: "The Poles did not show any joy... only the Yids, happy-faced, gathered at the houses where the Emperor stayed and upon his exiting a house shouted 'Hurray!'." [35]

Quite representative was the situation in another Belorussian town. Grodno had been populated by Jews since long before: the first mention of them in the town archives dates back to the XII century.

With the partition of Poland of 1793, the town was annexed by Russia. Jews were dominant in trade and industry and comprised the majority of the population. In Grodno there was one of the first Jewish printing shops and it was considered the center of Jewish culture. The town's residents were Poles and Polish-assimilated landowners who owned spacious and rich manors. Historically and geographically the town leaned towards Poland and looked at Russia with animosity. The masonic lodges of the Grodno province answered to the Poles in Warsaw.

During the French invasion the Catholic nobility sided with Napoleon: thus, in two counties — Slonim and Novogrud — two regiments (Bipinka's and Rayetsky's) were formed to join the French military. [36]

To celebrate the surrender of Moscow (September 2, 1812) the Poles hung huge banners on their balconies allegorically depicting the victory of Napoleon's forces.

Two months after the French left the Russian capital, Russian forces under the command of an 1812 hero, partisan and poet Denis Davydov suddenly invaded Grodno. Davydov rode into the town under a "Yid canopy" and was greeted by the Jewish residents. When he saw the banners shaming the Russian emperor on the balconies, Denis Davydov ordered the townspeople to gather and informed them of the outcome of the 1812 campaign. The Poles were ordered to surrender any weapons they had in two hours' time and wear mourning for their dead compatriots. They had been given two days to make and display new banners which would depict the victory of the Russian arms over the French and the Poles, and to top the triumph, the town priest, who had just recently blessed the French and Napoleon, was ordered to preach in the same church the praise to the Russians and to Alexander I. Finally, the commander ordered the civil power in the town to be given to the qahal. The Poles were promised that if they disobeyed the qahal, the town would be given to the mercy of the soldiers. The newly appointed town leader (a qahal Jew) was told to compile lists of collaborators. The Poles tried to complain about the "atrocities" of the partisan to General Miloradovitch, who was friends with Davydov and sided with him. Later, when the Patriotic War hero was introduced to the Emperor Alexander I, Feldmarschall M. I. Kutuzov reminded those present of the capture of the town, to which the Emperor uttered: "Whatever may have been, victors are not to be judged." [37]

Thus, the actions of Jews and Poles in the Patriotic War of 1812 were that historical condition that could not but determine their further relationship.

The rule of the qahal in Grodno was short: the administration was reluctant to punish the collaborationists. Soon, on January 22, 1816, Prince Drucki-Lubecki was appointed the civil governor of the town, and in June he also became the governor of Vilna. The prince was a devoted adherent of "the Polish party" and saw the Jews as a pro-government power. One of the tasks of the new governor was to discredit the Jews in the eyes of the Russian government.

THE BLOOD LIBEL AND RITUAL ACCUSATIONS

In 1815 the Russian Commissar to the government of the Kingdom of Poland Senator N. N. Novosiltsev introduced to the "Reform Committee" a bill on the Jewish question. While recommending the spread of crafts and agriculture as a way of economic development, the author of the bill demanded that Jews were granted unlimited citizen rights.

The governmental circles met N. N. Novosiltsev's bill with understanding; Prince A. N. Golitsyn in his letter to Novosiltsev noted: "The loyalty of these people to the Russian throne and their effort towards the benefit of the government during the past war were proven many times over and witnessed by the civil as well as military authorities, and gained the Jews the benevolence of the Emperor and, of course, give them the full right, equal with other His Majesty's subjects, to his protective laws." [38] However, the princes Czartoryski and Drucki-Lubecki, Zayonchenok, and the priest A. Staszic vehemently protested against the bill and pointed out to the committee the "harmfulness of

Chapter 1. The War of 1812 and Denunciation "Of All Russia"

Jewry" (in 1816 A. Staszic published an article with that title, in which he called Jews the reason for the decline of Poland and accused them of making Poland "the laughing stock of Europe" and "a Jewish country" [39]).

After the War of 1812, in the Kingdom of Poland, according to S. M. Dubnov, there was an outbreak of government-instigated ritual processes, and 1816 in Westland and the Kingdom of Poland became the year of a "ritual bacchanalia," as if an experienced hand "has sown the poisoned seed of the Middle Ages among the masses." [40]

In Miedzyrzec, Wlodawa, Lublin, Siedlice and other places, at Eastertide 1815 and 1816 children's corpses were found. Innocent people were arrested and charged.

On Easter Saturday, April 8, 1816, near Grodno, a body of a four-year-old girl was found, a daughter of a Grodno citizen Maria Adamovich. The Christians accused the Jews of a ritual murder. A member of the town qahal Sholom Lapin was arrested. Only in February of 1817, due to the efforts of N. N. Novosiltsev (who was personally acquainted with the Grodno Jews and co-owned some factories in the suburbs) and the Minister of Spiritual Affairs A. N. Golitsyn (the prince, a mystic and idealist, dreamed of baptizing the Jews and for that purpose founded the "Israeli Christian" society) the case was closed.

J. E. Przecławski remembered that a representative of the Jewish people Zundel Sonnenberg "complained of the libel, insulting to his co-believers," and cleverly attributed it to *"the hatred of the Poles for the Jews' loyalty to the government" (my italics — S.D.).* [41]

On March 6, 1817, all the governors of Westland received a government memorandum: "Concerning still present in some provinces gained from Poland accusations of Jews of murdering Christian children, assumingly to use their blood, His Majesty the Emperor considering that these accusations have previously been found false by independent investigations and the King's documents, issued his high ruling: declare to all the governors the royal will that from now on, no Jew be accused of murdering Christian children with no evidence, just on the prejudice that they, supposedly, need Christian blood." [42]

Prince Drucki-Lubecki was reprimanded by the Tsar for conducting a trial based on a "blood libel."

In 1822 the painter A. O. Orlovski (1777–1832), at a request from the Velizh Catholics, painted a picture *The Yids Bleeding a Tortured Child's Body*. One of the characters depicted bore a resemblance to a man well-known in the borough of Leczyca, and the painting itself was exhibited on the front of the church of the Order of Bernardinis.

After the complaint from the Jews the Russian administration ordered the painting removed. However, already in March, 1823 Orlovski created a larger painting with the same theme, and this time the characters were the spitting image of the borough's residents, including the rabbi of Leczyca.

This time the mob, encouraged by the retired lieutenant Wenceslas Dunin-Skrzynno, did not let the administration remove the painting. Soon, on the first day of Christian Easter (April 22), a three-year-old boy Fedor Yemelyanov went missing.

After ten days (of course, after the holidays were over) the child's body, covered in puncture wounds, was found in a bog. The suspects were two respectable citizens: the merchant Berlin and the councilman Tsetlin.

The investigation dragged on for almost a year and a half, and in the fall of 1824 the Vitebsk provincial court ruled: "The incident of the death of the soldier's son to be considered an act of God; all the Jews who were presumed guilty in the murder shall remain free of suspicion..." [43]

The local Uniate clergy headed by Metropolitan Jozafat Bulhak (he was a relative of J. E. Przecławski and a friend of Drucki-Lubecki) protested against the court ruling and the case was transferred to a known anti-Semite, Governor General of Belorussia Prince N. N. Khovansky (1777–1837); in the city, arrests, bribes and slander of witnesses broke out and the suspects were subjected to illegal methods of interrogation comparable to medieval torture.

Nicholas I, having ascended to the Russian throne, severely disapproved of and punished the often-fanatic Russian sectarianism, and, by analogy, believed there were secret groups among Jews that performed ritual murders. That is why the ruling of the new emperor was harsh, although consistent with the times: "Since the incident proves that the Yids use our tolerance of their faith to evil, to instill fear in them and as an example for others the Yid schools (synagogues. -S.D.) in Velizh are to be sealed until further notice and services are to be prohibited either in the schools themselves or at their locations." [44] At the same time, on prince Khovansky's report of repeated crimes committed by Jews (murder of children, desecration of sacramental bread and of church utensils, etc.) Nicholas I in October 1827 wrote skeptically: "We must find out who those unfortunate children were; this should be easy, if this isn't a filthy lie." [45]

Under the influence of multiple complaints of the Jewish population, in St. Petersburg distrust of the Velizh libel grew: it was noted

CHAPTER 1. THE WAR OF 1812 AND DENUNCIATION "OF ALL RUSSIA"

that "the committee, absorbed in its zealous prejudice towards Jews, was acting in a biased manner and dragging the case out unnecessarily." [46] As a result, the investigation was taken over by the Senate, and the de facto assistant to the Minister of Justice, Count V. N. Panin (1801–1874), based only on the legal side of the process, convincingly proved the unfoundedness of the charges and demanded immediate release of the innocent arrested. After V. N. Panin's report, the case was transferred to the State Council for discussion, and in 1834 the oldest member of the highest government body Admiral N. S. Mordvinov (1754–1845), who owned land near Velizh and personally knew many of the accused, [47] declared that the Jews had become victims of a conspiracy by religious and ignorant fanatics. The 80-year-old adherent of justice sent a memorandum "solely to inform His Majesty" with the deliberations and notes of the Department of the Civil and Spiritual Affair, whose president he was.

Pointing out that the accusations "uncover only a conspiracy to slander Jews," N. S. Mordvinov concluded: "The accusation of the Jews of horrific crimes had at its source malice and prejudice and was inspired by some strong power that can be traced through every step of the case." [48] At the meeting of the State Council its majority accepted Mordvinov's point of view ("Prejudice against Jews is too readily accepted as true and creates a basis for the entirety of the opinion." [49]), and then the Council decided to free all the Jews and ordered the Minister of Internal Affairs to confirm that in the provinces with Jewish population the ruling of 1817 (prohibition of conducting investigations of ritual murder charges) should remained observed. On this resolution of the State Council on January 18, 1835 Nicholas I laconically remarked: "Be it so," however, he refused to sign the order to the governors to stop conducting investigations of such cases because of his belief in the existence of fanatical Jewish sects. Thus, after nine years the innocent people were released (three of the arrested died in jail, most acted courageously during the investigation, and a real hero was the merchant Berlin's wife Slavka [50]), the synagogues were once more open and the police returned the scrolls of the Holy Scripture. Remembering the kindness of a number of Russian statesmen, the Velizh Jews introduced into the prayer to praise the patriarchs and prophets the following famous line: "Ve gam Mordvinov zocher le-tov" ("And we shall remember Mordvinov with kindness"). [51]

The Polish insinuations against the Jewish population were not limited to "blood libel." At the same period the Poles inspired certain criminal investigations (church robberies, desecration of the Holy

Cross, etc.). This is how the Slonim Affair started (no later than 1822): a group of Jews on their way to a traditional fair in a borough of Belva allegedly robbed a church of the regular (monk) canons.

As stated by J. E. Przecławski, the Jewish thieves were caught red-handed in a basement of a local woman's home while distributing their catch — they were breaking and cutting holy vessels and crosses. [52] (The investigation was conducted by a former Napoleon army colonel and the mayor of the town, one Konopka; his older brother General Ivan Konopka ineptly defended Slonim against... the Russian forces in 1812, and his younger brother served in Warsaw under the Grand Prince Constantine Pavlovich; his sister Julia was married to General Bezobrazov and, once widowed, married D. P. Tatishchev, the Russian ambassador to Austria. [53]) The intercession of Zundel Sonnenberg failed. Although the entire population of the town petitioned the mayor to conduct a thorough investigation of the circumstances, and Sonnenberg demanded that the suspects were released from jail, nothing helped, since the case, most likely, was a setup. [54]

For almost a century and a half, according to the legend, historians were convinced that Jews in Ukraine rented out churches.

Thus, in a book by V. V. Afanasyev about K. F. Ryleyev published as a part of the "Life of Remarkable Persons" series, it is stated: "A Polish sub-warden Czaplicki gave the Jewish lease holders the right to collect profit from the Orthodox churches of the town... The Union... of the szlachta made it possible to appoint persons of a different faith as church lease holders." [55] Later this legend changed: in the XIX century the Jewish lease holders turned into Jewish robbers and desecrators of church utensils. [56] We think that the real state of affairs should be distinguished from these popular beliefs. It is for a reason that the above-quoted J. E. Przecławski mentioned a beautiful Jewish widow, who in Ruzany with her *bachur* (son — *S.D.*) ran a den of thieves at her own tavern, *but her clients were Poles,* not Jews; besides, she had an affair with the gang's ataman. [57]

Let us remind the reader that during the Justin Karmelyuk rebellion, Jews not only gave shelter to the rebels and bought the robbed goods, but also participated in that movement that carried a distinct social character. Karmelyuk's primary assistant was "a baptized Jew Vassily Dobrovolsky," who later was sentenced to 50 strikes with a cane and to penal servitude. [58]

Several years later, in 1827, in the same Slonim county, during the observance of Purim, several Jews were arrested on suspicion of desecration of the image of Christ that stood on the road to the village of

Novosilki. The main accusers were the key officer Dombrovski of the Lukonitsa parish and the priest of the Yagneshits church, Malishevsky. They insisted that the Jews pulled down the image of Christ and "beat it instead of Haman."

Nine people were arrested and sentenced to penal servitude. The court's decree was affirmed by the notorious Prince Drucki-Lubecki, and after the affirmation by the Senate and the Committee of Ministers, the Tzar signed the sentence: eight of the convicts were flogged on November 9, 1828 (the ninth died during the investigation) and then deported to Siberia. [59]

Let us note an important fact. It is known that the French forces advanced along a front no wider than 50 km, through Lithuania and Belorussia, seizing on their way Vilna, Grodno, Slonim, Velizh, Vitebsk, and others. It is along that line that the Jews of Grodno, Slonim, Chavusy, Velizh, and Vitebsk demonstrated outstanding instances of heroism and courage while fighting for the Russian troops. [60] It is not a coincidence that in these particular towns the ritual charges were filed and processes were conducted, initiated by Poles. Meanwhile, neither in the southern Belorussia nor in Ukraine nor in the Baltics or Courland, the areas south and north of the French forces' movement, was a single known ritual charge filed or a bloody slander spread.

Therefore, the processes of the '10–'20s of the XIX century seem to be a consequence of the diametrically opposed positions of Jews and Poles during the Patriotic War of 1812. Another reason of active anti-Judaism in those areas was definitely the fight of the Polish nobility (many of whom were also freemasons) for its privileges, which soon in the Kingdom of Poland turned, according to a historian, into "a war because of Jews." [61] At the same time, the "blood libel" against Jews on the part of the Polish nationalists combined in a strange way with the "anti-masonic slander" against Catholics on the part of the Russian chauvinists. [62]

RUSSIAN FREEMASONRY AND SECTARIANISM

The natural penetration of the ideas of the era of Enlightenment and of the French revolution into Russia in certain sense caused the most educated segment of the society to aim "westward," while the "religious and dogmatic" and government-loyal circles (especially after Napoleon's invasion) saw in "westernizing" [63] a real danger to the throne and to serfdom. As we know, during the so-called period of classical freemasonry in Russia (the second half of the XVII through to the first quarter of the XIX centuries) many outstanding members of the Russian society became members of different lodges. At the same time, it was during that period that the guardian and patriotic officials thought of attempting to unite the ideas of freemasons with those of sectarians and infidels into a single compendium directed against the Russian state and the Russian people. [64]

P. I. Melnikov (1819–1883), who wrote under the name of A. Pechersky, was charged by the Minister of Internal Affairs S. S. Lanskoy with writing the famous *Notes on the Russian Schism* for the Grand Prince Constantine Nikolayevich and did a special research titled *Letters on Russian Schism*. While listing Russian sects, in Item D (*The Mystics*), he included among them the group called "Labziners," although the name of the group came from A. F. Labzin (1766–1825), the vice-president of the Emperor's Academy of Arts. a freemason and a mystic. Actually, according to Melnikov-Pechersky, the movement of Khlysts was also a kind of Russian freemasonry. Should we then be surprised that in his pulp fiction works he reviled the brotherhood of freemasons: "Both freemasonry and the Black Book witchcraft are the same thing. It originated from the warlock Bruce and is still thriving today... With them... if any man joins their faith, they require from him an oath and make him swear horrible oaths that he would not reveal their secrets to anyone: not to his father and mother, nor his kin, nor his tribe, nor his priest at confession, nor the judge in court. He would promise to endure the whip and the block, the axe and the fire, or the cold, yet not give away their cause and not reveal their secrets... if anyone converts to their faith, he says goodbye to the world and gives up everything..." [65]

Such a mix-up of freemasonry and sectarianism was very typical, but the point is that we "judge it by the documents from the hostile camp."

Let us remind the reader that along with the elite, masonic lodges often included "the dull people" (commoners — *S.D.*). Moreover, in the late XVIII century landowners often joined a masonic lodge together with their servants. Thus, A. F. Pisemsky in his novel *The Masons* tells of his uncle, a famous freemason Yu. N. Bartenev, whose manservant was also a mason. [66]

We should also mention that, due to a number of reasons, the mystical views of freemasons closely intertwined with ordinary religious mysticism. That is why, at the time, the Minister of Spiritual Affairs and Education in the government of Alexander I, Prince A. N. Golitsyn, supported the distribution of the masonic mystical books and their publishing (in particular, religious institutions did not create obstacles to publishing a freemason magazine *Sionsky Vestnik (The Messenger of Zion)*, and many members of *The Bible Society* were masons).

One of the zealous readers of mystical literature was E. N. Kotelnikov [67], a Cossack captain. Under the influence of A. Boehme and Jung-Stilling, he wrote a book titled *An Appeal to Men to Follow the Internal Call of the Holy Spirit* (SPb., 1820).

Nicely ornamented by vignettes by Count F. Tolstoy (the president of the Emperor's Academy of Arts) and illustrated with prints by N. I. Utkin, the book was distributed to all seminaries and spiritual academies on personal order of A. N. Golitsyn. However, Kotelnikov's second book (*The Beginnings with the God of a Sharp Heart in a Gold Crown*) was pronounced heretical and the author was arrested and, after he repented, exiled to his native village.

Kotelnikov broke his promise not to spread heretical ideas and was imprisoned in the Solovetsky Monastery. He became a monk and, although Nicholas I soon pardoned him, Kotelnikov died in the monastery.

The sect of Spirit-Bearers created by Kotelnikov incurred fierce attacks from the official Orthodox powers. The enemies of the Bible Society (and of freemasons) accused Kotelnikov of being an "illuminati agent," although the founder of the new sect considered his persecutors masons and servants of Satan.

One of the most consistent enemies of Kotelnikov, Metropolitan Seraphim, wrote about "spirit bearers" that they are, "in essence, also freemasons, illuminati, Jacobins and Carbonari," but "spirit bearers" were more dangerous, because "in the name of faith and God they conspired to destroy our Holy Faith and through that produce a revolution and use it to their profit." [68]

Warning the government of the secret enemies of the Fatherland, who acted in the name of good, Seraphim underlined the fact that Kotelnikov's idea had come from outside, for "there is no doubt that it was not invented in Russia but brought to us from beyond the seas and is managed and supported and spread in true diabolic ways by foreigners, who seek to topple our altars and the throne, and to destroy the power and might of Russia that scares Europe." It is noteworthy that Kotelnikov himself in his defense speech talked about… "followers of freemasons," among whom he named General Arakcheyev, Archimandrite Photios and Metropolitan Seraphim himself. [69]

Thus, regardless of the position taken by one camp or another, the basis for "harmfulness" and "anti-Russism" of the actions of powers-that-be as well as of their "exposers" were the ideas of the same groups — "freemasons," "carbonari," and "foreigners." In this situation of distorting the facts and of eclectic views of half-educated adherents of new sects and teachings, a new theory "synthesizing" polar images of freemasonry and sectarianism could not but appear. [70]

On February 8, 1816 Colonel V. I. Dibich, who in 1814 was a staff officer for special tasks to Barclay de Tolly and who later lived abroad in Messene, sent a report to the Feldmarschall General: as a "loyal son" of the Fatherland he decided to inform the government about his accidental discoveries that could have great consequences for Russia.

Attracting attention of the higher powers to the spread of republican ideas in the military and the recruiting of Russian officers to masonic lodges, V. I. Dibich specifically blamed Ignaz Aurelius Fessler (1756–1839), a "Jesuit and Jacobin" and a former professor of Hebrew at the St. Petersburg Theological Academy, who, after the fall of M. M. Speransky, who had invited him to Russia to teach, was exiled for his atheism to the Saratov province. In the opinion of the informant, there was nothing **more** dangerous than the actions of "this man, his way of thinking, and everything he is capable of." [71]

In his report Dibich told of masonic symbols and ranks of masonic lodge members. The masters, hiding their secret revolutionary goals from the lowest ranks, even worked out measures to "preserve their existence and, pretending to be innocent, bide their time until the right moment comes" [72].

The same day, February 8, he sent another report to his brother, Baron I. I. Dibich, the future hero of the Turkish-Russian war and Feldmarschall General. Justifying his actions by his oath, the colonel said that during his stay in France he had managed to infiltrate a society "kept secret, but by its actions quite obvious." [73] Speaking of immorality of the society he stated that this "cannot be proven by anyone, since any oral explanation given by an adept of a higher rank can be repudiated." [74] Apparently, both reports had documents attached that, unfortunately, did not survive, as well as notations by the colonel himself written in the form of a dialogue of an old high-ranking member of a lodge with a young apprentice.

Referring to the original sources of the teachings of secret societies in pre-Biblical times, Dibich tried to prove that all of them, from the Maya, pagan priests, sages, brahmin, Levites, Platonists, etc., to illuminati and Tugenbunders, strive for their own goals regardless of abuses. That is why any secret society gradually changes in time: it abandons its original good intentions and becomes dangerous to any state, because they present their intolerance "of injustice as freedom." [75] Manipulating the passions of the lower ranks, masters of lodges have devised ways to psychologically influence neophytes (rites of initiation, rules, and teachings). As a result, I. I. Dibich writes, they learn the character of the initiate and cleverly influence him: "They give pleasure to a sensualist, they trick someone interested in politics accordingly, to a kind man they open ways to being humane and to work towards happiness of the mankind, to a greedy spendthrift they give hope of acquiring treasure, to a dreamer they provide a chance to commune with the realm of spirits, and thus, everyone receives their own. If it turns out that the interests of the secret co-members don't allow for this to occur in the society one has joined, then on stage appear Rosicrucians or Swedenborgians or some other category, who, according to the change of pace, continue to keep the fly trapped in the web, and compete with each other, and everything remains the same. Thanks to that their common cause wins, because should something shameful be discovered, they say — well, those are not freemasons, they are Black Brothers, or some others, or that it is an illegal lodge, and meanwhile, was there ever an instance of final extermination of evil?" [76]

In the dialogue, a higher master "A" explained to the apprentice "B" that the main task of freemasons is the mastery of the art of rulers — the art of "ruling through people," [77] that is why a mason does not owe loyalty to any oath, homeland, monarch, or faith, for his homeland is "the entire world and not the little corner of it you were born in": "There will come a time when there will be no property except the reward for your labor, no material reward, except gratitude, no hereditary rights, except wider knowledge and larger ability to be useful, which are gained through socializing and being taught." [78]

Finally, the main task of freemasons, the master concludes, is the creation of a world monarchy, for it alone will give humankind the peace it desires.

Actually, both reports by I. I. Dibich were the first acts of defamation of freemasons in Russia. At the same time, the colonel's reports never mention Jews (with the exception of Professor Fessler, whose Jewish origins would later be pointed out by the anti-Semitists of the XX century).

Let us mention that these reports were preceded by a document that originated from the nobility close to pre-Decemberists: count M. A. Dmitriev-Mamonov, the last of his line, in 1814–1815 put together the 46 "Items taught in the interior Order," which resembled in their conquering ambitions a version of "The Testament of Peter I."

Undoubtedly, M. A. Dmitriev-Mamonov knew about freemasons first-hand, because in Item 25 he declared: "The gift to the Order of manors, lands and fortresses like to the Knights Templar, Teutonic Order and others, and naming the knights, Knights of the *Russian Cross.*" [79]

However, the manner of the plan definitely shows that its creator was mentally ill. And true, soon a guardian was appointed for the count. Re-drawing the map of Europe, the author of the state plan also paid attention to Jews — in Item 12 he suggested "moving half of the Yids of Poland to the unpopulated provinces of Russia and *converting them into the faith.*"

Several years after the defeat of the Decembrists the government had to return to the issue of "maliciousness" of secret societies.

In 1831 the former head of the office of the Ministry of Internal Affairs (the head of the secret police) Ya.I. de Saint-Glin was urgently called to Petersburg to testify about two reports "of the entire Russia" — "the foliant or volume" of the prince A. N. Golitsyn and the vast notes of M. L. Magnitsky.

"The work" of the prince was titled *On the Illuminati in 1831* and was made of two parts. After explaining in the first part the goals of the secret society, the author of the "foliant" claimed in the second part that Illuminati had seized the most important government positions in Russia and all the strings were pulled by M. M. Speransky, who for 20 years had protected the "foremost" Illuminatus, the famous Professor Fessler. In the margins of the "volume" the Emperor made notations in his own hand: "I require proof!" "Where is proof?" "Outrageous lie!" etc., since the author slandered en masse the persons close to the Emperor. [80]

Ya.I. de Saint-Glin managed to convince Nicholas I of the total absurdity of the report, for the secret police chief was much better informed in the matter than the prince. We should also mention one of the "foliant's" features: its author consistently referred to another report that belonged to M. L. Magnitsky and had been received by Nicholas I in February of 1831.

M. L. Magnitsky, a famous and outstanding person, graduated from the Moscow University and served in the Preobrazhensky regiment, and later worked for the Ministry of Foreign Affairs in Paris and Vienna (he was assigned to the staff of the Feldmarschall A. V. Suvorov and managed the commander's correspondence). Having earned the trust of M. M. Speransky, in 1810–1811 he, under the mentorship of the count, worked on putting together a reform project, and after the

Minister's fall was exiled to Vologda where he met Arakcheyev and became his confidant. Soon he took the position of the vice-governor of Voronezh and later the position of the civil governor of Simbirsk. Appointed a curator of the Kazan School District, M. L. Magnitsky became notorious after he simultaneously fired 11 professors of the Kazan University for "suspiciousness." However, in 1826 he was fired for misuse of government funds and went to live in exile in Revel.

In one of his articles, provocatively titled "The Fate of Russia," the disgraced nobleman proclaimed that Russia "did not regret that the Tatar period distanced Russia from Europe" and further explained: "She *is glad for it,* for she sees that *her oppressors the Tatars were her saviors from Europe.*

The Tatar oppression and distancing from the Western Europe were, perhaps, the greatest blessing for Russia... [81]

A memoir sent by M. L. Magnitsky to the Emperor on February 1 was titled: "Denunciation of a world-wide conspiracy against altars and thrones through public events and legal acts." In it he detailed the Illuminati plan to seize power and establish a new world order. The seven items of the plan described in detail the "malicious actions of freemasons." Thus, in Item 6 it said: "The goal of the order is to liberate people from their kings, nobility, and clergy," and Item 5 listed the steps to achieve this goal: "Illuminati must try to seize all official positions and have them occupied by their adherents." [82] Naturally, the former curator of the Kazan School District considered printing of books the evil that started the penetration of freemasonry into Russia. It is not accidental that, according to the informant, in masonic circles it was decided "to seize all the genres of literature and poison them all with the venom of Illuminati." [83] Consequently, from the West the roads of freemasonry led to Russians — Prince Repnin, Elagin, Novikov, Pozdeyev. Calling the Jacobins "the strike force" of freemasons, Magnitsky made a flowery claim that nobody in the world could resist them but Russia, for she "scares freemasons with her physical power, her spirit... of the true and unbreakable faith, her loyalty to... her rulers, sincere, heartfelt and sacred, because it is based on faith, on feeling, and on a thousand years of people's love." [84]

Four days later, on February 7, 1831 Magnitsky continued his report: having briefly recounted his previous memoir, he, as a friend and employee, took up denouncing his former boss, M. M. Speransky.

First of all, Magnitsky mentioned that Speransky was the leader of a conspiracy in Russia and, thanks to his patronage, the classic illuminati teachings were preached in the country with "hellish tricks" in school books as well as in scientific literature. Moreover, the informant said that the center of the world conspiracy was in London, where Illuminati founded a university where Christian theology was not taught, but "Yids" were accepted. [85]

Not quite satisfied with his first letters, a week later, on February 14, Magnitsky sent a new letter to the Emperor from Revel. In this letter he defined various types of Illuminati — political, spiritual, academic, and common.

Having pointed out the "ways" the political Illuminati invaded Russia (Yelagin, Shuvalov, Golitsyn, et al), he paid special attention to Emperor Alexander I's close circle, being especially ruthless towards N. N. Novosiltsev (for the set of liberal reforms he introduced) and the magazine *The Messenger of Zion* (a publication "thoroughly Illuminatian"). Naturally, Speransky was not forgotten this time, either, and was blamed for inviting the Hebrew professor Fessler. According to Magnitsky, Fessler was extremely dangerous, because, rejecting Christianity and striving to replace it with the teachings of Illuminati, the professor insisted that Christ was no Savior but "a son of an Essene who fooled people to establish his teachings." [86] Speransky received a "talisman" (a ring) from the hands of the honorable professor, which made the Minister the sole leader of Russian freemasons. Apparently wishing to make his report sound more realistic, Magnitsky "confessed" that he himself had not avoided the "cunning nets" of Illuminati and became a member of the lodge "Northern Star," although he immediately excused his misstep by reminding about the first report he made in 1811 (before the fall of Speransky), in which he denounced the lodge for "its dangerous foundations." Further in his letter Magnitsky listed nearly fifty high-ranking officials who were members of the secret society.

The opportunities for masonic propaganda grew since the foundation of The Bible Society, thus marking the appearance of "spiritual" Illuminati in Russia. The scholarly secretary of the society V. M. Popov (1771–1842) along with other members strove to substitute English Protestantism (Methodism) for "true Orthodoxy." Simultaneously with the spiritual Illuminati, the "academic" kind spread in Russia (through creating in 1816–1817 the first Lancastrian schools, where education was based on students teaching one another).

Naturally, the former "quencher" of the "fire of free thinking" in his own Kazan school district accused universities of teaching pantheism, materialism, and pragmatism, for studies of "precise subjects" (statis-

CHAPTER 1. THE WAR OF 1812 AND DENUNCIATION "OF ALL RUSSIA"

tics, economics, etc.) were bound to quickly convince students that "the persons of the government, clergy, nobility, and military are the groups that do not produce anything (drones of society)." [87]

Yet, arguably the most important thing about this letter of M. L. Magnitsky was the fact that, for the first time. Jews became part of "the world-wide masonic conspiracy."

That is why the book publisher Nikolai, a seller of "various lies," invited "the good Yid Mendelsohn" (one of the most active agents of Weishaupt) to work on *the World Library of Germany*. Pointing out dangerous heresy, Magnitsky placed the blame onto contemporary Jewry, which misinterpreted the Bible, especially in regards to prophecies of the coming of Christ. Jews, exploiting the fact that Christians did not know Hebrew, "published many outrageous writings against the people and governments in the guise of books of prayer. [88]

In fact, it was *Magnitsky who could claim priority in "discovering" the connection between freemasons and Jews,* although he never specified its details. Pointing at Jews as a demoralizing force, he stressed that Illuminati used them to achieve their secret goals. For example, in Item B that explained the means of spreading masonic ideas, Magnitky stated: "Through members and messengers traveling under various pretexts. People of that sort are mostly able to come to Russia as associates of trading houses, from which, for their cover, they can easily have some errands and such, for nowadays all Europe's funds have already been transferred into hands of Yids (the four Rothchild brothers) ..." [89]

Twelve years after he sent his "denunciations of all of Russia," in which M. M. Speransky was declared the main myrmidon of Illuminati, Magnitsky — a former employee and friend of the Minister — decided to publish an "obituary" (this time openly). In the Slavophil magazine "Moskvityanin" (1843) an article appeared titled "Reflection at the Coffin of Speransky." The informant of yesterday lamented the virtues of the deceased Minister: "This is a bier appropriate for a famous man, unmatched in our history in the variety and depth of his knowledge, his visionary mind, the brave and high flight of his thought, and his gift with words that combined power and simplicity with unique charm and which he possessed with ease and spontaneity with no need for rehearsal, in his understanding and clear presentation of the most complicated topics of state and in his direct participation in most important laws over four consecutive reigns." [90]

The difference between this "reflection" and "denunciation letters" seems to show in its author the model for future "seksots" (secret agents) and "laureates," of which the former informed "whom it may concern" in secret and the latter published their reports openly.

In any case, the basis was laid and later came followers and continuators. And those were never in short supply. Although M. L. Magnitsky's "creative work" was submitted to the "special archive" of the secret police, it almost immediately became known to garden variety anti-Semitists, of whom the foremost one was, undoubtedly, O. A. Przecławski.

Unlike Yu. Delevsky and many others who believed that the myth of "Jewish-Masonic conspiracy" first appeared in France in the '60s of the XIX century and was later adopted by Russian anti-Semitists, we believe that the history of social ideas in Russia contains enough facts and documents to prove that this "invention" was strictly domestic.

CHAPTER 2

The Great Secret of Freemasons

THE JEWISH QUESTION AND RUSSIAN LITERATURE

Until the XIX century, a stereotypical Jew in the world literature by Christian authors, regardless of their ethnicity, was based on certain myths. *Literary images of Jews* were dual in nature: on the one hand, the Old Testament history required "the high style" of depiction, on the other — the Gospel tradition imposed "the low style." The traitor apostle Judas Iscariot, who sold Christ to his persecutors for thirty pieces of silver, was a blueprint for many "familiar traits": treachery, bigotry, greed, amorality, cowardice, snitching. Interestingly, an image of a Jew in non-Christian literature of the Arab world did not carry these mythologems. [1]

In the Russian literature of the XIX century that was rapidly adopting European standards, naturally, the Jewish type was copied off already known characters created by Chaucer, Dante, Shakespeare, Molière, Byron, Goethe, and many others. At the same time, multiple variations on Biblical characters, psalms, and tales in one way or another, helped create in a number of oppositional works the image of a Jew who became a carrier of specific revolutionary ideals (for example, Wilhelm Kuechelbecker's *Zerubavel*, some imitations of psalms by F. Glinka, M. Lermontov's *Spaniards*, etc.).

However, these peculiar philosemitic attempts were an exception. Indeed, upon finding in Pushkin's *Black Shawl* (1820) the phrase "despicable Jew" and the line "I gave him gold and cursed him," it is easy to conclude that the great Russian poet's attitude towards "Yids" was "invariably decidedly negative": "Pushkin's contempt was unconscious, instinctive, and undoubting." [2] However, firstly, Pushkin deliberately included a subtitle "a Moldavian song" (so, the "I" in *Black Shawl* belongs to a Moldavian, not a Russian); secondly, the "despicable Jew," to whom the protagonist "gave gold" and whom he "cursed" could hardly have knocked on his door of his own initiative (consider the jealous and murderous nature of the protagonist: compare this to the image of Giray in *The Fountain of Bakhchisarai* and Aleko in *Gipsies)*; thirdly, in the "international" cast of the song (a Moldavian, a Greek, an Armenian) everyone, including the slave, are "bad guys," although romanticized. The distance between the real author and the protagonist stands to reason, unless we believe that all qualities of characters are, at the same time, those of the author. Another example that "proves" Pushkin's anti-Judaism is usually the image of Solomon in *The Miserly Knight*. But in this case, as well as in the "Moldavian song," the point is not "the stereotyped understanding of the character" [3], but the Western European stereotype of a usurer Jew. However, Pushkin gave Solomon not only wisdom, but also a psychologically precise understanding of a son's hatred that has grown to the extreme and is realized in the following scenes. Therefore, the suggestion of murder by poison characterizes not as much the personality of the usurer as the fact that he prophetically guessed the son's readiness to commit patricide.

The Jewish theme is represented by Pushkin in his creative works — in *Black Shawl* and *The Miserly Knight, The Gabrieliad* and *A Lamp in a Jewish Shack..., When an Assyrian Lord...* and an epigram for Bulgarin ("Be you a Yid, it's not that bad..."). His sketch of the poem *You Have Enlightened Your Mind With Education...*, apparently dedicated to A. Mickiewicz, he somehow connected with the end of the Polish poet's foreword to the third part of *Dziady*. [4] At the same time it is important to note that as soon as a Gospel myth enters the context, the meaning of the words "Yid" and "Jew" becomes negative (the only exception being, perhaps, the first draft of *As the Traitor Disciple Fell Off the Tree* (1836) in which the image of Judas Iscariot is not defined by his ethnicity), although in situations free of it both words become neutral. We believe that Pushkin's attitude towards Jews was neither anti-Judaic nor Judeophilic. Suffice it to bring up the author's line from *The Robber Brothers* ("Among them is seen... a Jew in black curls") and a character's line ("Whether there walks... a rich Yid or a poor priest..."), to come to this conclusion. It is not incidental that in *Songs of the Western Slavs,* in the presence of folk superstitions of Yid magic (*Theodore and Stamati*), Pushkin thought it necessary not only to comment on the line "the Yid pours water on the toad" ("All peoples

Chapter 2. The Great Secret of Freemasons

considered a toad a venomous animal"), but also to include Mérimée's comment on the line from *The Battle at Zenitza-Velika* ("They began... to hang Yids from trees."): "Yids in Turkish areas are always subject to persecution and hatred. During the war they were harmed by both Muslims and Christians. Their fate, as mentioned by Walter Scott, is akin to that of a flying fish." [5] To Pushkin, who took lessons of "pure atheism" and wore a signet ring inscribed with a Jewish word for "talisman" and who started learning Hebrew and dreamt of translating *the book of Job*, the Jewish/Yid question was not straightforward for the exact reason of him not judging their role in the Russian life from governmental and political position.

N. V. Gogol, who grew up in Little Russia and in whom contempt towards "the enemies of Christ" was instilled "with his mother's milk," naturally, depicted a Jew in the boundaries of Gospel myths, adding to them the Little Russian "tales," which became strong stereotypes in the Ukrainian folklore. Thus, for example, appeared a legend of Jews leasing out "holy churches" [6], through which Taras Bulba and Yankel meet: "Now they are in lease by Yids. If you don't pay Yid ahead, you can't hold mass... And if the doggone Yid doesn't mark a holy Paskha with his vile hand, you can't bless that Paskha..." [7] However, Gogol understood well that Jews simply found themselves between a rock and a hard place. The wrath of Zaporozhians against ksiądz, who harnessed "Orthodox Christians into shafts" and punished "the colonels and the hetman," fell on the "pagans": "'Hang all the Yids!', came from the crowd... and the crowd rushed to the suburb desiring to butcher all Yids... The poor sons of Israel, having lost their already miserable spirits, hid in empty gin barrels, in ovens and even under the skirts of their she-Yids; but the Cossacks found them everywhere." Of course, Gogol hardly sympathized with the "poor sons of Israel," yet he noted that it was Yankel's "internationalism" ("We are like brothers to the Zaporozhians...") that was the real reason for the pogrom: "What? the Zaporozhians to be brothers to you?.. You wish, damned Yids! Into the Dnieper with them, gentlemen!" Gogol motivates saving of Yankel by a circumstance important to Taras: the Jew had once given to Taras's brother Dorosh eight hundred sequins to ransom him from "the Turkish captivity." However, Bulba muses: "There will always be time to hang the Yid," and Gogol, summarizing the slaughter of innocent people, underlines the real reasons for the pogrom: "Now everybody... at the advice of the elders, the kurin leaders, the kish otamans and the will of the entire Zaporozhian host, suggested they march to Poland and take revenge for all the evil and the shame to the faith and the Cossack glory, to plunder the cities, to burn the villages and crops, and spread the word of them over the steppe." Without sympathizing to the Jews, Gogol still thought it necessary (either for expediency of the plot or due to his contradictory nature) to mention that Yankel was not at all "of miserable spirit": "Taras Bulba saw that his Yid Yankel had already set up a table under a canopy and was selling flint, wicks, and black powder... "'What a damned Yid!' Taras thought and, approaching him, said: 'Fool, what are you doing sitting here? Do you want to be shot like a sparrow?'" In response to this "kindly treatment" Yankel admits to Taras that among the Cossack wagons is his own wagon with various useful supplies and that he plans to "supply provisions on the road at such a low price as no Yid has ever charged before." The Zaporozhian only "shrugged his shoulders" and along with the author "marveled at the spry Yid nature." One should think that, based on the final scene of Chapter IV it would be difficult to conclude that Jews were "naturally craven" while demonstrating "spryness of nature" (if only in trade operations). In any case, Yankel's actions in Warsaw also defy definite assessment. Taras Bulba, after the capture of Ostap, decided to see his son no matter what, and "turned up in Uman" in front of the "dirty, smeared" house of Yankel. The author's characteristic of the "well-known Yankel" is extremely sincere: "He was already a landlord and an innkeeper here; he had gotten his hands on all the local gentlemen and nobles, sucked most of their money out and strongly marked his Yid presence in the country. For three miles in any direction there was no house in good repair: everything was falling down and degrading, and only poverty and rags remained, as if after a fire or plague, the entire land was devastated. And if Yankel were to live there another ten years, he would devastate the entire voivodeship." Such a characterization of "Yankel's fault" to the voivodeship, undoubtedly, in Gogol's opinion, justifies the pogroms by the Cossacks and the szlachta. However, the thing is, that the "economic" damage of the "Yid presence" (landlordship and innkeeping) was not the only and, consequently, dominant, definition of the image of a Jew, who, seeing Taras and remembering the two thousand red gold pieces of reward on his head, immediately "felt ashamed of his greed." Gogol, of course, could not help but use the myth of the "eternal thought of gold," which "like a worm, wraps around a Yid's soul." At the same time, following creative truth, the author unexpectedly puts words into Yankel's mouth that differ little from his accusatory action towards the Yid, but now aimed at Taras: "'Ah, what a glorious coin! Ah, what a nice coin!' he said, looking a gold piece over and biting into it. 'I think the man from whom sir took such nice pieces of gold did not live an hour longer in this world and went to the river right away and drowned there after losing such nice gold pieces." This two-sided fault of the main characters (the ruinous actions of Yankel and Taras's robbery) shows not only a shade of "equalizing," but also an unconscious understanding by Gogol of the general unfairness of the Christian hatred of Israel, even though the words are said by Yankel and not him: "'Catch a Yid, tie up the Yid, take all the money from the Yid, throw the Yid in jail!' Because everything that's evil is blamed on the Yid; because everyone treats the Yid as a dog; because they think if one's a Yid, he's not a human being."

Unfortunately, the researchers that accused Gogol of anti-Judaism stressed only the "black colors" of the Jewish theme in Gogol's novel, while refusing to see the many details of the author's sympathy for the deprived and defenseless residents of Warsaw and Uman: on Mordecai's face "there were so many signs of punches received for boldness, that he, without a doubt, had long lost count of them and treated them as birthmarks," "Mordecai had lost his last lock of hair... Yankel often covered his mouth with his hand as if he had a cold," Taras "agreed... to change his clothes... the outfit had been prepared by the sagacious Yid." The Zaporozhian sincerely says about the Yid's smartness and cleverness: "'Listen, Yids!..' he said and there was excitement in his words. 'You can do anything in the world and get anything, be it at the bottom of the sea; and it's long been said that a Yid can steal himself if he so wishes...'" And this tirade is followed by the words of Mordecai: "When we and God want something done, so it shall be done." The fact that the Zaporozhian did not get to see his son was not the Jews' fault, but Taras's, who in response to the hajduk's hurtful words gave away his Orthodox origins: "You are a dog yourself! How dare you say that my faith is not respected? It is your heretical faith that is not respected!" (compare: "These are dogs, not people. And their faith is one that nobody respects," or "doggone Yid" or "dirty Yid," and the Poles are "damned half-believers," etc.). The stress of the narrative in this episode is not on the "sorrowful thought" of Yankel about the wasted gold pieces, but on the hurt and anger of the Zaporozhian: "Why did you have to annoy him? Let the dog bark. His is such people that can't help cursing. Oy vey iz mir, what luck does God send to men! A hundred gold pieces just to have us chased away! And my brothers would have their peyot pulled out and his face turned into a horror to look at, and nobody gives a hundred gold pieces." (it's not the Jews who took the money and tried to meet Taras's request who are *without honor*, but the hajduks who took the bribe and broke their promise).

It should be mentioned that Yankel stood by Taras, as a good friend, during Ostap's execution. Therefore, we cannot speak of any definitive attitude towards the Jewish theme, although, of course, some untruths as well as following the "popular opinion" are obvious. It is not incidental that Gogol included "the shameful governing of Yids in the Christian land" (innkeeping and leasing) into his list of the offences towards "(Russian) nation" ("mockery of their own rights," "shameful... humiliation," "insulting the faith of our forefathers," "desecration of churches," "atrocities of foreign lords, "for the Union"), although before, when talking about life in the Zaporozhian Sich, he noted: "Only the Yids, Armenians, and Tatars encouraged by powerful greed dared to live and trade in the suburb... Although, the fate of these greedy hucksters was quite pitiful." It is possible that, while understanding the "bloody life" of that "fierce century," Gogol still was unable to accept as God's punishment the actions of those who "hearkened to none... and lifted their infants on their pikes off the streets and tossed them into the same fire." Taras's captivity is the highest judgement and, although "there are no fire, torture, or power in the world that can overpower the Russian power," it is doubtful that the heroic death of the Zaporozhian justified the "disrespect" of the black-browed Polish ladies who "could not find refuge even at the altars themselves": "Taras set them on fire with the altars." That is why his death, at the stake and not on the block, puts the ataman at the same level with the victims of the atrocity and stresses the common guilt of the "hardening" in which they "do not sense "humanity and humaneness." [8] In this sense the negative traits of Jews, according to mythologems, do not explain their "disloyalty" to both warring sides, but, quite the opposite, judging by Yankel and his friends, they sympathize with the oppressed rather than the oppressors. Of course, the absence of a positive image of a Jew in the works of *great authors* is unfortunate, but, apparently, this is a consequence of historically formed and ethnically and religiously colored notions and mythologems.

The Jewish theme in the creative works of Pushkin and Gogol sufficiently proves that their anti-Judaism was "Christian" by nature, yet by no means nationalistic or political. The appearance of the image of a Jew in the Russian literature of current interest in the XIX century did, of course, influence the sharply negative traits of the Jewish characters, however, they were, in one way or another, oriented towards "evangelical" allusions. But the *absence* in the image of the Jew of any social and political definition that accused other ethnicities of anti-governmental or anti-patriotic actions requires careful treatment of the notion of "an anti-Judaist," or we would have to put the entire European culture and all its creators in the dock. No good can come from such a "frontal" approach.

The reason for the Jews being "apolitical" among different tribes and peoples was their situation, *historically* connected to economic infrastructures and not to any governmental and political institutions. At the same time, for *any nationalistic* work, the opposition of positive to negative *based* on the character's ethnicity is basic and final. [9] But, being such a *postulated norm* of chauvinistic views, such opposition is present as a "categorical imperative" and, due to this circumstance, is devoid of any individual appraisal. [10]

It is different if the "categorical imperative" is joined by the specifics of "governmental and political" as well as "historical and social" exclusiveness of the *eternal hostility* of "the aborigines" and "the aliens." The consequence of this "symbiosis" is the truly "zoological" hatred of "the aliens" (not necessarily Jews) by "the aborigines," always dressed in the guise of "history," religious fundamentalism, "the eternal truth" and declared "the Holy war" between good and evil. That is why, however negative or positive the characters of the Jews appear in various creative works, their images themselves do not prove either anti-Judaism or Judeophilia of the author unless they are assigned *the historical and political blame* for the country's misfortunes. All other qualities of Jews defined by mythologems or stereotypes should hardly be considered a" crime," in other words, anti-Judaism. Otherwise, anti-Judaism gains a *mystically* unambiguous meaning of the same, favored by anti-Judaists, idea of "eternal hostilities," even if Zionistically interpreted.

F. V. BULGARIN'S NOVEL *IVAN VYZHIGIN*

Almost simultaneously with the "denunciations of all Russia" by Golitsyn and Magnitsky, who warned the government of the danger of spreading freemasonic ideas and who, still indirectly, included "Yids" into the masonic conspiracy, Russian pulp fiction turned up the stories that in one way or another touched upon the "secrets" of freemasonry and Jewry.

For the first time in a Russian novel, Jews and freemasons are encountered in a famous work by V. T. Narezhny *The Russian Gil Blas, or The Adventures of Prince Gavrila Simonovich Chistyakov*. The first three parts of the novel were published in 1814 and were immediately taken out of circulation. Twice more (1835 and 1841) this novel was banned by censors. What was all that about? V. G. Belinsky in his article "Russian literature in 1841" called Narezhny the "progenitor" of Russian novelists of the XIX century. For our purposes it is very interesting to know that this predecessor of Gogol was likely the first Russian philosemitic author and this was one of the reasons (if not the main one) for banning *Gil Blas*. A censor wrote in 1841: "In the entire novel all persons, without exception, of noble blood and higher class are described in darkest tones; contrary to them, many commoners, including Yanka the Yid, demonstrate honest and honorable actions." [10A] Let us not overestimate the author's social protest, though. Narezhny is ruthless in his depiction of common people — peasants who are all drunkards, thieves, idlers, oathbreakers, arsonists, and murderers. And indeed, the only decent people are Jews: the tavern host Yanka Yankelevich and his nephew "Joseph the beautiful". The odious person of a tavern host under Narezhny's pen turns into the tragic figure of the Wandering Jew, persecuted, beaten, robbed by the same peasants he had done good to. Such an image would not appear in Russian literature for a long time yet.

As far as freemasonry, it is represented in the novel as a caricature. One of the novel's characters is invited to join the secret order "Society of Benefactors of Light," which is called masons by the "mindless crowd." At the same time, they are the enlighteners of the world, friends of mankind and rulers of the Earth, possessed of high secret wisdom and knowledge of the affairs of European royal courts and familiar with the intentions of "boyars" and "the works of the world under the sun."

It should be mentioned that Leo Tolstoy undoubtedly read at least some pages of Narezhny's novel with particular interest, since the description of initiation into a lodge as well as the patronizing attitude towards the "brothers" is played by both authors in similar ways despite them being separated by more than half a century.

In regards to combining the Jewish and the masonic themes, A. F. Weltman, an author almost forgotten by the '70s of the XIX century, is of interest to us. His novel *The Wanderer* (1831), while demonstrating a certain familiarity with the everyday life of Moldavian Jews, contained mystical and masonic features and romantic high style of narration. [11]

Coachman Berka, who accompanies the protagonist in his "wanderings" and in his search of the "mysterious maid" (Sophia), plays a dual role in the novel: on the one hand, Berka is a simple servant who may or may not be ready to transport the quartermaster from place to place, and on the other, he is a keeper of some mystical secret and leads his master to "mysterious worlds." About the first face of the coachman the author writes with kindness and irony:

"I sighed deeply and awoke. I looked around. Where am I? — I was lying in the wagon; the horses, loose, were calmly eating hay. There was a forest to the right; to the left... noise... a lone inn... Where was my Berka? the trickster!

I walk into the inn and everyone is drunk!

And so is Berka! What am I to do?

The poor lazy bastard could not tell

Mordecai from Haman!" [12]

An interesting detail is the generally sober Jews all drunk at the inn and it was timed by Weltman to a specific event: during Purim, a good Jew had to get so drunk that he could not tell the curses to Haman from the blessings to Mordecai. This detail only proves that the author did know Jewish traditions and holidays.

Particularly curious is the "mystical chapter" CCLXII. Awaiting "the approach of the material ego" the protagonist finds himself in an unfamiliar world, whose attributes were supposed to be the letters of the Hebrew alphabet as explained by Kabbalah, which Weltman was certainly familiar with:

"To the left there were some buildings.

'What borough is this?' I asked the coachman.

'Alef!' he responded." [13]

'Alef is the first letter (and in astrology means "mother") and a mystical synonym to the "heavenly realm." [14] Here, in this mysterious world, the Hebrew letters echo the mystical events, one of which is the protagonist's marriage to the maid (apparently, Sophia — S.D.).

"Daring not to lift my gaze, I noticed that the beautiful young creature gestured for me to sit... Everyone was silent and everyone's eyes were on me... My impatience overcame me...

'I do not know which God looked upon me kindly and blessed me with being here?' I said quietly to the taciturn maid. She looked at me gently and breathed out 'Alef!'

'Alef! 'Alef!' the hall whispered.

I shivered with cold terror.

'I do not understand these mysterious words,' I continued. 'Everything here is a mystery to me. Please explain or allow me to leave such charms.'

'Bet!' the girl said quietly. 'Bet! Bet! Bet!' quietly echoed thousands of voices.

I stood up.

'I cannot bear this!' I cried.

'Gimel!' cried the girl and threw herself at me.

I was struck dumb.

'Gimel! Gimel! Gimel!' the hall echoed loudly.

Suddenly an old man in white robes appeared; his snow-white hair fell from under his two-horned cap of an ancient priest and rested on his shoulders. He approached me and took my hand and put the maid's hand in mine and began slowly: 'Alef, Bet, Gimel, Dalet, He, Vav, Zayin, Het, Tet, Yod, Kaf, Lamed, Mem, Nun, Samekh, 'Ayin, Pe, Tsadi, Qof, Resh, Shin, Tav!'

Everyone presented repeated these words. I was overcome with horror, my vision went dark, daylight disappeared and everything was covered in darkness. The maid's hand grew cold in mine...

'Aw!' I cried and awoke. 'My God, it was all a dream!' I said and jumped up happy to get rid of *Alef, Bet, Gimel and the rest of the Hebrew letters."* [15]

Of course, there may be various interpretations of this chapter. At the same time, the critics gave fairly good reviews to the novel, and Belinsky even called the poem *Eskander* included in the novel "one of the most precious gems of our literature." [16] Weltman himself sent a copy of his book to Pushkin with a comment that it is difficult to figure out from the novel whether he "wandered or whored." [17]

Very different in meaning and tendency were creative works of F. V. Bulgarin (1789–1859), who was one of the first Russian authors to speak against Russian Jewry per se. In 1829 in St. Petersburg a moralizing satiric novel *Ivan Vyzhygin* was published and it brought the author the fame of the "first prose writer" in Russia.

F. V. Bulgarin was born into a Polish family and studied at a privileged cadet school in Petersburg, despite the fact that his father (a friend of Kosciuszko's) had been exiled to Siberia for the murder of a Russian general. Bulgarin joined the military service and participated in the battles of 1805–1807, and then deserted the Russian army and ran to Warsaw where he joined the Polish legion as an officer and with it took part in the Italian and Spanish campaigns. In 1812 the Polish legion became part of Oudinot's corps that operated in Lithuania and Belorussia. It is known that after seizing Paris in 1814, Alexander I gave "permission to the Polish troops that had fought for Napoleon to return to Poland with their commanders and under their banners." [18] Among the "rehabilitated" was F. V. Bulgarin (how he

Faddei Bulgarin (1789–1859)

managed to avoid execution for deserting the Russian army remains unknown). After a short stay in Warsaw, he permanently moved to Petersburg in 1820.

Apparently, anti-government trends in the Russian society played a large role in the fact that a former deserter, who had carried arms against the Emperor's forces, was accepted by the opposition and trusted. It was at that time that Bulgarin met and became friends with K. Ryleyev, A. Griboyedov, W. Kuechelbecker and others. Terrified by repressions, executions and exiles, Bulgarin, after the defeat of the Decembrist Rebellion, became a secret agent of the Third Department while using his job as a special assignments officer at the Ministry of Education as a cover.

However, as early as 1829, Pushkin and his friends learned of Bulgarin's "part-time job" from the former "arzamassians" D. V. Dashkov and D. N. Bludov, who became Ministers to Nicholas I. [19]

Joining the team of N. I. Grech's magazine *Syn Otechestva*, Bulgarin soon achieved recognition in literary circles: the essays and articles by the fairly gifted journalist evoked continuous interest.

In 1825, together with N. I. Grech, he began publishing a new Russian commercial newspaper. The circulation of *Severnaya Pchela* (*The Northern Bee*) was anywhere from 4,000 to 10,000 copies and proved the incredible success, which allowed Bulgarin to become the "dictator" of literary tastes. A clever businessman of capitalist inclinations, he was familiar with the foundations of Wester European commerce and introduced advertising into Russian press and became, in fact, the "father" of the Russian newspaper feuilleton.

His newspaper was very obviously patriotic and pro-government (with its behind-the-scenes owner being the chief of the Third Department L. V. Dubelt [20]) and, undoubtedly, was the government's "loudspeaker," and often the "informative" editorials evoked vehement protest of all democratic and oppositional forces. Thus, publishing of Bulgarin's lampoon of Pushkin, who "tosses rhymes at everything sacred and flaunts his free-thinking in front of the mob, at the same time secretly crawling at the feet of the powerful" (*The Northern Bee,* March 11, 1830) [21], brought on a sharp retort from the poet — first, in a feuilleton "On Vidok's Notes" (*Literaturnaya Gazeta, #20, 1830, "Smes'" (Mix)*) and then in a famous epigram:

> It's not a shame that you're a pan.
> Kosciuszko's one, Mickiewicz's one!
> Be you a Tatar, that's all right:
> There is no shame at all in that.
> Be you a Yid, that's not so bad.
> Too bad you are Vidok Figlyarin.

The personal insult from Bulgarin was exacerbated by another sharp pain: *Ivan Vyzhigin,* published in 1829, was greeted with praise everywhere, whereas the first published prosaic works of Pushkin received almost no attention. This must have been the reason for Pushkin to accuse "Faddey Benedictovich" of "cunning": "*Ivan Vyzhigin* still existed only in the venerable author's imagination and yet T*he Northern Archive, The Northern Bee,* and *Syn Otechestva* were already singing great praise to it.

Monsieur Ancelot in his travels that attracted everyone's attention in Paris declared this not-yet-existing *Ivan Vyzhigin* the best Russian novel. Finally, *Ivan Vyzhigin* came out and *Syn Otechestva, The Northern Archive* and *The Northern Bee* praised it to high heavens. Everybody rushed to read it; many even finished it..." [22] Moreover, Pushkin's disgruntlement shows in his private letter to his wife of December 8, 1831: "I was going to take a winter coach, but I was told... I had to take a summer one... and they put me in a four-seater carriage with two friends... One of my companions was a merchant from Riga, a kindly German, who suffered from mucus every morning and who spent an hour at the station coughing it up in the corner. The other one was a Yid from Memel who traveled at the expense of the first. Imagine the merry company. The German got drunk precisely thrice a day and twice a night. The Yid entertained him with pleasant conversation for the whole trip, for example, retelling *Iwan Wijiguin* in German (ganz charmant!). I tried to ignore them and pretended to sleep. [23]"

We may recall that in late October in St. Petersburg *The Stories of the Late Ivan Petrovich Belkin* by Pushkin himself were published. A year earlier Pushkin explained to Pletnev: "I wrote five novellas in prose... which should be published as Anonymous. I can't put my name on it or Bulgarin will get angry."

CHAPTER 2. THE GREAT SECRET OF FREEMASONS

So, Russian literature was fully given to Bulgarin and Grech. [24] Therefore, it is not surprising that the feuilletons signed by the name of Feofilakt Kosichkin, the epigrams and epistolary *tales* by Pushkin in 1830–1831, in one way or another were inspired by the success of Bulgarin's moralizing and satirical novel, who was one of the first to sense the Russian reader's loss of interest in poetry...

At the same time, *Ivan Vyzhigin,* written in the spirit of a trickster (adventure) novel, while never having played any significant role in the history of Russian literature, was indeed a literary sensation in 1829–1831. One of the important parts of the plot was the landowner and nobility circles of Belorussian boroughs, which the author remembered from his childhood and which naturally fit images of Jews.

However, having been raised in a Polish family, Bulgarin used the stereotypes that had been created in Polish literature. Perhaps this is why Jews in his novel were, according to a critic's witty remark, especially "Vyzhigin-ish." Also, Bulgarin "treated and entertained... the simple and patient Russian audience with sparks of tavern humor..." [25]

In the course of his adventures the protagonist of the novel visits a rich Yid, Movshe (Chapters VII–VIII). Vyzhigin, analyzing the Jew's sources of riches, comes to a generalization: while despised and persecuted, Jews could only have become masters of Westland through cheating, robbery, and fraud. By encouraging the poor aborigines to drink, Yids learn local "secrets," the people's needs and connections, and use that in their fraud to become the "real owners of the landowners' property," thus submitting "to their Yid influence all affairs and circumstances in which precious metals or paper bills appear on stage." [26] Let us stress that this was not about a single Jew swindler, but about a whole people that, in the author's opinion, does not and cannot possess a single positive trait. Very typical is the ending of the episode when the Yid attempts to convert the protagonist into Judaism and, of course, fails.

The influence of such a "Jewish stereotype" on later pulp fiction was unarguable and decisive (without Bulgarin, novels by Vs. Krestovsky would have been impossible). It is not a coincidence that S. S. Okreyts whom elderly Bulgarin blessed to take up creative writing, as well as J. E. Przecławski, left warm memoirs of Vidok Figlyarin, since they fully supported his concept.

Pushkin, sensing Bulgarin's hatred towards all aliens as an orthodox guardian of the monarchy (hence the mentions of a Pole, a Tatar, and a Yid in his epigram), finished the second feuilleton of Feofilakt Kosichkin with an outline of *The Real Vyzhigin*. Among the listed chapters, those that hint at Vidok's life story ("Upbringing for Christ's sake... The first lampoon of Vyzhigin... Ubi bene, ibi patria... Vyzhigin the sneak... Mr. and Mrs. Vyzhigin buy a village with their hard-earned money...," etc.) are especially curious. Pushkin's warning ("Meanwhile, I believe I have a right to proclaim the existence of the novel... It will go into print or remain a manuscript, depending on the circumstances") made Bulgarin give up further lampooning and informing on the poet, although it did not at all mean that the editor of *The Northern Bee* gave up slandering Jews.

THE REAL VYZHIGIN (J. E. PRZECŁAWSKI)

Bulgarin was not an exception among those Polish ultra patriots, who, after "looting of Moscow" and "defections," repented and became "decent men" (Pushkin). At the same time, Vyzhigin's contribution to the Russian anti-Semitic literature has barely been studied, although, no doubt, these natives of Westland played the leading role in the negative depiction of the minority in the Pale of Settlement. It is not a coincidence that one of the most "shadowy" figures among the creators of the Russian myth of "Judeo-Masonic conspiracy" was another "real Vyzhigin."

Josef Przecławski was born in 1799 in Ruzany of Slonim Uezd in Grodno Governorate. He came from an old Polish family of Glaubicz, although it is hard to say if the Glaubicz family was purely Polish or "mixed," since Przecławski himself pointed out his kinship to a Belorussian — the Metropolitan of the Greek Uniate Church, Bishop Josaphat Bulhak of Brest.

Josef Przecławski
(1799–1879)

His father, Anthony Przecławski, according to the trustworthy testimony of the poet Adam Mickiewicz, was famous for his incorruptible honesty and outstanding justice.

He was the chairman of the local (uezd) court and later of the regional court of appeals, but mostly dealt with arbitration: disputes between landowners could last for dozens of years, and since Anthony was known for his honesty and fairness, which was also testified by Adam Mickiewicz, it was decided to call upon him as a mediator and completely abide by his decisions.

Ruzany belonged to Count Franciszek Sapieha and Anthony rented from him a large mansion and the borough itself. In the mid-XIX century over 1500 Jews lived there (according to the 1897 census, they comprised 70% of the town's population).

Przecławski saw the life of Jews since he was a child, and many ritual murder accusations in the neighboring Grodno and in Ruzany itself, naturally, shaped his attitude towards the infidels. His Catholic environment and the atmosphere of the Poles' hopes during the French invasion largely contributed to shaping his character.

Disappointment in Napoleon and the certainty that the continental blockade "benefited only Yids" pushed Przecławski into the opposite camp of Russophiles: later he repeatedly declared friendship between Poles and Russians, disapproved of the West's instigation and warned his compatriots against empty dreams about France's assistance in fighting Russia.

Not incidentally, in his *Memoir* Przecławski quoted a Polish legionnaire who, having learned about the French's defeat in the war between France and Prussia, exclaimed: "... serves these braggarts well! God is punishing them for involving us in perdition twice." [27]

Przecławski's tutor (as with many of his peers) was serviceman in Napoleon's military, the chief surgeon to the Neapolitan King Joachim Murat, a doctor of medicine and surgery Petazzi-Bordeaux, who instilled in the curious child a taste for sciences, especially botany and chemistry, and passed on to him his vast knowledge of humanities.

In September 1815, Przecławski entered the Vilna University (there he became friends with Adam Mickiewicz) and as early as in 1818 graduated with honors and a degree in philosophy from the department of physics and mathematics.

The financial situation of the family after his father's passing in 1814 was not brilliant, and Przecławski had to enter into service: on November 5, 1818 he became a secretary to his kinsman Bronsky, the Uezd Marshal in Slonim.

Soon the 18-year-old youth was recommended to the masonic lodge as an exception (the order only accepted those 25 years old and older) by Count Adam Soltan, an influential Novogrudok mason, and became one of the founders of the lodge in Slonim where he, with Soltan's support, achieved fairly high ranks.

Freemasonry was wide-spread in Poland. Becoming independent in the period of the Duchy of Warsaw, after the Vienna Congress it signed a union with the freemasons of Lithuania, who, after the defeat of Napoleon's forces, took up charity (they were helping the disabled, the families of killed soldiers, prisoners of war, etc.).

The common interest in mysticism, the search for the elixir of life and the philosopher's stone enticed the curious youth. [28]

N. N. Novosiltsev noticed the conscientious young man (later Przecławski painted quite an unfair image of his patron and caused a storm in the Russian nationalist circles). Nevertheless, the membership in a masonic lodge and informal socializing with outstanding people and statesmen favorably affected the youth's views and it was then that he realized the hopelessness of the Polish party openly fighting Russia.

Complicated property disputes of his uncle Ferdinand Borzymowski made Przecławski quit his job in May of 1822 and, upon his mother's insistence, travel to Petersburg with a letter of recommendation from N. N. Novosiltsev, to take care of this business. It is hard to say how Przecławski developed such a negative view of Jews, and yet throughout his life he believed that everything bad happens because of them. This ideé fixe caused him to twist the essence of the dispute he came to Petersburg to settle. According to Przecławski, the opposite side of his uncle's case was represented by a beautiful young woman "of Jerusalem origin," a Ms. S. (all persons in Przecławski's *Memoir* are named by their initials or only by their last name's initial), who was a mistress of the director of the Department of Justice I. V. Zhuravlev (a *raznochinets* who made a brilliant career thanks to M. M. Speransky). Her name was Theophania Stanislawowna S., and among her patrons was not only "Zh.," but, likely, Arakcheyev himself. For a long time, she received help from K. F. Ryleyev, who dedicated a collection of poems to "Ms.S." It is known that she was Polish by origin and no Jewish blood was found in her not only by Ryleyev and N. Bestuzhev, but also by a modern anti-Semitic researcher V. Afanasyev. [29]

Later her involvement in espionage for Arakcheyev was uncovered. Having come to Petersburg with N. N. Novosiltsev's recommendation, Przecławski was not a "poor orphan" facing superior forces of "powers-that-be." To disprove that it is enough to name the young man's patrons: The State Council member V. S. Lenski and the well-known Prince Drucki-Lubecki.

However, Przecławski's life in the capital started not with a litigation, but with him showing up at the Polish masonic lodge of *The*

Chapter 2. The Great Secret of Freemasons

White Eagle that was headed by the famous artist and mystic Jozef Oleszkiewicz (1777–1830).

His title of *Maitre en Chair* he inherited from a Senator Count Adam Rzewuski and all the lodges in Petersburg recognized his leadership: when Jozef Ivanovich, holding the highest rank in the order, visited "other lodges, he was greeted with special formality and honors (seven stars and iron cover)." [30]

The dispute that had brought him to Petersburg was drawn out and went on for two years.

During that time, he made some new and important high society acquaintances and often visited with the future Minister of Education Admiral A. S. Shishkov, who was married to close kin of Przecławski either on his grandmother's or his mother's side; in any case, in his *Memoir* he calls Julia Osipovna née Narbut "Auntie."

S. T. Aksakov in his memoirs sincerely pitied the forefather of "slavophiles":

"Aleksandr Semyonych... married, despite his advanced years and illness, a Pole and a Catholic, J. J. Lubarzevska, which surprised and upset all those close to him... Shishkov, a sworn enemy of Catholics and Poles, was surrounded by them. The new spouse flooded his home with completely different sort of people than before, and I could not bear to watch the respectable Shishkov among various mustachioed types, arrogant and self-assured, talking nonsense and treating him too familiarly." [31]

It was during that time that the "respectable" admiral energetically demanded the liquidation of the status of Jewish representatives and in the late 1825 finally got his wish. [32]

At the same time, Przecławski, while describing his pastime and activities [33] at the Imperial public library, mentioned that the library's riches had been acquired by robbery and confiscation of libraries of bishops (Zaluski) and princes (Czartoryski).

He paid a special attention to studying his "favorite subject, occulta," [34] and read almost everything the library had on it, from the Pyphagoreans to Cornelius Agrippa, [35] pursuing "one problem conceived long before, and through incessant labor, finally reached its solution": "This event had a huge effect on the future of my inner man. All I can say about it is: neither my research nor the results thereof had anything to do with Hermeticism." [36]

Even before the Senate's final decision on his case, on February 24, 1824 Przecławski entered into service at the Ministry of Internal Affairs as a minor office clerk and for the next 40 years held governmental positions.

The office supervisor M. K. Mikhailov, who was friends with his patron V. Puslovsky, and the Ministry manager V. S. Lanskoy moved the young man up the career ladder, and after "two years of boring dealings with Barbarians" (supervising Kalmyk cases) he was appointed as chief of a department. [37]

As an official of the Ministry of Internal Affairs Przecławski was present at the execution of the Decembrists on July 13, 1826 on a crownwork of the Peter and Paul Fortress, and left most interesting memoirs of that event.

As a student at Vilna University Przecławski had met Adam Mickiewicz and they became friends. What's more, Cyprinus (Przecławski) was Mickiewicz's guide in Petersburg when the Polish poet turned up in the capital on his way to the place of his exile for Philomathic activity.

Cyprinus introduced Mickiewicz to the artist and mystic Oleszkiewicz, and in 1828 (after Mickiewicz returned from his southern exile) helped edit the poet's collection of poetry and was a witness to Pushkin and Mickiewicz's personal acquaintance. [38]

In 1830, together with F. Malevsky and A. Parchevsky and with Mickiewicz's blessing, Przecławski started participating in the publishing of a Petersburg Polish language newspaper *Tygodnik (Weekly)*, and later became its sole owner until 1859.

The paper was a success and came out twice a week.

Przecławski involved in this work many prominent Polish authors, including the Metropolitan Golovinski, Count Henryk Rzewuski, N. Malinovsky, Romuald Hube, E. Sturmer (pen name), M. Grabowski, Józef Kraszewski, K. Bujnicki, et al.

Przecławski himself wrote pointed critical and satirical articles on political subjects that he never signed with his own name, but used Roman characters: "J.E.G." — Jozef Emanuel Gerba, "G" — Gerba, or "Glaubicz," "E.G.," etc.).

His pen-name *Cyprinus* came from the name of St. Cyprian (circa 210–280), to whom the public assigned a collection of aphorisms, and who, in his youth, dealt in magic. [39]

Tygodnik first came out on the eve of the Polish uprising of 1830, and later Przecławski assumed a decidedly anti-rebel position. Many of his articles were re-printed by the Russian press: the paper "became an organ of the most energetic condemnation of the criminal Warsaw movement and never stopped doing its best to oppose revolutionary

CHAPTER 2. THE GREAT SECRET OF FREEMASONS

doctrines, which, under the banner of false patriotism, involved a large part of Polish people in crime and destruction." [40]

Of course, such a position required certain courage from the author and doomed him to exile from Polish circles.

The emigrant tribunal sentenced Przecławski to death and the sentence was carried out... *in absentia*: on the Beautillion Field in Paris a portrait of Cyprinus was publicly burned.

Tygodnik, though, earned the full trust "of the government and displayed every evidence of trustworthiness and loyalty." [41]

And, although "trustworthiness and loyalty" did not save Przecławski from many deletions (normally those were burned in the Third Department due to their nonsensical content) and censorship of the newspaper's mail, still *Tygodnik* received *the title and rights* of the official organ of Kingdom of Poland (with this began the financial flourishing of the paper).

When, after the suppression of the Polish uprising a committee headed by I. L. Turkul was formed to revise and create laws for the Kingdom of Poland, [42] Przecławski was invited to be its member, and starting in 1840 he became the office director while at the same time being a member of the Special Committee at the Ministry of Education (in that field he earned the Order of St. Vladimir, 4th grade).

On March 16, 1862 he became a censor and a member of the Ministry of Internal Affairs council on book printing and his colleagues were A. V. Nikitenko, I. A. Goncharov, and F. I. Tyutchev.

This successful career of Przecławski was a consequence of the pro-government position he took on many principal issues (freedom of press, transparency, etc.).

His report to the censor committee evoked a negative reaction even from I. D. Delyanov (who later became a most reactionary minister of People's Education and the creator of the percentage system for Jews), who noted that "if he (Przecławski — S.D.) was to be followed, it would become decidedly impossible to express in literature any opinion on public affairs," for "this gentleman declares himself a zealous adherent of darkness and voicelessness." [43]

"'The project' was written... smoothly," however, A. V. Nikitenko also called it "ignoble and unintelligent." [44] In his journal he wrote: "I got into a heated argument with Przecławski: this gentleman breathes hatred toward any thought and press in general and suggests most severe measures.

"He was supported by Timashev (the Chief of the Gendarmerie Corps in 1856–1861 and later the Minister of Internal Affairs in 1868–

1877 — *S.D.*). I told him: 'Don't even think to employ terror. Neither governmental nor any other terror ever leads to anything good. Przecławski is the worst of all.'

"He, obviously, is fighting to be important. Although, devil knows: he is a Pole and, perhaps, just wants to harm the government itself by convincing it to use reprehensible cruelty." [45] In the same entry Nikitenko made a notable footnote: "After Ohryzko's exploits anything seems possible." [46]

Let us remind the reader that Jozafat Ohryzko (1826–1890), an inspector at the Department of consistent taxes of the Ministry of Finance, a collegiate councilor and publisher of a Polish newspaper *Slowo,* was arrested upon the insistence of M. N. Muravyov the Hangman for printing illegal literature for the Warsaw Committee and leading the Polish revolutionary activity in Petersburg. His arrest caused a commotion in the highest dignitary circles of Russia. [47]

Apparently, the shrewd Nikitenko, known for his anti-Polonism, suspected Przecławski of being a provocateur, because even he could not explain such "reprehensible cruelty" of Przecławski. (It is noteworthy that Przeclaski — "this gentleman" — was the very official that allowed the magazine *Sovremennik* to publish N. G. Chernyshevsky's novel *What Is to Be Done?* when Chernyshevsky was already a prisoner in the Peter and Paul Fortress.

It is interesting that Przecławski himself, while talking about this episode, thought it necessary to blame a bureaucratic confusion, although he did not only know the author well but left a most interesting and deep analysis of the novel. [48] Therefore, Nikitenko's hint at Przecławski's provocateur "streak" was not totally unfounded.

If we consider the fact that the publishing of the novel *What Is to Be Done?* had no negative consequences for Przecławski, one should ponder a certain double-dealing of this "adherent of darkness and voicelessness" that allowed the "Gospel" of the Russian freedom movement to be published.)

Przecławski himself described his situation quite precisely: "My position in the headquarters as a Catholic and the kingdom official (he means the Kingdom of Poland — *S.D.*) was somewhat exceptional." [49]

Przecławski spent 40 years in government service. During that time, he became a Privy Councilor (the 3rd class in the Table of Ranks after Chancellor and Active Privy Councilor) and was decorated with various orders for his "loyal adherence to service" (among Przecławski's decorations was the 5th-ranking Russian Empire order of "White Eagle"). Przecławski died in Tver at the age of 79 in 1879 and in his will, he had asked for a handful of Slonim soil he had kept all his life to be placed in his coffin.

This biography of a state official by himself would not be of any interest had Przecławski not left behind notes on the Jewish question and such memoirs of him meeting outstanding persons of his time which would allow us to judge the character of his "anonymous" literary activity that *had direct relation to the genesis of The Protocols of the Elders of Zion.*

THE PROVOCATEUR'S CATECHISM

In 1872 *The Russian Archive* first published an article by a retired Privy Councilor of the Ministry of Internal Affairs, J. E. Przecławski, "Notes on Mr. Berg's Article in *The Russian Archive* of 1870." [50]

By 1874 *The Russian Archive* had published multiple extracts from his memoirs under the title of "A Kaleidoscope of Cyprinus's Memoirs," later announced as "A Memoir by J. E. Przecławski" in *Russkaya Starina* (*Russian Antiquity*).

From 1874 to 1890 multiple essays on historical personalities and the events in pre— and post-reform Russia were published (Cyprinus's manuscripts were delivered to *Russkaya Starina* by his son A. O. Przecławski, [51] who cared much about his father's literary legacy).

The publication of Przecławski's first articles ("Jozafat Ohryzko and his Polish newspaper *Slowo*," "A few words on Mr. Berg's response to my remarks on his notes about the Polish conspiracies and uprisings," "N. N. Novosiltsev," "Adam Mickiewicz," "1811 and 1912") evoked a lively polemic among Russian nationalists, who believed that he "with all his obvious respect of Russians and insistence on his being unprejudiced is not always free of the desire to poke at the Russian self-esteem and to prove the moral and intellectual superiority of the Poles over Russians." [52]

His memoirs of Pushkin and Mickiewicz brought on particularly strong attacks, since "slavophiles" saw in them "belittling of virtues" of the great Russian poet and magnifying those of the Polish genius. [53] On top of that, while hypocritically praising the Russian people's obedience to "the powers-that-be," Przecławski declared through Mickiewicz's "mouth":

"One could think that it is cowardice and slavery; but no... a people that respects the authorities so instinctively and, in obeying them, forgets its own power is a great people...

"That is why the Russian people are stronger than any other: the individual strengths concentrate into a single idea and act in a definitive manner." [54] That is a very dubious compliment...

Fierce criticism was brought on by the pages of the memoir about N. N. Novosiltsev who had done so much to promote the career of the young Przecławski.

N. N. Novosiltsev (1761–1836) is a controversial figure in the Russian history. In the early years of Alexander I reign he was a member of the "Privy Committee" which its members jokingly called "The Committee for Social Salvation," while their opponents called the young liberals "a Jacobin gang," because one of the committee's members, P. A. Stroganov, while in Paris in 1790, joined the Jacobin Club. [55] One of the "Privy Committee" members was Prince Adam Czartoryski.

N. N. Novosiltsev, the president of the State Council since 1832, earned the notoriety among historians as a reactionist, a cruel repressor of the national self-awareness of the Poles and an uncompromising colonialist.

Such opinion of the "imperial commissar at the administrative council" was born in a large part in connection with Adam Mickiewicz.

The authority of the revolutionary poet who fought for the freedom of Poland, naturally, outweighed any objective evaluations of N. N. Novosiltsev's deeds.

In the famous foreword to Part III of *Dziady* Mickiewicz wrote: "Around 1822 Alexander I's policy of suffocating any and all freedom began to shape, strengthen and acquire definite direction.

It was at that time that all over Poland oppression of the Polish people started and became more and more cruel and bloody.

The senator Novosiltsev, whom Poland still remembers, stepped up on stage. He was the first to accept the Tsarist government's instinctive animal hatred for Poles as a right and saving policy and followed it in his actions, whose goal was to destroy Poles as a nation...

Having been sent to Lithuania by Tsesarevich Constantine with unlimited powers, Novosiltsev was simultaneously the prosecutor, the judge, and the executioner." [56]

Following his university friend, the revolutionary Mickiewicz, the respectable "adherent of darkness and voicelessness" Przecławski confirmed that N. N. Novosiltsev's activity was instigatory in nature

Chapter 2. The Great Secret of Freemasons

(as opposed to, for example, the advice of Prince Drucki-Lubecki) and provoked the Polish uprising of 1830.

Moreover, according to the laws of "romantic portrayal," the imperial commissar was depicted in *The Kaleidoscope* by Cyprinus as a sort of "monster" in both soul and body (a drunkard, a Céladon, a freak, a dwarf, etc.). [57]

P. V. Kukolnik (1795–1884), brother of the famous playwright N. V. Kukolnik, a professor of the Vilna University, refuted Przecławski's tale of the circumstances that directly related to his family. Using his family's history as an example (his family was Uniate until 1821 and later converted to Orthodoxy) in his article "Anti-Cyprinus: A Memoir of N. N. Novosiltsev" P. V. Kukolnik insisted that Novosiltsev's "financial impropriety" was a slander of the fantastically rich senator, who was first cousin to P. A. Stroganov, and had no need of any financial schemes. [58]

Let us remind the reader that in 1815, after the amnesty of the Polish regiments that had fought for Napoleon, Alexander I gave a "liberal" (for those times) constitution to the "Kingdom of Poland"... joined with Russia, and in 1818 charged Novosiltsev with creating a project of a "constitution for Russia." [59] This project, known as "The State Charter of the Russian Empire," was "in many respects very similar to the Polish Constitution" of 1815, from where Novosiltsev adopted "most of the articles and even many terms." Moreover, the Charter contained the "guarantees" of freedom of religion, of press, security of person and property, and Article 81 established or, rather, confirmed "a root Russian law: nobody shall be punished without due process of law." [60]

It is noteworthy that S. G. Pushkarev in his footnote on Novosiltsev's Charter says: "During the Polish uprising of 1830–1831 the Polish revolutionary government found Novosiltsev's text in Warsaw and published this constitutional project.

When General Paskevich took Warsaw in 1831, he found there the text of the Russian Constitution and informed the Emperor Nicholas of his discovery. The Emperor was very disturbed by his brother's "revolutionary" experiments getting published and ordered to gather all the printed copies of the Charter, if possible, and send them to Russia, where they were burned. [61]

Of course, if you think of the Charter project as an instigation and the introduction of censorship and the arrests in 1820 of opposition activists, who fought for independent Poland, a provocation, then Novosiltsev deserves condemnation. However, such condemnation from Przecławski (a believer in Polish-Russian brotherhood) was exactly a *self-exposure of the memoirist himself.*

No less ridiculous seem the accusations of Novosiltsev of bribery. In 1827 Jews raised 20 thousand gold pieces to give to Novosiltsev. The imperial Commissar was supposed to block the law of recruitment of Jews in exchange. The memoirist, to prove his point, referred to the story of a Grodno province rabbi Morduch Leisbovich (printed so in the original — *S.D.*), with whom Przecławski allegedly took lessons of Kabbalah. Morduch was in Petersburg, but his mission ended in failure, for the Jewish recruitment bill was passed (no mention of the rabbi Morduch Leisbovich is found in Jewish historical literature. [62])

This episode would not have been worth elaborating on, had it not possessed some quite particular signs of a defamation of an image of a decent person that are found in many such "researches" by anti-Semitists. [63]

In the Russian record of falsification and libel Przecławski arguably takes the first prize. It is not a coincidence that almost simultaneously with *The Exposure of the Great Secret of Freemasons* (1882), *Russkaya Starina* published Chapter VI of the essays out of the book *A Memoir of J. E. Przecławski,* [64] whose table of contents was put together in Bulgarin's manner: "Count Perovsky. — Moralizing of taverns and convenience stores. — Gasophobia. — Writings on the Skoptsy and the Yids. — Zundel Sonnenberg, a representative of the Yid people. — The Yid mind. — Qahals. — Sadducees. — Jacob Frank and his followers. — Karaites. — Jewesses."

The story about L. A. Perovsky (1792–1856), the Minister of Internal Affairs and an important manager of Nicholas's era, logically precedes the main topic of the publication, which is the government's measures to "stop crime" among which the crimes committed by Jews are the most dangerous.

Moreover, for Przecławski the *official*, the main achievement of the Ministry of Internal Affairs under Perovsky was the fact that "the time in office of this minister was also marked by creation, upon his order, of two quite remarkable items of administrative bibliography:

1. "A study of the heresy of the Skoptsy," SPb., 1842 (printed at the highest decree),
2. "The investigation of the murders of Christian infants by Jews and of using their blood." (printed at the order of Mr. Minister of Internal Affairs in 1844). [65]

Chapter 2. The Great Secret of Freemasons

"A study of the Heresy of the Skoptsy" was called by Przecławski "a thorough job" by N. I. Nadezhdin (1804–1856), the former publisher of *Telescope*, where the *Philosophical Letters* by P. Chaadayev were first published, who had already abandoned the ideals of his youth by 1843 and began editing the governmental *Magazine of the Ministry of Internal Affairs*, in which opportunities to fight sectarianism were explored. [66]

Having briefly characterized this "thorough job," Przaclawski mentioned the influence of old Kabbalah doctrines on the Skoptsy's teachings, as well as the influence of ancient Gnosticism and Manichaeism, while stressing that these "ancient and too abstract mystical teachings could not have been unknown to the one conducting an investigation of the heresy of the Skoptsy." [67]

This *lapsus linguae* ("investigation" instead of "study") is remarkable. It appears that the author is anxious to move on to "Jewish crimes," and the reference to Kabbalah, Gnosticism and Manichaeism is as necessary in the "Investigations..." of the ritual murders as in the "Study..." of the Skoptsy's heresy.

Naming N. I. Nadezhdin as the author of the "Study...," Przecławski, it seems, should have also stated the name of the creator of the "Investigations..." But the memoirist names no-one. This cannot fail to disturb.

The thing is, this work is usually attributed to the director of the Department of Foreign Religious Denominations V. V. Skripitsyn or the ethnographer and author V. I. Dal. [68] This issue has not been resolved, although in the bibliography of V. I. Dal listed by Melnikov-Pechorsky *The Investigations...* are absent, and V. Porudominsky [69] and Yu. Gessen [70] believed that Dal's name was simply used by the Black Hundred. Indeed, "*The Note on Ritual Murders*, wrapped in medieval darkness," would soil Dal's name, unless the legend that this note is a fruit of his labor was dispelled." [71]

Przecławski personally knew V. V. Skripitsyn and disapproved of his actions: "To be a good director of this department," he wrote, "one must, at least, study the essential basics of each denomination whose spiritual affairs he manages: this is the starting point and the alpha and omega of his position."

This was precisely the knowledge that Skripitsyn, in Przecławski's opinion, lacked. [72] Still, Przecławski never mentioned that Skripitsyn took any part in putting *The Investigations...* together, and most likely the department director had nothing to do with it. [73]

In 1846, the Ministry of Internal Affairs printed a work by a famous Russian Turkologist V. V. Grigoriev, *Jewish Religious Sects in Russia*. The scholar admitted that the book was a usual compilation of a number of foreign works, the same way *The Investigations...* were a compilation of some Polish books. [74]

So, it is very likely that Skripitsyn could have gone to N. I. Nadezhdin with a request to review the subject of ritual murders, especially since, to an educated scholar, such compiling work should not have seemed difficult. [75]

Still, this theory should be supported by thorough study of the whole scholarly legacy of Grigoriev, who became famous first of all as a Turkologist.

In *Jewish Religious Sects...* Grigoriev thought it necessary to note the obscurity of the material itself: "For us Russians, familiarizing ourselves with this subject has... a local interest, for, since the Jews lost their fatherland and their state independence, they wandered and dispersed all over the face of the earth, and in no one country have they congregated in such numbers as they do in the areas of the former Kingdom of Poland that were later partly joined with Russia." [76]

This remark is interesting, because Przecławski used the same explanation to begin his story, for getting familiar with the Jewish question "is of interest and use to the Russian society." [77]

Having taken up the subject of Jews, Przecławski informed us that the author of *Investigations...* had studied 26 different works in six languages and "managed to gain information from Jewish religious books that were kept in secret." [78] (By the way, it is known that B. I. Dal did not know any Hebrew, [79] and his "authorship" should be doubted for this reason, at least.)

Further, Przecławski retells the "hypothesis" that the crimes (nearly unknown in Western Europe), of which Jews were accused, were undoubtedly "lawful" according to the Babylonian Talmud, and their frequency in the Kingdom of Poland could be explained by the fact that it was populated by "old school" Jews, rigid in their ancient fanaticism.

Referring to "Foreign Quarterly Review" of 1842 and reminding of his participation as a witness in the Grodno case in 1816, the memoirist accuses "Hasidim" of the addiction to ritual murder.

According to him, this "sect," founded in 1760 or 1761 by Mr. Israel Bashlem (obviously a typo), practices "something monstrous": Allegedly, in "Likale Amuvia" (most likely, also a typo) — a book by Baal Shem Tov's disciple Rabbi Jacob Joseph of Polonne, *Toledot*

Chapter 2. The Great Secret of Freemasons

Yaakov Yosef, Likutei Amarim, a Collection of Statements, Moral Instructions, and Interpretations Bashlem strives to prove that a human must sin as much as possible to get close to God, because God occupies the top step and a sinner — the bottom one; this "ladder" is a circle whose bottom and top steps touch, and, therefore, God and a sinner become the touching links.

That is why Hasidim, according to Przecławski, consider themselves holy and despise and hate people of other faiths and, first of all, Christians. [80]

Let us note that Przecławski mixed together particular features of three different, and mutually exclusive, branches of Judaism: Sabbatianism, Frankism, and Hasidism.

It is noteworthy that in regard to the issue of procuring blood through ritual murder Przecławski uses a relevant passage from *Investigations* ("The words of some Jewish sympathizers that if that were true the Yids would not have to kill and could always procure blood in any barber shop, is not entirely unfounded; the mystery of this violent ritual requires precisely Christian martyr's blood of an innocent infant") [81]) and interprets it ("But this argument is entirely unfounded, for the precise requirement is to procure blood through torture") [82]). He does the same when answering the questions regarding the use of blood (Item 3) and Jews' guilt proven during the trials (Item 4), although he adds something that is missing from *Investigations*: Przecławski declares that the main reason for Jews going unpunished is their ability to do their business with the help of the golden calf whom they have been worshipping from times of old," and who "gave them the key of the same metal to open doors and hearts," [83] and uses as an example Case 117 from *Investigations* (The Grodno case of 1816).

In *Investigations* the conclusions of "anonymous" are in direct opposition to the government decrees. Yu. Gessen failed to pay attention to this in his time. The Grodno case became a triumph for the Jews and their acquittal was officially confirmed by the government. The Velizh case (that takes up almost a half of the book) also ended favorably for Jews as a result of active interference of Mordvinov and the Vice-Minister of Justice, Panin.

Perhaps that is why Przecławski decided to reinforce the *Investigations'* author's claim that Jews' "crimes" were proven by including extensive footnotes with additional "proof" of their guilt. Thus, pointing out that the author of *Investigations* was not familiar with the theologian Gerres's work *Mystique divine, naturelle et diabolique* that was published later, Przecławski mentioned the case of William of

Norwich in England (1144) and the trials that led to banishing of Jews from Spain in 1492.

In this light, Przecławski's claim that Count Perovsky went to consult on ritual murders ... State Secretary Turkul, who was Preclawski's own boss during the Kalisz process (that is not mentioned in *Investigations*), and who particularly trusted Przecławski and brought him along to report to the Emperor, is quite interesting. [84] Such footnotes reinforced the accusations (and their provability) of Jews of ritual murders. Besides, the only ten printed copies of *Investigations* (to be presented to Nicholas I, the heir apparent, the Grand Dukes and the members of the State Council) were secret in nature and its editing could only be entrusted to an exclusively trusted person, which, undoubtedly, could have been J. E. Przecławski. [85]

Przecławski's memoirs include enough obvious proof of the author's part in *Investigations*, at least as its editor. Hence the various tales of being acquainted with Jewish public figures and Jewish traditions that, according to Przecławski, prove "the maliciousness of the Jewish people."

However, in essence, while talking about the existence of "secret" Jewish societies whose members are connected either by initiation into sectarian mysteries or by adherence to mystic and messianic ideas, Przecławski uses almost all the "arguments" that, in one way or another, became the "corner stones" not only for *Investigations* but also for *The Protocols of the Elders of Zion*.

ACTA PROCONSULARIA

Przecławski, while looking into the case of the Slonim Jews robbing churches (the police caught them red-handed at splitting their loot in "a cellar of a Yid woman"), "discovered" that the Jews set up catacombs under the town's ghetto in the manner of those in Paris, where they hid the evidence of their crimes.

Entrusting the reader with this "secret," Przecławski concluded: "Therefore, the Slonim Yids were members of a true secret society, and we can safely assume that such undergrounds must also exist in other towns, where Jewish residents occupy separate blocks." [86]

According to Przecławski, the sect of Frankists was an example of a Jewish "secret society."

Following in his speculations an article in *Foreign Quarterly Review* (1842) and, possibly, the book by V. Grigoriev *Jewish Religious Sects*, Przecławski tells in detail of the activities of Jacob Frank and of a dispute in Lvov, which resulted in the sect's leader's and his followers' conversion to Christianity, which allowed the neophytes to join the most prominent Polish families. [87]

That is why Frank "became a true benefactor of his tribe, and some of his followers justifiably recognized Frank as the Messiah awaited by Jews." [88]

To comprehend the true meaning of such a conclusion by Przecławski it is sufficient to quote L. Korneyev, a modern anti-Semitist: "According to the Judaic dogma, Zionists believe that "the true Jewish" origin is gained through the Jewish mother. They also approve of non-Jews marrying Jewish women, believing that "goyim" husbands can become pro-Zionist agents, and their children may become direct supporters of Zionism.

Besides, Zionists have the support of rabbis who see in mixed marriages a strategy for "penetration of Jewish seed into goy society" and confirm their arguments by references to the Tanakh." [89]

Thus, Frank's "benefaction" that opened ways for Jews to mix with Polish aristocracy, pursued the goals of "the secret doctrine" of rabbis.

It is not a coincidence that Przecławski saw "seeds" of evil in Jewish origin.

While talking about the adventures of a Frankist Alexander Krysinski, he states: "If, by misfortune, such a malevolent charlatan has a Polish surname while, like Krysinski, having nothing to do with the Polish ethnicity in his origins, the Russian society that does not know the difference, will attribute all the despicable acts of such person to his supposed Polonism." [90]

At the same time, Przecławski was very familiar with Polish genealogy (in the past, Count V. N. Panin, already the Minister of Justice, had received from Turkul the information on Polish nobility collected by Przecławski) and made obtaining a certificate of nobility easier for his fellow Poles. He knew that the three greatest geniuses of Poland — Adam Mickiewicz, Juliusz Slowacki and Frederic Chopin — had mothers who came from Frankist families. [91]

Przecławski must have read many works by religious authors, most likely, Chateaubriand, (1768–1848), [92] for in his *Memoir* he mentioned noble features of Jewish women and their remarkable beauty (especially of those from Vilna, Mogilev on Dniester, and Berdichev). Besides, according to him, upon marrying a Christian man, they did not pass "the Yid type" to their offspring. Przecławski found an explanation for this phenomenon in "theological" ideas: for example, according to Chateaubriand, Jewish women kept their beauty, magnanimity, selflessness, kindness and loyalty only because they did not participate in "deicide," and cried and wailed in protest against Christ's crucifixion. [93]

Following in V. V. Grigoriev's steps, Przecławski contrasts Orthodox Jews and Hasidim with Karaim (or Karaites in his spelling), who insist that they are not affected by the curse ("His blood on us and children of ours") that Jews inflicted upon themselves by the execution of Christ, because they, the Karaim, had left Palestine before His coming. [94] That is why the pure Semitic type of Karaim is remarkably beautiful: "Their visage has a clever and serious look and none of that quite unpleasant... half-smile... that is characteristic of all Talmudists and affects even their remote, baptized descendants." [95] To support this opinion, Przecławski says that Lord Beaconsfield (Benjamin Disraeli), for example, is a spitting image of Feigin, a shopkeeper in Petersburg, and both have a repulsive type of face. [96]

The compilatory nature of the "work," and the extreme negativity of the evaluation of "the Jewish character," was not an obstacle for this anti-Semitist's wide generalizations.

Thus, speculating on "the Yid mind," he believes that a Talmudical education "refines" Jewish children's abilities, but points them "in the wrong direction."

As he does in *Investigations,* Przecławski refers to *Sanherdrin* (Part 5, 59) and points out that Talmud teaches to stay away from and hate infidels.

At the same time, he bitterly admits that Jews are "free from two vices of Slavs: laziness and drinking." [97]

Such speculations of Przecławski lead him to "the discovery" of a secret. Referring to *Yid Qahals,* a book he read in 1875, without naming the author and misspelling the book's title, [98] Przecławski declares that Jewry represents "a huge secret society," a state within a state (status in statu): "Wherever it (the qahal — S.D.) is permanently installed, all Christians and other residents walk under its power, unaware, and swaddled, as if in spider web, in an invisible yet strong net of monetary relations." [99]

According to Przecławski, long ago the Sadducees [100] created a program for enslaving other peoples by rejecting their laws and their governmental and societal rules in pursuit of the end goal of "reverting" humankind to its primitive state. [101]

J. E. Przecławski, an ethnically Polish Russian patriot, a former freemason, an acquaintance of many public figures of the times of Alexander and Nicholas, a "friend" of Mickiewicz and Ohryzko, the editor of a Polish newspaper and a renegade of "the Polish affair," in his search of the reasons for the hopeless and, consequently, useless fight of Poles against the Russian Empire could not but come to the conclusion of "a diabolic conspiracy" of the Jews of Westland: the fight between these two Slavic peoples, in his opinion, was not only Jewry's gain, but a means for the "persons of Jerusalem origin" to achieve the goal of ruling over them.

Having established the "malevolence" of the Jewish people, Przecławski gave his idea a philosophically complete form:

"Their creed, or, rather, their program, implied denunciation of all faiths, all laws, and all state and societal rules...

"The reader can't help seeing that Jewish Sadducism is precisely our modern communism, internationalism, social democracy, and nihilism.

"Among the Jewish people Sadducism does not exist as a separate sect any longer, because Sadducees' teachings became cosmopolitan and took on the form of an ubiquitous conspiracy against religion, order, and property. Nowadays we often see the horrific realization of this hellish plan in real evil doings." [102]

Unfortunately, researchers, while dedicating a big part of their works to borrowings and plagiarism in *the protocols of the Elders of Zion*, pay almost no attention to the fact that one of *entirely Russian* sources of this "forgery of the century" was a powerful political and philosophical branch of the national ideology. Essentially, without understanding the dialectic of the Russo-Germanic and Anglo-Franco-Russian relations in the '60–'80s, it is impossible to discern the real historical ground from which the creations of the "adherents" grew and exerted utmost influence on the concept of "worldwide conspiracy" (first and foremost among them, *Memoir* by J. E. Preclawski, which described the '20–'50s, but was published in the late '70s).

CHAPTER 3

Zealots

PAN-GERMANISM AND PAN-SLAVISM

The ideas of "chooseness" and "messianism" found their ultimate expression in a frightening and prideful phrase that had been once attributed to a Jewish kahal and was later paraphrased by nationalists: "A fight of one against all." But, as any nationalistic principle brought to the absolute, a conflict of "a loner" with everyone else could only be used in a crisis situation of an impending real catastrophe. That is why the Polish uprising of 1863 and the Russo-Turkish war of 1877–1878, as well as the Russo-Japanese war of 1904–1905, were the reference points for intensity of the "holy war."

Let us remind the reader that one of the most important "sources" of the zealots' concept in their "holy war" against not only Jews but all aliens was at the time *The Polish Catechism* that was allegedly found on the body of a dead confederate and that appeared in Russian in 1863. P. I. Bartenev published it as an addendum to Yu. F. Samarin's *Jesuits and Their Attitude Towards Russia* (1868), with the following foreword: "*The Polish Catechism*, a miserable practical application of Jesuit teachings, first became known... during the latest Polish rebellion of 1863 and the following years." [1]

Due to the lack of a Polish original, J. E. Przecławski, after analyzing the text, came to the conclusion that this "document" had been forged by the circles close to Muravyov-Vilensky the Butcher. On October 26, 1972 he published an article in "St. Petersburg Vedomosti." "The Russian Archive" soon came out with N. Bitsyn's response ("A remark on the *St. Petersburg Vedomosti* article about *The Polish Catechism*" [2]), in which Przecławski's conclusions were refuted. The argument between Polonophiles and Polonophobes drew out and was never re-

Chapter 3. Zealots

solved. Nevertheless, *The Polish Catechism* was used by "zealots" at different times and on many occasions not as much against Jesuits (Poles) as against Jews.

As is typical of "programs" of such sort, the author of the catechism referred to examples from ancient history: "Remember, brothers, that Phoenicia and Venice ruled the world not by the strength of their arms but by their intelligence, education, and riches..." [3]

This was followed by 13 suggestions put together by "a man experienced and loyal to his motherland":

1. ...In the lands taken, landowners must try their hardest to not let go of their lands... to not let the Russian element develop there... do their best to make them (Russian landowners —*S.D.*) sell their wrongfully acquired lands and leave this region...
2. ...Since Russians are for the most part uneducated, lazy, and careless, Poles must try to educate themselves to always have an advantage over Russians... and thus subdue these crude people morally.
3. ...serving his motherland in Russia, every Pole represents a great mission...
4. ...any measure that may lead to the impoverishment of our fatherland's common foe is not only allowed, but necessary... by stealing from the Russian treasury you weaken the enemy state and enrich your motherland...
5. ...To achieve... your goal any means are allowed... use flattery everywhere as a powerful tool against a Russian as long as you profit from it...
6. ...serve (in the Russian military — *S.D.*) until such time as the sources of your enrichment are gone, after which... leave the service... so your treasures cannot return to the hands of your enemies.
7. ...refuse, however, to occupy the highest government positions, but try... to become an assistant... to the highest statesmen... in the first case, the government will look upon you with distrust... in the second... all the government secrets will be known to you and, consequently, to your compatriots...
8. Be your boss's right hand in everything... Upon gaining their confidence... it will be easier for you to secretly favor your brethren.
9. ...When our agents have penetrated all Russian offices this way... it shall be in our hands...
10. ...remember that Russia is your foremost enemy, and an Orthodox is a schismatic, so do not feel ashamed of being hypocrite... but

secretly take revenge on every Russian: he... will never be your friend and will always support his government in abusing you...

11. ...Should any schemes of yours be discovered, blame the Germans: through this you will redirect the blow... and will avoid suspicion.
12. ...A Russian, as simple and crude as his nature is, holds himself in high esteem and is annoyed at being called a barbarian; to get rid of this hated name he would stab his own brother. Skillfully play with his pride and use it.
13. Should you have to deal with a strong and clever enemy... try to destroy him... with assistance from an *influential German*. The German... will help you in that and your enemy will perish thinking he owes his fall to German influence... and you, free of suspicion, will gain a comrade in an enemy and he will help you in your plans with dedication. [4]

The Polish Catechism (with time people forgot it was Polish) became the main "model" for accusing Jews of "secret conspiracies" and a "secret war" against Russian patriots (first of all, against the "zealots" themselves). [5] However, in the case of Poles, who fought for their motherland's independence, one could appeal to their country's history of existence outside of the Russian Empire, whereas in regard to Jews, who did not have their own national "plot" within the Russian territory, it had to be proven that their existence was determined by the "Vatican principle" based on being a "status in statu."

Moreover, the economic "harmfulness" of Jews who "enslaved" the natives, and the self-rule (status in statu) of the Jewish way of life were rather related to the Gospel myth than to any particular political and state institutions and events. In this respect it is noteworthy that the inglorious Crimean war (1853–1856) never gave birth to any rumors of Jews having aided in Russia's loss, and, consequently, the ideological transformation of the Gospel myth was caused by a number of other trends related to external political events on the international stage.

Born "at the border between the '30s and '40s of the XIX century" in the Habsburg Empire, "the national movement of the Slavic people" in Austria-Hungary did not promote the "idea of independent ethnic states" and only had one goal: "to gain recognition of their ethnic rights and a certain autonomy inside the Austrian state." [6]

This social movement later became known as Austro-Slavism.

Later, the international events post-1848 and the political processes during the time of consolidation of German princedoms (before the Franco-Prussian war of 1870–1871) gave rise to chauvinistic nationalism in Germany, and one of its branches was "pan-Germanism" whose banners carried the slogan of a "Slavic danger": "The term "pan-Slavism" (or, more precisely, Austro-Slavism) appears in the early '40s of the XIX century among Hungarian (more precisely, Austrian — *S.D.*) and German nationalist bourgeoisie that was wary of the Slavs' national liberation movement." [7] The point of this term was that to the Russian government was attributed "an aggressive plan of uniting all the Slavic lands under the Russian rule." [8]

The Tsarist government could not approve of such an "accusation," if only out of diplomatic concerns. At the same time, by shifting the point of pan-Slavism from "lands" to "Slavic peoples" the ideologists of Slavophilia turned a diplomatically negative "plan" into a positive "idea" of uniting Slavs with Russia. In fact, there was an abyss between the German and the Russian definition of pan-Slavism: for Germans it was a form of imperial expansion *policy*, while for Russians it was a form of *ideology*. Russian Tsarist autocracy, while denying the accusations of "imperial expansion," was hostile to pan-Slavism in its German version, [9] but approved of its internal ideology. It is sufficient to mention that consistent existence of mass media of conservative type and of obvious Slavophilic sort, mostly newspapers such as "Vest'" ("News"), "Russky Mir" ("Russian World"), "Grazhdanin" ("Citizen"), not to mention "The Moscow Vedomosti," has been recorded since 1863. [10] And Alexander II's personal support of the editor of "Den'" ("Day"), "Moscow," "Moscovite," and "Rus'" I. S. Aksakov, who for twenty years (1860s-1880s) constantly preached the idea of united Slavic nations, gave grounds to believe that pan-Slavism in its Russian version was very close to the government's point of view.

The Internal Affairs Minister P. A. Valuyev in his report to the Emperor Alexander II of 22 September, 1861, suggested, as an experienced provocateur, a change to the Russian media: "International records show that there comes a time in a country's development when the power of the government alone is not enough to suppress ideas that undermine social order...

We need the cooperation of the part of society that is inspired, or may be inspired, by the opposite ideas. By opposing one side to the other, the government can rule both in greater security and, by protecting social order, retain the necessary space for exercising its own power." [11] That is why it is no surprise that pan-Slavism found its legal niche in the right-wing media ("Nashe Vremya"/ "Our Time," "Grazhdanin," "Golos"/ "Voice," "Den'" et al.). By encouraging, "at the current state of minds," the founding of a magazine "whose conservative tendencies spread... beyond the conservative views of the government itself," P. A. Valuyev was first of all concerned about revolutionary propaganda in the democratic press. [12] In this situation shaping the Russian version of pan-Slavism became the foremost task for Slavophiles. That is why the ideological mechanism of the transformation of pan-Slavic ideas explains a lot.

The idea of a state's exclusiveness itself was typical for empires: "the middle" one (Germany) and "the eastern" one (Russia). However, while in Germany religious opposition between Catholics and Protestants was balanced, and political unity was built upon the *internal ethnic* community of German princedoms, in Russia the Catholic and Uniate population of Poland and part of Ukraine was an ethnic minority (not to mention the Muslims of Middle Asia and the Caucasus; their colonial status in relation to the empire is obvious). That is why the concept of ethnic unity of Slavs *inside* the Russian Empire collided with the problem of religious *denominations* of Catholics and the Orthodox, while a number of Slavic peoples resided outside of the Empire as part of other countries. It was "The double knot" (religious and national) that defined the character of pan-Slavism: the "Slavic exceptionalism" in its "imperial" concept had to be based on political expansion on one hand and on the religious principle of "chooseness" on the other.

In the late 1868, N. Ya. Danilevsky brought the final manuscript of the book *Russia and Europe* to Petersburg and it was published, a chapter at a time, in the magazine "Zarya" ("Dawn") (V. V. Kashpirev, the editor) during 1869. One of the first reviewers of the book, N. Strakhov, wrote: "*Russia and Europe,* certainly, has to be attributed to the school of our literature that is called Slavophilic, for this book is based on the idea of spiritual uniqueness of the Slavic world. Besides, the book embraces the issue so deeply and fully that it can be called an entire catechism or a code of Slavophilia... *Russia and Europe* are the book to study for anyone interested in Slavophilia. With the appearance of this book, we cannot say anymore that the ideas of the uniqueness of the Slavic race and of Europe as a world strange to us, of the goals and the future of Russia, etc., that these ideas exist only as magazine rumors, hints, daydreams, phrases, and allegories; no, Slavophilia now exists in a shape strict, clear, and defined, in a form as exact and logical as any other teaching in our country hardly possesses." [13]

Having rejected "*the common thread* in the evolution of humankind," N. Ya. Danilevsky came to the conclusion about separate civilizations existing in history: "Finding and listing these types presents no difficulty... These cultural and historical types, or unique civilizations, are, in chronological order: 1. Egyptian, 2. Chinese, 3. Assyrian-Babylonian-Phoenician, Chaldean, or Ancient Semitic, 4. Indian, 5. Iranian, 6. Hebrew, 7. Greek, 8. Roman, 9. New Semitic, or Arabian, and 10. Germano-Roman, or European." Further, pointing out that these cultural and historical types "correspond to the greater linguistic and ethnographic families, or tribes, of humankind," Danilevsky declares: "The Slavic tribe is the seventh in... the Aryan family of peoples. The larger part of Slavs (no less, if no more, than two thirds) comprise a politically independent unit — the great Russian Tsardom... Slavism is a term of the same grade as Hellenism, Romanism, and Europeanism."

As far as the "Jewish type," while *not once mentioning the role of Jews in a development of any civilization,* including the European (Germano-Roman), let alone in the political picture of the contemporary opposition of Russia and Europe, Danilevsky categorically states: "Religion stood out as something special and highly important only in the Jewish civilization... Only religious activity of the Jewish people remains as its legacy for its descendants... Jews never produced anything that deserves the attention of their contemporaries or their descendants... But the religious side of their lives and activity was sublime, and so perfect that this people is fairly named God-chosen. Among these people grew a worldview that subordinated the most highly developed civilizations and which was meant to become the religion of all people in its united, eternal, never-ending form... Therefore, we can call the Jewish cultural and historical type not just overwhelmingly, but exclusively religious."

The "Catechism of Slavophilia" created by N. Ya. Danilevsky in the mid-1860s was aimed at pan-Germanism as a power and a civilization aggressively anti-Slavic, and insisted that the "immortal" role of Russia, who strived to be the modern Tsargrad (Constantinople) and whose capital was to be moved to the Bosporus in case of pan-Slavic victory, in her *stand against entire Europe was* first and foremost a natural and historically grounded state *right* of one of the contemporary cultural and historical types (the Slavic federation of peoples).

The absence of any evaluation of the history, culture, and place of the Jewish people in the contemporary world in N. Ya. Danilevsky's work is, in essence, the acknowledgement of only "past," religious, merits of Jews who gave the world "one faith in one God."

On the other hand, the co-existence of the Jewish "religious type" with other cultural and historical types (Germano-Roman, Slavic, etc.) is immanent: in the struggle between pan-Germanism and pan-Slavism there is no place for any other! That is why "the new theory of global history" [14] that largely relied on the political picture of the world of the 1860s, with its real geo-political competition between the German and Russian empires, was indifferent towards the Jewish people and the Jewish question in Russia. Remarkably, this "code of Slavophilia" contained no mention of "the Judeo-Masonic conspiracy."

Conceptually, in the situation of the opposition of pan-Slavism to the modernized cultural and historical "Germano-Roman" type with its slogan *"Drang nach Osten,"* the author of *Russia and Europe* needed neither Jews nor freemasons. Moreover, according to N. Ya. Danilevsky, attributing the historical role of the "global starter" to any "privileged" political, ideological or religious movement was pointless and anti-scientific, since the main conclusion of his book is "as self-sufficient and as amazing in its simplicity and sobriety as this theory as a whole. Slavs are not supposed to renew the whole word and to solve historical problem of all the humankind; they are only a specific cultural and historical type with which other types can co-exist and develop." [15]

With the gradual change of the political situation (Austro-German war of 1868, Franco-German war of 1870–1871, Russo-Turkish war of 1877–1878, the assassination of Alexander II, and convergence of Russia and Germany in the 1870s), Danilevsky's *general* postulate of cultural and historical types of pan-Germanism and pan-Slavism became a *particular* case of Russia's opposition to Europe.

"The Eastern question" was posed by Russia and not Europe, because, despite the fact that *European countries never united* to overtake Russia, "only united Slavs can fight a united Europe," and the conditions for such union were "a common language that can only be Russian" and, of course, the "historical lot" of Russians who must become "the main safekeepers of the living tale of religious truth, Orthodoxy."

The concept of a "conspiracy" ("dominion," "opposition," "struggle," etc.) with the epithet "global" as an objective power threatening Russia appeared in geopolitics *before* the bogey of "Judeo-Masonry." However, later the ideological "vessel" created by Russian patriots and Fatherland's zealots could be "filled" with anything from pan-Germanism to Europeism to Judeo-Masonry. The discovery of a "global Jewish conspiracy" was determined not by its real historical existence, but by its necessity for justifying the real changes in the Russian Empire's geopolitics.

The chronological and "conservative" (from the point of view of the modern Soviet imperial mindset) confusion that was intentionally introduced [16] into the history of connections of two *antagonistic* ideologies (German and Russian) was meant, precisely, to blur the "genetic" transformations in pan-Slavism, which used the *initial* fight with pan-Germanism of the 1860s in a "new" manner in the 1880s (in light of convergence of Russia and France [17]): as the Orthodox safekeeper of the highest patriarchal values, Russia was declared "the only power" to oppose the fatal and Satanic role of Europe. Naturally, in this situation the "Judeo-Masonic" conspiracy that used to be "esoteric" (a domestic enemy) acquired also the meaning of "exoteric" (a foreign enemy). Without identifying the "domestic" and "foreign enemy" as *one and the same*, the global mystico-national concept of collision of pan-Slavism with pan-Judaism (among which, naturally, ranked European countries (but not peoples) would not have been possible.

Now it was possible to talk about pan-Slavism whose enemy was at times England, at times France, or, again, Germany, or in modern time, America. It did not matter at all who was the enemy; the most important thing was that only Russia was *the carrier of pan-Slavic values* and opposed first the "liberal" and "lascivious" Europe and later, the "bourgeois" and "capitalist" world. In this situation of Russian (Orthodox and imperial or Soviet Communist) exclusiveness of a *single* "cultural and historical type" that opposed *everyone* else, it was necessary only to point out the ingredients of evil that were supposed to be found in the political enemies. Those could, naturally, be Jews and freemasons long before the creation of the International or any other international institution, even the League of Nations and the UN.

Actually, the creation of the Russian version of the "Judeo-Masonic" conspiracy first against *just* Russia and later, in the years of revolutionary tribulation and world wars, against the *whole* world would have been impossible without politicization of the Russian idea of pan-Slavism in the mid-1870s — early 1880s. [18]

In France, Spain, Italy, or England, with their *actual* lack of ideas of "pan-France-ism," "pan-Spain-ism." "pan-Italian-ism" and "pan-Anglicism," the works of garden variety anti-Semitists in its "esoteric" essence could not become a basis for state policy. However, in Russia with its fertile soil of pan-Slavism and of pan-Germanism in the Second and Third Reich, the idea of a "Judeo-Masonic conspiracy" (that, of course, had seized power in the neighboring, and hostile, countries) came to politically resistant fruition. That is why multiple borrowings by Russian authors from foreign sources in the 1870s, to which are sometimes attributed the "basic importance," [19] was only the *fertilizer* for the fully mature and independent domestic revelations that were, in time, accepted by the "civilized" Germany as a cure for Bolshevism as well as a tool in a struggle against its own domestic political enemies. [20]

Thus, the political anti-Semitism that was born *in Russia* in the late 1870s grew in the perfectly original *domestic* soil of pan-Slavism. Any creative reworking of European sources by Russian pulp fiction authors was not as much a formative factor as an *adaptation* of a national-chauvinistic ideology to world history that revolved around a "Judeo-Masonic conspiracy."

I. A. BRAFMAN'S *KAHAL BOOK*

Despite the existence of the common stereotype of a Jew in the Russian literature of the first half of the XIX century, we have no reason to believe that a *new* interpretation of Gospel mythologems that could have turned into a political and ideological version of a "state crime" had been formed before the Emancipation Reform of 1861. In fact, such a statement would require a number of "documents" on conceptual self-exposure of Jews' historical "maliciousness," with evidence of their political hostility. Besides, Jewish theme in itself could hardly become acute without being connected to the main issues of the time. However, both links that were necessary for the birth of *The Protocols of the Elders of Zion* appeared in the late 1860s: on the one hand, Russian nationalistic idea was complete in the concept of N. Ya. Danilevsky (1869), and on the other Jews were first proclaimed *personae non grata* in the *Book of Kahal* by the convert J. Brafman (1883). The process of popular development of the new interpretation culminated in the publication of the anonymous *Exposing the Great Secret of Freemasons* (1883), in which "Jerusalem nobility" was presented as enemies of the Tsar and the Fatherland.

Jacob Brafman (Iakov Aleksandrovich Brafman) (1824–1879) was born into a family of a rabbi in the shtetl of Kletsk near Minsk and received elementary education in a cheder. He was or-

I. A. Brafman (1824–1879)

phaned young and, afraid that the qahal would betray him to military recruiters, he took to the road and kept moving from place to place until he was 34. In 1858, he converted (according to some sources, Brafman first converted to Lutheranism and later, Russian Orthodoxy). Naturally, the neophyte immediately became a missionary to Jews. Unlike the Jewish sources, the author of the apologetic article about Brafman believes that Brafman was multilingual and attributes to him the knowledge of Hebrew, Chaldean, Arabic, German, Polish, and French. [21] When Alexander II visited Minsk in 1858, Brafman sent to the Emperor his notes on the Jewish situation and then was summoned by the Synod to Petersburg for explanation. Metropolitan Filaret invited him to Moscow and recommended him to the post of professor of Hebrew at the Minsk Theological Seminary. One of the Metropolitan's orders was "to find the means to remove obstacles met by Jews wishing to convert to Orthodoxy." [22]

During the Polish uprising of 1863 and until 1865, Brafman, while being an active missionary (his "catch" was a few dozen "lost souls"), was a member of a committee that deciphered Hebrew papers. In 1866 he started publishing proselytizing articles in *Vilenskii Vestnik (The Vilna Messenger)*, among them "The View of a Jewish Convert to Orthodoxy on the Reform of Jewish Everyday Life."

The same year he was appointed to the post of the censor of Jewish publications in Vilna, and in 1868 he published his first book on "scientific" anti-Semitism *The Local and Universal Jewish Brotherhoods*. Brafman's insistence that Jewish communities were "a state within a state" were met with sympathy by the Vilna School District Curator I. N. Kornilov, a famous geographer and later the president of the Slavic Committee of Petersburg. Kornilov convinced the assistant to the Minister of Education, I. D. Delyanov, to use Brafman as a man knowledgeable in the Jewish question and a zealous Christian.

General K. P. Kaufman, the Governor of Westland in 1865–1866, ordered Brafman to collect qahal acts. Brafman presented his boss with documents and notes. To investigate Brafman's accusations of the land's Jewish communities, the so-called Vilna Committee was created and K. P. Kaufman (and later his successor, General A. L. Potapov) demanded that Jews were included in it. The Jewish representatives tried to prove Brafman's incompetence and defend the rights and traditions of their people.

However, this did not stop Brafman. He had his collected documents translated into Russian, with the help of rabbi schools' students, and in 1869 published them under the title *The Book of the Kahal*.

Jewish writers vehemently criticized the book and insisted that Brafman had partially distorted the qahal acts, that his translations were inaccurate and that even the publisher's commentary suffered from mistakes and, at times, intentional falsehoods.

Still, the Russian administration fully trusted the book: K. P. Kaufman in his conversation with I. Gordon said that several dozens of copies had been sent to Turkestan to be distributed at public institutions and officials were mandated to read it and familiarize themselves with Jewish way of life. [23] State officials later referred to *The Book of the Kahal* as to a code of law and it was reprinted several times.

In 1876 Brafman published an article in the semi-liberal *Golos (Voice)* that strongly attacked the Society of Spreading Education Among Jews. A special place among these attacks was given to criticizing the actions of Alliance Israeli that was presented as an "almighty and global" body of Jewish self-administration.

The later printings of *The Book of the Kahal*, amended with additional material that reinforced its anti-Jewish mood, as well as Brafman's articles and speeches, in the opinion of every author who wrote about him, encouraged the growth of anti-Semitism in Russia (it is sufficient to mention that in 1877 F. M. Dostoyevsky wrote an invective in *The Writer's Diary* against Jews who flooded Russia "as a whole qahal," "created" a state within a state and "seized" all financial affairs [24]).

Translated in its entirety into French and Polish, and in extracts into English and German, *The Book of the Kahal* became a great help for European anti-Semites as well.

For his meritorious service to the government and participation in the work of the Committee for All-Estates Military Conscription Brafman was decorated with the Order of St. Vladimir IV Class in 1871. He received "monetary gifts" from the government on multiple occasions. After Brafman passed away, his son Alexander became his successor in the work to "uncover the Jewish maliciousness." The foreword to *The Book of the Kahal* in many ways served as a "scholarly basis" for the "zealots" among pulp fiction writers (B. Markevich, Vs. Krestovsky, etc.) and opinion journalists (A. Shmakov, S. Nilus, etc.).

It is interesting that in 1928, G. Schwarz-Bostunitsch remarked that "a convert rabbi (anti-Semitists somehow considered every converted Jew a rabbi — S.D.) Jacob Brafman uncovered part of "Yid secrets" in the famous *Book of the Kahal* that was published in Petersburg and bought out by Yids." [25]

Chapter 3. Zealots

The Book of the Kahal contains 285 qahal acts of the Jewish community of Minsk, dated 1794–1803.

Many of these were mangled in translation and in the editor's commentary that was supposed to prove "the independence of the qahal," many of its decisions were interpreted arbitrarily.

In his foreword Jacob Brafman presented a number of theses whose point was to define the "corpus delicti" of the Westland Jews. Thus, for instance, a quote from Act 797 in Brafman's translation ("It is decided to renew *the reign of our Sovereign, morainu*, our teacher and the great rabbi of Israel, so he remains the rabbi and president of the *beth din* of our town for ten more years" [26]) was interpreted as "our Sovereign" (*morainu*, rabbi, teacher) opposed to "their" Sovereign, and therefore the community was subordinate first of all to "its own" ruler and only secondly to the "goy" Tsar. According to Brafman, this thesis means the Jews prefer obeying their community law to obeying the state law. [27]

The executive body to "our Sovereign" was a qahal council and the judicial body was a beth-din that was subordinate to the qahal leaders. That is why qahal Acts 155 and 156 referring to punishment of the disobedient, as well as the rulings on "secret persecutors," [28] were interpreted by Brafman in accordance with the general concept of Jewish self-governing.

Referring to the tractate *Sanhedrin* (Chapter 7) "on four types of capital punishments," Brafman hyperbolizes the all-powerfulness and cruelty of the qahal and states: "We would be better off keeping quiet about such a shameful feature of the ancient structure of a Jewish community (he means the types of capital punishment: stoning, burning, striking with a sword, and strangulation — S.D.), if the documents and facts did not clearly prove that this monstrous system of frontier justice that uses government offices and authorities as blind tools in the hands of Jews who pursue anti-government goals is still functional in the underground activities of Jewish institutions." [29]

That is why, Brafman points out, young members of a Jewish community are eager to fulfill any ruling of the beth-din, even if it contradicts the law of the land these Jews reside in. [30]

Naturally, the fact that Jews have their "own tsar" and their own "punitive" and, on top of that, "secret" bodies is the reasoning behind Brafman's main conclusion: Jews represent a special "state," independent from Russia's official institutions, and qahal that subordinates smaller "brotherhoods," is a powerful and well-organized machine whose activity is aimed not only at regulating Jews' private lives, but also at those who they live amongst. Not possessing the ability to rule all Jews and non-Jews, the qahal strives for "indirect power" and its weapon is private property.

Thus, commenting on Act 132, Brafman refers to a Talmudic tractate Bava Batra ("the property of a goy is as free desert") and the legal responses of 1552 by Joseph Kulun ("the property of a goy is as free lake") and insists that the qahal considers the residents of their area, "both Jewish and Christian," and their property as a kind of its own "state" or "official" property which it manages "on a kind of legal basis." [31]

Jewish press immediately pointed out the author's lack of integrity. As far back as 1870, "Novoye Vremya," "Den'" and "Deyatelnost'" mentioned that Brafman arbitrarily abridged or added to the texts in translation and subjectively interpolated certain fragments. The Jewish critics Shershevsky, Seiberling and Morgulis proved that Brafman barely knew Hebrew.

At the same time, publishing genuine documents of Jewish life in the XVIII–XIX centuries, Brafman "invented" a new method of "scientific" compilation, which turned out to be quite "genius" indeed. Building up his commentary of the decisions of the servants of religion of the XVIII century on quotes from Talmudic tractates of the II–VII centuries and on the thoughts of Jewish religious thinkers of the XII–XVII centuries, Brafman was trying to prove the eternal and unwavering character of a Jewish community whose leaders not only preserved their independence from governmental and social institutions but economically enslaved their own people as well as outsiders.

The "commentary" of a convert "rabbi" was made accessible to everyone and his "scientific method" was so simple and sufficient to expose the Jews' maliciousness that Russian anti-Semitic pulp fiction writers could not but exploit Brafman's "discoveries."

Brafman's book filled in the gap in the chain of "exposures" while exposing not just a single sect (for example, the Sadducees) but the entire Jewish people against whom *a Jew* has testified.

SATAN'S ELIXIR

While in the literature of the first half of the XIX century the image of a Jew was fragmentary and peripheral, in the 1870s it started to move towards the center, because any discussion of the Jewish question in the Russian society would turn into a discussion of two powerful ideological trends: conservative/Orthodox and revolutionary/nihilistic. For writers from Slavophilic circles the Jewish question in its social and political pragmatism was tightly bound with Christian mythologems, which to some degree dictated possible kinds of "final solutions," and it was noticeable, for example, in Dostoevsky's *The Jewish Question, Pro and Contra, Status in Statu, Forty Centuries of Being, But Long Live Brotherhood!* etc.

However, while Brafman's *The Book of the Kahal* set up the starting position of the definition of the "domestic enemy," the "anonymous" work *The Great Secret of Freemasons* that was first published in the magazine "Vek" (1883) and 25 years later appeared as a separate volume under the subtitle "From the papers of J. E. Przecławski" (1909) clearly defined the enemy's image.

In his memoir, realizing that the reader might find an idea of "a global conspiracy" a bit fantastic, Przecławski decided to "start with a trump card": "There is one unpublished work that proves that full realization of the Sadducees' doctrine is now the ultimate goal of one ancient secret society that is present almost everywhere and is biding its time under nice pretense." The editorial stuff of "Russkaya Starina" believed it was necessary to reveal the secret of "an unpublished work," and they added a curious footnote to his memoir: "The literary work mentioned here belongs to the pen of the late Joseph Emmanuel Przecławski himself, and it occupied him in the last years of his life." [32]

Let us remind the reader that *Memoirs* were delivered by the late author's son to "Russkaya Starina" *on February 3, 1883*. Simultaneously, two issues of "Vek" published by M. M. Filippov came out with "certain extracts" [33] from *Exposing the Great Secret of Freemasons*. [34]

The connection between these two "works" published in 1883 (the 1st and 2nd chapters from *The Great Secret of Freemasons* and *Memoir* by J. E. Przecławski) was "neutralized" in 1909: "Among the papers my late father, Privy Councilor Osip Antonovich Przecławski left behind I found, among others, a quite extensive manuscript titled *The Great Secret of Freemasons* and a letter to him from... Vladimir Dmitrievich Filosofov, dated November 7, 1873, in which he directly entrusted my father, on his own behalf as well as on behalf of his brother Alexander Dmitrievich Filosofov's widow, to make this manuscript public through printing. This leads me to believe that its author was no other than the — by then — late Alexander Dmitrievich Filosofov, although I have no other indications of this." [35]

It would seem that such a categorical "leads me to believe" and a quite doubtful "have no other indication" (of course, not from the father's correspondent but from J. E. Przecławski himself) are logically contradicting, and the indication of the *presence* in the deceased's archive of a letter from State Secretary V. D. Filosofov, without *presenting* its copy or at least some quotes, has no legal power. Although, when publishing (as "anonymous") the "work of A. D. Filosofov," the publisher mentions his name only once in the foreword and prefers a more appropriate type of "camouflage" — "the author of the manuscript," while putting out on the title page a meaningful phrase: "From the papers of the late J. E. Przecławski" and, most likely, picking epigraphs from the New Testament by himself. [36]

However, firstly, the "author's" title (*The Great Secret...*) was kept as the title of the "manuscript" but replaced as the title of the book with a general editor's *Exposure of the Great Secret...*

Secondly, among A. D. Filosofov's "admirers" were not only his family members (brother and widow of the "author") and his commentators (father and son Przecławski), but also "several high-ranking persons" (among them General Alexander Drenteln [37] and the State Co ntroller T. I. Filippov [38]), who declared "their full solidarity with its author's views." [39] Thirdly, *anti-Polonism* of some paragraphs *matched the time of the manuscript's compiling*, that is, the time after the pacifying of the last Polish rebellion in 1863 [40], as well as the life story... of the publisher.

This last circumstance is extremely important. Let us remember that back in the day, after the first Polish uprising (1831–1832), Przecławski senior was sentenced to death by his compatriots "for treason," and during the second uprising, his Russian colleagues alleged that Cyprinus, a Pole, wished to provoke the government into using "reprehensible cruelty." [41]

In any case, the anti-Polish and anti-Catholic utterances in the manuscript could hardly belong to a zealous Catholic and a "secret patriot." His son, however (Przecławski's wife was also Catholic), became a militant *Orthodox and a Russian chauvinist* and could think it necessary to "amend" the text with negative opinions of Poles and Catholics while preparing the book for printing in 1908.

Lastly, offering in 1909 a manuscript "outdated" by 50 years (a footnote by Przecławski junior to the foreword), the publisher paid special attention to the always relevant political pragmatism: "Furthermore, I find it necessary to add that if I, by now exposing the freemason's secret, may incur the wrath of Russian and even Western European Jewry (although the author's and mine denunciations concern exclusively the sect of Sadducees and, perhaps, the sect of Zionists whose teachings don't seem to stray too far from that of Sadducees), I still do my best to fulfill my intention, convinced that my passivity in this case would go against my consciousness and I would commit a great sin before the Lord my God and my Motherland." [42]

Formulating the goals and tasks of publishing *The Great Secret of Freemasons* in 1909 (after the surfacing, in 1905, of the *Protocols of the Elders of Zion* [43]) Przecławski-junior stated that the manuscript was "a scholarly, rather than literary, work," [44] and declared his strictly "conservative" view of the Russian Tsarist autocracy: "Our government is still strong, the Orthodox faith is unwavering in our people, and the loyalty of the people, the military, and the majority of our nobility to the Tsar and our trust in him is preserved." [45] At the same time, he juxtaposed this "scholarly work" to multiple literary and "documentary" writings of pulp fiction and opinion authors of the early XX century [46], insisting that the priority in exposing "a global Judeo-Masonic conspiracy" belonged to the owner of the manuscript, Joseph Przecławski, and... to him as the publisher. [47]

However, the "plot" of this publication whose late author A. D. Filosofov passed it on to a third party who, in his turn, enriched it with footnotes and then left it to his son, etc., had long before become a literary stereotype. Although we like the publisher have no "indication" as to the authorship, we can assume that the text and the most interesting footnotes were written by Joseph Przecławski himself, and the literary arrangement of the publisher's "plot" belongs to his son.

The book contains eight chapters [48] and each of them is devoted to examination of a core point in the history of Russia, Freemasonry, and Jewry. At the same time, the "point of view" chosen by the author is astonishing not as much due to its bias as to its lack of logic.

By defining utilitarian, scientific and social progress and their respective "subjects of crafts, science and citizenship" as parts of civilization, the author stated that "in Russia, three state eras and three state rulers matched" his scheme: Peter I, Nicholas I and Alexander II. However, since destructive actions of freemasons are illustrated by Polish rebellions, the omission of the actions of Catherine II, who participated in every division of Poland and joined most of it to Russia, as well as those of Alexander I, who defeated Napoleon and his Polish allies, appears strange and "ill-intended."

The logic also appears paradoxical. Peter's reign was a past long gone for the author, but the reign of Nicholas I was a time in history that he directly took part in. Should we then be surprised that to him "the Charter of Russian Laws" (that had been developed by

J. E. Przecławski under the supervision of... a mason and liberal reformer, M. M. Speransky) remained a "colossal memorial." No less precious to him is the time of the Great reforms of Alexander II (Przecławski-senior's zealous service brought him to the top of his government career). It would seem that such a consistent upward trend in Russia's development should have led one to think of common welfare that came as a result of social progress. It is here, however, that a surprise awaits. In fact, instead of a praise to the new "progressive" reality there sounds... a funeral march: "In our society everything is sort of scary, unnatural, tense; under the calm surface elements of decay are moving and it seems as if someone's invisible touch paralyses actions of our government or turns them into things harmful to our country; anyone can feel the approach of a storm, but doesn't see where it's coming from; everyone is anticipating something and secretly fearing something in the future. Well, there are reasons for fear: the state of mind has grown and the well-calculated and craftily organized propaganda has adapted to our soil which was followed in the XVIII century France by the birth of a bloody monster whose name is Revolution."

Thus, the "bloody monster" turns out to be a fruit of progress and the "state of minds" is only a consequence of well-calculated and crafty propaganda.

Moreover, having gone through the three stages of civilization, in the XIX century Russia found itself in the situation of XVIII century France. The paradox is the fact that benevolent actions of "state persons" encourage forward progress of crafts, sciences and citizenship and they, in their turn, assist in the birth of the devastating force of revolutionary changes in society.

Yet, having proved this fact, the author immediately replaces the causality of "evolution" (historical progress) and "revolution" (state regression) with mutually exclusive tendencies of "the power" (Tsarist autocracy) and "the democracy" (the people). Additionally, whereas the "august will" of monarchs pursues positive goals of *gradual* liberal reforms, the "malicious will" of persons without a position of state, is guided, naturally, by "intrigue, egotism, and tyranny." Henceforth, the point of understanding history lies in exposing the "secret" of those individuals and various parties that strive for power.

In Chapter 2 the author lifts the "cloak of ancient Isis": deliberate "destruction of religious and moral foundations that could not be good for any society" is the very "direct cause of the French Revolution," which, in the author's opinion, was ignited by a "conspiracy against truth." Exposing this conspiracy is the "subject" of his reasoning whose

Chapter 3. Zealots

pattern is surprisingly simple: the Christian world is opposed by the "atheistic" (masonic) world led by adherents of Judaism.

Of course, it would have been much easier for the author to describe the "conspiracy," had he not had to "study" the intermediary link ("the order of freemasons"), since the antinomy of Christianity and Judaism has become, after a thousand years, a "common point" for anti-Semitists of all types and ethnicities.

However, firstly, "the author's denunciations as well as mine refer exclusively to the sect of Sadducees." Secondly, "no source of Jewish literature ever mentions Adoniram." Thirdly, "the essence of the Masonic doctrine is only the teachings of Judean schismatics and not Moses' Law." Fourthly, "to comprehend the true meaning of the order of freemasons there is no need to absolutely insist that the Judean people are now directly and deliberately participating in the actions of the order." And lastly, "we know from the Old Testament Hebrew writings that before Christ no unusual mysteries existed among Hebrews."

And yet, the single and all-consuming idee-fixe of the authors of *Exposing...* is the *a priori fault of the Jewish people in every trouble of the Christian world*:

a) "in the official denunciation of Jesus the Savior as a Jewish criminal that was justly executed";
b) "Jews cannot but sympathize, with all the energy of their secret historical thought, with the total decline of Christianity and weakening of state foundations among Christian nations";
c) "we cannot but recognize their eternal animosity towards all other ethnicities... their constant resistance to authorities both civil and spiritual";
d) "striving to erect a global Judaic monarchy on the ruins of Christianity soaked in the blood of new martyrs, the monarchy with its vengeful God that used to smite whole generations and nations by Jews' hands";
e) "Hebrews... are preparing for Christians the fate of a purifying sacrifice for the actions of their ancestors";
f) "only the Jews enjoy the material advantages of modern civilization..." and the proletariat, "this rotten, infectious parasite of modern humankind, created by laziness, insolence and intrigue, is entirely unknown in Jewish society, cunning but hard-working and business-like";
g) "the coming and rule of... the Messiah... over the Jewish people is impossible without preceding moral destruction of Christianity";

h) finally, whether "modern Jews have anything to do with the order of freemasons, the writer has no positive knowledge, but there is no doubt that they cannot remain indifferent witnesses of the fall of Christianity that is happening in front of their eyes."

Such an idee-fixe in itself was neither original nor exclusive. A different matter was exposing "the new Judaic intrigue" — "a Judaic initiation" that lay at the "foundation of the masonic order."

Of course, using certain items of Jewish symbolism, Jewish names and words, some later apocrypha (not only Jewish in origin), interpretation of the New Testament events and many others in masonic "rites" as well as in their descriptions should have sooner or later "indicated" the "Judaizing" character of "freemasons."

However, to declare freemasonry a "secret" weapon of Hebrews, deliberately used by them against the Christian world, could have occurred only to someone for whom a person's "Jerusalem origin" meant not only social alienness but political unreliability.

Moreover, with the lack of direct and objective proof of a "Jewish conspiracy" against Christians, *exposing* "intermediary" links (activity of "secret societies," including Masonic ones) between historical periods of rejecting the Savior's messianic role in the ancient Hebrew world and Jews' participation in revolutionary movements in Europe in the XIX century should have happened just in a place where conflict between Jewry and "native population" (i.e. in the Kingdom of Poland during the Patriotic War of 1812) was of distinct *colonial* character.

In this sense, the guilt of the Jews who had stayed on the Russian side during historical events determined the measure of their guilt as participants of revolutionary movements against Tsarist autocracy. In both cases the harm from the "Jerusalem tribe" was clear for the renegade Przecławski who had been one of freemasons and revolutionary compatriots, and him the retrograde who missed Nicholas I, the educational reformer of Russia, and who looked at the liberal reforms of Alexander II with suspicion.

It was a different matter in the case of freemasons, whose interstate and international movement encompassed all the levels of society, regardless of its members' belonging to "powers-that-be" or their ethnicity.

As with the "ancient guilt" of Hebrews, freemasons' participation in the bloody events of the French Revolution determined the measure of their "guilt" in the "most recent political events," and the ideology of a zealous Catholic and loyal government official only prompted the logic of "exposure."

Borrowing from Jews of their holy books (the entire Old Testament with added, non-canonical for Jews, "scriptures"), ritual elements and traditions, and of a number of liturgical and theological methods spoke significantly more "against" Christianity than against Freemasonry. (Undoubtedly, the "author" of the exposure of the "great secret" was an educated man who had also been raised on theological works and well-studied in the history of Christianity. And yet, he never doubted the "Hebrew origin" of the New Testament, although it is in the birth of Christianity that he should have seen the possibility of a "Jewish conspiracy" aimed at achieving "world domination." [49])

At the same time, such an idea could not have occurred to any *practicing* Christian. But the absolutization of the *opposition of two faiths*, based on the same ancient (pre-Christian) sources and preserving their antagonism since the time of "Judaic" persecution of the Second Temple period and Christian persecution in the following centuries, appeared to be the only *meaning and content of history*. [50] That is why Freemasonry (as well as Christianity), which used symbols, apocrypha, proverbs and signs of Judaic origin and which accepted some Christian realities in a *heretical* manner (in the opinion of both Catholics and the Orthodox), according to the "exposer," could not help but take the side of Judaism.

The quintessence, or the "fifth element," of Freemasonry was, presumably, the legend of Adoniram, in which the Biblical tale of building the Temple was transformed, according to the author of *Exposing...*, into a rite of the bloody murder of Solomon's rival, and became a "symbolic foundation for the entire Freemasonry": "The matter is, first of all, that since the death of one Adoniram (in a footnote: or just Iram, which means "noble." — *S.D.*), a son of a widow from the tribe of Naphtali, the former chief builder of Solomon's Temple who was treacherously assassinated... by three Hebrew workers, Hebrews have lost some secret word without which a Hebrew temple was impossible to finish." To freemasons this word is *Mac-benach* ("the flesh is smitten"), and in the rite itself "one cannot but recognize... the symbolic language of Jews resembling both the Biblical and the Talmudical writing systems."

Still, the author admits, the legend was most likely created after the Resurrection of Christ: firstly, because "no source of Jewish literature... mentions an Adoniram," and secondly, because "this legend... includes hints obviously aimed against the Four Evangelists' stories of the Resurrection of Christ."

Later, S. A. Nilus [51] suggested a literary translation of this legend according to the book by J.H.E. Le Couteulx De Canteleu *Les Sectes et Sociétés Secrètes*, and G. Bostunich amended that translation according to its version in the novel *The Masons* by A. F. Pisemsky. [52]

The "scientific" analysis of the legend allowed G. Bostunich to arrive at a fair conclusion:

"If you look at the legend of Adoniram from a purely literary point of view, you shall have to recognize it as a product of a later time...

"Aside from the contradictions to the church legend, the authors also contradict the Holy Scripture..."

Then (in accordance with the theory of a "Judeo-masonic conspiracy) he introduces significant "noise and interference": "...most likely, this legend owes its origin to the Greek-speaking Levantine Yids who had adopted some elements of Islam, which, in its turn, took them from the Yids (do not forget that Mohammed first learned about Christianity from Arabian Yids)." [53]

The most important part of this sentence is arguably the "chain" of the carriers of the legend: from Levantine Yids to Islam to Arabian Yids.

Although G. Bostunich categorically notes that "the legend respects history even less than the Bible," [54] this did not stop him from resorting, in his own words, to "such re-making and interpretation that often it was hard to know which was more astonishing: the naivety of one or the stupidity of the other." [55]

Despite such a severe judgment, the legend (as the cornerstone of freemasonry) was declared not as much the content of the masonic rite of initiation as... the body of the crime of "malicious" Jewry:

"Let us rip away the remnants of the allegorical curtain that conceals reality: the death of Adoniram... is the fall of the Old Testament Judaism; the three Hebrew workers who murdered Adoniram are the three disciples of Jesus who... spread the news of the Resurrection of Jesus crucified by Jews... Abidal the patricide represents Christian teaching that destroyed ancient Judaism from whence it came..."

In this interpretation (G. Bostunich fully agreed with it and attributed the authorship of *Exposing...* to A. D. Filosofov [56]) the legend of Adoniram, adopted by freemasons from "Levantine Yids," called for revenge against Abidal, i.e., Christian teaching:

"Thus, the order of freemasons is a power united with the Judaic tribe; thus, Jews or their powerful allies, in their turn, are preparing for Christians the fate of a purifying sacrifice for the actions of their ancestors."

By presenting freemasons and Jews as "the enemies of Christian teachings" it was possible not only to introduce an "eternal" historical conflict into the dichotomy of these hostile powers but also to allow religious Christians to see in this conflict a shadow of the Apocalyptic prophecy of the war of "the sons of Light with the sons of Darkness," the war of Christ's host with Antichrist.

However, J. E. Pzeclawski's publications (both of his lifetime and posthumous) neither in the early 1870s nor in the mid-1880s could not yet become an "instruction manual" for reactionary circles in Russia due to a number of reasons. Firstly, the revolutionary movement was not yet as wide-spread as it would be in the 1890s. Secondly, influencing public opinion in the liberal times of Alexander II was made significantly harder because of "the great reforms." Thirdly, due to their *unscientific character* (remember the remarkable letter/afterword by A. O. Przecławski in the 1909 edition to the professor from Kazan regarding the absence of references to published works [57]), the conspiracy and, consequently, the "Jewish initiation" had to be tested first in pulp fiction and opinion journalism and in the end become, **thanks to these writings**, a "generally known theory" that did not need scientific formalization.

GOG AND MAGOG (B. M. MARKEVICH AND V. V. KRESTOVSKY)

Prejudice towards "Christ-sellers" and exaggeration of "Jewish danger" for contemporary Russian life, caused by participation of Jewish youth in revolutionary movements, were "conservative" in content as well as form. That is why only in the historical situation of the 1870s, Judeophobia acquired distinct geopolitical features of a fully conscious concept. From then on, it was not about some "ethical and mythological" malevolence of Jews, but government-postulated untrustworthiness of aliens towards Russia.

This point of view was expressed by a mediocre pulp writer B. M. Markevich (1822–1884) and a talented opinion journalist and novelist Vs. V. Krestovsky (1840–1895).

B. Markevich came from a Polish family. He studied at Richelieu Lyceum in Odessa. He served as a special assignment official for about 30 years and held a court rank of chamberlain.

He was fired for accepting a large bribe (over 5,000 roubles).

B. Markevich worked for "Russky Vestnik" for a number of years and, unlike M. N. Katkov, was a consistent anti-Semite. Although "democratic media" hushed Markevich's creations, A. K. Tolstoy, while strongly disapproving of anti-Semitism of the author of "anti-nihilistic novels," considered him one of the most important writers. In the *History of Russian Literature of the XIX Century* edited by D. N. Ovsyaniko-Kulikovsky, B. Markevich was given considerable attention.

In 1884, "Russkiy Vestnik" printed the first few chapters of B. Markevich's novel *The Void*, which completed his trilogy (*A Quarter of a Century Ago* — 1878, *The Turning Point* — 1880–1881). His death stopped him from finishing the novel and his family asked Vs. Krestovsky to finish the Afterword.

The stereotype of an anti-nihilistic novel was worked out in the late 1860s. This is how A. M. Skabichevsky characterized the storyline of an anti-nihilistic novel.

Representatives of aristocracy and high nobility are depicted in a very attractive manner. It is in this class that the salvation of a destabilized society lies and it is this class that remains "true to authentic Russian cultural traditions."

The representatives of the movement of the '60s are depicted as careless nihilists who reject religion, family, property, state and who mock everything that is holy and precious and are capable of any crime for material gain... Salvation of the Fatherland begins in a liberal sitting room in the provincial seat where the protagonist "bursts into a tirade on the decadence of modern mores..."

Then the protagonist takes up a federal or local government job as (insert the list of the author's favorite posts) — a mediator of peace, a court official or a special assistant to the Governor, and here "begins the hero's real fight against the evil that threatens the foundations and the edges." The evil is represented two-fold: firstly, as "a cunning Polish intrigue impersonated by Mr. Brzekserzynski who, under the pretense of serving his Fatherland, thinks only of spitefully taking revenge on the novel's protagonist" for his humiliation in front of a blue-eyed maiden; secondly, the evil is depicted as "a many-headed hydra of nihilism that is shown in the novel as *moutons de Panurge* of unbridled duns that excite peasants and sneak outrageous proclamations into the hero's pockets and, finally, threaten the hero's life itself," all under the influence of the Polish intrigue... Contemporary events serve as variations of the above...

When the author pays most attention to the Polish intrigue, the hero is sent to play the hero in Westland; if the novelist stresses the *moutons de Panurge,* the hero is placed in the 1860s Petersburg and interacts with nihilist student circles or even men of letters... Social heroic acts

CHAPTER 3. ZEALOTS

B. M. Markevich
(1822–1884)

V. V. Krestovsky
(1840–1895)

are intermixed with the hero's love affairs, since he, stereotypically, also possesses the gift of winning women's hearts… In the end, love for the blue-eyed maiden defeats all other temptations. The blue-eyed maiden is an example of the perfect Russian woman who strives for the perfect family home and diligently protects its foundations. With this spouse, perfect in every way, our hero, weary of the unequal battle, goes to his estate and devotes the rest of his days to raising future protectors of the Fatherland. [58]

Accusing the revolutionary camp of wishing to depose the existing government, Markevich used "the Polish intrigue" and showed in his novel quixotic bureaucrats and local liberals, only slightly changing the names of high-ranking officials from the government circles close to Alexander II: A. F. Timashev "Mityashev," A. A. Polovtsev "Pechenegov," L. S. Makov "Savva Leontievich," etc. One of Markevich's positive characters, General Torokurov, expressed the credo of the author himself: "None of the planted… European trees sprouted strong roots in the soil that is alien to them in its chemical composition…" While Markevich did not describe "the Jewish question" per se, he showed some "despicable Jewish types" in the novel. Thus, a talented pianist N. G. Rubinstein (in the novel, "Nikolai Grigorievich Edelstein") is shown as a notorious and cynical womanizer, and a One-year volunteer (EF), baptized Jew Schefelsohn ("a Jew of Jews"), naturally, turns out to be a despicable provocateur. [59]

In the novel, the anti-government conspiracy is headed by a figure with some Jewish features nicknamed Wolf, and the contemporaries could see in him a resemblance to a famous member of *Narodnaya Volya* ("People's Will") Zhelyabov. Wolf uses a fake passport in the name of Lev Gurievich Bobruysky and is on the roster of students of the Technological Institute. One of the party leaders, Wolf believes that the party follows Moses's law: "an eye for an eye, a tooth for a tooth." [60] In the protagonist's opinion, the party is led by a "mysterious Dalai Lama" who remains as unknown to him as Wolf himself is unknown to the pawns that he autocratically moves in the name of the will of a secret "executive committee." [61] With his morbid pride and desire for power, he had a hard time putting up with the opposition to his suggestions by his peers in the revolutionary hierarchy which he explained by the "obvious" influence of that authority, a higher one for them and unknown and, therefore, hateful to him. [62]

Introducing Wolf's thoughts on the "unknown" leader, [63] Markevich brought forth a remarkable idea which was later picked up by his "co-author" Krestovsky: that revolutionary movement *as a whole* was inspired by Jews and that is why during the Polish uprising of 1863 they led socialist and defeatist propaganda among Russian soldiers. [64]

It is for a reason that Weiss, Polyachek and Aronchik are listed among political immigrants and terrorists. [65]

However, in the history of Russian literature, B. Markevich still cannot be recognized as the writer thanks to whom anti-nihilistic novels not only became a banner of the police department bureaucracy but also defined the main direction of the strike against the revolutionary movement in which the Jewish minority was represented absolutely disproportionally. That writer was the author of *Afterword* to B. Markevich's novel *The Void*.

Vs. Krestovsky was born to a noble family in Kiev province. His father served as a commissar at the Petersburg military hospital. At first the boy was raised by the family of his mother Maria Osipovna (nee Tovbich). In 1850 he entered the 1st Gymnasium of St. Petersburg. A famous teacher V. I. Vodovozov noticed the student's literary talent and assisted him in publishing his poems and translations (especially good were his translations of Horace and Heine). This decided Krestovsky's fate for a while and he, without much effort, studied at the philological department of Petersburg University for two years. His college pal was soon-to-be-famous critic D.I Pisarev. Krestovsky dropped out of college and fully devoted himself to literary work.

CHAPTER 3. ZEALOTS

In 1864–67, he published his first "physiological" novel *The Slums of Petersburg (The Book of the Fed and the Hungry)* in *Sovremennik*. The *Slums of Petersburg* immediately attracted attention by its scandalous descriptions of the life of the "refuse of society" and vividness of the characters of different ethnicities.

Naturally, some of them were Jews: "Near Obukhov Bridge and around the Church of Ascension, especially in Kanava and Podyacheckaya, Jewish population sticks — every step of the way here you meet the sly and anxious miens and long coats and camelot overcoats of the children of Israel." [66]

One of the characters, Amalia Potapovna von Schiltze, as some suspected, "a Zhitomir Jew," had "hazel, fat eyes in thick eyelids of a Jewish shape" and spoke "mixing French, German and Russian phrases and words with a Jewish accent." [67]

The "king of our finances," a banker and baron David Georgievich, hosted a group that was depicted as grotesquely as the host himself. For a detective "of Yidish descent" the author "picked" an accent: "Yests, Your Honahr!.." [68] Not unkindly, Krestovsky described a mob searching for Jewish doctors suspected of spreading cholera.

It is interesting that Soviet editors excluded Chapters XVIII–XXII from the 1935 edition of *The Slums of Petersburg,* presumably, for their anti-Semitism. In reality, they were rather unhappy with the appalling naturalism of the scenes of horrible abuse of a child who later was cooked alive by Christians, which was not very realistic, although Krestovsky stated on many occasions that he was ready to provide documented proof of every fact in his novel.

There are also freemasons in the novel (Prince Jacob Chechevinsky), however, they have nothing to do with Jews.

Not free of imitating Eugène Sue's *The Mysteries of Paris*, Krestovsky's novel, in its turn, became a "template" — in 1868, there appeared *The Slums of Kiev*, whose author chose to remain anonymous.

In 1868, Krestovsky joined the Yamburg Uhlan regiment as a Junker. For six years he was engaged in serious historical research and wrote *A History of the 14th Yamburg Regiment* and later, in 1874, at the personal wish of the Emperor Alexander II was transferred to the Guards, to write a history of His Imperial Majesty Leib-Guard Uhlan regiment. Simultaneously he finished his novella *Grandfathers* (historical pictures of the reign of Paul I) and wrote the dilogy *The Bloody Pouf* that included the novels *Moutons de Panurge* and *The Two Forces*.

The time he spent in Westland during the Polish uprising of 1863 provided the nationalist writer with abundant material. It is not coincidental that "Polish intrigue" would consistently come up in his works (Polish schemers are also described in *The Slums of Petersburg*).

That is why in 1870, when Krestovsky's first anti-nihilistic novel *Moutons de Panurge* came out in Leipzig, it became clear that the "zealots" of the imperial triad of "Autocracy, Orthodoxy, Nationality" had gained another zealous adherent. One of the nihilist leaders depicted in the novel was a Jew, Moses Frumkin, "a great practician in the matters of this world." [69]

A chatterbox and a demagogue, Frumkin considers himself a "cosmopolitan," which does not prevent him from viewing the revolution as a way to get rich. At the same time, when his life is in danger, this godless atheist vehemently crosses himself and pretends to be an Orthodox Christian. In the writer's opinion, Frumkin was a typical underground activist who used the "moutons de Panurge" of nihilists for his own gain.

Alexander II's personal liking of Krestovsky allowed the latter to serve as the Tzar's historian with the Commander-in-Chief of Russian forces during the Russo-Turkish war of 1877–1878. His letters from the war theater were regularly printed in *Pravitelstvenny Vestnik* (*Government Messenger*) and later were published as a book.

By the early 1880s relations between Russia and England became strained and Krestovsky, attached to Admiral S. Lesovsky's naval squadron that set out in search for a convenient naval base near the shores of the modern Indonesia, took up the position of the secretary for the Pacific fleet. He sailed around the world. After that he stayed in Japan for six months. Unfortunately, his reports about the country of the Rising Sun and about the danger of a war with the Japanese were not heeded by Russian government. During his time in the Far East Krestovsky also put together a memorandum on the tasks of colonization of South Ussuri Krai. In 1882 Krestovsky received a new commission and arrived in Turkestan. Governor General M. G. Chernyaev, for whom Krestovsky served as a special assignment assistant, sent him on a diplomatic mission to Bukhara, and in 1887 Krestovsky's essay "Visiting with the Emir of Bukhara" appeared in the press.

The writer, quite objectively, described the civil right deprivation of the Bukhara Jews under the reign of a medieval ruler. Calling the Bukhara Jews "the only Russian party" awaiting the arrival of Russian forces, Krestovsky notes that, of course, if Bukhara joined the Russian Empire, it would "significantly expand their trade and property rights and deliver the person of a Jew from the humiliating position he is currently placed in under the Muslim regime." [70] At the same time, Krestovsky remained true to his attitude towards "Yiddies" and thought it necessary to note that Muslims' hatred towards Jews is by socio-economic rather than religious reasons, since "even here, a Jew is a malicious usurer, a broker, a secondhand dealer and huckster, an owner of secret disorderly houses, a supporter of lascivious behavior, and a smuggler of wine and vodka prohibited by the Quran, who openly trades only in silk." [71]

After his service in Central Asia, Krestovsky took a position with the Ministry of Internal Affairs and went on two inspection trips in Central Russia (Tambov, Tver and Vladimir provinces) and in the Caucasus.

Finally, in 1884–1892 he published over 200 articles in the newspaper *Svet* and the magazine *Grazhdanin* (until 1881 F. M. Dostoevsky actively participated in the magazine's affairs), and in 1894 Krestovsky became the chief editor of *Varshavsky Dnevnik* (*The Warsaw Journal*). A. I. Herzen branded the pro-government *Varshavsky Dnevnik* as "a refuse pit. a shelter for spies and provocateurs, the organ of Muravyov and Berg, who robbed Poland."

Strenuous work undermined Krestovsky's health. He died in 1895 at the age of 55. His body was brought from Warsaw to Petersburg and interred at the Alexander Nevsky Lavra.

The writer's eventful life and his travels around the multi-ethnic empire provided nutrition and material for Krestovsky's literary talent. And yet, odd as it may seem, he was truly interested in one topic only, and in it the resourceful writer was surprisingly monotonous and obtrusive. Moreover, the political tastes and "policing" ideology that permeated the storyline of Krestovsky's novels to some extent prevented him from becoming the author he could have become. His name remains in the history of Russian literature and Russian social thought only as that of an author of anti-nihilistic and anti-Semitic works.

The Jewish characters from *The Slums of Petersburg* and *Moutons de Panurge* moved to Krestovsky's novellas and short stories and gradually turned from ethnographic curiosities to negative and fatal types. The original sarcastic attitude of the author towards the characters of his "Jewish tales" was typical for the genre of everyday and ethnographic sketches. Thus, mocking the cowardice and vanity of Solomon Solomonovich, Krestovsky not only saddles him with a terrible accent ("Our Rahshah") and a personal item of silverware due to his "treyf" surroundings, but pays him his due for his honesty ("The Tale of Solomon Solomonovich and I Traveling from Chaushki-Pakhaly to Gorny Studen"). Elkes, "a good Yid," is kind, servile, often selfless, although "this man had a very special, peculiar and at the same time typically Jewish mindset, which, for the most part was expressed in his slyness" ("Mishter Elkes").

The old sutler Heike is quite pleasant. She provides officers with necessities and is subjected to a *herem* by the qahal for refusing to hire an uhlan as a watchman for the cemetery to "ward off" an epidemic ("Madam Heike"). Funny and dignified is the character of "Itzhak the Yid" who helps out a confused Lieutenant and does not want "the Yid share" ("Who is better?" — "Dedicated to my friend Itzhak Yankelevich Shtraletsky"). These two stories, and many others, as well as the essays and novellas written before the Russo-Turkish war, did not forecast at all the sharp turn in the traditional attitude towards other ethnicities that Krestovsky took in the late 1870s-early 1880s.

The writer himself admitted that the Russo-Turkish war and the spread of revolutionary movement that led to the tragic assassination of Alexander the Liberator played the main part in the new vision of stereotypical characters that smelled obnoxiously of onions and garlic, spoke broken Russian, made profit from buying stolen goods and were dishonest merchants and suppliers.

While preserving the "innate features" of an anti-nihilistic novel, Krestovsky turned it political, or rather, geopolitical, since the fate of the Fatherland became the fate of *Christian civilization as a whole.* That is why he juxtaposes the "world conspiracy" of one side to the "conservative" resistance of the other. Moreover, the Polish intrigue so favored by nihilist writers turned out to be propelled by an entirely different one, that of the Jews. This "discovery" of Krestovsky was not only timely to the police department, but also of current interest to the imperial nationalist circles.

A witness and reporter of the Russo-Turkish war, Krestovsky (like many of his contemporaries) was astounded by the fact that the post-reformation Russia, face to face with a decaying Asian tyranny, only due to a colossal effort won a truly Pyrrhic victory in the Balkans.

Russia's losses were over 200,000 soldiers, not counting the wounded, and immense war expenses bankrupted the victor. Besides, instead of expected drop in opposition due to a military triumph of the Russian government, the revolutionary movement became more active and gave inevitable rise to terrorism whose first victim was the Tsar himself. The catastrophe of March 1, 1881 made many "zealots" present memorandums to the new Emperor Alexander III the Peacemaker. [72]

Among these, the memorandum of the famous Count N. P. Ignatiev is of a special interest:

Chapter 3. Zealots

"In Petersburg there exists a powerful Polish-Yid group that holds in its hands banks, the exchange, the attorney bar, most of the press and other social affairs. By many legal and illegal ways and means they hold huge influence over officials and the state of matters as a whole. Certain parts of this group are involved in embezzlement and prohibited activities...

"Preaching blind imitation of Europe, the members of this group, while cunningly maintaining neutrality, use the extreme instances of forbidden activity and embezzlement to promote their remedy: widespread rights for Poles and Jews and Western-style official institutions.

"Any honest voice in the land of Russia drowns in the Polish-Yid screams that we ought to listen only to the 'intelligent' class and that Russian demands should be rejected as 'backward and unenlightened.'" [73]

For Krestovsky such an interpretation of the current situation was nothing new.

Moreover, the "Slavic idea of liberating the Balkan brothers" itself was, in his opinion, a provocation by the world Jewry that "cornered" Russia, and the war became inevitable due to two reasons: firstly, the war was meant to weaken Russia, secondly, it was meant to enrich Jews.

The means for the world Jewry to push the country to a disaster was the revolutionary movement in Russia.

Describing the protest of December 6, 1876 and noting that it was "Polish-Yid," Krestovsky commented:

"Young Jewish 'students' and 'protesters' took a most active part in this matter. In the past, Jewish names in political processes showed up only occasionally, but now there was a whole group...

"Here the goal of Jewish agitators to connect the purely Russian popular task of brotherly aid to Eastern Christians with the revolutionary goals of 'Land and Liberty' became abundantly clear...

"The puppeteer's strings of this Yid march, apparently, reached in from abroad where they counted on a win-win situation: if the Russian government gets scared of the movement that engulfed their people and abandons the Slavic cause, it will become extremely unpopular at home and Russia's prestige among Slavs and the trust of the Christian East would be undermined for a long time, if not forever, and this will clear a path to the Balkans for her adversaries; if the Russian government jumps headlong into a war, even better: a war would weaken Russia financially and martially, take away its freedom of operation for a time, and provide huge earnings to European exchanges, especially

German ones, and, of course, to Jews, while enslaving Russian finances to every Bleichroeder..." [74]

Believing the war to be a "Jewish affair," Krestovsky "proves" it by embezzlement and speculation:

"The Moscow lending and accounting bank headed by Landau, a Yid, embezzled 7 million roubles to the profit of a Berlin Yid Strusberg by lending the money to him for known false collateral... In late March, an over 2 million embezzlement was discovered in the Petersburg 'Credit Union Society,' and so on...

"The Bank of Kiev was embezzled by its Yids Zioni, Liberg and Schmulevich...

"At the same time a large sacrilege was happening: robbing of churches and stealing of icons...

"During the Holy Week in Petersburg, in St. Isaac's Cathedral diamonds worth 4,000 roubles went missing from the icon of Mother of God, and on the very Easter Sunday a bejeweled bishop's mitre was stolen from a cathedral in Odessa...

"Traces of many such thefts were later found with Jewish goldsmiths, moneylenders, and innkeepers..." [75]

Such an interpretation of events makes Krestovsky's conclusion quite natural:

"And, really: there are Yids in political trials, in the street protests, in the liberal press and among attorneys, and also in bank collapses, in various cases of theft and sacrilege, in total embezzlement of the treasury and the military, and in the rusk and herding businesses that brought thousands of Russian peasants to beggary there are, again, Yids, and even the Red Cross couldn't avoid them! This has outraged Russians to the bottom of their hearts... (they — *S.D.*) inevitably started considering 'the Jewish question in Russia' for the first time...

"Here everyone for the first time consciously sensed the warning of 'The Yid is coming!' and this 'Yid' seemed more frightening than any war and any European coalition against Russia." [76]

Thus "golem" was created: the only and frighteningly powerful *enemy* of Russia and the Russian people was a folk that made up no more than 1.5% of the population of the empire, deprived of basic legal and political rights, and herded into the Pale of Settlement, a folk that preserved not only a "mythological" hatred for Christians and all-encompassing love for the Golden Calf but a "desire for vengeance" for the centuries of humiliation and abuse. The war between "the sons of light" (Russians) and "the sons of darkness" (Yids) had been declared. That is why powerful, ambitious and proud members of "the enemy tribe" and not caricature images of "Jerusalem nobles" nor grotesquely pitiful Yid types of Westland nor perversely placid types in "camelot overcoats" became the characters of Krestovsky's anti-Semitic novels. [77] His trilogy (*Egyptian Darkness, Tamara Ben-David, The Triumph of Ba'al*) for the first time in Russian literature provided a foundation for the geopolitical view of "the Jewish question" and simultaneously defined the Russian approach to its "final solution": the political history of the Russian Empire turned out to be none other than a war of Gog and Magog.

"THE YID IS COMING!"

On the front page of the Sunday, March 23, 1880 issue of Suvorin's paper *Novoye Vremya* was printed a "letter to the editor" titled "The Yid is coming!" (possibly, inspired by the editor himself).

The author of the letter, noting the harmful domination of Jews in railroad business, finances and banks, in industry, among attorneys and other professions, and bringing up "statistical data" in the form of tables, insisted that Jews strive for education with the sole purpose of occupying, if not the top ones, then at least the middle rungs of the social ladder.

The "letter" caused a wide-spread stir in Russian and Jewish press. Responses began to appear in the media: "More on the Yid invasion," [78] "The way we Russians oppress Jews," [79] "Jews weeping on the banks of the Dnieper," [80] "Welter is coming" [81], etc.

Yet, arguably, this letter, inspired by the *Novoye Vremya* editor, became a declaration of intent only after Vs. Krestovsky made it the slogan for his trilogy.

The plot chosen by Krestovsky was uncommon: a Jewish girl falls in love with a "goy" and not only leaves her father's home (*Egyptian Darkness*) but becomes a Christian (*Tamara Ben-David*); later, seeing that as a Jew she has no place in Russian society despite being a Christian, she becomes a rural teacher and, desperate, answers "the call of the blood" and asks her grandfather for help (*The Triumph of Ba'al*).

Although the last part of the trilogy remained unfinished, Krestovsky managed to express everything that formed the basis for the author's most important warning: "The Yid is coming!"

Krestovsky's innovation was demonstrated not only through his courage in choosing an outstanding person — and of Jewish origin to boot, but also in the fact that the "primordial enemy" was shown from the inside (*Egyptian Darkness*).

This task required that Krestovsky introduce into the story such unusual for a Russian reader material as multiple Yiddish-isms and Bible-isms, detailed descriptions of Jewish everyday life and Jewish mentality, and various footnotes.

Moreover, his main "achievement" and his "most important" discovery was a commentary that, for the first time in Russian pulp fiction, used so much Jewish literature and Jewish sources: the books of Tanakh and teachings of wise men, references to medieval commentators and interpolation of contemporary traditions, and, finally, "scientific" writings of Brafman and esoteric sketches of Bogrov.

At the same time, the protagonist's fate and the complications of the storyline allowed Krestovsky to offer his reader some "historical digressions": for instance, to present the Berlin Congress of 1878 as "a thief" of the fruit of Russian victory, to "determine" the reasons for Russia's fighting for her "Slavic brothers," and to "uncover" the moving gears of the "Jewish conspiracy" in the revolutionary movement (*Tamara Ben-David*). In the third part of the trilogy (*The Triumph of Ba'al*) the writer decided to "explain" the economic consequences of "Jewish domination" in rural areas: robbing of peasants by the *zemstvo* liberals "the Yiddies": the local physician Goldstein, the pharmacist Guenzburg, the inspector Mikwitz, the road supervisor Lifshitz, etc. Naturally, the "fateful" goal of Jewry, according to Krestovsky, is their "vengeful desire" to destroy Russia from within.

That is why every political case is "permeated by various types of political crimes committed by the Jewish element." [82]

"Gog" (Jews) of Krestovsky is to blame not only for the economic troubles of the country but also for direct extermination of Russians through spreading epidemics and "overtreating" (the Doctors Affair of 1952 goes way back). In the writer's accusing speech (him being fairly "free-thinking" and not clerically inclined) a very traditional detail is, however, present: the infidels and the aliens encroach upon the "holiest of the holy" of the imperial triad — the Orthodoxy!

The mythological anti-Semitism of the past (the fight of Christianity against Judaism) acquired not only new justification, but presented itself as Alpha and Omega of the fight of the poor Magog against the omnipotent and omniscient Gog.

Although Krestovsky's opinion writing is directly related to F. M. Dostoevsky's *A Writer's Diary* (by the way, Dostoevsky found the courage, despite his own anti-Semitism, to call Russians and Jews to cooperation — "But long live brotherhood!"), the author of the trilogy was convinced that because of *Jewish expansion* neither compromise nor peace between Jews and Christians was possible.

Making Jewish hatred of Christians and Jewish desire for revenge his main idea, Krestovsky, long before *The Protocols of the Elders of Zion*, created a "black and white" version of historical existence.

The first chapters of the novel appeared in the January and February 1881 issues of *Russkiy Vestnik*. The March issue contained no continuation of the novel due to the assassination of the Emperor Alexander II. In the opinion of the editor-in-chief, an extreme nationalist and Polonophobe M. N. Katkov, who nevertheless considered fair the demands to emancipate Jews, further publication of the novel could provoke conflict between Russians and Jews. Indeed, in the summer and fall of 1881, a wave of pogroms swept over southern Russia. Krestovsky agreed with Katkov's arguments and *Egyptian Darkness* saw light only in 1889. [83]

Krestovsky's colleague from *The Warsaw Journal*, Yu. Elets, who in 1900 prepared the last part of the trilogy (*The Triumph of Ba'al*) for printing, referring to the author, formulated the basic idea and theme of the trilogy as follows: "The three novels are dominated by one thought: to show the power of Jewry in our social life, and total powerlessness and lack of grounding of our Slavic race that due to its kind-heartedness and carelessness could not oppose Jewish unity and energy with either strong convictions or strong resistance or give moral support to a neophyte Jew in her new environment..."

The author did not name the first novel *Egyptian Darkness* at random: he wanted to define the chaotic state of our society in the late 1870s and the moral darkness that the proselyte entered. [84] In essence, the "darkness" was "Egyptian" not only for Jews but also for the Orthodox Christian world. In this double rejection of either side of the "barricade," Krestovsky was the only one among the anti-Semitic writers: the rest of them believed the "darkness" was approaching only because of "Jewish expansion." Moreover, Krestovsky's rejection of "Slavic values" to a certain extent discouraged the "zealots" from using his trilogy the way they would have liked, and his novels soon passed into the archives of history. One of the reasons for this oblivion, undoubtedly, was the author's Germanophobia, which did not allow him later to be made into a Nazi ally. [85]

Egyptian Darkness began with a story of Sabbath celebration in a rich Jewish family (*Shabbos Kodesh*). The evening meal was traditionally attended by three strangers invited by Rabbi Solomon: a learned preacher (*lamdan* or *maggid*), a homeless pauper and a young *yeshiva-bocher*. After a nutritious supper the *lamdan* gives a "light musar for dessert" — a sermon, which, in Krestovsky's opinion, laid out the strategic goals and tasks of the "conspiracy" of the Jewish people against Christians (*The Word of Rabbi Jonathan*). [86] The basis of the sermon were various "sources" — a forged letter of Cremieux, a rabbi's speech at a Prague cemetery, or, more precisely, an "imperial" forgery — a speech by a Simferopol rabbi allegedly given in 1859: "Rabbosai!" he began with a pleasant smile. "I shall speak... of the tasks and importance of Jewry in the world and of our future..." The "Earth program" is explained by Jonathan in *pesukim*:

1. "Gradual, over many centuries, congregation of the riches of the world in Jews' hands, gradual overtaking of markets and exchanges of the Old and the New Worlds, until, finally, we become financial rulers of the Universe";
2. "Nowadays, the enemy that surrounds us still remains in Egyptian darkness. Therefore, here is the task: to weaken and, whenever possible, to *exterminate those* among whom we, outsiders, settle. To that end we must strictly obey the laws of brotherhood and mutual support among ourselves and never to enter into any communication or agreement with non-Jews...";
3. "So, rabbosai... *world domination* is the task and ultimate goal of Jewry... We must strive for it!.. Really, just think of what we would do, if we understood our goal narrowly and strived only for Palestine and restoration of the Jewish Kingdom in her modest borders?.. No, that would be the death of the Jewish idea, of the Jewry, since in the borders of little Palestine it would become a nonentity among powerful states and nations";
4. "The Jewish network must entangle all inhabited countries... a Jew... must be the same everywhere: brotherly as if of one womb, persistent... tenacious... mutually supporting one another, defensive, protective, covering mutual sins and mistakes and striving for the same cherished goal... This is guaranteed to us by the great names of Nesi'im... who created and solidified the world union of Jewish brotherhood... the qahal of qahals, in other words, *Alliance Israelite Universelle*";
5. "This is the way it is... everyone... consciously or unconsciously serves one and the same great purpose and goal of Jewry...

Chapter 3. Zealots

acting to subvert this hated Christian world... Fighting against it is possible and therefore a must... Not with iron, but with gold. Not with a sword, but with a purse."

It is easy to notice that such grand and vast goals declared by a fanatic, define Jews' "right" to consider themselves "chosen" and, consequently, their ends justify the means; that is why a Jew is allowed anything, including fight for "our civil rights," but "use these rights only to preserve our individuality in every way": "we may even... sacrifice our unique appearance and even...outwardly accept a different religion."

"Outlining" such a grand and satanic plan of action of "Christ's enemies," Krestovsky, in the chapters of his trilogy devoted to opinionated review of historical events, never abandoned his "search" for Jewish involvement in them and Jewish responsibility for them.

However, this consistent accusation of *Jews* of crimes against Russia and the Russian people somehow turned strange and mystical: the failure of Russia's foreign policy became a triumph for Europe; at the same time, the failure of Russia's home policy was defined by specifically Russian economic and social circumstances.

Moreover, the "share" of Jews in this "Egyptian darkness" was balanced, according to Elets, by Krestovsky's wavering: "what measure of power to give the qahal," since his protagonist "never found any of that which she had eagerly anticipated and searched for among Christians." [87]

That is why, despite the author's bias ("maliciousness" of the Judaic tribe), the inability of the Russian people to solve its political and social issues was clear to him and most likely became a large part of the reason why the trilogy was never completed.

At the same time, Krestovsky, who so colorfully and eloquently presented the "world Jewish conspiracy against Russia," in fact, "borrowed" from "Yids" the idea of "chooseness" for his Fatherland: his people and the Russian Empire are pictured standing up against the rest of the world and all other peoples.

This paradox of an anti-Semite who was frightened by the fanaticism and global thinking of Rabbi Jonathan and had tried the robes of God-chooseness and, naturally, God-fatedness on the "Third Rome," showed not only the "patriotic" and "conservative" ideas of Russia's *messianic role*, but also an ordinary and nationalistically colored inferiority complex:

"Among these peddlers and "sham marriage" arrangers are quite conspicuous Armenian, Georgian and Jewish last names of various Kardashovs, Chekoidze, Kikodze, Gamkrelidze, Jabadari, Prince Tsitsianov, Princess Tumanova, Hesya Gelfman, Mlle. Figner, Mlodetsky and others." [88]

Russian readers, while inadvertently heeding "his heated warning of "The Yid is coming!" [89] at the same time could discern in the author's theme the bellicose voice of a racist:

"A mass unstoppable cry of rapture and a storm of "hurray!" ...

Yesterday and today, she saw for herself and for the first time understood what the Russian Tsar and Russian people were, what kind of power they were, and what great moral ties bound them together.

As a Jew, until then it was alien and incomprehensible to her; as a Christian, she understood this power and those ties with all her heart at that moment." [90]

Most likely, Krestovsky did not realize the direct analogy between his made-up "conspiracy" of Jews and the real "mission" of the Russian people that he expressed, the people for whom all other peoples and nations — "Polies," "Yiddies," Romanian "figures" with their Romanian "Little Paris" ("for Romanians call their dirty half-Gypsy/half-Yid capital no less than Little Paris"), typical "pea-eating English," "sly Greeks," furious "hordes of Suleiman" in "sight of many distant flickering lights of Tsargrad... where almost a thousand years hence Oleg's Russian troops stood," "poor Sepoys," Serbians who believed they could "put an end to the boundless Russian despotism," "Bulgarian politicians' whose "backs had not yet healed from the Turkish whips of yesteryear," not to mention the eternal "German adversary" and the "ungrateful ally" the French, all in all, this "mixed bag of Europeans," [91] is, at best, an object for "taking care of," at worst, the adversaries and enemies of tomorrow.

Should we then be surprised that these poor things, having been overtaken by "Jewish domination," *to the last man did not wish to understand* that only Russia could be at the head and only Russia had the right to judge, punish, and bless countries and peoples?! Instead, "a European Areopagus was to convene in Berlin for some reason, with Russia as the accused...

"The Congress of Berlin indeed seemed... 'an open conspiracy against the Russian people ...'

"Still, Berlin achieved its goal...

"France turned away from her... Slavs slipped out from under Russian influence... Austria-Hungary received a handout... England pocketed Cyprus and restricted Russia in Asia Minor..." [92]

On the one hand, there was *Alliance Israelite Universelle* that appeared in every European country, and on the other, all European countries, according to Krestovsky, expressed surprising unanimity in regard to Russia: first, it found itself pulled into a war and then deprived of its spoils.

This is how the author defines the united front of Europe and *Alliance Israelite Universelle* against the lone "warrior" for the honor and glory of Slavs.

In his concept, Russia, as well as Jews, enters a fight against *the entire world*. The animosity between "outsiders" and "natives" in every country (the Jewish conspiracy) is the flip side of Russia's feud with Europe. Such a paradox in the development of anti-Semitic ideas was very convenient and prepared the way for *The Protocols of the Elders of Zion*.

From then on, every nationalist (Russian, German, French, Italian, etc.) could use it: it was enough to point to the "Jewish world conspiracy" to readily explain the reasons for the confrontation between any one country and the rest of the world.

CHAPTER 4

Enemies of the Human Race

AGENT PROVOCATEUR (S. K. EFRON-LITVIN)

One of the specific features of anti-Semitic pulp fiction (as well as opinion writing) is diffusion of similar ideas and plots. Not pretending to be original, creators of novellas and novels about Jews, as well as various "critics" of Jewish lifestyle and Judaism, shamelessly borrowed all they could from one another and completely ignored the fact that they were "discovering" something their predecessors had discovered long before.

This phenomenon may explain the colossal number of articles, brochures, books and volumes that engulfed publishing houses and bookstore shelves. However, if "scientific works" of the late XIX century [1] hardly played the main part in creation of *The Protocols of the Elders of Zion*, pulp fiction, undoubtedly, was not only its "midwife" but also its "wet nurse." That is why in the myth of a "world conspiracy" of Jews pulp fiction element dominates, and among the pulp fiction authors of the late 1890s who played the part of "zealots" and "prophets" stands out the dark figure of a convert and renegade, S. K. Efron-Litvin.

Efron was born in 1849 in Vilna province, in a very religious Jewish family and, possibly, was related to one of the publishers of the *Brockhaus and Efron Encyclopedic Dictionary*, and, therefore, to the Vilna Gaon. [2] Efron's pre-baptism first name is unknown. His grandfather was a rabbi. At the age of 12 Efron entered the Vilna college. The youth was deeply impressed by the Polish uprising of 1863 and his novel *In the Woods and Underground* (SPb., 1893) was largely based on the author's memories. A student of the Rabbinical college (which later was transformed into the Jewish Teachers Institute), Efron wrote for "Vilensky Vestnik" (*The Vilna Messenger*). The youth graduated from the college at the age of 20 and was going to enter Petersburg University, but was late for the entrance exams and started teaching Russian and arithmetic at a Jewish school (*Talmud-Torah*) in the town of Slonim. Starting in 1869, Efron's writings were published in Russian press: his first short story, "From Jewish Life," appeared in "Vestnik of Western Russia" (##9 and 11). In the early 1870s he moved from Vilna to Petersburg and became a guest listener at the Mining Institute.

Striving to be a writer, Efron took his "accusatory essay" to "Russkiy Mir" (edited by General M. G. Chernyayev) and Chernyayev liked the essay very much, although he did call the author, who spoke poor Russian, an "impudent Yid."

This did not stop the famous general and the beginner writer from becoming friends and remaining friends until Chernyayev's death. The editor of "Russkiy Mir" predicted Efron's literary fame, supported him financially and even paid for his tuition.

However, after three years at the Mining Institute, not having completed the course, Efron suddenly left Petersburg and moved in with his parents in Vilna. Then, as suddenly, he left for Moscow in the hopes to enter the Moscow Imperial Technical College, but literary engagements attracted him away from studies yet again. Here he began actively working with "Sovremennye Izvestiya" (*The Modern News*), whose editor was a known anti-Semite N. P. Gilyarov-Platonov. [3]

Most likely in the late 1870s or early 1880s, Efron was baptized, but it is difficult to judge the sincerity of his decision.

Metropolitan Anthony insisted that when he knew Efron, this "baptized Jew" was a consistent and worthy Christian "of Jews" who pitied his brothers ("Israelites") remaining in religious delusion. [4]

At the same time, "liberal chatter" ended badly for Efron with the end of Alexander II reign: he was arrested on a charge of "revolutionary propaganda." However, he was soon released.

Having gotten off easy, Efron later liked to mention that his liberalism had never gone as far as demanding a Constitution, for he never "wished for a rule of lawyers and talkers and other types of predator *raznochintsy* with their wolf appetites and their compliant consciousnesses." [5]

In any case, since then Efron kept right-wing friends only: Chief Procurator of the Synod K. P. Pobedonostsev, State Controller T. I. Filippov, Slavophiles M. N. Katkov and S. F. Sharapov.

Like many renegades of that time, Efron was a double apostate: both religious and political. His path, according to A. R. Kugel, a theatrical critic who knew Efron well, was similar to the path of another political renegade, L. Tikhomirov. [6]

This could explain Efron's bifurcation in the early 1880s: while pitying his "delusional brothers," he still published a sharply critical article by Z. Minor on an anti-Semitic book by I. Lutostansky (ref. "Vilensky Vestnik," 1879) and defended Jews from accusations of ritual murders by publishing *Alilas Dam, A Grandfather's Tale* ("Moskovskaya Nedelya," 1881, ##1–5).

Still, his criticism of various aspects of Jewish life never reached the extremes of G. Bogrov: the examples are the short stories *A Victim of Halizah* and *Divorce* published in "Sovremennye Izvestiya" (1879, ## 3,69, 70–71). Efron did not refuse to meet with revolutionary emigrants, either, and later wrote essays about them. [7]

He could simultaneously publish a story full of respect for his fellow Jews like *My Uncle Reb Shepsel-Eizer* in the Jewish magazine "Voskhod" under his real name S. Efron, and another story, *Atonement,* full of hatred and malice towards them, in "Istoricheskii Vestnik" of A. Suvorin, under the pen name S. Litvin.

Literary critics met S. Efron-Livin's creative works differently: some, like S. Ginzburg and Yu. Hessen [8], refused to acknowledge his literary talent, while others praised his gift.

Thus, D. V. Tutkevich repeatedly quoted S. Efron-Litvin, and believed that "as far as the psychology of a Jew, Krestovsky is much weaker...," [9] and V. V. Rozanov noted (on the short story *Atonement*) that, despite ideological alienation from Judaism, the writer was still connected to it by blood, because "the author's gift is serious as it should be in the case of a serious man." [10]

Every S. Efron-Litvin's work is built on a familiar template. Usually, as the author conceives it, the best representatives of Jewry (most often women) would start doubting the truth of Judaism and decide to convert to Christianity. The qahal, of course, would do its best to persecute the apostate.

Both happy and tragic endings were possible, depending on the author's wish: thus, in the novella *Rebecca's Marriage* the story ended with her baptism and marriage to a "noble goy"; however, in the novella *Sacrifice* (which is surprisingly similar to Krestovsky's novel *Egyptian Darkness*) an apostate girl, persecuted by fanatics, commits suicide. [11]

In 1897, S. Efron-Litvin's book *Among Jews* appeared in Petersburg. Its title came from the first novella in it that had been first published in 1896. [12]

CHAPTER 4. ENEMIES OF THE HUMAN RACE

Ten years later it became clear that the basis for the plot was a literary version of the theft of The Protocols of the Elders of Zion.

A Jew, a "commercial advisor," one Moses Borisovich Berdichevsky offered an unemployed teacher the position of a tutoress in his family, which consisted of him, his wife, two daughters aged 8 and 10, and his millionaire father-in-law Bobruysky.

By the way, the last name of Wolf (Zhelyabov) in B. Markevich's novel *The Void* was also Bobruysky.

Having made sure that the prospective tutoress spoke fluent German, Moses Solomonovich set a mandatory condition: the teacher, a Russian girl, must present herself to the family as a Courland Jew.

According to Berdichevsky, his father-in-law, a man of old habits, could not let an infidel into his home. Although playing such a role was uncomfortable for the young teacher, she accepted the offer due to her financial hardship.

Pesha, as they started calling her, charmed the old Jew and as his secretary learned the secrets of the qahal: the frail Jew turned out to be "only" the leader of a world conspiracy.

When Pesha met old Boruch, she sensed his extraordinary personality (the story is told from the first person): "He uttered the last words with such strength and such deep understanding of his power that it seemed to me that he became completely transformed from a fragile tiny old man into a higher being, strong in body and spirit, who was capable of destroying any obstacles in his way by any means necessary and would not stop for anything or fear anyone…

"Yes, I fully realized that in front of me was a Yid strong and vengeful and as threatening as Jehovah whom he worshipped."

Having gained the old man's trust, Pesha enters a room thoroughly hidden from visitors (the room resembled a shed with barred windows where in a corner stood a huge iron wardrobe tightly secured to the wall) and learns from Boruch: "All secrets of Israel are concentrated here… not an hour will pass and you shall be entrusted these secrets… Here's all my secret correspondence from all over the world… Here are letters from Vienna! Here, from Berlin!.. Here, Paris!.. Here, London!.. Here, from New York!.. Here, Constantinople!.. Here, from Jerusalem!.. Here, Madrid!.."

Then the tutoress tells us: "He sorted through his letters and continued to name various cities of the world where the letters had come from. The letters that were written in Hebrew he moved aside and the ones in European languages he spread before me.

"See, how many godly Jews fight against infidels and give their time and their money... It is a matter of life and death! And we shall win, because with us is the Lord who gave us Torah on Mount Sinai, who put us at the head of all nations and elevated us above everyone else and promised us the world as our inheritance! We, a regal people, will defeat everyone, enslave everyone and shall rule over every language. The unholy will perish by their passions Satan gave them, and we shall prevail through our virtues that the Lord Sabaoth Himself bestowed on us..."

The secretary worked for two hours and, among trivial papers, found letters of quite strange content:

"Those were letters of entirely different character that contained various secrets of various governments and details of preparation of bills and activities of extreme importance. The former required opposition and the latter had to be supported by all means. Entire programs of action in regards to a government of a certain country were laid out.

"Reading these letters, I realized what a terrible power was concentrated in the hands of Jews and how they used it to harm the entire humankind! Scattered all over the globe, they caught all countries in a strong net and, like a spider, suck all healthy juices dry out of their victims. Common interests of Jews all over the world united them to fight other peoples! They, undoubtedly, are masters of the world or, at least, believe they are. Further familiarizing myself with the content of that correspondence... I concluded that every country is ruled by Jews!.. But what outraged me most was the terrible hatred and arrogant contempt these messages carried for everything non-Jewish!.. Who could have thought that this illiterate little Yid held in his hands all the threads of European politics and knew all the secrets of European governments and that he himself... was a prominent member of the most powerful organization called the World Qahal!

"Who could have thought that world-famous political and financial leaders addressed this shabby little Yid with utmost respect and reverence and gave him assignments of utmost importance and asked for his advice and direction. And yet, it was so...

"Still, let them be, these European correspondents who told him how Jewry undermined morality, prosperity and religion of countries and people strange to me... How did I feel, however, when I learned what the World European Qahal was doing to harm my own Fatherland?!

"Meanwhile the letters from Vienna, Berlin, Paris, London and other large centers told what measures had been taken by Jews to fail our recent external loan; how the qahals of all the important centers of Europe worked together and made even the Rothschilds offer an ultimatum to the Russian government against their will: to support this loan only if the government agrees to emancipate Jews!

"And what resources these underground activists, these moles working in their holes and cracks, possessed!.. In only two or three hours, I learned so many Jewish secrets and became so familiar with the underground workings of Jewish qahals and I held all the threads to their schemes in my hands."

Of course, the woman protagonist was an adventuress. On the one hand, her situation was scary, frightening, and confusing. On the other, the old man that instilled those feelings in her [13] attracted her and made her revere him:

"I was flattered by his trust and inwardly proud that this scary Yid before whom everyone trembled... made me close and treated me as his equal...

"This was mixed with pangs of shame: I knew that I served as a weapon of terrible evil and helped the old man in his despicable doings to harm humankind. Nevertheless, I continued to diligently assist him in his office and with enthusiasm I myself did not quite understand, I became involved in his affairs and did my best to deserve his approval."

However, afraid of the old man's revenge in case she was discovered (remember that Pesha was a false Jew) the tutoress made copies of some important documents and stole a number of originals. Then she passed her loot to a trusted person in Petersburg.

The plot of Litvin's novella became known to Russian public in 1897–1898 and, surprisingly, *preceded* the versions of the theft of *The Protocols of the Elders of Zion* that appeared in the early 1900s. The strategy and tactics of the "world qahal," proved with "genuine letters" to Boruch are the text of *The Protocols* themselves.

It is no coincidence that Gregor Schwarz-Bostunitsch, the editor of a Nazi leaflet Welt-Dienst, later called Efron-Litvin an important witness of their "authenticity" and "the history" of *The Protocols*. [14] It is probable that the "former rabbi" could be one of the editors in the Russian Department of Police...

Several years after *Among Jews* came out, a scandal over the performance of the play *The Sons of Israel (Smugglers),* which Efron co-authored with the famous translator of Lessing's *Nathan the Wise* and even more famous anti-Semite V. A. Krylov, broke out. Colonel Piramidov, the head of the Security Department, who was present at the theater, noted: "No, this is not a march of protest. This is a real revolution." [15]

The critic A. R. Kugel characterized the play in a similar manner: "This, of course, was not yet an overture to a revolution... this was tuning the instruments before the overture." [16]

Meanwhile, it is known that Efron-Litvin read the article in defense of the play at the Black Hundred newspaper "Svet" office (after all, he himself was the secretary of this paper for many years), and he gave a copy of *Sons of Israel* to the actor P. N. Orlenev (the date of the autograph is 20 April, 1901, i.e., several months after the performance on 23 November, 1900). [17]

Five years after the scandal in Suvorin Theater, Efron wrote to his co-author whom he met through the editor of "Istoricheskii Vestnik," S. N. Shubinsky:

"You as an ethnic Russian will be forgiven that which shall never be forgiven me... You could have written that unknowingly... I will be scolded and accused of lying, and rightly so..." [18]

We should specifically mention the instant of plagiarism that remained unnoticed by many critics from every camp. The thing is, in August 1899 "Istoricheskii Vestnik" published a memoir by M. P. Mezhetsky, a former officer and later an investigator, titled *The Smuggler. Scenes of Life at the Western Border*. The events described in the memoir took place at the Russo-Prussian border in 1856–1857. [19]

In Mezhetsky's tale there was everything that later could be found in the play: Jewish smugglers, an incorruptible Russian investigator, shots fired from both sides, triumphant justice and punished sin. The co-authors, in order not to be caught red-handed, added Krestovsky-like fantasies to Mezhetsky's moderate anti-Semitism.

Little is known about S. Efron's later years. He became a monk and after the revolution turned up in Yugoslavia in the Monastery of St. Paraskevi near Šabac where he lived from June 7, 1921 to June 23, 1925. His death was noted both by Jewish newspapers and magazines [20] and the monarchic press.

It is telling that the newspaper "Dvuglavy Orel" (*Two-Headed Eagle*) informed its readers that the late Savely Konstantinovich Efron (Litvin) had once been called to the Department of Police to translate some documents seized from Jews, compared to which *The Protocols of the Elders of Zion* would look perfectly innocent.

The author of the article "The Secret Acts of Judaism" mourned the fact that Jews had managed to steal back such condemning evidence of their "maliciousness." S. Efron did put together a report on the documents' content and personally handed it to Purishkevich in 1918. However, this report, in its turn, was stolen by the Black Hundred leader's secretary. [21]

The monarchical logic was "impeccable": that which could be stolen from Jews, naturally, could be stolen from non-Jews. Therefore, the point was not whether the documents were present or absent, but that someone at some point described the "condemning materials." That is why the further "investigation" into the "worldwide Jewish conspiracy" could use not only literary versions of their "authenticity" but also statements of the authors of those versions as evidence of their authenticity. We've come full circle.

From then on, there was no distinction between "literature" and "reality": that which was made up by pulp fiction writers could be declared "a document," which, in its turn, became the basis for a new pulp fiction tale. Of course, these "widely known" facts did not require neither references nor explanation.

THE TRANSFIGURATION OF SATAN

The timeline of creation of *The Protocols of the Elders of Zion* from the moment of their "stealing" to their first publication is known (1897-1903), although their final putting into shape takes up another decade, and if we consider their new, 1922 release in Germany, we should be talking of two decades. That is why in *The Protocols* we must discern genetic roots of the ideas that had been appearing over *25 years* and sprouted during the three completely opposite historical situations; pre-revolutionary (1897-1903), revolutionary (1906-1911), and post-revolutionary (1917-1922).

The fact that it was in 1903-1909 that almost all basic "documented" works on the "worldwide Jewish conspiracy" came out in print, tells us who needed to find a final solution of the "Jewish question," and why.

Norman Cohn, an English researcher of *The Protocols of the Elders of Zion* noted: the first to be printed was a somewhat abridged "anonymous version" under the editor's title *The Program of Jewish Takeover of the World* in a Petersburg newspaper "Znamya" from August 28 to September 7, 1903. The paper's editor P. A. Krushevan claimed that his "Protocols of the meetings of the world union of freemasons and elders of Zion" were a translation of a document written in France.

Two years later, the same version, this time unabridged, came out as a brochure (censor permission of December 9, 1905) under the title *The Root of Our Trouble* and the subtitle "Where the root of the modern disturbance in the social formation of Europe in general and Russia in particular lies. Abstracts from ancient and modern protocols of the World Union of Freemasons." In January of 1906, a new edition of the brochure came out that listed the editor's name as G. V. Butmi and had a different title — *The Enemies of Humankind* and the subtitle "Protocols retrieved from secret stores of the Main Office of Zion." (Where the root of the modern disturbance in the social formation of Europe in general and Russia in particular lies.) As Norman Cohn writes, "three more editions of this version appeared in 1906 and two more in 1907." Besides, in 1906 in Kazan there came out a reprint subtitled "Abstracts from ancient and modern protocols of the elders of Zion of the World Society of Freemasons." [22]

From the first publication in Krushevan's paper to the "Kazan" version, the authorship of **the compilation** of *The Protocols* was assigned alternately to freemasons and to "the Office of Zion." The second edition of S. A. Nilus's *The Great Within the Small and Antichrist as a Close Political Possibility* (first printed in 1903), which came out in December of 1905 (censor permission of September 28, 1905) had an addendum of the same "protocols" (that were absent from the first edition) but this time under a "historical" title *The Protocols of the Elders of Zion*. Nowadays it is impossible to determine who was the first to acquire this "secret document" — P. A. Krushevan (1903) or S. A. Nilus (1905), although later the discovery of this "document" was fully ascribed to the "learned hermit" Nilus, based on the author's commentary.

In the post scriptum to the newspaper version, the translator warned the reader not to confuse the Elders of Zion with... representatives of the Zionist movement. Yet, in every edition of S. A. Nilus's works, "of Zion" is synonymous to "Zionist" and in the 1917 edition ("It is close, at the door") there is a remarkable footnote: "Only now I have learned for certain from Jewish sources that these *Protocols* are none other than a strategic plan to take over the world... presented to the council of elders by the "prince in exile" Theodor (?) Herzl in the days of the 1st Zionist Congress which he called in Basel in August of 1897." [23]

It is quite possible that Krushevan's "version" and Nilus's publication *went back* to the same "protograph" and it is doubtful that either of them borrowed their version from the other. The Department of

Police *could offer* its "laboratory experiment" to wide range of readers of an anti-Semitic paper on the one hand, and to the Tsar and his close circle as part of a work of mystical fiction, on the other. Nilus's version (not Butmi's) influenced "world history... when... it reappeared in a slightly changed and revised form and **in larger volume** under the title *It's Close, At the Door...* in 1917." [24] That is why *The Protocols of the Elders of Zion* should be considered as *part* of Nilus's book and not as an *independent* newspaper version.

Among the most popular sources of proof of a "Jewish conspiracy" borrowed from European literature is usually an abstract out of *Biarritz* by a former police agent Hermann Goedsche (1815–1878) who wrote under the pen name John Retcliffe, titled "The Jewish Cemetery in Prague and the Council of Representatives of the Twelve Tribes of Israel." The first Russian translation of "the speech of Rabbi Eiger" (as this abstract became known) appeared in 1872, and later various authors (Major Osman Bey, [25] K. Volsky, [26] A. Kaluzhsky — A. M. Lavrov, [27] Ya. G. Demchenko, [28] S. Rossov, [29] V. I. Protopopov, [30] et al.) used Retcliffe's "literary fantasy" as a well-known historical document.

While including the notorious "Rabbi's speech" in "Addendum" in 1906, G. Butmi explained to the reader: "In London, at the end of the past century there came out the book by John Retcliffe *Review of Political and Historical Events of the Past Decade.*

This creation was translated into French. The French press, not waiting for the complete translation due to a certain interest in certain places, reprinted it on its pages. Thus, in the Paris papers and magazines there appeared a translation from English of a speech (from Hebrew) by one of the rabbis, highly interesting and enlightening for Russia for the truth of which the above-mentioned author accepts responsibility...

This monstrous document was at a certain moment mailed as a printed copy in French to the office of... "Novorossiysky Telegraph" ... and printed in #4996 of this paper on January 15, 1891... The speech itself dates back to the time of Sanhedrin of 1869. [31]

Przecławski Junior, when publishing his *Uncovering of the Great Secret of Freemasons*, thought it necessary to veil the literary origin of the rabbi's speech: "In the Northwest country among Jewish and Russian population there circulates a huge number of copies of a "speech of a rabbi to his fellow Jews." We include this speech (possibly, apocryphal) as a sample of that written literature which never fails to deeply influence both Russian and other ethnic masses." [32]

Translation of "the solemn speech" from Hebrew to English to French to Russian and its subsequent publication in newspapers was essentially *proof of its authenticity* for Butmi, while for Przecławski Jr. the mere fact of the popularity of this "speech" in "a huge number of copies" was *the basis for documental nature* of this sample of "written literature."

It is easy to notice that in both cases the principle of "sanctity" of a printed and distributed word that had been mocked by Pushkin was working: "We all think: How can this be stupid or unfair? This has been printed." [33]

The fictional nature of the genesis of the "basic document" of the prosecution made Nilus resort to a disguise. In the *Necessary Explanations* to *The Protocols of the Elders of Zion* he included a large abstract from an article by K. I. Tur that had been published in "one of the November 1910 issues of *Moskovskie Vedomosti*" and which categorically stated:

"About five years ago Russian media discussed secret Jewish programs in the form of "The Prague Speeches" of the 1860s..."

Thus, the question of the origin and, consequently, the appropriateness of use of Retcliffe's "literary fantasy" was resolved. It would seem that the "zealots" could have quoted not an Anglo-French but their own homemade source, the speech of Rabbi Jonathan from Krestovsky's *Egyptian Darkness*, with the same effect.

The main points of Retcliffe's "document" were *transformed* into separate "protocols" of Jewish Sanhedrin: "theoretical ways and means to achieve Jewish domination" that were only hinted at in *The Prague Speeches* were supported by "examples and events of many years of experience" that were included in *the Protocols of the Elders of Zion* which were "almost contemporary." We should not forget this structural and genetic connection between "the rabbi's speech" and "the protocols."

Neither the history of the publication of the body of the "protocols" [34], nor the act of their *creation* in the laboratory of the Russian Imperial Department of Police (as was the case with the "rabbi's speech") did not exclude the *possibility of their inclusion* into a certain dogmatic and mystical concept precisely because its "cornerstone" was not the "basic document," but the "word of the church": "The Church of Christ has already proclaimed with its universal voice the approaching danger of the "baptism by fire" to the world"...

But before the second coming of the Lord in His glory and the Judgement Day "another shall come in his own name," i.e., the Antichrist, who, having come from Jewish blood, shall become the

King and Lord of the entire world, a messiah of the House of Dane of Israel on whom lies the blood of the true Messiah and whose fates are still ruled by Pharisees and Scribes, who are the sworn eternal enemy of the entire non-Jewish world."

Most researchers distinguished *The Protocols of the Elders of Zion* from Nilus's book as an "independently existing" text. [35]

However, they should be considered in the *religious and mystical context of the worldview* of the "scholar from Optina Monastery."

The author of *The Coming Antichrist* was right to preemptively refuse to answer the question of the authenticity of *The Protocols*:

"I could possibly be accused, and fairly so, of apocryphal nature of the presented document.

"Yet, if its authenticity were possible to prove legally and it were possible to find the persons at the head of the world conspiracy who hold its bloody threads in their hands, the "mystery of iniquity" would be ruined and it must remain whole until it is accomplished in the 'man doomed to destruction.'

"For a thinking Christian observer isn't that enough evidence of the authenticity of 'the Zion protocols' around him?"

For a religious fundamentalist like Nilus, "the mystery of iniquity" was the only evidence of "authenticity" without which the belief in "the man of lawlessness" cannot exist and, therefore, the belief in the second coming of Christ cannot exist, either.

The distance between "free" interpretations of separate *Protocols of the Elders of Zion* and scholarly understanding of their origin and their meaning in the context of the book is as vast as that between the Nazi "solution" to the Jewish question and Nilus's hope that with his book he "did not excite... animosity towards temporarily blinded Jewish people."

Despite multiple attempts at developing the myth of a "worldwide Jewish conspiracy" in the 1980s-1890s, it is necessary to note that this myth in itself had been *rational and materialistic* before Nilus's "apocalyptic" book came out.

Indeed, ritual murder charges against Jews used to be brought on only if a crime was actually committed.

"The eternal fight" between Judaism and Christianity justified the rise of the "world qahal" (and its activity in "enslaving" Christians) by political and economical means.

In the same way, exposing "the great secret of Freemasons" in one way or another related to a quite *materialistic and real* "conspiracy" against the powers-that-be.

Rational and materialistic accusations required only such evidence as documents, testimonies, clues, etc., which could have been overturned during the investigation.

Mystical and messianic anti-Semitism required none of that.

Jews' fault was not in something they actually committed, but in the *self-sufficiency* of mystical views and Christian myths, according to which any sin could be imputed to Jews. That is why mystical and messianic anti-Semitism is irreal on the one hand, and based on religious ideology, on the other.

Anti-Semitic literature of France, England, Austria, and Germany was represented by a significant number of names (Count Joseph Arthur de Gobineau, Chevalier Gougenot des Mousseaux, Georges Vasher de Lapouge, Paul Anton de Lagarde Boetticher, Hermann Ahlwardt, Houston Stewart Chamberlain, Willibald Hentschel, et al.) that became popular in Russia in one way or another.

However, European countries could not be the birthplace of mystical and messianic anti-Semitism, although later many of them swiftly caught the "bacteria" of the universal "final solution" to the Jewish question.

The reason why mystical and messianic anti-Semitism was born in Russia and in no other country, lies in the *historical experience* of Moskovia developing into the Russian Empire. As an idea of the dominated (and the domineering), the assimilated (and then the assimilating), the baptized and the baptizing, the belief in "holy Russia's" messianic fate became *a national trait of the Russian character*. [36]

The image of Russia in her mystical and messianic aspect is presented in Alexander Blok's *The Skythians* (1918), [37] although he was not the pioneer in that field. Pushkin wrote in his article "On the worthlessness of Russian literature" (1934) that Russia "was given a high purpose... Her vast plains devoured the might of the Mongols and stopped their invasion at the very edge of Europe; the barbarians did not dare to leave the enslaved Russia behind their backs and returned to their Oriental steppes. The emerging Enlightenment was saved by the torn and mortally wounded Russia..."

In a footnote he stressed:

"And not by Poland, as European magazines recently wrote; but Europe was always as ignorant about Russia as it was ungrateful." [38]

Of course, starting the count of the time of the "emerging Enlightenment" from the mid-XIII century (the Tartaro-Mongilian invasion of Rus') is a falsification. [39]

Chapter 4. Enemies of the Human Race

The Oriental expansion, known in world history as "the great Mongol and Turkic migration," successfully reached Rome after conquering the "vast plains" *of Rus' that did not yet exist.*

"The Asian hordes" not only failed to stop the creation of European civilization but, rather, facilitated immediate assimilation of multitudes of various tribes of invaders. The Ecumene of the Roman Empire, torn apart by the Goths, Huns, Alans, Vandals, Suebi, and other barbaric tribes, became the cradle of *Medieval* civilization, and Christianity became a world religion. After the invasion of "Asians," Europe saw an extremely important process of shaping of European nations and states with such institutions that ancient people had no idea of and that facilitated the "development of a civilization unlike the Greco-Roman" [40].

One of the paradoxes of history that should be recognized as such is the fact that *anti-German* action conceived in the Russian Imperial Department of Police turned *anti-Russian.* The main question of *The Protocols of the Elders of Zion* was not identification of the sources of the "forgery of the century," but the way the "Russian version" (i.e., particularly national) *turned out to be acceptable*, in the first place, to Russia's "original enemy," Germany. The fascist propaganda of Goebbels and Rosenberg managed to turn *The Protocols* into an "international document" and dissolve the specifically "Russian idea" of the "Scythians" messianic role in their plans of *Aryanization* of Slavs...

Yet, for *eschatology* it is absolutely unimportant *what* "material" and "document" is, for the logic of the anticipation of "the second coming" of the Savior is based on the "Apocalypse" and the many centuries of its "commentary."

Historical environment of "competition" between Orthodox Christianity and other Christian churches encouraged not only the birth of the myth of the "third Rome" but also development of a *national and messianic* conviction which is most precisely formulated in the self-definition of "Holy Rus'." [41]

"Having overturned the old idols... humanity in the West has eliminated... the image of the True King... and got into state close to anarchy. A little longer, and the support of the constitutional and representative and republican scales will break and the scales will tip and pull all world nations down with it to the bottom of the abyss of world wars and unbridled anarchy. The last fortress of the world, the last shelter from the approaching hurricane is once Holy Russia, the home of the Virgin Mary: even now, in the hearts of many sons and daughters of our Motherland, their Holy, pure Orthodox faith is alive and burning brightly, and even now the incorruptible and loyal autocratic Orthodox Tsar, anointed by the Lord, stands as the keeper and protector of His Kingdom."

With this juxtaposition of one *holy* nation of the Russian Empire to European nations mired in anarchy, the messianic destiny became a factor of national standing apart, or "chooseness." At the same time, the New Testament tradition required not the nations, but churches to unite against "Jewish efforts to lure Christians away from Christ": "Jews consider themselves chosen by God and despise non-Jews and have never been and will never be practicing "brotherhood and equality" that they preach. This sermon is nothing but an evil trick of Jewish leaders... This pestilence penetrated the greatest fortress of Orthodoxy on earth, Russia. *This consistency in spreading anti-Christian ideas proves that some dark power leads the troops of those rising against Christ...* Such enemies for Christians are *Jews* who of old persecuted and opposed Christ and His Holy Teaching. Jews believe in their future domination of the world and realize that this domination can be hindered by people united into one great family of followers of Christ."

Such "dual" standard (inside the Christian world, holy Rus' against Europe; outside it, Christians against Jews) defined the catechism of a new apocalyptic vision whose point was not Christ's fight against the Antichrist but the fight of all Christians (with Orthodoxy at its lead) against Jews. The only thing needed was to ascribe to this strictly modern interpretation of *Revelation* the historical *constancy* of "eternal war at the end of time": "According to the data of secret Jewish Zionism, Solomon and other Hebrew elders, 929 years before Christ, conceived a theoretical political plan of peaceful conquering of the Universe by Zion. As historical events developed, this plan was reworked and amended by the adepts of the cause." Moreover, for "greater glory" S. A. Nilus enrolled Paul the Apostle as "one of the more gifted disciples" into the ranks of the "adepts" of the "Jewish domination" doctrine. (Although, later "zealots" will bring this slip *ad absurdo*: Christianity itself will be declared a "Yid business" of conquering the world. [42])

CHAPTER 4. ENEMIES OF THE HUMAN RACE

THE "SATANIC AFFAIR" (S. A. NILUS)

The publisher of the "canonical" text of the "apocryphal document" Sergei Alexandrovich Nilus was born on August 25, 1862 (Julian calendar) and called himself a son of a wealthy landowner from Orlov.

Nilus insisted that his paternal family came from a Swedish prisoner of war in the times of Peter I and his maternal side went back to Malyuta Skuratov (of which fact Nilus was extremely proud). [43] His family members are unknown, with the exception of his brother Dmitri Alexandrovich, the Chairman of the Moscow District Court. Both graduated from a gymnasium in Moscow and the Law Department of Moscow University.

After graduation, Nilus worked for a short time for a law department in the Caucasus, but had to leave due to his difficult temperament. He tried to take up agriculture, but this turned out to be impractical and he abandoned this enterprise as well.

Nilus used the remnants of his family's estate to take abroad Natalia Afanasyevna Volodimirova, a married woman, and they lived for a long time in Biarritz. There Nilus, 21, and Natalia Afanasyevna, 38, had a son who was later legally adopted by his father.

S. A. Nilus (1862–1929)

Having received *The Protocols of the Elders of Zion* from P. Rachkovsky through Juliana "Justina" Glinka, he became a passionate promoter of the idea of a "Judeo-Masonic conspiracy." According to Alexandre du Chayla who knew Nilus from the Optina Monastery, Nilus was fluent in several Western languages and well-read in modern foreign literature.

Despite his continuing affair with Natalia Afanasyevna, upon his return to Russia Nilus married a lady-in-waiting to Empress Alexandra Fyodorovna, Elena Alexandrovna Ozerova, a daughter of a chamberlain and a former Russian envoy in Athens. Her brother, Maj Gen D. A. Ozerov, was the butler at Anichkov Palace. Connections at court allowed Nilus to publish the second edition of *The Great in the Small* in 1905, this time including *The Protocols*. In 1911, at the

V. S. Solovyov 1853-1900

expense of an old believer from Kozelsk, Nilus re-printed his "work" under the title *The Coming Antichrist*.

Nilus lived in Russia through the Revolution and the Civil War. He never emigrated and died "in his own bed" on January 1 (14), 1929 (according to some sources, in the village of Krutets of Vladimir region, on the eve of the day of Seraphim of Sarov [44]). Nilus's name was known to Bolsheviks: he was arrested several times but released due to his obvious insanity. A memoirist, a Zionist Jew, remembered that on Easter in 1926 he received from the Jewish community a care package of food, which he shared with his cellmates among whom was Nilus; he could not miss the opportunity to remind the publisher of *The Protocols* of "the presence of Christian blood in matza." [45]

Nilus considered himself to be a student of Vl. Solovyov and not only referred to *The Three Conversations* [46], but devoted to this philosopher's work a whole chapter in his *The Great in the Small* (Chapter VIII): "V. S. Solovyov on the end of the world and Antichrist. V. L. Velichko on V. S. Solovyov," and in Chapter X, while posing the question of the second "fearsome and glorious coming of Our Lord Jesus Christ," Nilus quoted the fragment from Vl. Solovyov's *The Three Conversations* about choosing "the man of the future" and concluded that "this answer... does not fully solve the above-mentioned issues."

Judeophilia of the Russian philosopher Vladimir Sergeyevich Solovyov (1853–1900) is common knowledge. This circumstance gave rise to all sorts of theories, including his Jewish origin. [47] But of course, this was not the case. A thinking Christian philosopher ought to have paused sooner or later before a global mystery, the Jews. That is why as late as in his middle years Solovyov began studying Hebrew under the mentorship of Faivel Meer Getz. Solovyov studied not only etymology and grammar, but expressed vivid interest in elaborations and interpretations of Talmudical and rabbinical commentators and read the treatises *Pirkei Avot, Avodah Zarah, Yoma,* and *Sukkah.* [48] In 1886, he informed his teacher: "I continue with my Hebrew reading. Besides *Torah* and historical books, I read all the prophets and psalms... Now, thank God, I can at least partially perform my religious courtesies by adding Hebrew phrases to my daily prayers." [49]

CHAPTER 4. ENEMIES OF THE HUMAN RACE

Studying Jewish sources naturally influenced the views of the philosopher. This is confirmed by most scholars of Vl. Solovyov's legacy. [50]

In the miserable pogrom-filled 1880s, Solovyov, unlike many idealists, sought an opportunity to help Jews and collected, in Moscow and Petersburg respectively, 60 and over 50 signatures of public figures under his petition to protect the persecuted, although he could not publish this quite moderate petition under the existing circumstances. [51] He holds the honorable place of the first Russian to openly read a public lecture on the historical importance of Jewry at St. Petersburg University on February 18, 1882. [52] In his memoir, Professor V. Speransky stated that the Chief Prosecutor of the Synod, K. P. Pobedonostsev, reported to Alexander III that "that insane Solovyov" even tried to put together a march in defense of oppressed Jewry. The Tsar wrote in his own hand next to Solovyov's name in the prosecutor's report: "a pure psychopath." [53]

Vl. Solovyov repeatedly tried to bring the Jewish question from the realm of theory to practice and in a conversation with S. Yu. Witte resorted to the following arguments: "The troubles and misfortunes of various states are in a certain way dependent on the grade of hatred and unfairness that those states demonstrate towards Jewry: persecution of a nation that God had laid His hand on cannot but invoke His vengeance." [54] The philosopher was also interested in Zionism. He was greatly impressed with Theodor Herzl's *Judenstaat*. However, while he sympathized with the revival of the Jewish state, Solovyov envisioned it only as theocratic one, and led by either an anointed Tsar of "the house of David" or, at the very least, a High Priest and Sanhedrin. [55] On his deathbed Solovyov, as his contemporaries testified, prayed for the Jewish people [56] and his last words were "Shema Israel." [57]

Solovyov's philo-Semitism made even the Black Hundred respect him. For example, M. O. Menshikov (1859–1918), who was later executed by Bolsheviks, wrote: "Vladimir Solovyov could not but love Jews as a poet and a thinker; the history of this people is too magical in its endurance and destiny, its role too central in the life of our spirit, its fate too *tragic*. But this was not all that made his close ties with Jewry. As far as I understand Solovyov, he himself, in the noble sense of the word, was a Jew, secretly, so to speak, in his heart and its holy tunes. His soft Slavic soul was significantly transformed by the Biblical roots of Christianity and he could be called a Jew possibly more than many modern Jews." [58]

On November 12, 1900 the Society to Spread Enlightenment Among Jews honored Solovyov's memory in a synagogue. He had been their honorary member. The rabbi, A. N. Drabkin, PhD, made a speech, and after him spoke N. I. Bakst and M. I. Kulisher. The latter reminded the audience that upon accepting the honorary membership, Vl. Solovyov told the representatives: "The day shall come when all nations shall follow Israel."

The Jewish college set up four scholarships in his name and hung up a portrait of the philosopher in the assembly hall. [59]

Solovyov's philo-Semitism deserves to be mentioned, because one of his writings, however ironic it may sound, played an exclusive part not only in the development of the "Judeo-Masonic conspiracy" myth but also in Nilus's arguments.

In the spring of 1899, Solovyov began working on *The Three Conversations*, in which he included his novella about the Antichrist. The foreword that the philosopher wrote on Easter Sunday in 1900 became his last work.

Although *The Three Conversations* are mainly aimed at the teaching of Leo Tolstoy, which, in the philosopher's opinion, was pseudo-Christian and started to spread just before the coming of the Antichrist, Solovyov did not forget freemasons. Solovyov's authority in Russian society was great and, undoubtedly, *The Three Conversations* played its part in establishing the myth of a "Yid-Masonic conspiracy" in the minds of the Russian *intelligentsia*. G. Bostunich justly noted that it stood to reason that in his novella about the Antichrist "the genius Russian prophet" and "one of the greatest philosophers of the world" foresaw the creation of the League of Nations as "the crown jewel of the masonic schemes to enslave the entire world." [60]

Indeed, in the novella about the Antichrist the philosopher "foretold": "Shortly... an international Constituent Assembly of the European countries' union was to take place in Berlin. This union, having been established after a number of wars abroad and at home... which had significantly changed the map of Europe, was in danger of confrontation not between nations anymore, but between political and social parties.

"The bosses of general European politics who belonged to the powerful brotherhood of Freemasons sensed the lack of common executive power. European unity that had required such hard work to achieve threatened to fall apart at any minute. *Comite Permanent Universel* [61] was not unanimous, because not all slots were occupied by true initiated freemasons...

"Then the 'initiated' decided to establish an autocratic executive power with sufficient mandate. The main candidate was an unofficial member of the order — 'the coming new man' ... *The coming new man was elected almost unanimously as a lifetime President of the United States of Europe...*" [62]

Still, the most important thing was not as much the "prophecy" as the fact that *The Three Conversations* became the foundation for Nilus's book long before the "masonic" League of Nations was created. Nilus, attempting to solve the contradiction between Solovyov's "prophecy" and reality, wrote: "This baffling question is further complicated by the fact that 'the other' (Antichrist — *S.D.*) must be accepted by Jews as a universal concentrated power, while this power is still 'dispersed' and still calls itself 'the persecuted tribe'; that this 'coming new man' must become the lord of the Universe and dominate the entire world which is still divided into powerful national and ethnic entities..."

The fact that three months after *The Three Conversations* came out of print, Solovyov unexpectedly passed away, could not but be mentioned by "his friend Vassily Lvovich Velichko." Nilus quoted the conversation between the philosopher and the biographer in his book:

"Curiously, once, after reading the manuscript of... the novella to his friend, he suddenly asked:

'What do you think he will do to me for this?'

'Who?'

'The interested party. *Himself!*'

'Well, that's not going to happen any time soon.'

'Sooner than you may think.'

"Solovyov's friend who told me that, himself a bit of a mystic as all believers are, added anxiously:

"'Mind, however: several months after this question, our Vladimir Sergeyevich was no more; someone did knock this crusader out of his saddle.'"

It would seem that Nilus, having quoted this fragment, should have commented on it: this is how "the devil's servants" get rid of their opposition. However, considering Solovyov's philo-Semitism, he only indirectly hinted at the possible identity of "himself," and that only in the footnotes to V. L. Velichko's memoir. Velichko survived Solovyov "by only two or three years": "It is worthy of attention that both Solovyov and Velichko died fairly young and in the prime of their physical and spiritual power. These deaths were mysterious and puzzling." However, this hint did not go unnoticed. Bostunich, in his habit of blaming everything on freemasons and Jews, dotted the i's: "Witte was poisoned by freemasons... in 1917. If they never held back with their own, it is not surprising that they systematically eliminated outstanding Russian people. Thus, they killed the philosopher Vl. Solovyov following the publication of his last book *The Three Conversations*." [63]

At the same time, "zealots" are reluctant to remember that S. A. Nilus, for example, accomplished his "heroic religious act" and gave "poisonous weapon" to murder millions, but still lived 24 more years after the first edition of *The Protocols* and died at 67. Justice never happened and the "almighty" Yids and freemasons never took revenge on the "Hermit of Optina."

"A CONCENTRATED UNIVERSAL FORCE"

To consolidate mystical and messianic trends (Christians of all countries against Hebrews and Orthodox Christians against all other Christians) for the purpose of "proving" a world "conspiracy," Nilus had to use *The Protocols of the Elders of Zion*, presented as a document, and not *The Prague Speeches* (a direct "literary fact") as the main "document" of the accusation, of which he "forewarned" the reader:

> "In 1901 I happened to receive from a man close to me, now deceased, a manuscript... (In a footnote Nilus solemnly remarked: "My God-loving reader, pray for boyar Alexei's rest in peace." — S.D.). The person that passed this manuscript to me testified that it was an exact copy of the translation of genuine documents that had been stolen by a woman from one of the most influential and initiated leaders of freemasons after a meeting of the "initiated" somewhere in France, this lively nest of the masonic conspiracy."

Prince N. D. Zhevakhov pointed out that the person in question was "the leader of the nobility of the Chernsky Uezd of the Tula Province, Alexei Nikolayevich Sukhotin, who gave the manuscript of *The Protocols* to S. A. Nilus, his neighbor and friend" and specified the "origin" of the manuscript: "The same circumstances are described in a somewhat different way by the prosecutor of the Moscow Synod Office, Chamberlain F. P. Stepanov, in his letter printed in Mrs. L. Fry's *Waters Flowing Eastward*. [64]

F. P. Stepanov writes: "In 1895, my Tula neighbor, the retired Major Alexei Nikolayevich Sukhotin, presented me with a manuscript copy of *The Protocols of the Elders of Zion*. He told me that a lady he knew (he mentioned no name), who was living in Paris, found *The Protocols* at her friend's (presumably, a Jew) house, and, before she left Paris, translated it in secret and brought the only copy of the translation to Russia and gave it to him, Sukhotin.

First, I made a hundred copies of it on a hectograph, but this edition was barely legible and I decided to have it printed at a printing house... in that I was helped by Arcady Ippolitovich Kelepovsky who at the time was a Special Assignments Officer to V. C. Sergei Aleksandrovich...

It was 1897..."

"The signature of F. P. Stepanov was witnessed by the elder of the Russian colony... and raises no doubt of its authenticity. F. P. Stepanov's daughter, Princess V. F. Golitsyna, whom I recently contacted, insists that the manuscript of *The Elders of Zion*... was in Russian; that the first edition, as a manuscript... was also in Russian; that the manuscript her father received was, most likely, the authentic manuscript which Al. N. Sukhotin had received from an anonymous lady; that it is unknown whether it was first translated into Russian from some other language; that S. A. Nilus received the same Russian manuscript from her father that her father had earlier received from Al. N. Sukhotin." [65]

Another version of the "origin" of the manuscript is told in a book by F. V. Winberg: "...when it became known that Zionists decided to gather in Basel in the autumn of 1897, the Russian government... sent a secret agent there": "The latter bribed a Jew... who at the end of the meeting received an assignment to deliver the secret reports to Frankfurt am Main... The messenger spent a night in a small town where the Russian agent waited for him with a group of copyists who copied the documents that night..." [66]

Thus, the "zealots" themselves date the origin of *The Protocols* to different years (1895, Stepanov; 1897, Winberg; 1901, Nilus). However, the exact date is not, of course, the point. After all, the difference of six years is insignificant. The point is the political situation of the late XIX century in which *The Protocols* originated. That is why some circumstances are definitely present in every "memoir," albeit in different ways.

Firstly, *The Protocols* were *secretly* copied/translated, in one case, in Paris by a friend of a "most influential freemason" or a Jew (Nilus and Stepanov), while in the other it was done by a Russian agent either abroad on the way to Frankfurt am Main or in Virbalis on the way out of the country (Winberg and Zhevakhov). It is, however, important, that many mention the involvement by the Department of Police in the appearance of *The Protocols*. [67]

Secondly, the "apocryphal nature of the document presented," fully understood by Butmi, Nilus, Zhevakhov and other "apostles," was not, in their opinion, enough to deny the *authenticity* of *The Protocols*, for the "secret power of lawlessness" was present in the "environment" and in the "world and domestic events."

Thirdly, the deciding factor for making *The Protocols* public was the forecast of "the coming" that determined the character of the modern history in mystical as well as in political sense.

Finally, the main argument of the "defense" in the "case of authenticity" after the revolution became the argument of the failure of the Russian government to appreciate in time the imminently coming rule of the Antichrist (Bolsheviks).

Thus, Zhevakhov, referring to the article by Colonel Dobronin (1934) on the firing of the Governor of Simferopol by Baron Wrangel in 1920 for the permission to distribute *The Protocols* in the city, concluded:

"This article not only disproves the slandering the Russian government, that, allegedly, falsified *The Protocols* for its pogrom goals, but also proves the ignorance of the Russian excuse for generals...

"To allow that *The Protocols* were falsified by the Russian government would be to accept that not only Soviet Russia, but the entire world, with the exception of Germany, is ruled by the orders of the Russian Department of Police..." [68]

This was, indeed, a senseless "assumption," since the publication of *The Protocols* never pursued any purposes *directed* by the gendarmerie or the government, which, however, does not eliminate the main goal of this political provocation: to *compromise* the revolutionary movement as such under the slogan of a world Yid conspiracy.

It is believed that *The Protocols* were "fabricated sometime between 1894 and 1899": "The country, undoubtedly, was France, which is proved by many references to French cases.

The place was probably Paris... a copy of Jolie's book in the National Library is full of notations that are surprisingly similar to the borrowings in *The Protocols*.

Therefore, this work was done during the Dreyfuss trial, between his arrest in 1894 and his amnesty in 1899... this forgery is obviously a work of a Russian... a person oriented towards the Russian political right wing." [69]

So, *The Protocols*, created in the pre-revolutionary situation on the eve of 1905, became "an astounding document" in the apocalyptic world of revolutionary changes after 1917.

This is probably the only historical perspective under which the "creative history" of the document should be considered.

In the first editions of 1903–1906, the number of deviations in the text, the discrepancies in page numbering in "the manuscript" and the printed editions, the references to the Talmud or their absence, testified for the fact that the publishers *adapted* the "manuscript" to their views and gave it the contextual nuances that could serve as arguments in their *Credo.*

A modern researcher insists that comparing Nilus's "version" with the "hectograph fragments found in the Wiener Library shows that Nilus's version appears to be the closest to the original, although it was not the first printed edition." [70]

However, Nilus's main innovation that should be recognized is the fact that in his edition of *The Protocols* he gave them an "apocalyptic" image by placing a "brief summary" after every subtitle (the Protocol so-and-so) and then duplicating the ideological context of the abstract in the margins next to the text. Let us remind the reader that the "symphony" that usually accompanied the "New Testament" texts played an important part of solidifying in a believer's mind the continuity of the testaments by the Gospels and the apostles about the first Coming of the Messiah and the prophetic fragments of the Old Testament.

Nilus explained this "structural" revision of *The Protocols* by the fact that "at first glance they could seem what we would call platitudes...

"Also, I should not fail to mention that the title of the manuscript does not quite match its content: these are not protocols of meetings but a report by someone in power, divided into parts that are not even always logically connected...

"The origin of the manuscript... indicated by me allows for a satisfactory explanation of this. According to the Holy Fathers, the work of the Antichrist was supposed to be a parody of the work of Christ..."

It was the latter circumstance that decided the "structural" shaping of *The Protocols* which were meant to be seen as a *parody* of... John's *Revelation,* but the author's "notations in the margins" and their ideological context were to refer to the "prophetic" text of the book *The Great in the Small.*

Let us note, first of all, that Nilus made the text of *The Protocols* more *"subjective"*: instead of the blurred "we" in Butmi's edition (referring to a certain consensus) in Protocol 1, 3, 4, 5, etc., ("I" is only used in Protocol 2), Nilus's "Ecclesiast" ("one speaking at a meeting") prefers first person singular. Because of this "correction," Nilus achieves an important effect: his "speaker" symbolizes dictatorship, despotism, and totalitarianism of a mind of a ruler.

As it has been mentioned, after the "summary" and before the number of a protocol, notes in the margins serve as an original reference to the author's text.

It is only in this "structural" context of *continuity* of Nilus's "prophecy" and *The Protocols* that it seems possible to appreciate the "parody of the work of Christ" as told by a "Hebrew elder." Indeed, if the author's text is the new "Revelation" of the coming of the "Antichrist's kingdom on Earth," then their essence, *Christian*, in Nilus's opinion, is opposed by the *anti-Christian* model of the morals, philosophy, and actions (strategy and tactics) of the "son of darkness."

That is why the "notes in the margins" appear to be "paraphrases" of the author's text that, as odd as it may seem, distort, in a manner of parody, the same "messianic" goal of a Russian chauvinist: world domination.

The "dualism" of the apocalyptic "work" of Nilus (Christ and Antichrist/the author's text and *The Protocols*), at the moment of its "historical" publication *could not be* appreciated precisely due to its "orientation" towards the era preceding revolutions and world wars.

This explains the lack of *The Protocols'* popularity before 1917. But, with the growth of Bolshevism in Russia (1917–1923) and fascism in Germany (1921–1924), both regimes, although to different degree, strongly disapproving of the belief in "the second coming," Nilus's "work" lost its *main* component — the *mysticism of a Christian*, without which the "immanent" *Protocols* became the foundation of "pure" Judeophobia whose victims turned out to be not some mythical rulers, "scribes and Pharisees," but the entire Jewish people.

The continuity between the first part (the author's text/ *The Protocols*/"The necessary explanations") and the second ("The Secret lawlessness"/"The Seal of Antichrist and the Number of the Beast 666"/"A Few Words on the Day of the Second Coming of Our Lord Jesus Christ and the End of the World") is a device of "parallel" positioning which allows for the "great legend" of Adoniram to be genetically compared to ancient historical "testimonies" (*The Word* of E. Sirin, the notes of 1848, etc.), "The Seal of Antichrist and the Number of the Beast" to *The Protocols,* and "A Few Words..." to the "Necessary Explanations."

Such parallelism is the structural principle of *The Protocols*. That is why, for instance, the notes in the margins are purposefully similar (in parenthesis are the numbers of the protocols — *S.D.*): "The right in the power" (1)/ "The right of the powerful" (1)/ "The right of the powerful as the only right" (15); "Freedom as an idea" (1)/ "Abstraction of Freedom" (1)/ "Freedom" (3)/ "Freedom and faith" (4)/ "The Masonic definition of freedom" (12)/ "Freedom of thought" (17); "Terror" (1)/ "Terror. Who serves Freemasonry?" (9)/ "Executions" (15)/ "Victims" (15)/ "Cruelty of punishment" (15)/ "Arrest on first suspicion" (18).

The texts of *The Protocols* are composed in such a way that, if necessary, they can be reorganized based on "ideology and topics" of their subdivision: jurisdiction, economics, politics, history, contemporary events, etc.

In itself, such "combination" of the texts of *The Protocols* proves their *fictitiousness*, because logical discrepancies noted by Nilus in the foreword become not an "attribute" of the mind of a "powerful one" but the *principles* forced into *The Protocols* from the *outside*. This is precisely because one should not either try and legally prove their authenticity or "look for particular persons" at the lead of the "world conspiracy," since in this case "the secret lawlessness" will be broken and without it, in Nilus's opinion, "the end of the world" cannot come.

Moreover, the "solitaire" combination of the texts allows for any of its fragments to be used without any connection to the others.

The practical advantages of this compositional device were that anti-Semites could "pull" any "card" out of *The Protocols* and it would always be "the trump" in a dishonest scheme.

Having created in the first part of his book a "contaminated" text of a logically whole narration ("The coming Antichrist and the kingdom of the Devil on Earth") and a logically discreet one ("The Protocols of the Meetings of the Elders of Zion") and then returning to the logically whole "Necessary Explanations," Nilus, naturally, could not have predicted that his "layered cake" would be "eaten" "layer by layer" or, more accurately, that his followers would pick their favorite "frosting" ("The Protocols of the Elders of Zion") out of various paragraphs and use it as "a concentrated universal force." [71]

Unlike the editions of *The Protocols* published by P. Krushevan, G. Butmi, or references to them by G. Bostunich and N. Zhevakhov, Nilus's *The Great in the Small* (with all its addenda) is not a "document" of political reality of the events of 1895–1905, but a *fact of one of literary trends in Russian pulp fiction*.

In this regard the book is comparable to John Retcliffe's *Biarritz* or Vs. Krestovsky's *Egyptian Darkness*.

For *all* "zealots" the issue of the "Yiddo-masonic conspiracy" was at the same time the issue of the relation between the 'Yid" books of the Old Testament and the books of the New Testament.

Moreover, the idea of this antagonistic positioning of the Testaments was the "cornerstone" of interpreting the Apocalypse as a dual reformation of the world at the "end of time": the coming of the "kingdom of the devil" and the "second coming" of the Messiah.

The "zealots" who "forewarned" about the coming reign of the Antichrist, naturally, used this dualism of the Apocalypse to concentrate the attention of patriots *on the first step only* of the eschatological prophecy. Their fight against the "Yiddo-masonic conspiracy" was declared a fight "pleasing to God," for even *before the judgement* of Christ they put themselves on the same level as those "which had not worshipped the beast, neither his image, neither had received his mark upon their foreheads, or upon their hands;..." (Rev 20:4)

We should specifically mention two circumstances that served as philosophical and mystical "antinomies" without which *The Protocols of the Elders of Zion* could have never existed: on the one hand, the Old Testament (i.e. Judaism), while juxtaposing the religion of the Hebrew to beliefs and traditions of other tribes, established the *nationalistic* principle of "chooseness" (an ontological consequence); on the other hand, the New Testament (i.e. Christianity), that preaches monotheism to pagan peoples, established the *international* principle of "universal" humankind (a gnoseological consequence). Moreover, Judaism as well as Christianity never forgot this inner contradiction of the basic principles and tried to solve it in different ways in one or another mystical concept.

It is not coincidental that in the Apocalypse the "national" ("the sealed" tribes of Israel) and "international" ("the saved people" for "witnessing of Christ") are equal attributes of "New Jerusalem": "And I heard a great voice out of heaven saying, Behold, the tabernacle of God is with men, and he will dwell with them, and they shall be his people, and God himself shall be with them, and be their God." (Rev. 21:3)

At the same time, with Christianity turning into a "world religion," the Old Testament thesis of the "chooseness of Israel" was in the Slavic world almost immediately interpreted by the adherents of the new teaching as "alienation of Yids," and the Judaic opposition between Israel and the goy was turned into a New Testament opposition between Christians and Israel: "Here we are praising the Holy Trinity with other Christians, and yet Judea is silent. We praise Christ and the Jews curse Him. People worship and the Jews deny." [72]

Chapter 4. Enemies of the Human Race

Reprinting his work in 1911 under the title of "The Coming Antichrist," Nilus repeated his call: "We must pray! Something terrible and elemental, like heavy leaden clouds, presses its incredible weight on the once clear horizon of Orthodox Russia."

Then he brought up the notes of N. A. Motovilov ("the night of October 26, 1844") of Motovilov's conversations with the Holy Father Seraphim of Sarov: "He often mentioned to me the Holy King, Prophet and Our Lord's Forefather David and would then achieve amazing spiritual joy... Often he would switch from David to our great Emperor and spend long hours talking to me about him and the Tsardom of Russia."

The mention of the Psalm-singing King is extremely important for the entire "diachronism" not only because of the Christian tradition that traces Jesus Christ's origins to David, but also because the "holy King" would later be juxtaposed (especially in the *Legend of Adoniram*) with his son, King Solomon.

At the same time, the idea of autocracy (the principle of "anointment" and hereditary throne), according to Seraphim of Sarov, is mandatory in order to establish the roots of "our great Emperor" from "the holy King David," not only because of the dogma, but also because of patriotism which is one and the same with "Orthodox piousness."

That is why interpreting the words of Abishai "We are many and you, Lord, are one... if you live, Israel is whole and hale" is the basis for service to the Tsar as an "Orthodox virtue."

It is notable that in Motovilov's text, this Biblical episode is distorted (only Abishai is ascribed the heroic act of fetching water from Bethlehem "while a band of Philistines was encamped in the Valley of Rephaim"):

15 David longed for water and said, "Oh, that someone would get me a drink of water from the well near the gate of Bethlehem!" 16 So the three mighty warriors broke through the Philistine lines, drew water from the well near the gate of Bethlehem and carried it back to David. But he refused to drink it; instead, he poured it out before the Lord. 17 "Far be it from me, Lord, to do this!" he said. "Is it not the blood of men who went at the risk of their lives?" And David would not drink it.

Such were the exploits of the three mighty warriors.

2 Samuel 23:15–17

"These three" are named as Josheb-Basshebeth, Eleazar, Shammah, and... Abishai. 2 Samuel 23:8–11;18. Considering that an Old Testament example was necessary only to praise "the diligence and zeal of the loyalists" of the Russian Emperor, the holy Father's inaccuracy and the goal of it is quite understandable. Thus, the "Old Testament layer" in Nilus's creation carries an important function of justifying the "God-givenness" of autocracy. Naturally, any *anti-autocracy* trend in this case is at the same time "satanic" and *anti-God*!

The "New Testament" and "Christian apocryphal" ideas are represented in Nilus's book by *The Word* by Ephrem the Syrian who died in 378 AD. It should be noted that the saint's hymns and teachings were created at the time of Christological debates *inside* Christian churches and aimed against Monophysites, arianites, followers of Origen and other heretics. (For example, Origen's eschatology was based on "restoring of all existence at the end of the world; as at the beginning everything was "very good" and there was only a world of pure and free spirits, and only later, as a consequence of their devotion to God cooling, some πνεύματα (spirits) became ψυχαί (souls) and required bodies, and some spirits even went as far as demonic fall" [73]). To Ephrem the Syrian "the end of time" means resurrection of people from the dead rather than restoration of "pure spirit": "The graves shall open and in a blink of an eye all tribes of the Earth shall awaken." Then Satan "with all the demons... and all who have accepted his seal, all the unholy and all sinners, bound, shall be brought in for Judgement." Undoubtedly, Ephrem the Syrian's *The Word* is an example of early Christian apologetics that rose after the First Council of Nicaea of 325 AD during many arguments with heretics which were partially solved at the First Council of Constantinople in 381 AD.

Therefore, it is clear that Ephrem the Syrian's interpretation of *Revelation* is intra-Christian and not anti-Judaic.

Indeed, the image of the serpent as well as that of the "defiled maiden," while borrowed, are interpreted in the spirit and through the events of *The Apocalypse,* in which members of the twelve tribes of "sons of Israel," unlike "people of other languages," bear on their foreheads "the seal of true God," the God of Israel, and, therefore, are not susceptible to Satan's "temptations." But that which was obvious to the Syrian, to Nilus is precisely the *casus belli* in his anti-Judaic ideology:

"Centuries have passed since the above-mentioned testimony about the Antichrist of St. Ephrem the Syrian: terrible storms have raged over humankind's eternal spirit; more than once the Christian world trembled in anticipation of the coming of the 'despicable' 'the man of sin and son of perdition'; and the Old Testament Israel, stiff-necked, temporarily blinded by the Talmud, Kabbalah and theomachy, has managed during this time to excitedly accept and reject in despair twenty-five false messiahs... and the real Antichrist has not appeared yet even to us, the sons of the XX century worn out by lawlessness; our Savior has not come to judge the living and the dead."

However, "the Old Testament Israel" was not alone in its accepting and rejecting of "false messiahs" (a phenomenon well known in the Christian world), and prophecies of "the end of the world" that had *persistently* circulated at the time of every historical cataclysm were based on the judging of "sinners" from the religious point of view and not national or political.

At the same time, quoting the "outstanding letter" of the hegumen Anthony (Bochkov) of the Chermenets monastery, Nilus picked the lines that make Russia stand out among the entire Christian world:

"Pagan time is near its end. All European scientists now celebrate the liberation of human thought from the bonds of fear and obedience to God's commandments... If "free" Europe prevails and destroys the last fortress, Russia, then, see for yourself what we can expect. I dare not speculate and only pray to merciful God to spare my soul from seeing the reign of darkness."

Nilus's "contribution" to Christian eschatology was precisely that he was the first to "doom" not just the "infidels," among whom should be Muslims, Buddhists, and worshippers of other "gods" alien to Christianity, but the "Old Testament" *Israel* for its non-religious views, since, according to Nilus, the "Jewish tribe" "had been prophesied to be chosen by God among people to own the Earth as an indivisible Kingdom of Zion."

In this *power over the Earth* as well as in *desire of that power* are "Alpha and Omega" of Nilus's mystical "discovery." For Nilus, undoubtedly, the only lawful rulers were not just Christians, but *Orthodox* Christians — the holy Rus' led by "the anointed by God" (*de facto* the *possible* Messiah).

Noteworthy is the commentary of Elder Ambrose to a dream of A. P. Tolstoy, included by Nilus. Tolstoy read those words in the "book" by Protoiereus M. A. Konstantinovsky:

"Sixth, after three celebrated names of Rome, Troy, and Egypt, the name of *Russia* is mentioned...

Then follows the Bible: no other country is mentioned. This may mean that *if even in Russia, in spite of God's commandments and for other reasons, piety runs out, then does follow the final realization of that which is written at the end of the Bible, i.e., in the Revelation of St. John the Divine."*

The real paradox for the nationalist Orthodox position of Nilus is the antinomy of *anticipation* of the "prophesied" second coming of Christ (with the preceding short reign of the Antichrist) and *resistance to it* (or, more precisely, the call to prevent the victory of Antichrist in the form of the "all-powerful brotherhood of Freemasons" or "the Elders of Zion").

According to *The Revelation of St. John the Divine*, "God's plan" was precisely for the believers to "comprehend and hear" the foretold test of their faith: "And, behold, I come quickly; and my reward is with me, to give every man according as his work shall be." Revelation 22:12

A true believer was not allowed to forget about the *mandatory* coming of Antichrist's rule and the *inevitability* of the reward for those "not written in the Book of Life" (including "the elders of Zion," should they happen to be "Satanists").

Nilus, despite the grave warning of the Apostle (*18* For I testify unto every man that heareth the words of the prophecy of this book, if any man shall add unto these things, God shall add unto him the plagues that are written in this book: *19* And if any man shall take away from the words of the book of this prophecy, God shall take away his part out of the book of life, and out of the holy city, and from the things which are written in this book. Rev. 22:18–19), adds and takes away as he understands it: "The unclear became clear... Secret after secret began revealing to my human weakness in which the great power of God was realized, and only through this great power I *learned that this world and all in it, the past, the present, and the future, could be comprehended in their entirety only in the light of the Lord's Revelation* and those who devoted their lives to His service in spirit, verity, piety, and truth.

"But before the second coming of the Lord in His glory and with His Judgement must, for a short time, come 'another in his own name,' the Antichrist, who, coming from Jewish blood, will become the king of the earth and the messiah of the house of Dan of the Israel on whom is the blood of the true Messiah and whose fate is still ruled by the scribes and the Pharisees, and which is the eternal enemy of the entire non-Jewish world."

Nilus's logic is built upon various falsifications: *all* modern Jewry is named descendants of only *one* "tribe of Israel," the house of Dan; it is to this tribe that Nilus attributes spilling of Jesus's blood, although there is not a single proof that Pharisees and scribes belonged to the house of Dan, and most likely they were, according to Hebrew tradition, *Levites* ("*2* And Ezra the priest brought the law before the congregation... *4* And Ezra the scribe stood upon a pulpit of wood... *4* ...and the Levites, caused the people to understand the law... *8* So they read in the book... *9* ...and Ezra the priest the scribe, and the Levites that taught the people..." Nehemiah 8:2-9) and not Danites; the accusation of Jews of the Antichrist's coming *"from Hebrew blood"* equally became their "promise" that Christ came from the *"tribe* of David."

Judaism, being a religion of a single people, naturally, was lacking anything international and opposed itself to the surrounding *heathen* world, whereas Christianity became a worldwide religion and lacked anything ethnic, but, because of this, found itself opposed to ethnic beliefs of non-Christians, including Jews.

That is why Jewish belief in the Messiah "is permeated, according... to the Gospels, by ethnic and political motives; the best Israelis (among Christians — S.D.) for example, Zachariah and Christ disciples (the Apostles — S.D.), etc., were not free of it." [74]

However, there was another circumstance that explained the difference in understanding "chooseness" in Orthodox Christianity and Judaism.

Let us remind the reader that for the Hebrews and Muslims the peak of their national glory — the "Great Israel" and the Arab Caliphate with all its Pan-Arabian unions, by the *mid-XIX century* were things of the ancient past.

The Christian Eastern and Western Roman empires also became history, and only the Ottoman Empire and Russia (aside from Austria-Hungary) could lay claim to this title on the political map. That is why Germany's ambitions to create "the Second Reich" appeared as an anachronism, because the "imperial" concept itself — where many ethnic minorities are ruled by the laws of one major ethnicity — soon was to transform into the concept of federalism — a union of many equals.

Nilus's mystical concept laid out in the "main part" of his book *The Great in the Small*, essentially, was not only anti-Semitic but anti-Christian.

The apologist of "the truth about the Jewish conspiracy" and Nilus's biographer, Prince N. Zhevakhov stated bitterly that "the responsibility for the sad fact of Jewish domination of Russia lies with the official church of Russia." [75]

Still, this *mystico-political concept* of a "worldwide Jewish conspiracy" based upon John's *Revelation* about the last battle of God's host (Christians — the Orthodox — Russians) with "the beast" (Israel — Hebrews — Yids) at "the end of time" hardly suited the Orthodox church in its *content* ("the chosen people" — "sons of Satan") and *form* (Nilus's "prophecies" lacked "Biblical inspiration").

But the idea of *The Protocols*, conceived in the womb of Orthodox mysticism, could become... another heresy to Christians. [76]

APOSTLE OF HERESY

The anti-Christian (as a whole) and anti-Orthodox (in particular) essence of *The Protocols* has barely been studied.

The basis for Nilus's "prophetic concept" was the question of whether "'one in his own name' had to come for a short time: The Antichrist who, coming from Hebrew blood, should become the king and ruler of the entire Earth and the messiah from the house of Dan of the Israel on whom is the blood of the True Messiah and whose fates are still being defined by the Pharisees and scribes, and who is the eternal enemy of the entire non-Hebrew world." Arguing with V. Solovyov, the author "complicated" the issue by the fact that "...'one in his own name' must be accepted by Jews as a concentrated universal force while that force was still 'dispersed' and calling itself 'the persecuted tribe'... the Israel of Talmud." Then he stated: "*The Protocols* give a clear answer."

The general antinomies of the "prophet" were acquired from mythologems: Christ/Antichrist, Christianity/ "Talmudical Israel," the second coming of the Messiah/the reign of the Antichrist, power of spirit/power of gold, religion/atheism, good/evil, life/death, etc. The particulars came from... pan-Slavism: monarchy/republic, Orthodoxy/Catholicism, Europe/Russia, chauvinism (chooseness of "Russians")/worldwide conspiracy. [77]

The church was not interested in the political foundations of the "teaching," but the interpretation of the mythologems was to the hierarchs of the Orthodox church nothing other than obvious *heresy* of montaistic and manichaeic type. Nilus's Christian teaching, "mistakenly coordinated either with Judaism or paganism" [78], in the Apocalyptic picture contradicted both the Orthodox dogma and the orders of the Council. Moreover, it relied not on the "teachings of holy fathers," but on apocryphal (i.e., not legalized by the Church) interpretations, which Nilus presented as truly Orthodox.

Almost right away, before referring to Seraphim of Sarov, Nilus stated: "Most of our kind could but silently suffer and weep in the silence of their solitary prayer to God, unknown to the world... God spoke... to His people, the New Testament Israel, to Russia, the last keeper of Christ's Orthodox church and autocracy as the earthly reflection of the power of the Almighty God Himself, One in His Three Images, on Earth... Let us remind Russia of this word..."

Then he concluded:

CHAPTER 4. ENEMIES OF THE HUMAN RACE

"It is not the smoke from the incense that believers burn while praying to God that covers the land of Russia, but a coal stench of factories, plants, and steam engines...

"This stench of human pride rises to the heavens as a challenge to God, born from malice and curses of social hatred... Have we preserved Orthodoxy?.. Are we cherishing the Autocracy granted us by God? Are we keeping safe our God-anointed Tsar with all the might of our love? No. So what awaits Russia for betraying the faith and loyalty of our fathers?..

"Let these questions be answered by the cruel and terrible things that will follow in the next chapters... You keep your free will, reader: believe it or not as you will! But, having read carefully that which is in this essay, check it against the Word of God and against the contemporary events, worldwide and Russian, and consider yourself forewarned."

Should you agree with the author that his narrative has been *"checked against the Word of God"* and therefore is a Divine warning, you will have to recognize Nilus's book as *the last and full revelation of God*.

This opinion of one's own — modern — prophecy is the essence of Montanism: "God's revelation... has reached the last stage of its realization and action in order to, in the light of the imminent end of the world, prepare the community to the act of perfection and completion of all through new revelations and demands." [79]

Besides, the idea of a God-anointed autocratic ruler is surprisingly similar to monarchic heresy (as Jesus was born to the Virgin of His Father's *will*, so is the Tsar "given by God"). [80]

However, most prominent in Nilus's mystical concept are philosophical (but not social) views of Manichaeism (named after the Persian prophet Mani). [81]

Nilus's familiarity with them is abundantly proven by the addenda: "The Secret Lawlessness," "The Seal of Antichrist," and "The Number of the Beast 666."

Identifying freemasons with Jews and retelling the masonic *Legend of Adoniram* [82] ("son of the morning," the symbol of the image of "God's adversary," the devil, enters the fight for the beautiful Queen of Sheba with King Solomon), Nilus declares it to be *The Credo* of "the teachers of Israel. who condemned to crucifixion the Son of Man, the true Messiah, the Savior and God of the Universe."

Equating freemasons and Jews, first "discovered" by Przecławski Jr. (or, more precisely, masons as a weapon of Jews) was turned by "zealots" into a whole semantic mess of interchangeable schemes: Jews — masons — revolutionaries — liberals — republicans, etc.

The only basis for this was the fact that freemasons used various Hebrew "glosses" and symbols in their rituals. In this, freemasons were students of... Christians. Moreover, the principles of interpretation and re-interpretation were the same. If the Hebrew word "anointed" when translated into Greek could become "Savior" (Χριστος), then why couldn't a King's tax collector (שר מסים) Adoniram become "the son of the morning"? (1 Kings 5)

Although Adoniram, who was responsible for the levy not only to Solomon but also to the next king, Rehoboam, who was sent to negotiate with the rebels, was stoned to death (1 Kings 12:18) [83], *free interpretation* of the Bible *by vivid imagination* could have changed Adoniram into a victim of jealousy of a lustful king.

In conclusion, the author of the new "revelation" declared: "The secret of freemasonry uncovered by *The Protocols of the Elders of Zion*, the legend of Adoniram and, finally, the half-admissions of masonic leaders, proves that the goal of freemasonry is to found a new universal kingdom with a freemason-appointed king at its head, a patriarchal king of Zion blood, a messiah of the enticed Israel and a founder of a new testament with a god that neither Moses nor the prophets knew, on the ruins of Christian countries of Europe.

"'Ye are of your father the devil,' said the Lord and God's word cannot be changed.

"The coming messiah of Jews will be the adopted son of the devil, the Antichrist for whom freemasonry has already prepared the path to the rule over nations and tribes of the Earth."

It has already been mentioned that the juxtaposition of the Hebrew messiah (Mashiach, Izbornik XIII) and Christ of Christians is one of the oldest proofs of the antinomy Christ/Antichrist.

The Gospel phrase "Ye are of your father the devil" (John 8:44) referred only to Pharisees and scribes "of the Hebrew." At the same time, Nilus condemns the entire "enticed Israel," since "God's Word cannot be changed" (compare to "the scripture cannot be broken") John 10:35), although this condemnation in the Gospel refers only to "unbelievers in Christ," the Pharisees, and not the entire people ("Jesus should die for that nation" John 11:52; "The people therefore that was with him" John 12:17; "Jesus answered and said, this voice came not because of me, but for your sakes." John 12:30).

The antinomies Christ/Antichrist, God/devil, good/evil, light/darkness, Christianity/Judaism were themselves traditional.

However, by adding masonic symbols ("the Seal of Solomon," "the star of David") and cabbalistic "rites" ("tetragram," "pentagram") Nilus, following freemasons, arrives, in fact, at "open dualism."

However, as long as Christ is opposed by the Antichrist, the Divine is ascribed to one and the satanic — to the other. All other parts of the antinomies are grouped according to the initial dichotomy: The Divine includes good, light, Christianity; the satanic includes evil, darkness, Judaism and freemasonry (liberalism, constitutionalism, etc.).

But such dualism was, in fact, manichaeic: "The teaching of Manichaeism is as follows: 'two equal substances exist from eternity... the God of light is good and holy... the god of darkness is... Satan. His Kingdom includes five elements: total darkness, thick mud (silt, slime), stormy wind, destructive fire and suffocating smoke... *Christ who reigns in the sun*... comes down to people deceived by paganism and Judaism... His disciples... did not rightly understand His teaching...'

"Foreseeing that, Christ, Son of eternal light, Son of man, promised to send "another Comforter" (Παράκλητος)... Manichaeism fully rejected *the Old Testament...*" [84]

The manichaeic "markers" of the five elements of "the god of darkness" became for Nilus the markers of a "worldwide Jewish conspiracy": "A terrible force, like heavy leaden clouds... obnoxious stench... the fumes of pride... destructive storms... in a whirlwind of lawlessness... from the approaching raging hurricane... some dark force leads the troops of the rebels... the sun of the night... the world lies in evil... he and his actions are condemned to fire... In the Kingdom of darkness and malice... "Is it possible to fight the spirit of darkness...," etc.

No less characteristic for Nilus is the manichaeic thesis of descending of *Jesus Impatibilis* to the deceived: "God spoke to His people, the New Testament Israel, Russia, in Sarov...

Through the Saint himself the Lord told His word to Russia about how Russia must keep and protect the great secret in purity and holiness..." (Compare: "For my Christian sense of responsibility it is enough to... not awaken in someone's heart any animosity towards the Jewish people, blind until later days...)

Although properties of "transformational analysis" of religious and mystical views are not the topic of this work, it should be stressed that the foundation of all mystical teachings, whether it is Jewish Kabbalah, Masonic rites, or Christian Apocalyptic literature, is *one and the same occult exegesis.*

S. A. Nilus's book, which was turned by the "zealots" into an anti-Semitic gospel, is in fact a strictly occult work that has nothing to do whatsoever with religion. [85]

This is precisely why Russian theological circles never accepted Nilus's concept built upon the exegesis of Manichaeism.

Researchers missed not only the nature of Nilus's heresy but also the understandable dependence of his occult views on the Jewish principles of interpretation used in Kabbalah and characteristic of all mystics in general.

One of the pillars of European mystical thought, Jacob Boehme (1575–1624), who greatly influenced freemasons and theosophists of later generations, especially German, Dutch, and English, according to Gershom Scholem, shows a "surprising affinity with Kabbalah":

"Friedrich Oetinger... in his biography tells of him, a young man, asking the Kabbalist Koppel Hecht (d.1729) of Frankfurt am Main for the best way to start studying Kabbalah. Hecht responded that Christians had a much better book on Kabbalah than Zohar. Oetinger asked what Hecht meant and Hecht replied: 'The book by Jacob Boehme!' He also told Oetinger about the correspondence between his metaphors and metaphors of Kabbalah." [86]

Cursing the "magics of Babylon" — occultism, spiritism, necromancy, etc. — Nilus, in the name of exposing the Yiddo-Masonic conspiracy, "creates" a theory of a "symbolic Serpent" using an image... from Kabbalah.

Joseph Gikatilla's treatise סוד נחש ומשפחתו ("The Secret of the Serpent and His Trial" is the title of the "metaphor" in Warner's Leiden manuscript, 32) includes the myth of the origin of evil: "Know that the serpent, since its creation, represents something important and necessary for the harmony of the world, while it was in its place.

He was a great servant created to carry the burdens of domination and service.

His head towered over the heights of the Earth and his tail reached the depths of the nether land. In every world he had his appropriate place and made something incredibly important for the harmony of all *merkavot*, each in its place. And this is the secret of the *heavenly* (not earthly — S.D.) serpent, known from "ספר יצירה", who moves the spheres and rotates them from east to west and from north to south.

Without him no creation under the Moon could live. There would be no sowing and no sprouting and no motivation for any creation to procreate. This serpent dwelled at first outside the walls of the holy sphere and was connected with the outside wall from the outside, for his body was attached to the wall and his face looked outward.

It was not for him to look inward. His place and his law were to make things grow and procreate from the outside, and this is the secret of the Tree of Knowledge of Good and Evil.

And so, God warned the first man not to touch the Tree of knowledge of good and evil while good and evil were connected in it, one outside and the other inside.

He should have waited before removing the tree's prepuce, which is its first fruit, from it.

Adam did not wait and removed the fruit before its time and thus brought "the idol into the holy of holies" and as a result the power of impurity penetrated inside from the outside...

Know that all God's deeds, if they are in their proper place that is set for them and foretold for them, are good; if they rebel and leave their proper place, they are evil and so it says in Isaiah 45:7: "I make peace, and create evil." [87]

Isaiah's aphorism turned out to be true in the case of a mystic who made up a Yiddo-Masonic conspiracy and created evil.

In Kabbalah, the Serpent impersonates the "dualism" of the knowledge of good and evil (compare to Roman pagan god, two-faced Janus: one of his faces looked to the past. and another looked to the future).

The circle formed by the body did not close the "holy circle of the wall" but defined the "inside" and the "outside."

By turning the Kabbalistic image of the Serpent (most likely found in Blavatskaya's writings [88]) into a "symbolic serpent" — the Jewish Sanhedrin — Nilus, in fact, created a new myth that had nothing to do with the Bible and Orthodoxy. His "metaphor," by its nature, became a common "poetic metaphor" of literary imagination, and not meditation.

The Protocol #3 begins with a phrase about the "conspirators" being close to achieving their goal: "There is only a small distance left and the road we have traveled is ready to complete the cycle of the *"Symbolic Serpent,"* as we depict our people."

Then Nilus comments on the "idea" of the Symbolic Serpent." The representatives of Zion of the 33-grade decided to peacefully seize the world for the Zion by the cunning of the Symbolic Serpent whose head was supposed to consist of the Jewish Government, initiated into the secrets of the Elders (always concealed even from their own people), and the body would be the Judaic people.

Penetrating into the depths of nations on his way, the "Serpent" undermined and devoured (tearing them down) all non-Jewish state powers as they grew. This same he must do in the future... until his cycle is complete in returning his head to Zion and until, in this manner, the Serpent encloses and concentrates the entire Europe inside his circle and, through Europe, the rest of the world."

Such interpretation of one of the "metaphors of Kabbalah" had nothing to do with Jewish philosophical thought. Nilus not only used the name "Symbolic Serpent," but gave it a fantastical meaning, in no way connected to the Biblical tale of the original sin.

And the whole concept based on manichaeic heresy turned into the eternal fight of the "world evil" (Hebrews — Jews — the Elders of Zion) with the forces of good — Russian Orthodox church.

CHAPTER 5

TWENTIETH CENTURY SATANISTS

SPIDERS (E. A. SHABELSKAIA)

On November 4, 1905, Dr. Dubrovin and a wire-puller Purishkhevich created the Union of the Russian People in Petersburg. The government immediately gave it a RUB 2,500,000 grant. The Emperor Nicholas II sported a military coat with the Black Hundred lapel pin.

Naturally, in the atmosphere of total attack on "Yids and masons" in 1905 *The Protocols* were widely used (versions "edited" by G. Butmi as well as by Nilus). The climax for "zealots" was the fact that the Emperor did read *The Protocols* and left his conclusion in the margins: "What depth of thought! What foresight! What precise realization of the program! It is as if our year 1905 were guided by the hand of a Wise man! There can be no doubt as to authenticity. The hand of Jewry that directs and destroys can be seen everywhere." [1]

However, soon after the Minister of Internal Affairs Stolypin presented the Tzar with the results of the secret investigation into the origin of *The Protocols,* Nicholas II grudgingly and bitterly wrote on Shmakov and Markov's report on wide use of *The Protocols*: "*The Protocols* must be removed... A pure cause cannot be defended by dirty means." [2]

And yet the fact that Stolypin successfully proved the non-Jewish origin of *The Protocols* did not mean at all that they were compromised: for the majority of anti-Semites, they were documents that confirmed "Yid stranglehold."

Nilus's mystico-messianic book built upon intricate reasonings involving "the holy fathers" and on religious fanaticism relying on the

Great Rus', Orthodoxy and autocracy, could not yet become a *mechanism of real politics*. The Yiddo-masonic conspiracy had to be "fictionalized" in specific literary plots and characters. *Illustrative* function of literature in relation to ideology is not merely an invention of socialist realism.

The principal blueprint of "fictionalized art" (first, "the theory, then its "illustration") was created long before the "revolutionary method" of depicting reality.

As *Russia and Europe* by N. Ya. Danilevsky and *The Book of Kahal* by Jacob Brafman preceded novels by Vs. Krestovsky, so did various "works" by A. S. Shmakov [3], M. F. Shugurov [4], L. A. Tikhomirov [5], and A. I. Benz [6] precede novels by A. F. Amfiteatrov, V. I. Rochester-Kryzhanovskaya, E. A. Shabelskaya, N. N. Breshko-Breshkovsky, I. A. Rodionov and many others who brought to the reader the contemporary teaching of a "worldwide Yiddo-Masonic conspiracy."

However, it was pulp fiction and not theoretical articles by the zealots of "the root of our trouble" that turned *The Protocols* into a genuine document of the time: the "fiction" about Elders of Zion born in anti-Semitic pulp fiction later became "reality."

Such uncritical approach to any "printed page" as a proof of authenticity of an existing fact and the unwillingness to distinguish between fiction (literature) and history (reality) is a characteristic feature of ideological interpretations both of "theoreticians" of socialist art and those of anti-Semitism.

G. Bostunich was "absolutely documentary" and "factual" in using mystico-philosophical, fiction and political creations as a *scientific* basis for his "research": "Just as *The Protocols of the Elders of Zion* presented the program of militant Jewry, so do Pietro Chiari's *L'Uomo* (1755, Venice), Dostoevsky's *The Legend of the Great Inquisitor* and *Caesar's Column* by Ignatius Donnelly present the entire program of the militant Jesuits..." [7]

That is why ideas and images of pulp fiction became 'facts of life" which could be used later in scientific works about reality itself.

In 1906, *The Spiderweb* by V. I. Rochester-Kryzhanovskaya [8] was published in Revel (Tallinn) with a dedication to "The memory of my dear husband and colleague Sergei Valerianovich Semyonov."

The novel describes the years of the crisis before and during the Russian revolution while Russia is surrounded by enemies: Germans want to split Russia, Poles want to secede from the Empire or create a state within a state, Jews, the most active revolutionaries, want to destroy autocracy from within.

Chapter 5. Twentieth Century Satanists

Traditionally, while foretelling "landowner pogroms" in Russia, the writer expresses the most intimate thoughts in "prophetic dreams" of her protagonist: "...the filthy, shabby gang consisting mostly of Yids flooded the room and began tearing icons off the walls and ripping them and stomping them with their feet.

At this moment she noticed that another gang was dragging the bloody corpse of Rostislav with a gaping wound in its chest and then threw it at her feet, shouting: 'A dog's death to a dog! See, your saints did not save you and our Satan triumphs! Bow to him, sacrifice to him on his throne and you'll be happy!' Then diabolic laughter roared all around!." [9]

It is noteworthy that among anti-Semites the favorite praise of an author's creative work is a "gift of prophecy": writers, while narrating of the present, always foresee the future, which for some reason turns into one "victorious for the enemy," contrary to the desires and hopes of the author.

Thus, Bostunich thought it necessary to stress a *fact* little-known to the "so-called reading public (italics by Bostunich — S.D.)":

"Vera Kryzhanovskaya-Rochester, who was named an 'officer of the French Academy' by France for her novels and earned her death by starvation in Revel in 1924 from the Russian emigration, in her outstanding novel *The Wrath of God... foresaw and foretold* Balkanization of Europe and, in particular, the birth of the joke of the state of the Czechs ruled by freemasons (Masaryk, Kramář, Beneš), which, in the novel, even overtakes Vienna (naturally, in the novel, these 'also Slavs' manage to finish off this city, wonderful but already gutted by *Yids and esdecs*)" (italics by Bostunich — S.D.). [10]

By borrowing ideas from Slavophiles, Vs. Krestovsky, and Litvin, the author declares as her "Credo" hatred towards Peter's reforms supported by the class that's groveling before the West and betraying Holy Rus' — that "Yiddified *aphid* of society that is called *intelligentsia*, faithless and rotten to the core." [11]

Many decades later, reviving chauvinism, xenophobia, and hatred towards Yids (Zionists), Ivan Shevtsov would borrow from Rochester-Kryzhanovskaya the nickname for *intelligentsia*, "aphids," and make it the title of one of the first Soviet anti-nihilist novels.

Another author of "outstanding novels" was, in Bostunich's opinion, "a marvelous Russian lady writer, Elizaveta Aleksandrovna Shabelskaya, a fearless fighter for the Russian national cause, a devoted anti-Semitist and anti-Masonist, a pioneer of education of the rotten Russian *intelligentsia* in this subject..." [12]

In the history of Russian anti-Semitic pulp fiction Shabelskaya occupies a special place. Her contribution was tying **together** anti-Masonic, anti-Semitic and anti-intelligentsia tendencies.

She came up with a criminalistic title for her trilogy (like the trilogy of Vs. Krestovsky), *The Satanists of the XX Century*.

The life of Elizaveta Aleksandrovna Shabelskaya (1855–1917) is in itself a fascinating story of an **adventure seeker** that contains it all: running away from home, a marriage to a man she did not love, lovers from various political camps, breaking the law, stages of European theaters, secret police service, participation in the war, and a murderous son.

E. A. Shabelskaya
(1855–1917)

Her life seems to have come off the pages of Alexandre Dumas. Such is the outline of the life of a "marvelous Russian lady writer." However, Shabelskaya's creative biography has not been studied at all.

The most valuable information about her life can be found in Shabelskaya's confession letter to A. S. Suvorin [13].

(According to a Russian tradition, women's confession letters were usually addressed to "authors, the teachers of life."

These sincere appeals found reflection in the works of Dostoyevsky, Tolstoy, and Leskov.

The fact that Shabelskaya addressed Suvorin, whom she invited to be her "confessor" is in itself remarkable: by 1896 the former liberal had become a symbol of reaction and anti-Semitism.)

As we learn from the letter, Shabelskaya was born on 18 April (Old Style), 1855 in the village of Stupki of Bakhmut Ujezd of Ekaterinoslav province. At 14, she graduated from the Kharkov Gymnasium for Girls.

Having learned about her affair with one Vidamin, her brothers, in the attempt to rescue their sister, sent the 16-year-old Shabelskaya to Paris to study singing. Soon she lost her voice and transferred to the drama class of the music school, but two years later, when her brothers went bankrupt, had to abandon her studies. Unwilling to return to her home country, Shabelskaya became an operetta actress (she worked for Offenbach among others). Unsatisfied by the meager pay and under the influence of one Fedotov (the possible founder of the Buff theater), she returned to Russia and began working in *cafe chantants* in Petersburg.

For some time Shabelskaya even performed on the stage of Mikhailovsky theater, but, apparently, without success, because she left the capital and moved out to the periphery.

An excitable person, Shabelskaya was afraid of another failure and in her letter confessed that she carried "a gun in her pocket" on stage with the intention to commit suicide in case of such failure.

A great success came to her in Kharkov where she played the part of Katerina in A.N. Ostrovsky's *The Storm* and later she was hired to perform in Taganrog, Odessa and Kiev.

According to her letter, her life during that time was punctuated by lovers who offered to financially support her on the condition that she quit the stage. In 1882, she joined Korsh Theater, but could not compete with Glama-Meshcherskaya and Ryabchinskaya. After she left Korsh, fate brought her together with a famous German director, theorist and innovator Ernst von Possart.

He advised her to go to Vienna to study at a music school and take Professor Stribon's classes. In 1885–1888, Shabelskaya performed in theaters in Augsburg and Basel, and in 1888 she moved to Berlin where her theatrical debut was a great success.

There she met an outstanding theatrical critic and dramatist Paul Lindau who suggested she leave theater, but instead she left Lindau (according to Shabelskaya, he paid her for a year, but she never got any parts due to his scheming).

Finally, Providence took care of the actress: Maximilian Harden (1861–1927) became her lover.

He helped his girlfriend to start writing in German and Russian, and soon her plays, thanks to Harden, were put on the best stages of Berlin and Leipzig: *Berühmter Mann (The Bitter Fate)* in 1891, and *Agrippina* and *Jenerlichen* in 1892.

According to the letter, in 1896 Shabelskaya still lived in Germany ("but for my pity for Harden, I'd go to Russia and return to the stage"). [14] Later, Shabelskaya "thanked" Harden by including his caricature image in one of her novels.

Maximilian Harden (Vitkovsky) was a Jew who converted to Protestantism. Before 1891 he signed his articles with a pen name "Apostata." His views were adjacent to radical, and socialist democrats considered him their "loudspeaker'. However, he gradually separated from the leftists and became an unofficial conduit for the ideas of the elderly Bismark and an avid critic of "international socialism,"

"Judaizing liberals" and "Francomaniacs." In 1892, at the time of his affair with Shabelskaya, he founded the weekly publication *Die Zukunft (The Future)*, whose editor he remained until 1922.

At first, Harden and Shabelskaya's relationship was of a lovingly patronizing type. The actress, using Harden's closeness to Bismark and in influential circles, provided Russia with vital information. Thus, twelve years before the sensational case against Philipp, Prince of Eulenburg, she reported: "Of the trusted persons (of the Emperor — *S.D.*) the first is Philipp of Eulenburg. This friendship is such that some suspect a love relationship a la Ludwig von Bayern." [15] During WWI, Harden first assumed the annexationist position, but gradually moved to pacifism and thus brought on himself furious attacks from anti-Semitists. Along with Walther Rathenau (assassinated June 24, 1922), he became one of the first victims of the Nazis: on July 3, 1922 two terrorists wounded him eight times with lead and iron weapons, but doctors were able to save the journalist's life. He succumbed to the complications of his injuries several years later. [16]

Her relationship with Harden did Shabelskaya much good: she learned the rules of the backstage scheming and armed herself with the Black Hundred-style anti-Semitism of Apostata. In late 1896, Shabelskaya returned to Russia. At least, on January 1, 1897, Suvorin wrote in his diary that she had given him an abstract from *Frankfurter Zeitung* about his novel that had been translated by Shabelskaya. In Petersburg the actress met V. I. Kovalevsky (1844–1934) who at the time was the Director of Trade and Industry Department and later, in 1900, became the deputy to the Minister of Finance S. Yu. Witte.

Kovalevsky came from a peasant Ukrainian family. In his college years, he became close with revolutionaries and was even imprisoned in the Peter and Paul Fortress for sheltering Nechaev, although he later insisted that he had had no idea whom he had been hiding.

According to Witte, the big bosses never forgot Kovalevsky's past. His career began in the Ministry of State Property which he joined soon after graduating from the St. Petersburg Agricultural Institute in 1875. Witte took notice of a capable employee and, wishing to have him, went to plead with Prince Meshchersky: "But Kovalevsky... is not only a liberal, but a red." "Witte responded to me: 'The Emperor is of the same opinion, but he has stopped being a red and it would be a shame not to use such a capable man'." [17] After talking with Alexander III, Kovalevsky became the director of the Department of Trade and Manufacture. His career was interrupted when he was the deputy Minister of Finance, and Shabelskaya was to blame. "A very lively, extremely talented and hardworking man," Kovalevsky was an important asset in his position, but, according to Witte, "he, perhaps, would have made a brilliant career but for his weakness for the female kind, the weakness that has always allowed and is still allowing unworthy women to exploit him." [18]

Shabelskaya became rich over only a few years: she rode in carriages, she rented mansions, she "held festivals": "She gives out places," Suvorin wrote, "and assists enterprises for money. Near Sochi, she was given 67.5 acres of the best land (Kovalevsky helped Shabelskaya purchase the lot for 15,000 rubles and the enterprising con woman immediately resold it for 30,000 rubles — S.D.). God will forgive her, what with Sergei Alexandrovich and the Grand Dukes doing the same." [19]

Nemetti told Suvorin how Shavelskaya rented the garden and theater "at Demidov's house": "She rented them for 25,000 when Tompakov offered 30,000. The manager of the house said that he would definitely rent out to Shabelskaya, because she was allegedly in relationship with six ministers. Kovalevsky is digging his own grave with this wench." [20] Shabelskaya was "the gang leader" of some famous people, i.e., Duchess Drucki-Sokolski. In Kovalevsky's name Shabelskaya signed forged notes for a tremendous amount of 120,000 rubles, which were supposed to be recorded in Petersburg, Vilna, Warsaw, and Riga. But the con woman's brother (most likely, a Petersburg chess player M. A. Shabelsky) recognized her handwriting and in November 1905 a notorious case took place. Kovalevsky had to resign, but Shabelskaya got off easy, likely because she was already "sponsored" by someone at the police department.

In 1905, Shabelskaya took as her common law husband A. N. Bork, who was connected to "The Union of the Russian people" and belonged to the radical right wing. She began editing the Black Hundred newspaper for workers "Freedom and Order" and wrote militant anti-Semitic articles while being "generously subsidized" by the police department. [21] She also owned other publications of "The Union of the Russian People," such as "Russian banner" (unknown years of print —S.D.), "Brotherhood of freedom and order" (1906), "Russian Worker" (1915–1916). Under various pen names (A.B., Delargo, E. Sh., Proteus) she published in "The Bell" and "The New Time." At the same time. A. R. Kugel talked about her enterprising activities. [22]

In the newspaper "The Bell," whose editor was one Skvortsov, Shabelskaya began publishing chapters from her anti-nihilistic novel:

using episodes of her private life, her travels and her meetings with people of various political views, she decided to talk about the "worldwide Yiddo-Masonic conspiracy." [23]

The plot of the novel *The Satanists of the XX Century* is simple. A Russian actress, an offspring of an "aristocratic family," while touring Germany, attracted the attention of freemasons who wanted to use the beauty and talent of the young woman to achieve their criminal goals. However, the protagonist met Professor Rudolf Grosse and he "opened her eyes" to the truth about freemasons.

In his research titled *An Experience in the History of Knights Templar*, the professor insisted that freemasons were nothing more than a cover for the criminal activity of Jews who aimed at world domination. As a result, the professor concluded that every secret society of the world was in one way or another connected with the "affair" of Jews who had long before exchanged their faith in God for worship of Satan, to whom they made human sacrifices. Naturally, all revolutions past and present were the result of the "malicious" activity of Jews.

The professor's untimely death becomes the reason for persecution of the protagonist who had penetrated into the secrets of "the worldwide conspiracy": freemasons accuse her of murdering Rudolf Grosse and thus wish to do away with the poor actress.

Only chance and our heroine's prudence help her avoid death, and protection and aid from the German emperor finally put an end to the scheming of the freemasons. The truth prevailed. Freed from prison, the actress received a farewell audience with the emperor and happily returned home.

Following the first storyline Shabelskaya begins developing another one: the Russian actress's friend, a Jewess Termina Rosen, is caught in the nets of Yiddo-Masons. Now the reader gets a closer look at "the enemies of the human race." The author's imagination leads to the discovery of the "secret of secrets" of Yiddo-Masons, and of their methods and means to achieve their "cannibalistic" goals.

The central scene of the first novel is a meeting of the representatives of the Jewish High Council, among whom appear a notorious terrorist and leader of the Esser fighters Grigory Gershuni (1870–1908) [24] as well as, against Masonic code, the wife of Pompei Vrede, the beautiful Malka. In Malka the reader could easily recognize the wife of Count Witte, Mathilda Ivanovna, née Khotimskaya, Lissanevitch in her first marriage, a daughter of a Siberian owner of gold mines. The ravenhaired beauty arrived at the meeting, because Count Pompei Vrede himself could not leave Petersburg unnoticed. In place of the password

Malka presents a hundred-ruble bill (an obvious hint at Witte's occupation in finance): the letters on the bill could easily be formed into the word "Lucifer."

The leaders of beth din accept the "letter of credence" from the Countess and say: "Countess Malka... we recognize you as a full representative of the great Jewish self-defense society, the Bund that must turn into a weapon of conquering Russia, into the army of the victorious Israel... we appreciate the brilliant deeds of your husband and your assistance to our common cause." "The beautiful Countess" suggests that Russia be dragged into a war with Japan and her husband Pompei Vrede should take care of the Russians' defeat.

The Count himself had been present at one of the previous meetings: "Only one man looked very different, with his non-Jewish face, although there was much Jewish blood in his veins. This was a Russian count of German origin, an influential statesman, hated in Russia and glorified abroad. A son and grandson of pureblood Jews, Count Vrede favored in appearance the Russian countess who gave his grandfather a noble name to which she had been the only heiress, and who passed on to her son and grandson the typical Russian beauty that made everyone forget that the counts Vrede were a branch grafted onto the ancient family tree. Unfortunately, even a decidedly Jewish face can be changed easier than a Jewish soul, and Count Vrede, who so skillfully played the part of a Russian nobleman and patriot who would lay his life for the Russian autocracy, in essence was as much a Jew as the other twenty-six representatives of the world freemasonry, or, rather, the world Qahal." The description of the Jewish origin of Pompei Vrede clearly hinted at S. Yu. Witte. [25]

Of course, after Dobuzhinsky's and Chekhonin's caricatures of the powerful minister it is difficult to recognize Witte in Shabelskaya's portrayal. However, M. M. Vinaver recalled: "In a spacious office we were greeted by a tall, of almost Peter the Great's height, man with strikingly narrow, pointed head and with eyes colorless but confident, as if he did not expect anything new from his visitors, a calm man with authoritative voice, a man of tomorrow." [26] To the Black Hundred, Witte's freemason membership was "common knowledge." Having written down the report of the leader of the Union of the Russian People on the fact that, allegedly according to Witte, a guillotine for the Tsar had been brought to Petersburg, one of the most informed contemporaries, General G. O. Rauch noted in his diary: "Dubrovin insists that Witte belongs to one of the masonic lodges in Petersburg and is wholly in the hands of Jews... He could be right." [27]

S. K. Efron-Litvin, who knew Shabelskaya well, quoted S. O. Sharapov, whose views became the basis for the economic theory of *The Protocols of the Elders of Zion*, on Witte: "I figured out this gentleman long ago, and not from the rumors but based on an old personal relationship. He grew politically in front of my eyes and I knew very well where his gifts were created and where his brilliant reforms and his strong will and his technical prowess came from. But I still did not quite believe that Mr. Witte had no God or consciousness. I still did not believe that he could as easily betray Russia as drink a shot of vodka." [28] Soon, according to Efron, Sharapov did believe... At the same time, A. R. Kugel said that after the manifesto of October 17, 1905 was published, Witte invited Jewish representatives to his office. Pointing out the Emperor's promise regarding the Constitution, the minister suggested that the Jews... stop the revolution. To their amazed inquiry as to how they were supposed to do that, what with them, Jews, not participating in the revolution at all, the count responded angrily: "Don't play naive. Write to *Alliance Israelite* and explain that in the long run this revolution will only make Jews' situation worse." Kugel noted that these were the words of one of the most prominent men of the time and added: "So what were others, supposedly, saying?." [29]

Let us, however, return to *The Satanists of the XX Century*. The world Qahal is headed by Reb Hershel Rubin, a Yid with a thin gaunt face, a "blade-shaped nose," a toothless mouth, and a bald scalp. In his shabby clothes with *tzitzit*, filthy and repulsive, Hershel Rubin is considered a famous *tzadik*, a great kabbalist and the "light of Israel." Everyone worships him: "The beautiful snow-white face of Countess Malka bent to kiss the thin skeletal hands with swollen veins and dirty claw-like fingernails."

The characters, the plot, the figure of the protagonist (a woman who penetrates into the secrets of Jews), and the concept of a "conspiracy" are borrowed by Shabelskaya from other authors: Markevich, Krestovsky, and Efron. Following in the steps of Rabbi Jonathan from *The Egyptian Darkness* by Krestovsky, Shabelskaya makes the head of the High Sanhedrin D. Moore present a program whose certain items are almost word for word quotes from *The Protocols of the Elders of Zion*. For example, the first item of the program is printed media: "With the help of our newspapers and magazines we can assign great meaning to any trivial thing that is useful to us and ignore, and thus make them forget, the things most important for *goyim*."

Compare this with the theses from Protocol 2: "Let's whatever we convince them of play the most important part... For this purpose, we shall, through our press, constantly instill blind trust in us... The press embodies the triumph of free speech... But no state knew how to use this power; and now it is in our hands..."

Or the second item: "We can... take over education without which we cannot seduce Christian peoples enough to make them give up their resistance, their own good, and even their self-preservation. It is in schools that the souls of our future enemies are shaped. *Goyim* school must be changed so a child or a young man comes out of it poisoned by lack of faith, lasciviousness, and indifference to anything but beastly sensuality." Compare this to Protocol 9: "We have fooled, drugged and seduced *goyim* youth through raising them on principles and theories obviously false to us, and yet instilled by us..."

Following *The Protocols of the Elders of Zion*, Shabelskaya brings out images of conspirators of "other blood": a representative of *Dashnaktsutyun* (Armenian Revolutionary Federation) Emzeli-oğlu Davidian, a Spanish anarchist Ferrera, a Chinese revolutionary activist Li Ki-Ching, a convert to Judaism, and an Indian brahmin Rasikandra.

Protocol 9 talks about the multi-national army of conspirators: "We have people of all opinions and beliefs serve us: restorers of monarchy, demagogues, socialists, communists, and all sorts of utopians."

Still, the stand of the only "safekeeper of Orthodoxy," the great Russian people, against everyone else (and not only Jews) is known not as much from Shabelskaya's novel as from those who came before her: Danilevsky, Krestovsky, the convert Litvin. In this, she was not a pioneer.

To achieve this goal, "tracing old patterns to make new ones," Shabelskaya gave concrete form to the Jews' plans of conquest and introduced in her novel the slightly camouflaged images of her contemporaries: S. Yu. Witte, his wife, P. N. Milyukov (in the novel, Pavel Nikolayevich Sazikov), Prince Dolgoruky (in the novel, Dolgonogy), etc. In one of her characters (Naskokov) one can recognize the member of the State Duma V. D. Nabokov (the father of a great writer of the XX century). Due to all this, Shabelskaya's narrative claimed to be "true" as a work of realism.

Naturally, the reader, recognizing the "real life" details of great current interest, could also believe the previously unfamiliar material. A. R. Kugel wrote: "What else, for example, are all these "Books of Kahal," the creations of Nilus... if not novels like *The Count of Monte Cristo* with an added dose of malice? But people believe them; many are willing to, and do, assign nearly documentary qualities to this ridiculous fiction!." [30]

In his memoir, V. D. Nabokov described a notable episode from the post-February Revolution time. During a meeting of the Elders in Pre-Parliament he sat next to M. A. Vishnyak, who, upon noticing a group of grey-bearded elders (Natanson, Chaikovsky, Kutler, Martov, Vinaver, and Peshekhonov), according to Nabokov, whispered: "That's a true Sanhedrin."

M. A. Vishnyak had to amend: "Nabokov brought up my words in confirmation of the fact that the Council of Elders was dominated by Jews, like an ancient Sanhedrin that represented Hebrews. Meanwhile, my remark referred not to "Hebrews" but to the bearded and grey-haired elders... I mention that to show that even a great memoirist like Nabokov, disappointed in his past, was capable of implying meaning into the events that they never originally possessed." [31] (On March 22, 1922, Nabokov put himself between his friend P. N. Milyukov and the terrorists of the Black Hundred and was killed. One of his murderers was Shabelsky-Bork, the son of the "outstanding lady author").

Whereas for Krestovsky, Litvin, Rochester-Kryzhanovskaya, Shabelskaya and other adherents of the "Yiddo-Masonic" conspiracy doctrine *literary fiction was "reality,"* for many of their like-minded fellows' reality itself became "literature."

Thus, L. Korchmiy, the author of the foreword to Shabelskaya's trilogy that came out in print in 1934–36 in Riga, while commenting on her prophecies about Russia perishing from internal turbulence and war, chose to support her "literary fiction" with a reference to "documentary truth": "It was impossible to guess at this conspiracy plan in all its details, like Shabelskaya describes it; she possessed very sensitive material and somehow reached into the innermost secrets of freemasons and used them in full in her novel." [32]

Another anti-Semitist, Col F. V. Vinberg, in his book *The Roots of Evil* confirmed a "historical event": on December 16, 1916, on the eve of Rasputin's assassination, in his apartment showed up "a Russian woman, a staunch patriot, an old writer who knew many secrets of freemasons for which fact she had suffered much torture and grief in her life."

She warned the favorite that he would be punished for his service to the satanic Yiddo-Masonic forces. [33]

It is not difficult to identify the "Russian woman" described by Vinberg as E. A. Shabelskaya.

A most popular Soviet writer, V. Pikul, who had undoubtedly read Vinberg's works, recreated this "staunch patriot's" visit with the Imperial couple's favorite:

Chapter 5. Twentieth Century Satanists

"Between December 1 and 16, the phone rang in Rasputin's apartment. A melodious female voice asked:
'Excuse me, is this the apartment of Rasputin?'
'It is. And what is it you want?'
'Could you please tell me when the funeral service for the late Grigory Efimovich is being held?'
Rasputin was dumbfounded.
When he recovered, he cursed the female voice colorfully and hung up. Who was this woman? Why did she call? The author does not know." [34]
The borrowed apocrypha worked according to an old recipe for all false witnesses: admit one thing and insist on another.

The author readily admitted to knowing neither the woman, not her purpose. That only made his *knowledge* more convincing: someone warned Rasputin about his impending doom. Neither Vinberg, nor Pikul cared that these apocrypha could be easily disproved: Shabelskaya was not mentioned in any of the police spies' reports on all Rasputin's visitors on the eve of his assassination...

The first novel, *The Satanists of the XX Century*, that gave the name to the trilogy and was printed in the newspaper "Kolokol" (The Bell) in 1911, was published as a separate volume in 1912 and later forgotten. G. Bostunich, regretting the oblivion of a "fascinating novel," hurried to state: "This novel, as well as another one, *The Red and the Black*, was *totally* (italics by Bostunich — S.D.) bought out and destroyed by Yids for telling under its cover the terrible, authentic, and scholarly truth." [35]

In the years when Ya. Sverdlov, L. Trotsky, L. Kamenev, and hundreds of other Jewish officials, big and small, chekists, agitators, and executioners were counted among higher Soviet statesmen, as many Jewish lives were ended as lives of other peoples. Of course, this is not a "merit," although it should be remembered and *blamed* on the rulers, as well as the famished innocent peasants of Ukraine and the exiled Tatars of the Crimea and the executed Polish officers in the forests of Khatyn.

The Nuremberg trials of the Nazis for "crimes against humanity" was called "a trial by history" by journalists. However, it was not a trial *of* history, for on the bench next to the German generals there were no original criminal, "Bolshevism"; the genocide of Jews began not in 1933 when Nazis came to power in Germany, but in 1917 in Russia. [36]

BETWEEN TWO WARS

After 1917, Russian geopolitical mechanism was an ideological mix of cause-and-effect relation between historical events and ethical and legal norms of coexistence of different states. And, the "Yiddo-Masonic conspiracy against the world" was assigned the main part in the process.

Singling out the "Soviet" Jewry made it impossible to use in the USSR the thesis of "worldwide" nature of Jews. That is why, denying "Soviet Jews" the right to be a separate ethnicity, [37] the political authorities of the USSR had to avoid using *The Protocols* before 1949. However, turning a "Soviet" Jew into a cosmopolitan ("rootless" (?), although Jewish Autonomous Region in the USSR already existed, and so did the state of Israel) was predetermined by the "international" ideology of the Bolsheviks.

However, *The Protocols of the Elders of Zion,* aimed only at "Jewish takeover of the world," were extremely dangerous to the Soviets. Having "absorbed" considerable multinational masses but never becoming Jewish, Georgian, or Latvian, the Bolshevik power *presented* indisputable "proof" of its *actions being based on the methods* developed by "the elders of Zion." [38]

That is why the geopolitical situation created by the Bolsheviks' victory in Russia became the "growth medium" in which the bacteria of a "worldwide Jewish conspiracy" were destined to fully develop.

Firstly, the world became "two-colored" and split into those "for" Moscow and "against" it.

Secondly, the Russians who lived in Russia in international family of brother peoples of the USSR, had to consider themselves "internationalists," but those who had emigrated, could keep the holy banner of their ethnic purity and blame the events on Yids, Latvians, Caucasians, or any other tribe.

Thirdly, after the Keiser was deposed in Germany and a patchwork federation of republics was formed, the ideals of pan-Germanism in the struggle for "living space" became very Russian-like: fighting "Yiddomasons" meant fighting the bolsheviks. [39]

Jews in the post-1917 Russia were declared "Soviet" (at the same time, there was no such thing as a "Soviet Ukrainian" or a "Soviet Udmurtian") based on a *non-ethnic* feature.

Jews in Germany were identified as "the fifth column" and, in the eyes of Germans, the difference between "external" and "internal" enemy had to disappear. "The Jewish conspiracy against the world" became a *"world conspiracy against Germany"* (and the Bolshevik Russia, already "overtaken" by Jews, served as an example). It was supported not as much by the geopolitical situation as by the *Russian version* (and none else) of *The Protocols of the Elders of Zion* that had already become HISTORY (after the revolution of 1917). [40]

It should be noted that the proof of the Russian Imperial Department of Police's participation in the birth of *The Protocols* [41] was, at the same time, a sort of rehabilitation for the "revolutionary" coup d'état of the Bolsheviks. That is why, in the geopolitical situation between two wars, the "investigations" conducted by Yu. Delevsky (1921–1923) and V. Burtsev (1938) could not affect the emigrant reader in any way. However, connecting the "Jewish conspiracy" (*The Protocols*) to anti-Soviet topics of N. Breshko-Breshkovsky or I. Rodionov (not to mention the "theorists" E. Brante, [42] G. Bostunich, N. Zhevakhov, and V. Akhmatov [43]) made their works not only "patriotic," but "progressive" (against the background of the "friendship of peoples" cemented by *millions of victims* of the Bolshevik terror and of the Soviet policy of 1920s-1940s. [44])

The publication of Nilus's book in the white-emigrant digest "Louch Sveta" ("A Ray of Light") in 1920 became the starting point for the revival of the cause of the Union of the Russian People. The author's text of the book *The Great in the Small*, with its mystical and messianic interpretation of the apocalyptic war against the Antichrist, was not necessary. The point was not the religious prophecy of the second coming of the Savior, but a real and quite material *crusade* against Jews as a whole, and the Soviet Russia in particular. It is no coincidence that G. Bostunich politically separated these two objectives in the subtitle of his research: "The Mystical Truth and the Real Truth." [45] *The Protocols of the Elders of Zion* (*an anonymous text*), on the other hand, turned into a "Jewish catechism" and became the basic document of ethnic phobias, whose "carrier" was the publishing house "Novi Sad."

Here's a question: Why did Yugoslavia become the "main printing shop" for anti-Semitic literature between the two wars? It has not been studied enough. The economic and geographical position of the state, the "tsarism" of Belgrade, the presence of a large colony of Russian White emigration were important, but not main one, circumstances.

Perhaps, studying of the history of the country broken up into duchies and princedoms that alternately aim for unification or federation and its *many centuries* of anti-Judaic and anti-Bogomilic literature with strong nationalistic trends, will someday give us an explicit answer.

In any case, Yugoslavia was the primary distributor of anti-Semitic literature in the Russian language in 1920s-1930s, the fact witnessed by publishing of anti-Semitic collections, apologies for *The Protocols,* novels and "scholarly works" along with other "revelations" of pulp fiction and pamphlets.

The "instigator" in the sphere of pulp fiction was Nikolai Nikolayevich Breshko-Breshkovsky (1874–1943), a professional author who became known before the revolution for his writings about athletes [46], about "the scandalous inner lining of high-society life" [47], and about Germano-Austrian espionage in Russia. [48] He was one of the first Russian screenplay writers and movie directors and emigrated in 1920. According to the memoir of L. Lyubimov, the son of Catherine Breshko-Breshkovsky ("the grandmother of Russia revolution") after 1933 "hurried to Berlin and... served in fascist propaganda institutions until he died in a bombing" in 1944. [49] In 1923, "Novy Sad" published N. N. Breshko-Breshkovsky's novel *Under the Devil's Star*. [50]

In the foreword (or, rather, instead of one) entitled "On the fight against anti-Semitism and all that...," the author, on the defensive (as it was customary among "zealots"), took the offensive: "Undoubtedly, some will call this book of mine a *pogrom* one. Most, the less zealous of that camp, will proclaim it anti-Semitic... But every smart and honest Jew... will admit that not only it has nothing of *pogrom*, but, quite the reverse, in several places the author denounces, and severely so, any pogroms or pogrom sentiments."

Apparently, the author meant the following deliberations:

"Ah, if we could take two squadrons on uhlans, surround Nalevki and give them an ultimatum... That would startle the Yids!"

N.N. Breshko-Breshkovsky
(1874–1943)

"And two days later," Vinarsky (the head of counterintelligence — *S.D.*) joined in, "telegrams would appear in the western and American press claiming that Polish uhlans committed a Jewish pogrom in Warsaw... No, Mr. Beizym, not in this case, nor in any more serious and wide-spread ones, no repressions! Not a single drop of blood, not a single smashed Yid mug! Nothing that would give Yids a reason to cry Polish pogrom and anti-Semitism... Pogroms stain the army, they stain men and take away innocent lives, and are, actually, just the other side of bolshevism. Leave pogroms to Petliura's gangs..."

Having announced to the reader that the "approaching bloody wave of pogroms" had to be fought "in a most energetic way," and that "the more difficult, complicated and... thankless task" was to "fight anti-Semitism as a whole," Breshko-Breshkovsky declares that the reason for "anti-Semitism in Poland, the anti-Semitism that has spread even into some socialist circles" is... Jews themselves [51]: "It's Jews' own fault. The relentless, dry, devastating facts and numbers are against them."

First and foremost, Jews are to blame for 80–90% of them being revolutionaries, and among those "a good half of those arrested and convicted communist Jews are rich young people." That is why Poles see in revolutionary minded Jews... *agents of the Soviets* who "relentlessly work towards destruction of Poland," although "we have... the most democratic Constitution..." and many Jews are "officers or even generals... serve in all ministries and have literally flooded our justice system..." Jews, unlike 200,000 workers of Warsaw, who marched on May 1 holding the "banners of their guilds," came out with "red standards" and "songs of praise to the Soviet rule."

Besides, when Marshall Fosch arrived on May 3, Jews "did not join the celebration" of the *Polish* Warsaw: "In both cases, Jews themselves turned out to be anti-Semites." Finally, in this subjectively interpreted "picture" of cause and effect, this fighter against anti-Semitism looks for support to a "proper Jew," who (the favorite idea of all "zealots") blames the revolution in Russia on his brothers:

"Through ten centuries Russia was being built and glorified...

"It grew and got stronger through that nameless Russian gray mass on whose bones Petersburg was built and whose graves are scattered over Turkestan, the Caucasus, and the steep slopes of the Balkan Mountains.

"We, Jews, strangers that overstayed their welcome, we never took any part in creating the giant Empire. So, by what right have we engaged so vigorously in its destruction?

"A master of the house, in his madness, may, although unlikely, set his own home on fire, but if his tenants start the blaze, they are in trouble!.. Even though most international gang leaders that sit in the Kremlin are Russian, still, their minds are Jewish... And, as a Jew, I insist that without our "Jewish mind" bolshevism would not have lasted two months in Russia. With this Jewish mind, however, and German machinery, encouraged by the sagging, narrow-minded and egotistic... Europe, it has entered its sixth year..."

The author stands with the "literal" words of his young Jew: "An all-Russia rebellion... Total despicableness, cruelty, cowardice, rudeness, and greed. But even more despicable was the defiant, impudent behavior of little Jews that suddenly showed up out of some holes... A *soviet* of worker and peasant representatives? My God, it was, to a person, a Gotsliberdan, including Nahamkes and Bronstein! In this Gotsliberdan were sprinkled a dumb Caucasian mule Chkheidze, an even dumber Russian fool Sokolov... and a Russian bastard Skobelev... Kerensky's petty bourgeois gang and "Gotsliberdan" could not but lead to the triumph of Bolsheviks. It would have been preposterous, had it happened differently."

Finally, Breshko-Breshkovsky offers his "recipe": "Let him be brave to the end and... say, looking straight at you with his clear shining eyes:

'Well, gentlemen, onward! Allez! Let's begin! Let's fight anti-Semitism!.. How? Very simple! Do not write "interests of democracy" all over the place, because anyone will interpret it as "interests of Jewry" ... Next, stop the insane bullying of several thousand exhausted Russian people... Then, do not dare to blasphemously mock... the name that is dear and holy to many Russians... To quench the hatred for Jews in the hearts of others, first quench the hatred for all that is dear and holy to a Russian in your own hearts..."

The foreword "On fighting anti-Semitism and all that..." appears to be that very "egg" that hatched not even a crocodile but the devil himself, "under whose star" Breshko-Breshkovsky's characters live. The plot of the novel is transparent: amazing Polish patriots (Beizym, Vinarsky, Liviysky, etc.) and no less amazing Russian refugees from the Soviets (Labenskaya, Prince Gagarin, Princess Barb, etc.) uncover chekists, disrupt the schemes of communists, and convict and execute "enemies of Poland and Russia," who, to the last person, are Jews.

The scene is laid in Warsaw in 1921–1922. Beizym, a Polish nobleman, an athlete, an actor, and an officer, returns to Princess Barb the jewelry stolen from her by the chekists, saves Gagarin and Labenskaya from starvation (and takes revenge for them on the "diplomat" Geller, a despicable sadist from the close circle of the no less despicable butcher, Zinovyev-Apfelbaum), and signs a contract for shooting a new movie for which he writes the screenplay and is going to star in, with Countess Sapari (naturally, connected to chekists).

In the name of art, Beizym has to act out a scene of wrestling a bear which is to be filmed at his family homestead.

The countess tells the vengeful Geller the time of the movie team's arrival and then (of course, being madly in love with Beizym) confesses her treachery to her lover. "Yids and communists" die, the vice has been punished, and the protagonist, Ignatius Beizym, and his girlfriend leave for Italy.

As it often happens with pulp fiction authors among "zealots," at the end of the "story" the protagonist, without a hint at self-parodying, admits:

"I've had enough of this bloody trash."

Of course, had Breshko-Breshkovsky not attempted to "reveal the philosophical depth of thought" of his characters, this trivial and forgotten novel would not be worth mentioning.

But, *Under the Devil's Star* is interesting precisely because it demonstrates such well-formed tropes of uncovering a "Yid" (without freemasons) conspiracy that can, from now on (without any "Jewish materials," "documentary excerpts from letters and journals, etc.) be a "recipe" for the "creativity" of fighters "against anti-Semitism."

The author does not need the obscure twists of *The Protocols of the Elders of Zion*, because Yids themselves are at fault for the anti-Semitism of those around them, so it is sufficient to talk about these despicable, treacherous, filthy, sinful, cowardly, unscrupulous degenerates of the human race.

At the same time, the invectives of the "good guys," as well as the self-deprecating monologues of the "bad guys," come together in a perfect and, in the author's opinion, indisputable picture of the *right* of Russians, Poles, and even the English and the French, to hate Jews. The "corpus delicti" is one of the versions of *The Protocols of the Elders of Zion*:

"Beizym shrugged: 'A Yid can only be a Yid patriot, not a Polish one. They proved it brilliantly when the red hordes advanced: I never saw them at the front lines, only in the rear...'

"Christian officers and Jews swapped places. Before, and not so long ago, the former would beat up the latter. Now, the latter beat up the former ... Young people were especially thrilled. The heroic actions of Arthur Montebianco (a political and financial figure of Zionism, Weissberg-Belogorov-Montebianco appears in Warsaw to 'secretly scheme' against 'the free and democratic Poland'— *S.D.*) inspired them to perform similar acts. A few days after his arrival in Warsaw, at night, a gang of Jewish students assaulted a Polish officer at his home, Nalevki. The lone, unarmed officer could not defend himself and, in the heat of the moment, the youths gave him a good thrashing.

"Montebianco stuck his unfinished cigarette into the ashtray...—
...Someone, I forget who, said long ago that there were two perfect organizations in this world: the German military and bureaucracy, and

the Catholic church. He forgot the third institution which... is even with Catholicism with whom it competes for world domination. This is us, Jews..."

Montebianco's speech is an example of a self-revealing "light musar" of Rabbi Jonathan from Krestovsky's *Egyptian Darkness*. Breshko-Breshkovsky's "innovation" is the fact that he added a quite modern political review (naturally, from the position of bolshevism) and... references to the program of *The Protocols of the Elders of Zion*. [52]

"Reactionist papers write: 'Jews, scattered all over the world, have their own secret government.' We respond in our press (and our press is 80% of all the papers on Earth [53]) that this is a lie and a malicious slander of anti-Semitic pogrom-makers. This is for the general public, and in reality, between us augurs, this is no lie at all... We have no army... what for? Why would we shed the blood of an ancient noble race when Christian armies are at our service...? Although, now we can say for certain that we do have our own army that was created through force and enlistment... the Red Army... Yes, it is our army with our leader at its head, Trotsky... Paraphrasing Bismark, we can say that Russian people are the fertilizer for Jewish might and greatness... the Red Army is our cannon fodder... We do not need monarchs, we need republics... The King of England, before taking an oath to his people and the Constitution, takes an oath to a masonic lodge... We need to keep things boiling, to keep authorities and idols crumbling, to keep blood shedding and the feud flourishing. In this unholy mess... our unity and our power over the world is solidified... When we say or write 'democracy' and 'interests of democracy' one should read 'Jewry' and 'interests of Jews.' Russian intelligentsia has served us faithfully in this..."

Thus, on the one hand, Germany and Russia became victims of a "Yid conspiracy," whose augur was the "Zionist" Montebianco, and on the other, the intelligentsia that spoke against autocracy, Orthodoxy, and the power of "Big Brother," served faithfully the enemy of the Fatherland. Essentially, intelligentsia replaced freemasons as the second component of the "great secret."

That is why it's not surprising that modern Soviet ideologists of anti-Semitism see Stalin's butchery of intelligentsia as a justified action.

"Obviously, Jewish ethnic consciousness is one of the main forces that now move this 'minority group.' Well, maybe we are dealing with a purely ethnic movement?

"It does not appear to be so... the "minority group" ... uses a certain group or class of people that currently tends to go through spiritual isolation...

"This can be a religious group (the Puritans in England), a social one (the third estate in France), or an ethnic one (a certain branch of Jewish nationalism here).

"And yet, just as noblemen and clerics played a prominent part in the French revolution, we can see many Russians and Ukrainians among leading proponents of the 'minority group' ... It appears... that Jewish influence plays an extremely important role, judging by the degree to which the literature of the 'minority group' is saturated with Jewish nationalist opinions." [54]

In this reasoning of the academician Shafarevich, it is easy to see a mathematical "substitution": at one time, for the "zealots" of the XIX–XX centuries, Yids and *masons* comprised the "minority group," then it was *Jews* and *intelligentsia*, and now it is Jews and the "leading *opinion writers*" ("authors"). Only the name of the "additional" component changes, whereas the "nucleus around which this layer crystallizes" remains the same — Yids, Jews, the "minority group."

The fate of *Under the Devil's Star* was not good. The "spiritual seer" and "Yid fighter" N. N. Breshko-Breshkovsky, as well as Krestovsky in his time, made a mistake: "To those who in a thousand years have never taken part in building our Motherland, we must bravely, without fear of being accused of a lack of democracy, say: 'Hands off!'

"Poland was built and raised up high for Poles... At the cost of an ocean of the Polish blood and through the Polish valiance and Polish genius, we have won the right to live as we wish, in our home and for ourselves, and not like parasite newcomers wish...

"I do not wish to over dramatize the situation, and yet I speak with full conviction: our homeland is in danger!.. The block of minorities is a Yiddo-Germano-Bolshevik serpent that has been sheltered on the breast of Poland.

"Yiddo-German-Bolsheviks do not surprise me. They are consistent in their desire to unbalance our home that is still developing... If all Poles, regardless of their party, consolidated in a powerful ethnic union, then, undoubtedly, we and only we would be masters of our own country... To my bitter shame and heartache, I have to stress that this campaign was not started by Yids only... but also by Poles...

"Whereas to the Pole Vinarsky the 'Yiddo-Germano-Bolshevik conspiracy' (an 'esoteric' alliance against Poland) and the 'Yiddo-intelligentsia conspiracy' (an 'esoteric' alliance of anti-national powers) appear to be mortally dangerous to the 'developing homeland,' to the Russian Gagarin the 'esoteric' alliance of 'Yiddo-Germano-Bolsheviks' is a barrier for his 'historical dream' of creating, together with Poland, a 'pan-Slavic union that would also include Serbians and Czechs and which would become something powerful and mighty and would dictate its will to Europe':

"Curse these Germans! Because of them Russia has become a wild desert. It's from them, Germans, that bolshevism comes... Germans, to our peril, sent us all this refuse in a sealed carriage, and now this refuse rules with their blessing and support...

"And now? Now that Bolsheviks rule in Berlin as if at their own home, when the despicable thief, the little Yid Sobelsohn-Radek, directs German politics and has the German government grovel before him?

"Now only complete idiots or complete treacherous bastards can think of an alliance with Germany..." [55]

Should one be surprised that a decade later, after 1933, Breshko-Breshkovsky's novel became "outdated"? Still, this Polish patriot calmly went to Berlin and began to promote the Nazi right to "ultimately solve" the Jewish problem, despite the fact that pan-Germanic tendencies led to the destruction of his "beloved homeland" which later was also divided between "Germano-Bolsheviks" ...

OCCULTIST EXECUTIONERS

Following a theoretical "innovation" (the reprint of Nilus's book), there began to surface various "creative" reworkings of plots of novels and of "speeches" of characters not only of long forgotten "Yid fighters" [56], but of the author's contemporaries.

In fact, for all pulp fiction "novelties" of the XX century, including the "bestsellers" of Soviet literature, *the similarity of storylines, narration devices, plot twists, and characteristics of style and personages* were nothing else but a way to prove that a "Yiddo-masonic conspiracy" was an objectively real phenomenon. However, presenting to the reader the myths and legends of anti-Semitic literature as *widely known facts and common knowledge*, the authors used a limited number of "facts," similarity of "logic," monotony of "quotes," and the same sources.

Remarkably, a typical trait of all the creations of anti-Semitic pulp fiction was direct borrowing from one another of the details of the "Yiddo-masonic conspiracy," decorated with "stylistic novelties" and carrying no references to their predecessors. The principal condition of such borrowing followed a strict rule: this *thesis (situation, ritual, tradition, etc.) is true, it has long been proved by such and such and requires no notations or references.*

The first signs of this were mandatory statements about creating out of "sense of obligation" and together with "insurance': the authors attempted to present themselves as possible victims of "Jewish revenge" for the "honesty and truth" of their works.

The publisher of the "manuscript" out of "the papers of the late Josef Przecławski" (*Exposing the Great Secret of Freemasons*) in his foreword specifically noted: "Then, I find it necessary to add that should I, now revealing the secret of freemasons, invoke the wrath of the Russian and even western European Jewry... I still, nevertheless, shall perform my duty in certainty that my passivity... would be a betrayal of my consciousness and a grave sin before Lord our God and my homeland." [57]

A brave Russian officer, imprisoned by Germans [58], G. Schwartz-Bostunich escaped abroad during the revolution and supported the publisher of *Exposing the Great Secret of Freemasons*:

"I know that publication of my lectures will bring a storm of outrage...

"I know that of the roses that shall one day cover my remains, only thorns await me in the valley of life. And yet, I cannot do otherwise...

"I foresee buckets of refuse and slander from Jews, who, in an old and tried way, will attempt to hush me and my work; and where they can't, they will declare me a fanatic and a madman; my book, as it also happened with the books of Dal, Diminsky, Shmakov, Nilus, Selyaninov, Lyutostansky, Shabelskaya, Butmi, Kalitin, Countess Tol, Tikhomirov, Archbishop Nikon, Col F, Vinberg, and other lovers of truth... they will attempt to buy out and burn... I foresee persecution, libel, slander, and curses, but I cannot abandon my oath..." [59]

In the second edition of the book Bostunich introduced a special sub-chapter "The Sentence to the Author of This Book" into the chapter "The Secret Society of Yids," in which he reported receiving a "black mark": "This sentence demanded that I immediately reject all my beliefs and unconditionally go over to the side of the "prince of darkness," or else face most grievous consequences..." [60]

His like-minded fellow, E. Brant, beseeched: "I know that Jews will bully me and that even my life may be in danger, but I consider it my duty to give as many Christians as possible, and also Jews, an opportunity to make sure that the monstrous rite of ritual murder among Jews is not a myth but a sad reality." [61]

It is easy to notice, in the forewords by two very different authors, the same plot that would later be developed into storylines of many works of writing: remember the protagonist of Litvinov's novella, the governess Pesha, who, afraid of the vengeance of "the old Yid Boruch," passed the compromising letters "from all over the world" she had copied, to her attorney in Petersburg; or the poor Rudolf Grosse, the hero of Shabelskaya's trilogy *The Satanists of the XX Century*, whom Jews murder just for writing a study of Yiddo-masonic conspiracy.

Even the concluding words in the work of the newest accuser of the "minority people," the academician I. Shafarevich, sound somewhat familiar, redundant, and *stolen*: "When... a bilateral process is out of sync, the same thing happens as does in nature: the environment turns into a wasteland and with it, the human being dies...

This is the end the "minor people" are pushing us towards by relentlessly working to destroy everything that supports the existence of the "major people." That is why creating a spiritual weapon of defense is an issue of national self-preservation...

But there exists a less grand task... *to tell the truth,* to utter, finally, the words that we have been afraid to say. I could not die content without having tried to do this." [62]

No less "redundant" is the image of the "ancient enemy," the Jew: endowed, through "predatory" epithets, with a repulsive appearance (for phrenologists and psychiatrists this appearance could be a "visual aid" in discovering symptoms of "bad illness") and as repulsive character traits (naturally, copied from evangelical mythologems), his image cannot but invoke in the reader a sense of disgust, contempt, and hatred.

Compare, for instance, the description of a *maggid* by Krestovsky ("At his right, limped, thin as a bent pole, *armer lamdan*, Rabbi Jonathan...

A lean, sickly yellowish face... his deep-set eyes glowed like coals from under his brow... *Armer lamdan* smiled smugly..." [63], and Litvin's description (a frail, helpless old man, an illiterate and worthless little Yid, ugly Methuselah, etc.) with similar portrayals in the works by Breshko-Breshkovsky and Rodionov. [64]

"Indeed, in his shaven, fleshy, asymmetrical face... with a large massive chin and a shock of reddish kinky hair over a low straight brow, in his bull neck and untimely fat, obese body with a significant belly that rounded under a blue satin quilted blanket... he lowered his fat, bare feet..." or "Behind him was a fat man... His shaved, fat, wrinkled woman-like face... On his short, meaty fingers... these flabby cheeks covered with red veins...he was disgusting... with his fat, woman-like chest, fat short legs and hanging belly..." [65]

"The visitor... sat in a chair at the table... The newcomer's obese body could not fit in the wide chair and he had to sit sideways, with his huge belly completely covering his thighs...

The remainder of reddish gray hair curled around his neck in a narrow fringe... The guest had a noticeable lisp and his speech was impeded by his large fleshy tongue... [his face] was monstrously ugly, disgusting and frightening in its general expression of *satanic malice, infinite contempt for everything and a rare ugliness:* square, disproportionally large... clean-shaven, crimson, and shiny.

And among all the above-mentioned appendages stood out a huge nose, shaped like a thick beak, and despicable shifting eyes glimmered from narrow, long eye sockets..." [66]

Still, while utilizing in one way or another the language material from the "shop of ready-made combinations," "outstanding" Russian pulp fiction writers, the "laureates" awarded not only the rank of Officer of French Academy, paid most attention (with a possible exception of Krestovsky) to "specifying" and "amending" the **body** of "Jewish documents." That is why, while thoroughly copying *The Protocols of the Elders of Zion* in which modal and subjunctive forms of verbs "we ought to" (#2–3), "we must" (#8), "we could" (#9), "we should" (#10), etc., together with simple future tense, indicated *intentions and wishes*, the compilers deliberately turned plans and programs into *already completed actions* of the "conquerors."

Thus, Bostunich stressed: "Because of Yids' scattering... their organization... their fusing had to become international... That such a secret international government exists, was sensed by our seer Dostoevsky..." And Montebianco, already familiar to us from Breshko-Breshkovsky's novel, declared: "For two thousand years, we... were accumulating hatred, energy, material goods... 'Jews, scattered all over the world, have a secret government'... Such organization as ours, with the incredible scattering of Jewry, is impossible without a unifying center from where orders and directives come..."

He was echoed by his "identical twin," Mr. Dikis from Rodionov's novel *Sons of the Devil*: "...and if someone decides to voice their guesses and assumptions about the existence of our secret authorities, that person should not even be discouraged, but laughed at and doused with refuse with contempt and nonchalance... The Jewish masses... do not suspect... of the existence of their own ethnic government which directs their lives and rules them through qahals and rabbinates... with the exception of the few initiated who receive the ruling directives..." [67]

In accordance with a Russian saying "The hat burns on a thief" ("God marks the crook"), the compilers often talked — *dixi et animam levavi* — about their own troubles and cares:

"I foresee also accusations of not working this topic fully and in depth and will say in advance that the issue of freemasonry is too profound and complicated to be fully studied...

"My work does not aspire to make redundant the works of my "predecessors, but, on the contrary, refers to them and calls forth my successors..." [68]

E. Brant wrote: "I shall be accused of plagiarism, for much of what I gave the reader I had taken from others, and of never bothering to check facts personally against originals..." But, commenting on this "fault," he only explained the latter accusation: "The originals, as well as some chronicles, have been checked enough by Jews themselves and their defenders, so there was no need to double check them... They will also say that I have no right to speak on the Jewish question, since I cannot read a single Jewish character. I shall respond to that by saying that my work is a compilation." [69]

It seems that combining the words "plagiarism" and "compilation" determines the history of creative labor of anti-Semitists to a great degree. No wonder one of the denouncers of "alcoholism, meanness, and savagery" of the Russian people, I. A. Rodionov, the author of *Our Crime (Not Gibberish, but Truth)*, subtitled "From the Modern Life of Commoners," which survived six editions, carried both sides of anti-Semitic "work" *ad absurdum*... [70]

The novel *Sons of the Devil* (compare to *The Satanists of the XX Century* by Shabelskaya and *Under the Devil's Star* by Breshko-Breshkovsky) is built entirely on the "teachings" of elders of Zion: one of the leaders of the conspiracy, one Dikis, initiates Lipman, a novice, into the history and secrets of the organization.

Retelling what he had read in the books by Butmi, Nilus, and Bostunich, the author decorates the "teaching" with minute details of Biblical and evangelical nature in an attempt to prove that Jews had "turned away" from the God of their forefathers already at time of the creation of Talmud:

"So... convinced of Jehovah's complete incompetence, our Pharisees concluded that there was no gain for Israel in following God and only then made a crucial decision...

"That is how Israel became God-hating and God-fighting..." [71] The apostates' ally was the devil and Hebrews turned from the chosen people into "sons of Satan."

The novel *Sons of the Devil* summed up the ideological development of *The Protocols*.

Everything fell, finally, in place: there was no longer need to hope that "temporarily blinded Jews" would see the light and that they, sooner or later, will accept Christianity (Nilus); it became possible to talk not only about sects or masons who obeyed a "secret government" which kept their people in ignorance of the goals and means of the struggle (Bostunich); or fight "anti-Semitism of Jews themselves" (Breshko-Breshkovsky). The "globally concentrated" investigation was finished and the only things left were to announce the sentence and execute it.

Rodionov's book appeared in stores in the early 1933, although the author pointed out that the conversation between Dikis and Lipman had happened in 1923. The decade of "brainwashing" turned out to be a success: in Germany, once "Yiddo-masonic," the power was seized by those for whom physical extermination of Jews was a program and the world domination schemes of *The Protocols of the Elders of Zion* [72] became a guide to action. The belief in the truth of *The Elders of Zion* and the genius of their program required only one thing: the *subject* of *The Protocols* ("malicious Jewry") had to be exterminated, and their *objective* ("the tale"), world domination, had to be made real.

CHAPTER 6

THE SOVIET VERSION OF ANTI-SEMITISM

REANIMATION

The anti-Hitler coalition's victory in WWII and another, similar to that of 1812, experience by Soviet troops of "freedom brought on the tips of bayonets" and of European life could not but reanimate a whole complex of imperial ideology (the famous Stalin's toast to "the great Russian people" in *Pravda* on May 25, 1945) in a situation of "internationalism": the discovery of another "global enemy" of Soviet pan-Slavism that culminated in the campaign against "cosmopolitans" and the Doctors' Affair of 1948–1953. [1]

This process ended with the change from a dictatorship of *one* to a "collegiate" rule of *many* (1953–1959), then a short-lived "thaw" (1959–1964), then a long-term "stagnation" (1964–1979); all this, by *historical logic,* encouraged the revival of "golem" in the birthplace of *The Protocols of the Elders of Zion.*

In this sense, the creation of the state of Israel and its stand against pan-Arabism was copied by modern anti-Semitists/anti-Zionists as a stand of "global Jewry" against the impoverished totalitarian camp of socialism.

The history of freemasons (mostly unknown to general reader in the Soviet Union either in theory or in historically documented sense) was represented only by a few articles (and those in the atheist magazine "Science and Religion"), which told in simple language about masonic lodges of the late XVIII-early XIX centuries.

The Soviet reader even learned the legend of Adoniram, illustrated by many engravings with masonic features, signs, and even a caricature of an initiation rite. [2]

Chapter 6. The Soviet Version of Anti-Semitism

There was even an attempt to "revise" Philip IV the Fair's massacre of Knights Templar.

Following the ideas of S. G. Lozinsky [3], A. P. Levandovsky, while questioning criminal investigation applying torture, terrorizing, and slandering, nevertheless "historically" excused the French ruler:

"Another circumstance indirectly speaks in favor of the 'iron king.'

"Four hundred years after the described events, the name of Knights Templar will be assumed by one of the most reactionist branches of freemasons (which, by the way, survived to this day), which, grounded in the USA, would tie its fate to global Zionism. Although, the history of neo-templarism is a plot of a different essay." [4]

The widespread campaign against Israel and the Zionist lobby in the governmental institutions of the USSR, with full and unequivocal support of Muslim pan-Arabism, similar to pan-Slavism in its ideas, made possible the revival of this issue.

The first "stone" was thrown by N. N. Yakovlev [5], and the next — by V. Pikul, whose novella *A Quiet Shot* was published under a pen name Yegor Ivanov [6]. Chauvinistic emigrant publications on the "Yiddo-Masonic conspiracy" became for them the basis for revising the official Marxist interpretation of the driving force of the revolution. Freemasons, according to these "reformers," disorganized the "rear guard," assassinated Rasputin, and forced Nicholas II to abdicate (apparently, only censorship prevented them claiming that it was freemasons who instigated labor strikes). Yakovlev even quoted bad poems about Rasputin's death found in the Empress's dresser (he hung his "graying head," hit by the "weapon of an invisible mason") and led the reader to the following conclusion: the "troubles" of the homeland (past and present) have been brought upon it by the "malicious agents" of the Russia's "global enemy."

This "stone" was followed by an avalanche of Pikul's "chronicle novel" *At the Last Frontier* [7], and a series of biographies in "Lives of Notable People" — Derzhavin [8], Bazhenov [9], Tatishchev [10, 11].

Fifty years of change, the formation of a socialist camp in Europe, and the "cold war," as well as the opposition of NATO and the Warsaw Pact, led to geopolitical reorientation. The former conflict "Russia vs. Europe" turned into the modern one "Russia vs. America." Freemasonry that used to be a "revolutionary force" now became a "reactionary force" and the "Jewish" conspiracy became Zionist. Finally, a modernized concept was presented, based on the example of... 1906: "It is in error that in his commentary," wrote Butmi, "the translator (apparently, the name of the translator of *The Protocols of the Elders of*

Zion was well-known among members of the Black Hundred — *S.D.*) asks not to mix the teachings of the elders of Zion in freemasonry with representatives of the Zionist movement, or Zionism, that had been founded by Dr. Herzl in 1896. It is in Russia that the Zionist-freemasons found a natural ally in Judaism." [12]

Former "Yiddo-masons" of the White Guard press (Trotsky, Zinoviev, Kamenev, etc.) and "cosmopolitans" of the Soviet press (Mikhoels, Markish, Bergelsohn, etc.) turned out to be agents of a unified "global conspiracy of Zionists." This revision of terminology led to... repetition of the "incantations" of the former denouncers of "enemies of Christ."

Thus, S. Losev and V. Petrusenko explained to the readers of "Ogonek" that Sirhan, the murderer of Robert Kennedy, was a member of a masonic lodge of theosophists and Rosicrucians, and noted in their commentary that the Order of Rosicrucians was born in Germany in XII century and the Anglo-Saxon branch of the order of "a red rose in the center of a cross" merged with freemasonry. [13]

V.A Pigalyov declared בני ברית (B'nai B'rith/ Children of the Covenant) to be the most influential lodge in modern freemasonry. Therefore, freemasonry was "for the most part ruled by global Zionism" and, although masons sacrificed part of their compromised organizations (the author of Bazhenov's biography was quoting, almost *verbatim*, the 1814 report of Col Dibich), they "did not really disappear but only changed their tactics." Pigalyov stressed that Soviet warriors should remember that Polish *Solidarność* was a work of Zionists who in 1968 initiated... a zionist *putsch* in Poland. [14]

A prominent Soviet "expert" on the "world Zionist conspiracy," E. S. Evseyev, entrusted the readers of "Sovetskaya Cultura" ("Soviet Culture") with his astonishing discovery: "Once, in a crowded book market in Cairo (almost like in Paris on the banks of the Seine — *S.D.*), I managed to acquire a rare Brussels edition of the so-called *Geneva Dialogues*. In the '60s–'70s of the past century this book made a racket and was widely known in France. The author, a French lawyer Maurice Jolie, who was directly connected to French freemasonry and inclined towards spiritualism and mysticism, built his work in the form of dialogues between the shadows of Machiavelli and Montesquieu. In these, he laid out the most urgent political issues in France at the time of Napoleon III. Many thoughts in the book seemed familiar to me, especially in the part that touched upon the state, the form of government, and political principles. It reminded me of a booklet by a Zionist "prophet" Herzl, *The Jewish State*. I compared the texts of these two publications... and some curious things surfaced: the "prophet" Herzl simply copied the work of the Frenchman Jolie." [15]

It is known that Maurice Jolie published his pamphlet twice, in Brussels and in Geneva. In 1921, a correspondent of *The Times* found a copy of the Geneva edition of *The Dialogues* in Constantinople. Through comparing the Geneva edition of Jolie's pamphlet to the Nilus edition of *The Protocols of the Elders of Zion*, the fact of plagiarism was established. In 1927, a future Hitler's minister, A. Rosenberg, published a work *The Congress of Global Conspirators in Basel*. Wishing to prove that *The Protocols* were an authentic "Jewish document," Rosenberg pointed out that "the founder of Zionism Theodor Herzl" had used Maurice Jolie's dialogues, and quoted specifically the Brussels editions of the Frenchman's work. (It goes without saying that none of those quotes of Jolie were ever found in the literary legacy of Herzl.)

While editing the Nazi leaflet *Welt Dienst* that was printed in the languages of German-occupied Europe, Bostunich, who by then had become an *Obersturmbannfuehrer* of the SS, in his article "The modern results of the study of the origin of *The Protocols of the Elders of Zion*" referred to "comparative analysis" by A. Rosenberg, based on the Brussels edition of Jolie's pamphlet. [16]

Therefore, we can conclude that E. Evseyev, who had discovered "most curious things," *indeed discovered for the Soviet reader... either the article by the* Obersturmbannfuerer *or the one by the* Reichsminister.

Whereas E. Evseyev, who did not live to see *perestroika* with its pluralism and revelations by the garden variety fascists of "Pamyat" ("Memory"), had to come up with a tale of a "market" in Cairo and finding the Brussels edition of Jolie's *Geneva Dialogues*, L. Korneev, an ideologist of anti-Zionism in the USSR, simplified everything: he quoted the forged letter by Crémieux on "a global Jewish conspiracy" from Selyaninov and Dikiy and had no intention to share the source of his knowledge with an "unprepared reader."

In his opinion, the publication of this forgery was a *self-sufficient fact*: "The Jewish teachings must fill the world. The net that Israel spreads over the globe will expand every day and the grand prophecies of our holy books will finally be realized. Our might is enormous. Let us learn to use it to promote our case." [17]-[18]

The reanimation of anti-Masonic and anti-Semitic (in Soviet terminology, anti-Zionist and anti-Judaic) ideas during the "shameful twenty years" (1964–1984) was an important historical ground for the birth of Russian fascism of the Nazi variety. [19]

This enthusiastic advance of patriots and fighters against "secret conspiracies" was moving as a wide front, capturing even the republics of the Union. [20]

The priority, of course, still lay with the "Big Brother," and in its vanguard in the recent decade (1979–1989) has rightfully been the pulp fiction writer Valentine Pikul and academician I. Shafarevich, the publicist. In this alloy of the names of a superficial, but good at a "fast plot" and favored by the authorities master of an adventure novel, and of a professional mathematician with a dissident past and amateurish ambitions, one can see, it seems, the perfected myth of a "global Jewish conspiracy," whose entropy determined sterility and senselessness of the "revelations" based on the "Orthodox" atheism, "international" chauvinism, and "monarchic" pluralism.

CHRONIC TOTALITARIANISM

The creative works of V. Pikul (1928–1990) is a variation of the writings by N. N. Breshko-Breshkovsky, with the only difference being that Pikul, trained by the Soviet Navy, was a militant atheist and his openly chauvinistic and anti-Semitic views were aided by his anti-religious tendencies.

Here, we must note a number of Pikul's military and historical works, the genre that became traditional since N. Danilevsky and Vs. Krestovsky.

The dominant anti-German theme is a consequence of Pikul's personal WWII experience; it allowed him to "revise" the pro-German views of emigrant anti-Semitists: *Bajazet* (1961), on the Anglo-Franco-German alliance against Russia in the Balkans; *By Plume and Sword* (1970), a novel aimed against Frederick the Great; *Slovo and Delo* (1974–1975), on "Yiddo-German" domination in the times of Anna Ioannovna; *The Battle of Iron Chancellors* (1977), aimed against at Bismark who created the Prusso-German military machine.

Two novels by Pikul were his creative rehearsal for the "Satanic theme" of Jewish participation in Russian history.

First Pikul published his novel *Out of the Deadlock* (1968); it talked about revolutionary events in Murmansk. Then, *Moonzund* (1973) came out; it talked about WWI in the Baltic countries.

Finally, in 1979, Pikul became a "superstar" for "patriots"; in the magazine *Nash Sovremennik* his novel *At the Last Frontier* was published. The novel immediately became an anti-Zionist bestseller.

CHAPTER 6. THE SOVIET VERSION OF ANTI-SEMITISM

Raised according to the indestructible Soviet Stalinist dogma, the author decided to arm the reader with "reliable methods of research and learning," following V. I. Lenin, having based his novel on the "authentic materials" and having checked questionable collisions against the "recent works of Soviet historians."

The reliability of "research and learning" was colored in ideological hues of "bolshevism": "decay," "court *camarilla*," "rot," "despicable Tsar's gang," "cruelty of these pogrom makers."

But don't even for a minute believe that by "pogrom makers" he meant those who organized Jewish pogroms.

No, this word was used in the directly opposite sense: Pikul's "pogrom makers" are Jews and traitors who plotted "Rasputininsm," the war, and... the revolution.

By keeping "the names in their historical authenticity" and insisting that "there were no fictional characters in the book," Pikul, by "authentic materials" and "checking" his sources and facts "against the most recent works of Soviet historians," also means not as much the scholarly aspect as the subjective selection of the materials and "checks" which were necessary for the author of the chronicle to achieve his *preset goal.*

Its mention comes through an image of Blok: "The ladies from the capital would hardly recognize now their idol in this soldier. No, it was not poems about the Beautiful Lady that he conceived at the crossroads...

"Now, in him, a mature man, a book about the last days of the Tsarist empire was being conceived.

> *Yes, we are Scythians, yes, we are Asians*
> *With our slanted greedy eyes...*

"...And on the corner... paper boys, in their ringing voices, were selling folk *lubki*, the fresh masterpiece of underground literature..."

The history of "Rasputinism" is represented in the dualism of the *named* "reactionist" events and characters ("God-anointed ones," ministers, murders, bribes, betrayals, lewdness, etc.) and their *unnamed* revolutionary counterparts:

"Perhaps the author may be reproached for not reflecting in the novel the cruel fight of the Tsarist Ministry of Internal affairs against the revolutionary movement...

It is so.

The author does not object.

"Still, he was writing about the negative side of the revolutionary era...

"The author consciously did not wish to fit two different topics under one title: the process of the growing revolution and the process of strengthening of Rasputinism..."

"At the same time, the dualism of the 'black (the told) and the white (the untold)' is only a 'veil' that hides another antinomy: Russian (normal) vs. anti-Russian (abnormal).

"The 'God-anointed ones' degraded to the point that the abnormal presence of Rasputin... seemed to them normal...

"The author, perhaps, does not fully understand the reasons for Rasputin's rise because he tries to be reasonable.

"To understand these reasons, one has, perhaps, to be abnormal."

The Protocols of the Elders of Zion naturally come to mind: in those, the "conspirators" (Jews) thought themselves normal and the *goyim* — abnormal, for whom was created "insane... literature... (that) could lead to such insane blindness..."

As Nilus wrote, it was scary to "look at modern day people tangled in contradictions and at the insanity that has seized them... their inner state of disorganization..."

Naturally, the "black" (the decay of autocracy, the camarilla, the corrupted officials, the irresponsible politicians, etc., on the one hand, and occultism, charlatanism, lewdness, greed, wordiness, etc., on the other) required the opposition of the "white."

However, by refusing to depict "progressive forces" of the revolution, the writer, who tried to "reason," had to use as his "white" ... the "black" with the "opposite sign" (loyalty to the government, chauvinism, security, totalitarianism, etc.).

That is how the *truly black* character of the "Tsarist gang" in this chronicle novel was opposed to the "black color" of the *fictional,* with "people loving" and "good nature" mixed in: "The revolution awoke in the people not only noble powers... but also brought to the surface of life much slime that had laid at the bottom of our difficult and deep history."

And although this "slime" gave birth to the Black Hundred, for the author those like-minded to Purishkevich and Dubrovin were "white": "Do not think that the Black Hundred are all narrow-browed revelers in long undercoats and aprons, who ambush students in dark gateways and smash their skulls in with iron crowbars. Although, such as these... existed in Russia, but they were only executing someone else's will. At the head of the Union of the Russian People stood reactionist doctors, writers, generals, lawyers, teachers, and industrialists, all people literate enough."

Chapter 6. The Soviet Version of Anti-Semitism

Let us not nitpick. Pikul's innovation lay somewhere else. He knew about the Nuremberg trials that pronounced harsh sentences on a doctor (Seyss-Inquart), a writer (Dr. Goebbels), a general (Jodl), a lawyer (Fritzsche), a teacher (Rosenberg), and an industrialist (Krupp), as well as about the trials of the "executors of someone else's will," that of Goering, Ohlendorf, Hess, and others, and he put the *logical emphasis* not on the social structure of the Union, but on the *distinctive feature* of those at its "head."

Not "educated," not "independent thinkers," not "well-mannered," but precisely "people literate enough."

Pikul did not have to explain their "literacy": the whole narration and all the features of the "literate people" proved that their literacy was only in understanding the "root of our troubles." *For a Soviet writer of the "time of stagnation" the spring of Russian history was wound by "global Zionism"* — according to Nilus, "the Talmudic Israel": "This same year (1895—S.D.), the department of police filed the first prophecy that, out of nowhere, had begun to spread through the court: *In the beginning of the reign there shall be troubles and misfortunes for the people, there shall be a losing battle, there shall come a great disorder and father shall rise against son and brother against brother, but the second half of the reign shall be light and His Majesty's life shall be long.*

According to the tale, this prophecy originated in the remote monastery of Sarov. Its author was a merchant's son Prokhor Moshnin who had been born in the midst of the Seven Year war and died after the execution of the Decembrists. His monastic name was Seraphim of Sarov..."

Embedding apocalyptic idioms (first, at "the end of times," troubles and misfortunes of the people, the war between the "sons of light and sons of darkness," a great disorder, father shall rise against son and brother against brother, and then, after the victory of Christ's forces there shall be a life of light and Christ's Kingdom eternal) into a modern background (the beginning and the second half of the reign, life of the Tsar), Pikul, *following* Nilus, pointed to the same source of the "ancient prophecy," Seraphim of Sarov.

Yet, either due to his atheistic upbringing ("The factory that produced gods was always on Earth"), or by agreement with Nilus's biographer ("*The Protocols* were regarded from the mystical point of view and few saw their political meaning" [21]), the mysticism of the "camarilla" (and, perhaps, of Nilus himself) Pikul ascribed to the "black," and the revealing of the political meaning of the "Zionist conspiracy" to the "white," i.e. himself and... the Black Hundred:

"Vulgarity can sometimes replace wisdom and insolence often excludes ceremony. Philippe (to give him his due) was a brave man... Philippe sneaked to Petersburg, closer to the gold... Meanwhile, the head of Russian foreign agents Rachkovsky... found such information about Philippe that he couldn't even risk entrusting it to a diplomatic mail courier... Rachkovsky personally arrived in Petersburg and took his report straight to Sipyagin. the Minister of Internal Affairs...

"'Philippe,' continued Rachkovsky, 'is an active member of the secret Grande Alliance Israelite, the center of the global Zionist organization... With his help, Zionism has penetrated where even you cannot get access...

"'What are you getting at?'

"'The fact is that this abnormal situation is dangerous for the Russian state. It is possible that foreign intelligence will from now on use the mystic inclination of our Empress to gain access to the court...'

"'Here is my good advice. Toss your dossier in here and I will stir it with a poker...'

"Rachkovsky acted differently. He went to the dowager Empress Maria Fyodorovna and handed her the dossier of Philippe.

"'Thank you, Pyotr Ivanych,' replied the Mother Tsarina. 'I shall pass it on to my son. Into his own hands...'

"Rachkovsky was soon sacked, and without pension!

"Nicholas II disdained his agent, and decided to support Philippe instead...

"The palace commandant Hesse, defending Rachkovsky, wanted to 'open the Tsar's eyes' to the charlatanism of Philippe, but the Emperor ordered him to be quiet...

"Philippe did not return, but he sent his student to Petersburg, a clever Zionist Papus..."

The autocracy refused to prevent its own death at the hands of Zionists, and the patriots of the Union of the Russian People had to deal with the conspiracy themselves. [22]

First of all, Pikul hinted that Rasputin, an agent of "Yiddo-masons," was "unclean": "The harsh order took long to reach the Tumen Ujezd: Immediately extradite Grigory Rasputin to Moscow. The paper looked official and the form of the Union of the Russian People (with the coat of arms and crown) alarmed the authorities...

"The priest Nikolai Ilyin was scared more than others... Wishing to get ahead of other calumny, Ilyin quickly threw together a report against Rasputin...

Chapter 6. The Soviet Version of Anti-Semitism

"But everyone was astounded by the Elder Belov, who learned from some papers that Grigory Rasputin was a son of a former Elder Efim Vilkin. Grandpa Silanty looked at everyone with his amber wall-eye:

"'I remember Yafim Vilkin. He later called himself Novykh.'"

Then, having noted the foresight of the "Unionists" ("The Black Hundred unanimously rejected Rasputin"), Pikul finally placed the figures of his "chronicle":

"Witte had to go, for he was suspected of connections to the secret 'Yiddo-masonic' society of Europe; his friendship with the Kaiser Wilhelm II and with the Zionist bankers Rothchild and Mendelsohn did not speak in favor of Witte-Semisakhalinsky. Witte was a criminal, but a respected one! ...

"To the Black Hundred he seemed intolerable as a dangerous liberal... It was Witte who had authored the 17 October Manifesto, whose consequences the Romanovs had to deal with..."

Witte was replaced by Stolypin, who "inherited a doomed legacy": "He was forty-four... Pyotr Arkadyevich Stolypin was a reactionist, but at times thought radically and tried to destroy the order of things that had stood indestructible for centuries." A Lenin quote clarifies Pikul's phrase about the order of things "indestructible for centuries": "A landowner and a leader of nobility... makes himself "famous" in the eyes of the Tsar and his Black Hundred camarilla... he organizes Black Hundred gangs and pogroms in 1905 (Balashevsky pogrom)."

That is why for the author "radicalism" of the Prime Minister was first of all radicalism of the Black Hundred: "'What is the meaning of everything?' said the president (according to Pikul — S.D.) with emphasis. 'If we want to see Russia as a great nation, if we believe in the special historical development of the Russian people, we must drastically change the main thing in our country... Who is our nobleman and landowner? This is crap,' said Stolypin with gusto."

Popular fiction in the Soviet times was not research: "The Russian reader has mastered the language of Aesop and that is why he inferred a political sense even in the bad weather forecast."

Self-confession?

Not just that. A sign of the author's times is that the reader is supposed to be insightful and discern in the *style* itself the nuances of thought. "A nobleman and landowner," along with the Yiddish word "dreck" (crap) is a synonym of a 'Jerusalem nobleman" (a Yid *dreck*), to which also belonged Zionist-sympathizing "refuse of departments and trash of offices" (notably, several pages further Pikul would utter a memorable phrase: "It is useful to remember that the German

General Staff insisted: 'There is no refuse, there are only human resources'"). However, having thrown in a reminder of the true meaning of the Black Hundred doctrine, Pikul, to avoid social trouble, turns Stolypin's conversation with the Tsar into a "chronicle streamed" of the agrarian reform.

The plot conflict of Stolypin and Rasputin (a highly educated man, G. I. Rossolimo, said: "I know that Stolypin did not fall under Grishka's influence. He became his enemy and that broke his neck..." — "Rasputin left Stolypin very offended... The premier has an evil eye. He looks at a man as if he was forcing a corkscrew into a bottle. I have met such people before. They happened in my way. Those are dangerous people...") was turned by Pikul into a conflict between radicals and noblemen (in Stolypin's sense of the word — *S.D.*)."

Rasputin, the "new political power in the empire," accepts a "rainbow check" first from Witte (semi-Jerusalem, i.e., "Semi-Sakhalinsky") and then also from his "well-wishers" who provided him with his favorite drink, madeira.

"Global Zionism already noticed in Rasputin a future influential favorite and the aces of stock markets gave him abundant credit... Later, spies of the German General Staff will take this beaten path to Rasputin... "There is no refuse, there are human resources!"

In *The Protocols*, the power of gold ("and Satan leads the dance") that is necessary to bribe ("at his feet the human race") is followed by a declaration about a "secret weapon" of the conspirators, seduction: "The goy people are dumbed by liquor and their youth is crazy with classicism and early lasciviousness, in which they were encouraged by our agents...

"...To prevent them thinking for themselves, we distract them with celebrations, games, revels, passions, and public houses... Soon we will begin offering contests through the press..."

The logic of *The Protocols* dictated to Pikul the storyline of his "chronicle novel": "Reactionism always goes hand in hand with the fall of morals... Among students there sounded a treacherous call: 'Down with revolutionary asceticism, long live joys of life!'... Russian papers were full of advertisements:

"'A single young lady searches for a decent gentleman with means; will pose in the Paris style'.

"'A gentleman of 60 (still vigorous) searches for a lady to spend time with at a resort.'

"'A young cheerful lady would like to accompany a single man on a train ride.'

Chapter 6. The Soviet Version of Anti-Semitism

'Everywhere, like toadstools after the rain, dark and immoral societies sprang up... Reactionism is not only a political pressure. It is the hollowing of the soul, a fracture of the psyche, inability to find one's place in life, wandering of the mind, alcohol and drugs, and a night in the embrace of a prostitute."

Naturally, in the "chronicle novel," as in *The Elders of Zion* (see Protocols ## 2, 12, 14), the press is assigned a provocative role: "In the evening, in the Winter Palace, the Premier was visited by the politely lisping Izvolsky, Minister of Foreign Affairs... Berlin was secretly promoting war and the German General Staff decided to "create in Russia a printed medium that would serve Germany's political and economic interests." It was not even necessary to start a new printed medium in Petersburg; it was easier to just buy you an old newspaper...

"*Novoye Vremya*," reported Izvolsky, "has been targeted. Today I got a call from Professor Pilenko... He said that the Germans were acting through Manasevich-Manuilov... My conversation with Pilenko was interrupted when the German ambassador himself showed up... Portales was obviously embarrassed...

"'This should remain between the two of us,' he said. 'I have found myself in a very awkward position. Berlin transferred to me 800,000 rubles for bribing Russian press.'"

And, although "Zionists vehemently hated" Vanechka Manasevich-Manuilov "for lack of tribal patriotism," he, bending over "a blank sheet of paper to mar it and to get paid for it," loyally served not only the Russian Department of Police and the "German General Staff," but, of course, also Rasputin, i.e., the Zionists ("behind Rasputin's back stands a secret society of a 'Yiddo-Masonic' sort"):

"The banker considered and decided to aid the Empress, and called in Manasevich-Manuilov, who had long been his secret agent (of which Beletsky did not know and thought him his loyal spy)."

The author V. Pikul did not exaggerate when he declared that his "chronicle" had no fictional characters and that many facts were checked by him against the works of historians (well known and not at all "recent Soviet"). The author hid only one thing: the main plot of the novel was the illustrative and documentary material of *The Protocols of the Elders of Zion*, with some small (according to modern times) deviations into Germanophobia, spy-mania, and policing. In any case, the "timely novel" of Pikul, during the active operation of "The anti-Zionist Committee" (a body of the KGB), did not contradict the general directive of the Party and government: "The fates of international capitals are very complicated.

But they are thrice as complicated when they go through the hands of Zionists. The money in this case surfaces in very unexpected places, as though it has gone through the depths of sewer systems. "Novoye Vremya" was already legally in the hands of Zionists, but Rubinstein had not begun to work yet..." "At one of Lithuanian manors Myasoyedov 'was caught in the act'... Myasoyedov, apparently, visited Rasputin on multiple occasions... and all his assistants, who were arrested with him, were connected to Rasputin's financial circle; if you also recalled that Rasputin's guard included German agents, the suspicions only grew..."

"They talked about mass production of forged dentist diplomas among Zionists..."

Klimovich arrested over two hundred swindlers in one night. They were illiterate, but had diplomas of dentists...

For Simanovich this came out of the blue; the Zionists were in a nervous state of turmoil and accused the judges of ingrained "anti-Semitism." "First of all," Simanovich admitted, "we looked for people who would agree to a separate peace treaty with Germany."

"Paleolog wrote: 'I will never forget the expression in his eyes... I saw in front of me the personification of the entire despicability of the security department. And right away he asked his secretary to bring out of the archives the secret dossier on Vanechka that held one too 'intimate' detail of Manasevich's life: in 1905, he — a convert! — was one of the initiators of Jewish pogroms in Kiev and Odessa...'"

Well, his writer's intuition did not fail Pikul: following the theses of *The Protocols* he could unfold before the reader a terrible picture of a molested, enslaved and betrayed Russia, whose main enemy were... Zionists: "...on the windowsill appeared the figure of Borka Suvorin... the Black Hundred publisher opened rapid fire with his handgun and yelled:

"People of Russia! The heathens have seized my paper!

"The machine of police investigation was put into gear... The underground connections of the financial bigwigs led very far, as far as Berlin... 'This case attracted the attention of the entire Russia', wrote Aaron Simanovich. 'I had to have Rubinstein's case closed, because it could be harmful to the Jewish cause!'."

And so, the novel *At the Last Frontier* finally defined it: *the case of Jews*, the main accused in the story of the *death* of Russian autocracy, and Russian revolutions, became the priority, and the witness for the prosecution was that dark force of the "camarilla and bureaucracy" that is "called reactionism between the two revolutions."

Chapter 6. The Soviet Version of Anti-Semitism

In 1979, the Soviet reader discovered Protocols of the Elders of Zion — not the apocryphal and "police and hysterical" *ones* but fact-checked and fictionally arranged.

The writings of V. Pikul, V. Kochetov, I. Shevtsov, and the opinion writers of "Oktyabr," "Molodaya Gvardiya," and "Kuban" in 1968–1985 prepared and fertilized the soil for the birth of monarcho-chauvinistic ideology of the "Pamyat" society, whose founding document was the article "Russophobia" by an academician in mathematics, the recent dissident, Igor Rostislavovich Shafarevich (1923-2017).[23]

Shafarevich brilliantly (which was uncommon among the ideologists of the Black Hundred and the "denouncers" of the white emigrant elite of the past), suggested a new solution to an old problem, based on the criticism of the "liberal, and cultural intelligentsia" movement, whose vanguard, in his opinion, was the "third wave" of emigration.

Through introducing the Soviet public to the previously unknown names and works of G. Pomerants, A. Amalrik, B. N. Shragin, A. Yanov, A. Sinyavsky, etc., and quoting the equally unfamiliar thinkers of the past (the Frenchman Augustin-Louis Cauchy, the German Max Weber, the Russian L. Tikhomirov, the Jew L. Pinsky) Shafarevich tried to achieve an effect of surprising novelty and independence of thought.

And a "cosmogonic" scope of his contemplations, illustrated by the Bible, philosophy, literature, history, and politology was supposed to give his work fundamental and conclusive character.

The Soviet reader, unfamiliar with the vast anti-Semitic literature of the beginning of the century (let alone foreign), obviously, would not catch the modernized *compilation* of the academician: the fight between the "Minor" and the "Major" peoples could be accepted as quite plausible and applicable to the processes happening in Russia.

However, if one compares the texts, the logic of Shafarevich's "Russophobia" and that of the works of "Russian patriots" turn out to complement each other.

Moreover, the *indirect* and, thus, obscure but obvious *similarity* of the concepts of Shafarevich and his forgotten colleagues deprive "Russophobia" of any claim to independence of thought.

Mathematically speaking, in his theorem the rules for proving Jews' guilt are the same, the only difference is the "space-time images" ("Yiddo-Masonic-intelligentsia conspiracy" — the conspiracy of the "Minor people" that includes Jews and the intelligentsia).

I. R. Shafarevich
(1923–2017)

Without touching upon the *criticism* of Shavarevich's choice of works of the authors of the "third wave" (the choice of mostly Jews speaks for itself), let us try to expose the mathematician's indirect logic and find its sources. In other words, we are interested in the "positive views" of the author and not in his polemics.

First of all, we should mention a certain idealization by Shafarevich of the history of his people. However, this is probably the nature of all nationalists. We can't either fault or praise a man for his love for his homeland. Yet, idealizations vary; some appear as exaggeration of certain positive things, others — as underestimation of the importance of drawbacks.

Asserting that the term "autocrat" did not at all mean "recognizing one's right to abuse of power and irresponsibility, but only expressed one's sovereignty and the fact that one did not pay tribute to anyone (specifically, to a khan)," Shafarevich mixed genetic phenomena with ontological ones. Although, he himself introduces a negative attitude towards the "term":

"An outstanding example of disapproval of a Tsar is the evaluation of Ivan the Terrible, and not only in chronicles, but also in folk tales... Peter I was called an anti-Christ among common folk precisely because of his willfulness which was seen by opposition as anti-traditional and anti-Christian.

"That is why the term "autocrat" as applied to Peter the Great did mean "abuse of power" (compare it to a religious term 'lawlessness' that defines the Antichrist)."

As contradictory is the thesis of the concept of "the Third Rome" ("Russia remained the only Orthodox Tsardom... the Tsardom of Russia will stand forever if it remains true to Orthodoxy"): "This theory did not possess any political aspect; it did not push anyone to any kind of expansion or to Orthodox missionary work. In people's minds (for example, in folklore) it was not reflected in any way."

Firstly, after the Council of Florence and the fall of Constantinople Russia, indeed, was the *only sovereign* Orthodox tsardom (although Orthodoxy still existed in Bulgaria and Macedonia).

Secondly, the fall of Rome and the fall of Byzantium ("the Second Rome") were caused not at all by their rejection of the "true faith" (Christianity spread throughout the Western Roman Empire during its agony, and in the Eastern part, Orthodoxy was the official religion; and the fall of Constantinople was not caused by religious reasons, either, which "Elder" Philotheus of Pskov understood very well). The strengthening of the Moscow Rus' at the time of Ivan III could not but give rise to allusions (and illusions).

For the monk from Pskov, the formula "Moscow is the Third Rome, and there shall be no fourth" (this is the formula in its entirety) carried a dual meaning. Equaling Moscow to Rome and Constantinople, Philotheus exaggerated the greatness of the Russian state; the Moscow Rus' at the time was neither an empire, nor "Russia" in the modern sense — from the Bug to Kolyma.

In size and population, the Polish-Lithuanian Kingdom was not inferior to the Tsardom of Moscow. On the other hand, the heresy of Judaizers and the associations with "the end of time" caused by them, defined the eschatological meaning of "the Third Rome"; after the victory of heretics and a short reign of "the sons of the Devil," in Philotheus's opinion, the eternal Kingdom of God was to come in which no Rome, no Byzantium, and no Moscow would exist and, consequently, the fourth *Rome* (apocalyptical) could not be.

Shafarevich simply passed over in silence the folklore, because "Moscow Centrism" ("The world, we know, begins at the Kremlin," etc.) was a well-known phenomenon in the XVII–XX centuries.

As contradictory is another thesis of the mathematician: "We can't find among Russians any specific hatred towards foreigners and foreign influence that would make Russians different from any other people.

"The fear for the purity of their faith was strong, as was suspicion of Protestant and Catholic missionary work.

"Here we can observe certain religious intolerance, but this feature does not at all make Russia of the time different from the West, whose level of religious intolerance was characterized by the Inquisition, St. Bartholomew's Day massacre, and the Thirty Years' War."

Of course, mentioning "specific hatred" (and why not "specific love"?) was necessary for the following reasoning on *Judaic hatred of Christians* (=religious intolerance), or, more precisely, according to Shafarevich, on Jewish hatred of Russians (=ethnic intolerance).

Patriotic euphemisms ("fear," "suspicion") are understandable. It seems that this thesis of Shafarevich by itself, in this limited historical form — limited to the time of the Schism which is compared to the Huguenot and other wars, is a consequence of the choice of a "point of view" according to which the Russian people (historically and ontologically) possessed the same moral and ethical virtues (a very fair thought) as *everybody else* (with the exception of Jews, of course):

"To limit pre-revolutionary Russia to Ivan the Terrible and Peter the Great is a simplification that completely distorts the picture (and what about limiting Jewish history to Biblical wars and massacres? — S.D.). Such a set of picked-out facts cannot prove anything." Let us agree with this, as well as with the author's insistence that "these arguments are borrowed."

Other arguments are: disproving feature of "slave submission" assigned to the Russian people as compared to... the English who had accepted the "brand new denomination" imposed by Henry VIII; affirming free-thinking of the Russian people shown by the fact that "secondary... changes in rituals introduced by the authorities were rejected by the majority of the nation... the problem has not lost its acuteness in 300 years"; disproving the "typical Russian" submission of the church to the state, since all forms of "unanimous obedience" (a term of A. Shragin) that appeared in Protestant countries were "precisely copied by Peter I"; disproving the Russian origin of the concept of a totalitarian state that "subordinates not only the economic and political activity of its subjects, but also their intellectual and spiritual life," because this concept was "wholly developed in the West"; disproving the claim that "messianism" ("a very old phenomenon") originated in Russia, since a *recent* and "very thorough research of this tradition... mentioned Russia only... in connection with the fact that western "revolutionary messianism" by the end of the century flooded Russia"; disproving the thesis of "predestination of a revolution in Russia," since "socialism was introduced into Russia entirely from the West."

In fact, Shafarevich's "disprovings" are a sort of *accusations* of "sin"... (according to N. Ya. Danilevsky ("Europeanizing is a disease of Russian life"), aimed at the West and, of course, at his Russian brothers (from Peter I to Bakunin and Herzen). [24]

Shafarevich makes claims against opponents *he picked himself*: "Russian history is considered by *our authors* (my italics — S.D.) exclusively from the point of view of the modern mind while entirely ignoring the demands of *historicism*."

Well, let us agree with the mathematician's position while paying attention to the well-known, or even *imitative*, "historicism" of Shafarevich himself.

Upon getting familiar with his work, one first of all notices an odd — considering the academician's "historicism" — choice of authoritative (=positive) names and... someone anonymous (the author of the "recent very thorough research" of messianism): Dostoyevsky, Vl. Solovyov, Tikhomirov, Augustin Cauchy [25], Max Weber, and the authors he denounces: Hobbes, Saint-Simon, Fourier, Ruge, Heine, Saltykov-Shchedrin, Byalik, Martov.

The "strangeness" of the choice of "prophets" and "enemies of the human race" immediately disappears, once the reader begins to realize that the academician (who must have experienced much fear in his dissident times) was afraid to name (and reference) in his *Russophobia* the author of the "very thorough research" of the traditions of "revolutionary messianism" — G. Bostunitsch [26].

The point is not only that the logic of proving (as well as certain examples) of maliciousness of the "minor people" (i.e., Jews) was borrowed by Shafarevich, but that the *entire camouflaging polemics with modern 'russophobes" was necessary to inject Russian patriotic circles* (not yet participating in the "Pamyat" society) *with* The Protocols of the Elders of Zion.

The "conspiracy" of Shafarevich's mindset is algebraic and that is why he uses "professional" devices he is familiar with. Let us list some of them.

This is a method of substitution of some terms (names, titles, situations, etc.) for others. If Shafarevich, referring to Cauchy, begins to talk about Calvinism in England in the XVI–XVII centuries and blame the Puritans (in their ideology we recognize the "familiar features of the "Minor people" ... even before the Creation, God predestined some people to be saved and others to perish eternally"), he needs this only to be able to say in conclusion:

"And indeed, Puritans called for a total do-over of the world... And, according to a plan known to them in advance. The call to 'build on a new foundation' was reinforced by the familiar to us concept of 'building a Temple,' in this case, the restoration of the Temple of Jerusalem after the return of the Jews from captivity... the real role of Calvinism... was in the fact that... the new group of the rich managed to overthrow traditional monarchy that had before the support of the majority of the people."

It is sufficient to compare this to the thoughts of Bostunitsch on the "Yiddo-masonic conspiracy" that was the "bane of humanity" in England ("It was them who, through the fanatic Cromwell, organized the English revolution of 1648, and as a result the Jews received equal rights in England and made the country their base for further Jewish advance..."), and on the fourth stage of conquering the world by the "symbolic Serpent": "... I believe that 1648...London, when the fanatic Cromwell (who, by the way, was a freemason himself) for the sake of his Puritan ideals did not hesitate to become a political hireling... of France, and a masonic hireling of Yids... and to send Charles Stuart, the King of England, to the block...," to recognize Bostunitsch's "masons" and "Yids" as Shafarevich's "Puritans" and "Calvinists."

These are the methods of multiple cross-referencing. Bostunitsch finished his study on an optimistic note, quoting not only the Gospel "Whoever is not with Me is against me" (like his enemies/brothers in the Soviet Union) but also Minin's word from the drama chronicle by A. N. Ostrovsky "Minin and Pozharsky" ("truely said the poet"):

> We must prepare first ourselves:
> To clean our minds with sweat,
> With fasting strengthen our will to act
> And pray to our speedy Helper;
> He gives us power of the mind and words...
> . . . .
> Then we shall go wake our sleeping brethren
> And with the word of God inspire their hearts.

Tears and repentance will revive us and our great homeland." Of course, a modern scholar, unlike a "recent" one, had to quote not the drama chronicle of Ostrovsky, but a Soviet author (secondary, but still "of Jews"), who aspires to lead people's opinion.

The "anti-patriotic" mood, as shown by a poem by A. Bezymensky from 1920s, in Shafarevich's opinion, "saturated literature as well":

> I suggest
> We melt Minin down
> And Pozharsky,
> Why do they need a pedestal?
> . . . .
> Look at them,
> the saviors of Russia!
> It might've been better to just let it fall.

This is the method of a "matrix" (adding "new" parameters, discovered at a later time, to the ones already "known"). Bostunitsch wrote about a typical Jews' striving "for extremes in everything, beginning with politics maximalism of terrorists before the revolution and of the chekists after), through literature (idiocy of futurism of Lifshits and others), art (cubism), and even more so, the perversion of the foundation of all: the religion of the Living God — into most disgusting satanism...," and Shafarevich "added" to this list of "idiocies" (from his own time):

"Our descendants will be unable to comprehend the influence of Freud as a scientist, the fame of Schoenberg as a composer, of Picasso as an artist, of Kafka as an author, and of Brodsky as a poet." However, he forgot that his "multitude" that is called the "Minor people" had to include not only Jews (Freud, Kafka, Brodsky) but also the intelligentsia of other ethnicities (Schoenberg, Picasso).

This is the method of "linear and spatial intersections." When Shafarevich points out the "evil" part of the "Minor people" in the case of *"final destruction of religious and ethnic foundations of life,"* he stresses that the literature of the "Minor people" is not a result of "an objective work of the mind" or an appeal to "life experience and logic."

To prove that, the author of *Russophobia* requires us to realize that this kind of literature "implies... colossal... concentration of social attention on certain events or people: from the Calas affair, when monstrous injustice of the sentence, denounced by Voltaire, astounded Europe (although the historians say there was no judicial mistake made), to the cases of Dreyfus or of Beilis."

Connecting a Christian trial (the Calas case), a treason charge (the Dreyfus case), and a "blood libel" (the Beilis case), Shafarevich pronounces his sentence:

"That is why we simply cannot allow... our desire to comprehend our national path to be stomped out, spitted on, and be pushed in the direction of clamorous journalist polemics."

Logical connection between the "destructive actions" of Jews (their crimes against faith, society, and person) and the role of the press ("journalist polemics") in their defense (the cases of Dreyfus and Beilis) has been borrowed from the paragraphs of *The Protocols of the Elders of Zion*, and the "corpus delicti" is presented according to Bostunitsch and his "desire to comprehend the national path':

"Cruelty and sadism are in the blood of the Yid tribe... *in the court records* of the West we also constantly stumble upon *court-proved* (italics by Bostunitsch — S.D.) cases of Yid sadism...

Now, when truth seekers have collected mountains of astounding proof... it would be naive to argue the existence of ritual murder at all...

The most recent case (that of Beilis — S.D.) is especially convincing and should take the veil off the minds of Judeophiles. For *the Yid press* abroad during the process has printed literally the following... 'The Russian government decided to declare war on the Yids in Russia... '".

Long before Shafarevich, the future *Obersturmfuehrer* warned: while Yids consider "the case of every Beilis their personal business, they all together and each one separately are morally responsible, and, once Russia is restored, will be responsible legally..."

This "mathematical" methodology of using the works of his predecessors would be incomplete if it didn't include various "interpolations," "overlaps," "combinations," etc.

We shall not speak of the Jews' "fateful role" that is tied to their belief in the "chosen people" and "its destiny to rule the world." The author of *Russophobia* was neither the first nor the last to repeat the formula of Butmi, Nilus, Bostunitsch, and suchlike.

Noting that "these were people of Jewish origin that made up the nucleus... of 'the Minor people,'" our author decided to prove their "eternal hatred" and "bloodthirst" with the examples he *found* in Bostunitsch's works:

"Well known are the sayings from Talmud and its commentary that... an infidel (*akum*) [27] could not be considered human..."

Let's go back to Bostunitsch: "As time went by, the Yid mass has become completely set in their rituals... the form ultimately killed the content, with the exception of those human-hating rules like: "Kill even the best of the goyim!" as Mekhilta says in *The Book of Zohar* (III, 14,3)."

We will not attempt to prove that *Zohar* has nothing to do either with Talmud or with its commentary, and the permission to kill an idolater *refers to a Jew, and only a Jew who became a pagan and an idolater* (compare: "The sons of Israel are idolaters outside their country").

"Applying" "Mekhilta's" formula to "goyim" (infidels/non-Jews) anti-Semitists, indeed, engaged in "profanation of metaphysical enthusiasm" or, as Shavfarevich writes, "substituting one thought with another." That is why he needed that word "akum" instead of Bostunitsch's "goy" to hide the source of his knowledge of Talmud.

Quoting Cauchy, Weber, and Samuel Lurie, as well as the anti-Soviet and anti-Zionist digest *Russia and the Jew* (of course, without mentioning the authors with non-Russian last names) Shafarevich did not think it necessary to refer to his main teacher and "informant," and not at all because of "interpolations" and "reworking" of someone else's ideas, but out of the *"humble"* quality of his discovery that he conceals from the unenlightened reader. That is probably why, against any scholarly ethics, the honorable academician presents his *plagiarism* as his own "knowledge," "conscience," and "study":

Chapter 6. The Soviet Version of Anti-Semitism

"For thousands of years, every year at Purim, Jews have celebrated killing 75,000 of their enemies... One can only imagine the impression such upbringing could leave in one's soul..."

Had Shafarevich peeked into the *Book of Esther*, he, to his joy, would have found many more victims of vengeful Jews, for it is said: "The Jews struck down all their enemies...

In the citadel of Susa, the Jews killed and destroyed five hundred men... the ten sons of Haman son of Hammedatha, the enemy of the Jews. But they did not lay their hands on the plunder... and they impaled the ten sons of Haman... and they put to death in Susa three hundred men, but they did not lay their hands on the plunder.

Meanwhile, the remainder of the Jews... killed seventy-five thousand of them but did not lay their hands on the plunder." (Esther 9:5–16). It is easy to calculate that Hebrews killed about 76,000.

Of course, Shafarevich, while profiting from "accuracy" would have lost in "quality": the number 75,900 of "their enemies" *did not include*, as the academician insisted, "women and children," unless, of course, one does not consider the "ten sons of Haman." However, it is unclear whether those sons were *children or adults*! This "detail" only underlines the fact that Shafarevich learned about the "bloodthirst" of Jews not from the *Book of Esther*, but from a "recent study" by Bostunitsch: "Revenge on a fallen and restrained enemy is a defining feature of this tribe. Their entire history speaks to it. The famous holiday of "Purim" (Shafarevich, as well as Bostunitsch, puts the name of the holiday in quotation marks, although they probably would not do the same with Easter — S.D.) ... is a mass celebration of the pogrom of defenseless Persians that this valiant nation executed. N. N. Pankhrai, a Jewish "*Wachtmeister* by upbringing and a pogrom maker by conviction" ... says that "all over the country Jews struck down 75.000 (note that there's a dot after "75," which to the mathematician Shafarevich should have had a different meaning and yet he kept it — S.D.) people and the ten sons of Haman were impaled."

The meaning of the holiday aside (the author of the "Public Letter to I. R. Shafarevich" B. Kushner was right: "On May 9, we celebrate not the deaths of millions of Germans..."), we should remember *Russian* chronicles: "And the Drevlians sent their best men, twenty in number, in a longship to Olga... Olga ordered a great and deep pit in a courtyard outside the city... And they were carried in the longship... And they were delivered to Olga and as they were in the longship, they were thrown into the pit... And she ordered them to be buried alive; and they were buried... And Olga sent for the Drevlians... the Drevlians picked the best men... and sent for her... Olga ordered the sauna to be prepared... And the sauna was prepared, and the Drevlians entered it... and the door was locked behind them and Olga ordered to set it on fire at the door, and all perished. And she sent for the Drevlians... Upon hearing this, they brought together many meads and boiled them... Then the Drevlians sat down to drink and Olga ordered her youths to serve on them... And when the Drevlians were drunk... she stepped aside and ordered her *druzhina* to cut down the Drevlians and five thousand were slain... The Drevlians... gathered three doves and three sparrows from every household and sent them to bow to Olga... And when it started to get dark, Olga ordered her warriors to release the doves and the sparrows... and so burned... at once, every house burned... And so, she took the city and burned it, and the city elders she took prisoner and others she killed..." [28]

The number of the victims of Olga's revenge for *only one man, her husband, killed by the Drevlians,* (20 plus 5,000 plus the residents of the city), apparently, is not as great as the number of the Persians killed. But what would the Russian people say if in the XX century they were blamed for Olga's actions at the time when Olga was not yet *baptized* (and, consequently, did not yet know about the "abominations" of the Old testament)?

Shafarevich, realizing the flimsiness of the accusation, chose to refer to modern examples of Jewish "bloodthirst": "More obvious testimonies can be found in literature. For example, "salutary hatred" is widespread in poems of the Jewish poet Hayim Bialik who lived in Russia... he wrote:

> Out of the abyss of Abaddon bring forth the song of Destruction,
> The song that is as black from the fire as your spirit,
> And spread among peoples, and everything in their damned house
> Poison with suffocating smoke;
> And everyone shall sow the seeds of decay in their fields
> Everywhere he goes and stands.
> If you but touch the purest lily in their garden,
> It will blacken and wilt.

...Often, we hear the following argument: many acts and feelings of Jews can be understood, if we remember how much they went through. For example, some poems of Bialik were written under the influence of a pogrom."

Firstly, Shafarevich quotes not a "poem" (as a whole work) but bits and pieces of... *various* poems by the Jewish author. Secondly, the first quote ("And that is why I locked inside your throat..."), indeed, comes from *The Tale of the Pogrom*, whereas the second one ("Out of the abyss of Abaddon bring forth the song of Destruction...") comes from the poem *The Scroll of Fire*. In it, as Bostunitsch noted, "is described how, after the destruction of the Second Jerusalem Temple, tribal chiefs do not repent but maliciously rebel against Adonai," and then pointed out: "Especially characteristic is a piece of advice of someone called The Terrible to twelve youths and maidens who wander the face of the Earth after the destruction of the temple," and quoted: "Out of the abyss of Abaddon..."

Shafarevich omitted the following lines of the quote he copied from Bostunitsch:

"And if your gaze should fall on the marble of their statues,
Those will crack in two;
And bring with you the bitter, cursed laughter
To kill everything that lives..."

The academician must have sensed that the second line was missing two feet and the quote could be inaccurate. Besides, the "source" followed the quote with a too drastic conclusion:

"This is their program, in the words of their bard: to kill everything that lives!"

This is a conclusion that does not at all match the quote, and Shafarevich could not but abridge the quote and keep quiet about... the source of his knowledge of Jewish poetry.

Attentive reading of Shafarevich's *Russophobia* and Bostunitsch's *Freemasonry* allows us to mark many "parallel" places that give us the opportunity to formulate the true goal and task of the author as a fighter against the "Minor people": *to adapt an old, compromised theory to a new situation.*

For this purpose, he had to pick opponents with Jewish (Yanov, Shragin) or Jewish-like last names (Sinyavsky, Abram Terz, R. Pipes) and "anti-Russian" (or, rather, anti-imperial) ideas, from modern literature, to restock his "testimonies" (Eduard Bagritsky, David Markish, Igor Guberman, Nina Voronel, et al.), and to present the ideology of the "Yiddo-Masonic conspiracy" to "conquer the world."

Indirectly polemicizing with Bostunitsch, Shafarevich corrected the "overly general formulas" of the *Obersturmfuehrer* (compare: "This entire revolution is a Yid business"/ "The revolution was not made by Jews only"), but kept the principal structure of Jews' ("the newcomers") "hatred" to everything Russian ("original") and the love of "patriots" for the "pre-revolutionary" (monarchic) rule.

Borrowing facts and ideas from Bostunitsch (Peter the Great's syphilis, Jewish-Latvian dictatorship, the "role" of Sh. Rappoport, the characteristic of Herzen, Ruge, and Witte; Schiff's dependence on the American company "G. Leb & Co.") and transforming the "setups" (the assassination of Plehve, of the Grand Duke Sergei Alexandrovich and of the royal family, Jews' participation in the revolutionary movement, the membership of VCIK, Politburo, and ChK, the "chooseness" of Jews and the principle of "self-defense" from them, etc.), Shafarevich found himself in a vicious circle of "ready word combinations."

In fact, a mathematician should have realized that any reasoning based on *The Protocols of the Elders of Zion* (no matter how patriotic its goals and well-meaning its purposes) presented elements of "spurious infinity," since any separate occurrence reflected the conceptual whole of the "Yiddo-Masonic conspiracy."

At the same time, it is Shafarevich's *Russophobia* that is the last link in the literary history of *The Protocols of the Elders of Zion*, and this leads to the conclusion that in a hundred years of anti-Semitic popular fiction in Russia *zealots and patriots could not bring anything original or innovative into the ideas and topics of the political and messianic concept of "Holy Rus'."*

Moreover, the collapse of the Soviet empire and the rejection of the state practice of "pan-Slavism," with concentrating on specifically *national* issues and *national* spiritual development, dooms the myths of the "Yiddo— Masonic conspiracy," the "Minor people," "malevolence" of other ethnicities (for example, Latvians or the Chinese), and "anti-patriotism" of the *intelligentsia* outside of ethnic features, to *degradation and degeneration.*

And although Shafarevich's work appeared ten years after G. Klimov's novel [29], many of the theses of *Russophobia* seem like a "reverse translation" of the ideas of *Prince of This World*.

Super-serious and globally learned work by the Soviet academician, not counting his plagiarism from Bostunitsch, may seem just a reworked version of a *parody by G. Klimov*, tragically joyful and openly mocking towards anthologies about the "Minor people," where he "describes a sort of a complex social disease which used to be called the devil and now is called degeneration":

"In the thematic catalogue there are hundreds upon hundreds of card entries for "degeneration" that refer to the two main parts of this complex: psychiatric disorders and sexual perversions...

But the most important was the fact that this largest library in America did not hold a single book that would describe degeneration as a whole. There are psychiatric disorders and there are sexual perversions, but the degeneration that consists of these two parts, that degeneration... is not there!

There is no key! And without this key you would understand nothing in this field."

In the foreword to Klimov's novel (on the endpaper of the 1980 edition, either from *Globus Publishers* or from the author) the reader is forewarned: "Although *Prince of This World* is just a novel, this book is meant for adults only. In legal medical literature on this subject there is also usually the following warning:

'For legal and medical professionals only, for clerics and teachers, as well as professionals in the fields of psychology and sociology'."

Then Klimov, according to a standard of antisemitic popular fiction, "aspires" to be "scholarly" due to "specific features of this book that requires special research and the author's archives."

After the epigraph, taken, naturally, from the *Apocalypse*, follows the "Introduction by the professor of modern Soviet literature of Stanford University," of course, a "PhD" and, naturally, "Russian," S. P. Novikov.

Finally, the "Afterword" of the book is by another professor and PhD (this time not in literature but in social psychology) from another non-existent American university. Moreover, the foreword and afterword have author's titles: "Forbidden Fruit" and "Poison Keys"; the "fruit" is idiomatically connected to "sweetness," so the epigraph to it should be "bitter": "...but you must not eat from the tree... for... you will certainly die," but for the "poison keys" Klimov found "sweet words": "But God knows... you will be like God..."

(The plot of the novel is built on the "parallelism" of the lives of two brothers: the older, Maxim Alexandrovich Rudnev, who was born before the revolution and made an astounding career from a GPU agent to an all-powerful "red cardinal"; and the younger, Boris, who was born after the revolution and remained near his brother either as an "inspector" or as a "curious professor" to his brother.)

The foreword by S. P. Novikov is a "calling card" of Klimov's parody.

Having mentioned the editor of the Argentinian paper "Our Country," Dubrovsky (could he be an illegitimate son of the founder of the Union of the Russian People Dr. Dubrovin [?] — *S.D.*) and the bravest editor of "Russian Life" (San Francisco), Delianich (*almost Delevsky and Bostunitsch* — *S.D.*), who insisted that such a novel "had never before been printed," the professor notes:

"I checked the catalogue of the Library of Congress in Washington... There is not a single book on the topic of 'the Prince' there."

This "novelty" of the topic (can the last name Novikov come from the word "novelty"?) made the professor to "closely study the origin of this book and its author." The "reviewer" could not keep up with either a biography of a literary historical narration and revealed a secret: "Klimov was at the head of one of... special projects...

He was the president of the Central Union of Post-War Emigrants (TsOPE) and editor-in-chief of the magazine "Svoboda" in Russian and the magazine "Anti-Communist" in German... In 1955, Klimov moved to America and returned to his occupation of electrical engineering.

At the same time... he creatively transforms his vast experience in the area of psychological warfare...

In the American books that analyze the work of the CIA, they write that in professional jargon... such work is divided into "black magic" and "white magic," with "grey magic" suspended in between.

The US propaganda is divided in the same way... These, apparently, were the affairs that the Harvard Project dealt with. In every serious scientific institution... if one team of scientists works on a project, another team of scientists... simultaneously works on a counter-project...

Klimov's novel was such a counter-project..."

As an example of the efficiency of the "counter-project" Professor Novikov tells the story of the arrest in the USSR of an American citizen, one Barghorn, "soon after the *Prince*'s walk-through publishing houses and official channels," since the most effective way to pass something on to the Soviet intelligence was to send a good material through Western intelligence agencies."

Klimov's "counterproject," "according to Novikov," was based on secret archives of the Soviet secret police or on the once of "some American super-intelligence agency." That is why there "were so many legends" around Klimov's book.

Their "assortment" is remarkable: "Some say that this book was not written by Klimov (sounds like Nilus's version — S.D.), but by a full team of Jesuits (almost like Samarin on *The Polish Catechism* — S.D.) ...

Some say the opposite: that the *Prince* deserves to be placed in the *Index Librorum Prohibitorum* (compare to: the reaction of the Orthodox church to Nilus's "work." — S.D.) ...

There are many guesses. Some pessimists even express a concern that, if there wasn't one before... there absolutely must be one now." To appreciate the "counter project" it is sufficient to remem-

Chapter 6. The Soviet Version of Anti-Semitism

ber Bostunitsch's statement that had *The Protocols* not existed, they should have been made up, since the events around us testified to their authenticity.

But the most important thing is not even the self-denunciations (undoubtedly, the "author" and the "reviewer" are the same person) or the parody nature of the foreword (and of the novel), but the *conscious absurdization* of all the "guilty" verdicts of *The Protocols*, which make Klimov's book a "counter project" to the writings of Pikul, Kochetov, Shevtsov, Kuzmin, et al: "The matter is, although this novel is about Soviet life, the divide is not along the line of communism/capitalism, but much deeper: along the line of that good and evil, which in the end, from the point of view of religious philosophy, are called God and the devil." In fact, combining the two hostile super-states into one whole, the "reviewer" dots the "I's," while nearly quoting Nilus and Bostunitsch: "Talking about the devil and the truth... they note that the truth about the devil is such a filthy thing that a single drop of it clouds a life... they say that the devil is only dangerous when we do not see him... that he is Nobody and Nothing..."

That is why the foreword ends "magically": "Would you like to have such a crystal ball to know the future? and to avoid such a future. Well, I will give you a way... Based on the reader's reaction to the *Prince*, you can see right away who they are. Some read it with great interest... Others grimace in disgust and run from it like hell... So, this is a tried-and-true method." And following the "methodology," he gives the statistics of "the enemies of the human race": "legionnaires" (from the Gospel idiom "his name is legion," which is a synonym to the name of the devil) based on... *The Protocols*, the "scholarly works" of E. Brant and G. Bostunitsch, and the "self-published" reasonings of the future "zealots" of "Pamyat."

Novikov's foreword is closely followed in its parody nature by B. V. Sakharov's afterword. The Woodhaven professor lays out the foundational ideas of the *Prince of This World* (i.e., *The Protocols*) in a "nomenclature and hierarchical" thesaurus: from mad rulers to "odd people": "To understand the mystery of Stalin and Hitler... we need to be familiar with the so-called "power complex" that creates the so-called "natural-born leader" ...

Here lies a paradox: a natural-born leader is a person least suitable for power.

It is this paradox that is the cause of almost all wars and revolutions in human history... The subject of the *Prince* is a very contradictory one...

Like Cain and Abel, one of the first victims ...of the cleansing was Abel Yenukidze... in the "Pravda" issue of 13 June 1935...

In the book by an American lawyer... are described thirteen historical processes... What a strange concentration of the number 13?

Dr. Kinsey's statistics give a partial answer:

"Every 13th American... at least for three years... was a pure homosexual" ... Of course, we must stress that NKVD had other departments besides the 13th... In Donald Corey's *Homosexuals in America,* it says that "after the Russian revolution all laws against homosexuals were abolished" ...

By the way... through the history of Christian civilization, the laws against homosexuals were abolished for the first time as a result of the French revolution. Hm, what a weird connection between revolutions and gays. (Academician Shafarevich in his *Russophobia* seemed to have tried to give an answer to this by discovering a unit of evil equal to one "Minor people." — S.D.)

So... 4% of pure homos are much more benign than 33% of secret or partial homos...

To this camouflaged category belonged comrades Lenin, Trotsky, and Stalin.

We can add Marx and Hitler... Both Lenin's and Hitler's marriages were childless. Marx, Trotsky, and Stalin carried an entire series of suicides and grave mental disorders... in their families...

Here is the paradox... an expanding legion of 37–50–75%." By dividing the world into the mad (less dangerous, since they are locked in mental asylums) and the mentally ill who are "unrecognized subjects" among healthy population, and by dividing the latter category into open and closeted (most dangerous) homosexuals, the American professor points out that the statue of Liberty, as well as American democracy, is a gift from some secret French societies." (The analyzed popular fiction calls these societies masonic and their members, according to Klimov, Novikov, and Sakharov's definition, are latent homosexuals — S.D.)

Then, leaning on either Jewish-American or Euro-American (Sakharov does not specify) data and referring to Nilus's, Shabelskaya's, Bostunitsch's, etc., favorite number of "enemies" of ⅓ of the population (according to the Revelation), the Woodhaven professor uses the "Biblical keys of knowledge": "This is where lies the terrible apocalyptic secret scripture...

If you believe certain clever institutions... in the press the number of these legionnaires, candidates, fellow-travelers, and sympathizers...

will be... all of 75%. And in a good civilized society this is the ruling party (Mr. Shafarevich, the "Minor people" were given demographic characteristics by the professor of sociology B. V. Sakharov, and not by you! — *S.D.*) ...

Should I be accused of repeating myself, I do it on purpose. *Repetitio est mater studiorum.* We are not here to read novels but to talk about the most difficult science in the world: the higher sociology, God and the devil, Christ and the Antichrist, the sources of good and evil, happiness and misery, life and death..."

The "thesaurus pyramid" of power, according to Klimov (and his interpreting professors), looks like this: at the top are "natural-born leaders," i.e. 100% latent homosexuals among the mentally ill; below are heads and executors of "clever institutions"; then, "legionaries" of science, jurisprudence, press, the "intelligentsia" of artistic world ("clever blotters" like Picasso, the apostles of the 13th department of the KGB: the "Jewlings" Lombroso, Nordau, Freud, Kierkegaard, poet-futurists, modernists, etc.), members of "secret French societies" (masons); and only then, red-headed statesmen (sadists and masochists), and, finally, Hershels, Yagodas, Yankels, Sverdlovs, and other organizers of "Zionist conspiracies."

Of course, the fact that at any level of the pyramid one can find an open or latent "Jerusalem noble" allows one to state that: "The smartest book of the world is the Bible... And the smartest book of the Bible is ... the Revelation... And in the Revelation, it is said twice that one third of humans will be destroyed for their various sins."

Consequently, "humanists," "Satanists," "Zionists," etc., make up this one third. As Comrade Lenin, a known "natural-born leader" with a splash of Jewish blood and a potential latent homosexuality (according to Klimov) to boot, said, *to work,* comrades! And let your name be Legion...

CONCLUSION

In his work the author strived to demonstrate the genesis of political myth in literature related to religious and historical comprehension of "secret societies," dialectics of revolutionary movements and organizations, and changing forms of government, and reflected in a *special form* of popular fiction and opinion writing aimed at the issue of coexistence of native ethnicities of the Russian Empire and the "exile people" within the same society.

In Russia, ant-Semitic literature was based on Gospel mythology and had as its social and historical sources the Poles' fight for national independence and the Westland Jews' goal of *international* distinctness, with the latter supporting the unity of the empire; these two trends were aimed in different directions.

The "betrayal" of Poland and "loyalty of Jews" of the Russian Empire in the war of 1812 was a most important originating condition of the transformation of the myth of Jewish "malevolence," and the spreading of masonic lodges in the Catholic circles of the Kingdom of Poland and penetration of masonic ideas into Russia (especially post-1812) with the following diffusion of "revolutionary" ideas of the Decembrists, asserted dominant influence on the joining of Gospel mythologems and masonic liberation trends in 1830s-1850s.

Meanwhile, the geopolitical transformations in Europe in 1830s-1850s and the process of shaping of the "Middle Empire" (Germany) with Prussia at its head, based on the idea of "pan-Germanism" that contained the controversy of "pan-Slavism," in the real historical and social situation, became the generating conditions for the myth of the opposition of one social and ethnic formation to the rest of the world, whose real counteragents, at first, were the competing states.

The formation of "pan-Slavism" that found its expression in the concept of "Russia and Europe" (the late 1860s), the change in the geopolitical relations between the Russian Empire and France and Germany, Russia's defeat in the Crimean War and the unprofitable

CONCLUSION

end of the Balkan War (1877–1878), affected the evolution of myth creation as well as the international alliance of anti-Russian forces: Yiddo-masonry that used to be an *internal* enemy, in the situation of developing revolutionary movement, was transformed by the ideologist of pan-Slavism into an *external* enemy.

This complex image of the "enemy" (revolutionary movement internally and the geopolitics of hostile states externally) in 1870s-1890s, together with the already formed "Yiddo-masonic" mythologem posing as "internationalism," became the final stage of the appearance of a strictly Russian nationalistic myth of a "global Jewish conspiracy," and, as a result, the Russian Department of Police produced certain "anti-state directive documents," a.k.a. *The Protocols of the Elders of Zion*.

The revolutionary situation in Russia made the police "developers" of the "guilty" verdict to the "Yiddo-masonic conspiracy" deploy the documents they had "confiscated from the enemy": the newspaper version (Krushevan/Butmi) was offered to the general reader and the book one (Nilus) — to the Emperor's court.

However, the efficiency of this ideological bomb was low: Stolypin's investigation and the indignation of Russia's liberal democratic circles nullified the police's efforts. The First World War and the Revolution of 1917, and Russian Civil War that followed it, refreshed the "stale ideas": on the one hand, *The Protocols,* in the hands of the defeated White emigrants, became a killer commentary to the Bolshevik coup and the following terror, on the other, the banner of "Yiddo-masonic threat" gathered together all the adventurers who sought their fate in the "corridors of power."

The main consumers of the "global conspiracy," as a hundred years before, were the ideologists of pan-Germanism and pan-Slavism. This fact allowed Mikhail Agursky to write a book with an eloquent title, *Ideology of National Bolshevism* (YMCA-PRESS, Paris, 1980).

The tragedy of the Jewish people that took six million lives, the devastation of the post-war years and the Soviet expansion that led to formation of a socialist camp in Eastern Europe, should have been able to denounce the myth of Jews as "conquerors of global domination."

Yet, founding of the Israeli state in 1948 and its immediate confrontation with Islamic Arabs whose ideology was pan-Arabism, and the anti-Semitic campaign in the USSR, Poland, Czechoslovakia, Hungary, and Romania in 1949–1952, initiated by Stalin and his government, became the main reason for the modern revival of *The Protocols of the Elders of Zion*.

In the situation of a state-wide crisis in the USSR and the currently observable crash of this "evil empire" (while the European countries tend towards liberal democracy), the strengthening anti-Semitism (and anti-Zionism) keeps reproducing the same ideas, images, and "documents" of a century ago. In modern geopolitics, with the exception of the ideologists of the *Russian society* "Pamyat" who strive for the "Slavic unity" with Ukrainians and Byelorussians who have no intention to rub elbows with them anymore, the ideas of *The Protocols* found their only shelter in the Arabic world.

At the same time, an analysis of Russian anti-Semitic popular fiction of the XIX–XX centuries allows us to note the following: literature built upon mythological and ideological foundation of the fight of "one people against the rest" is doomed not only to redundancy of images and topics, but to the "bad infinity" of plots and storylines that reflect *general* "qualities and phenomena" in *every* element.

Exhausting of popular fiction options of describing inter-ethnic conflicts in the era of the "black-and-white" hostilities between the "natives" and the "aliens" inevitably leads to *epigonism and plagiarism.*

And, as any phenomenon that is brought to absurdity, anti-Semitic popular fiction experiences internal corrosion in one way or another. This is reflected in the birth of *parodies,* since a parody in its essence is meant to be the *sum total* of existence and the "gravedigger" of a historical literary phenomenon.

ADDENDUM

The Protocols of the Elders of Zion
Short Overview

The *Protocols of the Elders of Zion* (hereafter: *The Protocols*) is a literary forgery commissioned by the Russian secret police in the late nineteenth century in order to "prove" the existence of a Jewish conspiracy to attain global domination.

STRUCTURE AND CONTENT. Two versions of the Protocols are known. The more widespread is the adaptation of Sergei Nilus, promulgated in 1903. The second version orders the protocols differently and has other minor discrepancies; it was published by Georgy Butmi de Katzman in 1905.

Nilus designed his edition in the style of Christian Bible publications, intending to enhance the emotional effect of the text: the reader would encounter an anti-Gospel or Satanic Gospel. His edition contains twenty-four "protocols" of the allegedly real, clandestine meetings of Jewish representatives, who discuss a strategy for seizing power throughout the world. Their ultimate goal is to concentrate global control in the hands of a "King of Israel" from the line of David, to be appointed by three "Elders" (or "Sages"). This King would rule humankind autocratically; in the case of his death or serious illness, the Elders would transfer power to their next elect.

The first ten protocols delineate a program for the subversion of Christian states. The conspirators' plot envisions the following as effective means of bringing about social collapse: propagandizing democratic freedoms and human rights, bribing the press, implanting a cult of money, establishing monopolies while provoking economic wars, and encouraging the secret activities of the Freemasons. The conspirators call for whipping up the arms race, furthering the growth of armies and police forces, provoking wars between Gentile ("goyish") states, and promoting anarchy, permissiveness, and debauchery. Freemasons would be used as an unwitting tool of destruction, remaining largely unaware of the fact that the true purpose of their lodges was to serve the establishment of an "international Jewish super-government." The conspirators express a conviction that democratic countries lie especially vulnerable to the contaminating influence of Freemasonry.

The next fourteen protocols (with some illogical repetitions) describe the transition to universal autocracy and new state structures. An autocratic form of government is extolled as ideal, as opposed to democracy.

The Nilus edition concludes with "clarifications" from the "translator," which state that the original protocols bear the signatures of "the representatives of Zion" (names withheld). They were purportedly extracted in secret from the book of protocols held in the repository of the "Head Chancellery of Zion" in France. The notes further provide a brief history of the supposed Jewish conspiracy, beginning with its alleged foundation by King Solomon and other "Elders" in 929 BCE. Paul of Tarsus is described as one active implementer of the will of the "Elders."

Alongside the absurdity of the very possibility of planning out such an aggressive takeover century or even millennia in advance, the educated reader also perceives a total lack of any traces of a Jewish "signature" in *The Protocols*. One finds no Biblical or Talmudic references; the eschatological divinations do not mention the coming of the Messiah or deliverance; the Jewish empire of the future receives metaphorical interpretation as an "apologia of the god Vishnu." Nonetheless, the forgery's very crudeness, combined with a rather artfully depicted atmosphere of conspiracy and sinister mystery, could exert a strong impression on already prejudiced people.

Judging by hints at specific events contained in *The Protocols*, they could not have been compiled earlier than 1895.

POLITICAL BACKGROUND OF THE CREATION OF *The Protocols*. Already in the Middle Ages, the phantom of a Jewish conspiracy resided in the Christian imagination. One of the most famous libels accused the Jews of poisoning the wells of Europe at the order of their elders in Constantinople and Jerusalem. Rumors of rabbis meeting in secret to prepare ritual murders and host desecrations circulated widely. In Spain, in Portugal, and later in other European countries, the focus of anti-Jewish accusations gradually shifted from the religious to the political. Presumably, it was then that the need for creating forgeries to justify persecution of Jews first arose. Thus, in the counterfeit correspondence between the rabbis of Istanbul and Spanish Jews dated 1485 (published Paris, 1583), the rabbis advise their Spanish co-religionists forced to convert to Christianity that they should educate their children in the professions of merchants, doctors, pharmacists, priests, and lawyers, in order to be in a position to harm Christians and eventually enslave them. This counterfeit was used to incite against the new Christians, and then reprinted repeatedly in the nineteenth century in France and Germany.

The notion of a Jewish political conspiracy against the Christian states gained a further edge after Napoleon Bonaparte convened a Sanhedrin in 1807. The works of Alphonse Toussenel, Roger Gougenot des Mousseaux, Édouard Drumont, Eugen Dühring, Adolf Stoecker, and others all elaborated on this idea from various points of view. From the 1860s on, reactionary circles in Germany developed the concept of a Jewish-Masonic conspiratorial pact to jointly undermine the foundations of the Christian world. It was later embraced in France and played a considerable role in the Dreyfus affair. In Russia, Yakov Brafman published *The Kahal Book* in 1869 (3rd edition: 1888), in which he accused the Jews of corporate exploitation of the Christian population.

In 1873 a secret agent of the Russian government, Vladimir Osman-Bey, writing under the pseudonym Frederick Millingen, published *The Conquest of the World by the Jews* in German in Basel. The following year the treatise appeared in Russian and was subsequently reprinted many times. The author asserted that the true goal of the Jews was world domination; the Jewish diaspora was voluntary and served the purpose of preparing an offensive against the human race. Millingen claimed that Jews had discussed plans for seizing control of the press at a "World Jewish Council" in Krakow in 1840.

The idea of a Jewish conspiracy found "artistic" reflection in the novel *Biarritz–Rome* (1866–1870) by the German writer Hermann Goedsche (pen name Sir John Retcliffe), which would comprise one of the direct sources of *The Protocols*. A chapter from this novel, entitled "The Jewish Cemetery in Prague," was translated into Russian in 1872 and republished many times, sometimes under the title "The Rabbi's Speech." This fictional text describes a "regular" secret gathering of representatives of the twelve tribes of Israel at the grave of a "holy rabbi." There they discuss plans for the subversion of Christianity and the establishment of a Jewish kingdom. Novels by some Russian authors, including Vsevolod Krestovsky (*The Darkness of Egypt*, 1881) and Nikolai Wagner (*The Dark Affair*, 1881; republished under the title *The Dark Path*), are also awash with the idea of a global Jewish conspiracy.

In the 1880s the antisemitic press gave wide circulation to the counterfeit "Crémieux Manifesto," described as dating from 1874. This text predicted an imminent victory for world Jewry: "The day is not far off when all the riches of the earth will belong exclusively to Jews." Since that time the Alliance Israélite Universelle founded by Adolphe Crémieux figured as a primary target of anti-Jewish attacks.

In 1879–1880 Hippolytus Lutostansky published a "study" entitled *The Talmud and the Jews* (3 vols.) in Moscow; it reflected the gross ignorance of the author. In 1882 *Vek* magazine published a treatise with the title "The Great Secret of the Masons," most likely authored by Osip Przecławski (in 1909 his son republished the treatise as a separate edition in Moscow under the title *Exposing the Great Secret of the Freemasons*). This work contained a whole range of fabrications about the supposed Jewish-Masonic conspiracy,[1] which later served as the basis for *The Protocols*. Prior to publication, the manuscript was inspected by high-ranking officials of the Russian Empire, including Chief of Gendarmes Alexander Drenteln.

By the 1890s the archives of the Ministry of the Interior had accumulated a significant number of internal reports and other materials "exposing" the Jewish conspiracy. Among them was a report from the archive of the Police Department entitled "The Secret of Jewry," dated 10 February 1895. Genrikh Sliozberg would later publish it as an appendix to the book of Y. Delevsky (pen name of Yakov Yudelevsky), *The Protocols of the Elders of Zion: The History of a Forgery* (Berlin, 1923). The heads of Okhrana (the tsarist secret police department), wanting to exploit the growing antisemitic movement for their own purposes, had orchestrated the fabrication of a "document" purporting to demonstrate, in language appealing to the masses, the leading role of "world Jewry" in the Russian revolutionary movement. They could thereby discredit the slogans of opposition parties. "The Secret of Jewry" set the task of fighting against the revolutionary movement as "exposing in the popular press the secret Jewish plot against the entire Christian world — and Russia in particular." The decision to resort to a provocative hoax had been made.

---

[1] This Russian expression employs an ethnic slur instead of the normal word for "Jewish." (*Here and further — translators notes*)

The fabrication of counterfeits had been widespread in Europe since the second half of the eighteenth century, some of them being produced for political purposes. The most sensational was close in time and place to *The Protocols*: the extravagant hoax by the French anticlerical writer Léo Taxil (pen name of M.J.G.A. Jogand-Pagès). In 1885 Taxil expressed remorse and returned to the bosom of the Catholic Church. By commission of the Vatican, he then wrote a number of works filled with the most ridiculous fabrications about the Masons (including "documentary confirmation" of their connection to the devil). However, in 1897 Taxil announced that all his anti-Masonic publications had been a hoax aimed at exposing Catholic obscurantism. Another forgery, the falsified gospel called *The Life of Saint Issa, Best of the Sons of Men*, was allegedly found in Kashmir. It was published in French in 1894 (Russian translation 1895) by the Okhrana agent Nicolas Notovitch, who was also the author of an antisemitic book entitled *The Truth about the Jews* (1889).

The practice of literary forgeries was similarly practiced in nineteenth-century Russia. The anonymous *Polish Catechism* (1863) ascribed to the Poles, whose anti-Russian uprising had just been suppressed, attempts to harm Russian interests in every way possible by penetrating the upper echelons of power. Its publication provoked stormy debates.

PREPARATION AND INITIAL DISSEMINATION OF *The Protocols*. The operation of creating *The Protocols* was carried out with professional adherence to the rules of conspiracy: none of the participants ever disclosed the secret afterward. Nonetheless, the investigations of Delevsky, Vladimir Burtsev, Pavel Milyukov, and Sergei Svatikov succeeded in discovering a number of facts related to the creation of *The Protocols*.

The Nilus edition refers to France as the original location of *The Protocols* manuscript. Princess Catherine Radziwiłł and Henrietta Herblet testified that the agents of the Russian political police. Matvei Golovinski and Ivan Manusevich-Manuilov (the latter a Jew baptized in early childhood), prepared a document exposing the alleged Jewish conspiracy in Paris at the instruction of the head of the Okhrana foreign service Pyotr Rachkovsky (who later became vice-director of the Police Department). The National Library of France holds a copy of Maurice Joly's book *A Dialogue in Hell Between Machiavelli and Montesquieu, or The Politics of Machiavelli in the Nineteenth Century* (1864) with particular notations most likely made by the authors of the forgery. Joly's tract dealt neither with the Jews nor with the Masons, but rather exposed in a grotesque form the tyrannical aspirations of the Emperor Napoleon III. However, the authors of *The Protocols* based the speeches of "the Elders of Zion" on the monologues by Machiavelli's ghost concerning strategies for seizing power. Nearly half of the text of *The Protocols* was plagiarized directly from Joly's book.

In all likelihood Rachkovsky, a great master of political provocation, initiated the creation of *The Protocols*. In his youth he had been a member of Narodnaya Volya[2] and proposed to utilize the weekly *Russkii evrei (The Russian Jew)* that he edited as the party's legal mouthpiece. Upon crossing over to full-time service in Okhrana, he began to publish and distribute the Black Hundreds'[3] leaflets from the Police Department. Rachkovsky was himself one of the founders of the Union of Russian People.[4] The professional writer Golovinski, who at the instruction of Okhrana was engaged in surveilling Russian emigrants in Paris, is believed to be the author of *The Protocols*. The journalist Manusevich-Manuilov, a long-time Okhrana agent, may have been privy to Golovinski's assignment and assisted him in carrying it out. In addition to Joly's book, the forgers also plagiarized other works, in particular pamphlets by the Jewish convert to Catholicism Elie de Cyon (1842–1912, physiologist scholar and conservative publicist) that had targeted the financial policies of Sergei Witte. It is unlikely that de Cyon himself participated in creating *The Protocols*, as suggested by some scholars: he would have been capable of carrying out such a commission with greater knowledge of Jewish realia.

In order to deliver *The Protocols* manuscript to Russia, Rachkovsky employed the services of the Okhrana agent Yuliana (Yustina) Glinka. A rumor was circulated to the effect that Glinka had managed to obtain a top-secret document from a secret Jewish repository in France. The baptized Jew Savely Efron (1849–1925, pen name Litvin) related this version of events in his short novel *Among the Jews* (published in *Istoricheskii vestnik*, 1896). Nazi propaganda would subsequently cite his book as evidence of the "authenticity" of *The Protocols*. In 1909 Nilus told his guest Alexandre du Chayla that in fact Rachkovsky had

---

[2] **Narodnaya Volya** (The People's Will) was a nineteenth-century Russian revolutionary organization that espoused violence and whose members assassinated Tsar Alexander II in 1881.

[3] **The Black Hundreds** (Chernosotentsy) comprised an ultranationalist, antirevolutionary, and antisemitic movement in Russia in the early twentieth century.

[4] **The Union of Russian People** (Soiuz russkogo naroda) constituted an extreme-right political party and a main political component of the Black Hundreds.

handed over the manuscript of the "document" to "a Parisian lady." Aleksei Sukhotin, a close acquaintance of Glinka, passed *The Protocols* on to Filipp Stepanov. In 1927 Stepanov recounted how he had first printed one hundred copies on a hectograph and then later, in 1897, used a print shop in Tula province to create additional copies (without specifying the year or place of publication). Nilus and Butmi received their copies of *The Protocols* from Sukhotin. Though Stepanov's small print run went unnoticed, the editions of Butmi and especially Nilus would in time become known worldwide.

The edition of Nilus with his preface was first published in the St. Petersburg newspaper *Znamia* (1903) by Pavel Krushevan, a well-known Black Hundreds activist and instigator of the Kishinev pogrom, under the title "The Jewish Program for Conquering the World." In autumn 1905 two further editions of *The Protocols* appeared simultaneously: one as part of Nilus' book *The Great within the Small, and the Antichrist as an Imminent Political Possibility*, which told the story of his "spiritual search," and another as a separate book edited by Butmi and entitled *The Root of Our Travails*. A second edition by Butmi bore the new title *Enemies of the Human Race*; its preface specified the date of the manuscript's "translation" as 9 December 1901. The translator's note stated that *The Protocols* had been signed by the representatives of Zion, who should not be confused with Zionists; the publisher, however, disputed the note.

In 1911 another edition of the Nilus version was published under the title *The Soon-Coming Antichrist*. In the foreword the publisher of *The Protocols* stated that he had received the manuscript in 1901; he allowed for the possibility of its unauthenticity: "Some may perhaps reproach me, and rightfully so, for the apocryphal nature of the proffered document." In 1917 Nilus published his book yet again, this time under the title *Here I Stand at the Door*. This edition declared that he had received the manuscript from Sukhotin and that *The Protocols* encompassed a strategic plan for world conquest developed by Jewish leaders and presented by Theodor Herzl at the First Zionist Congress in 1897.

In spite of the audacious efforts of its fanatical proponents, *The Protocols* did not garner wide support in Russian society. Even such leaders of the Black Hundreds as Mikhail Menshikov, a leading journalist at *Novoe vremia* whom Glinka tried to convince in 1902 that she had truly stolen *The Protocols* from the "Jewish capital" of Nice, turned their backs on the clumsy forgery. The disseminators of *The Protocols* also failed to enlist the support of the court. It is true that during the heat of the 1905 Revolution, Nicholas II received a copy of *The Protocols* and, according to a general of the gendarmes, scribbled on the margins of his copy such notes as: "What depth of thought! ...What precision in realizing the program! ...There can be no doubt regarding their authenticity..." The agents of the Okhrana foreign service who had "discovered" *The Protocols* were rewarded generously. Nonetheless, when right-wing politicians submitted a proposal for the extensive use of *The Protocols* in the political struggle, Prime Minister Pavel Stolypin ordered a secret investigation and reported its findings to the tsar, leaving no doubt that *The Protocols* were a forgery. Nikolai II wrote on the proposal: "Withdraw *The Protocols;* one cannot defend a pure cause by dirty means." The negative attitude of the Russian authorities towards *The Protocols* manifested itself strikingly in that no references to *The Protocols* were permitted even during preparations for the notorious Beilis Trial.

The Protocols found some resonance only in mystical circles. Pavel Florensky's master's thesis refers to the Nilus edition. Archbishop Nikon of Vologda asserted the authenticity of *The Protocols*. In fiction, Elizaveta Shabelskaya-Bork upheld the "anti-Masonic" tradition in her novels *Satanists of the Twentieth Century* (1909) and *The Black and the Red* (1911). She devoted many pages to descriptions of Jewish conspiratorial meetings headed by a character resembling Witte; the speeches of the conspirators reprised the monologues of the "Elders" in *The Protocols*.

During the First World War *The Protocols* spread beyond Russia for the first time. Grand Duke Nikolai Nikolayevich, an uncle of the tsar and commander-in-chief of the Caucasian front, was a notorious persecutor of Jews who ordered *The Protocols* translated into English and disseminated among the Allies. According to the memoirs of Chaim Weizmann, *The Protocols* attained great popularity among British officers stationed in the Middle East.

The year 1918 was a turning point in the history of *The Protocols*. The murder of the tsar's family by the revolutionary authorities of Russia stirred a new wave of mass and mystically tinged interest in the antisemitic forgery. Kolchak army investigators discovered in the room of Empress Alexandra Feodorovna Nilus' book *The Great within the Small*, which had been given to her a few months earlier, along with the Bible and *War and Peace* by Lev Tolstoy. This news was perceived in profusely monarchical Christian circles as a testament of the martyred tsarina denouncing the Jews as the true culprits of the tragedy. Editions of *The Protocols* appeared in Novocherkassk, Rostov-on-Don, and

Kharkov. The notorious anti-Semite Vladimir Purishkevich, who served in the propaganda department of the Volunteer Army, took a hand in disseminating them among White Army forces.

According to the testimony of Moisei Novomeisky and some others, Admiral Kolchak became obsessed with the idea of the "Jewish-Masonic conspiracy." As a result, new editions of *The Protocols* appeared in Omsk, Irkutsk, Vladivostok, and Khabarovsk. The White Guard press circulated various versions of the so-called Zunder Document (a new variation of the Crémieux Manifesto), which had allegedly been found among the papers of a Red Army commander. Propagandizing of *The Protocols* and other forgeries among the Whites and Petliura's troops provoked the most vicious series of anti-Jewish pogroms, resulting in an unprecedented number of victims.

After the Bolsheviks' victory, dissemination of *The Protocols* in Russia was banned. The forgery continued to circulate only in some underground nationalist, anti-Soviet circles. However, White emigres brought *The Protocols* to Europe, where they played a sinister role in the formation of right-wing ideological movements, especially National Socialism in Germany. Alfred Rosenberg, who left Russia for Germany at the end of 1918 and became an official ideologue and philosopher of the Nazi Party, combined the Russian Black Hundreds' ideology with German Nazism. In 1923 Hitler appointed Rosenberg to the post of editor-in-chief of the *Völkischer Beobachter* (*Nationalist Observer*) newspaper. There he published *The Protocols* and then actively promoted their republication in millions of copies in German and other languages. (Ludwig Müller von Hausen had published the first translation of *The Protocols* into German under the pen name Gottfried zur Beek in 1919; a second translation was made by Theodor Fritsch in 1920). Nazi propaganda in regards to *The Protocols* stirred up widespread anti-Jewish hysteria and provoked the murder of Walther Rathenau, who had been declared one of the "Elders of Zion."

It is difficult to overestimate the role of *The Protocols* in development of Nazi plans for "the Final Solution to the Jewish Question." However, their effect on the foundations of Nazi ideology is also apparent: Hitler and his entourage accepted the absurd conspiratorial plan to achieve world domination outlined in *The Protocols* as a revelation — and set out to implement it themselves.

In England the first translation of *The Protocols* was published in 1920; it ran to five editions. In 1921 Victor Marsden, a correspondent of the London *Morning Post*, published a new translation, which was also reprinted several times. Both the *Morning Post* and *The Times* ran articles claiming authenticity for *The Protocols*. In Boston in 1920 the automobile king Henry Ford funded the printing of half a million copies; his mass circulation *Dearborn Independent* newspaper also propagated *The Protocols*. Ford's book *The International Jew* elaborated on the conspiracy notion and circulated internationally.

In France, various translations of *The Protocols* were published beginning in 1920. During the 1920s, and even more so after 1933, translations of *The Protocols* (funded by Germany) appeared in Polish, Swedish, Danish, Finnish, Italian, Hungarian, Japanese, Arabic, and other languages and were widely publicized.

EXPOSING THE FORGERY. The orgy surrounding *The Protocols* evoked concern among the liberal Jews of Europe and America. Democratic circles of Russian emigres also protested the dissemination of the forgery and debunked it. In 1921 the Istanbul correspondent of the London *Times*, Philip Graves, discovered the main source of the plagiarism — Joly's *Dialogue in Hell*. The same *Times* that had recently advertised *The Protocols* now clearly demonstrated its forgery technique, publishing a comparison of the texts of the *Dialogue* and *The Protocols*. In 1921 journalists of *The American Hebrew* magazine published an interview with Princess Radziwiłł and Henrietta Herblet. In the 1920s-1930s articles and books by Milyukov, Anton Kartashev, Delevsky, Sliozberg, and Burtsev appeared in Russian, with detailed studies on the history of the forgery. The philosopher Nikolai Berdyaev strongly condemned *The Protocols*, Théodore Reinach in France and Lucien Wolf in England opposed the spread of *The Protocols*.

With the support of the general public, American Jewry took a stand against *The Protocols* in an organized manner. The American Jewish Committee condemned Ford's publications; other national Jewish leaders, along with U. S. Presidents Woodrow Wilson and Theodore Roosevelt, joined the protest. The journalist Herman Bernstein (1876–1935) and the financier Aaron Sapiro filed lawsuits against Ford on charges of libel and moral damage to the Jewish community of the United States. In 1927 Ford was forced to pay damages to Bernstein. He also apologized to the Jews of the country in a letter addressed to Louis Marshall and declared a recall and ban on reprinting *The International Jew* (which, however, did not prevent the publication of large-scale editions in Nazi Germany). Three court hearings in Bern (November 1933 — May 1935) dealing with a lawsuit filed by the Jewish communities of Switzerland against local Nazis who disseminated *The Protocols* caused an even greater public commotion. After hearing the arguments of both parties, the court deliberated on the issue of the authenticity of *The Protocols* and declared them "a counterfeit, plagiarism, and nonsense," sentencing the Swiss Nazis to a fine. In 1937 the Supreme Court in Bern rejected the defendants' appeal and thus upheld the decision of the court of first instance.

MASS DISSEMINATION OF *The Protocols*. The court cases in the US and Switzerland managed to prevent further dissemination of *The Protocols* in democratic countries. Nevertheless, anti-Semites continued to reprint *The Protocols* and translate them into ever more languages. A tendency to link the creation of *The Protocols* with the new Zionist movement also grew stronger. Authorship of the monologues was attributed to Herzl, Max Nordau, and most frequently Ahad Ha'am. After the Nazis seized power in Germany, dissemination of *The Protocols* became a national priority; in 1934–1945 all schools in the country taught *The Protocols*. The special Welt-Dienst (World Service) bureau was established to publish antisemitic leaflets, including (among other compositions) *The Protocols* in all European languages. By the time of the Nazi occupation of European countries, *The Protocols* had been reprinted in huge numbers in order to indoctrinate the conquered peoples. The Propaganda Department of the so-called Russian Liberation Army under General Vlasov was also involved in promulgating *The Protocols*.

After the defeat of Germany and its allies, the international community learned the truth about the Holocaust, and the Nuremberg Trials condemned the practice of Nazi genocide. The publications of *The Protocols* had been stopped. However, it did not take long before Arab nationalists wishing to discredit Zionism rekindled dissemination of *The Protocols*. In Egypt, Syria, Saudi Arabia, and other Islamic countries *The Protocols* came to be reprinted over and over again. The phantom of *The Protocols* also reappeared in Communist countries in the late 1940s and early 1950s, along with persecution of the Jewish intelligentsia (the "anti-cosmopolitan" campaign, the "Doctors' Plot," the Slánský trial, the "Crimean Affair," etc.), though the forgery itself was not brought into play. However, in 1968 *The Protocols* were sold openly in churches in Poland; soon after, the notion of a "thousand-year Jewish conspiracy" resurfaced again in the Soviet Union in Yury Ivanov's book *Beware! Zionism* (Moscow, 1969). Since that time, Soviet propaganda adopted the "struggle against Zionism," interpreted in the spirit of *The Protocols* as the struggle against a worldwide conspiracy, as one of its most important directions. Attacks on Masons in light of ideas in *The Protocols* appeared in works by Nikolai Yakovlev, Oleg Mikhailov, Vadim Pigalev and others, while the authors Ivan Shevtzov and Valentin Pikul elaborated on the topic of the Jewish-Masonic conspiracy. The 1975 United Nations General Assembly resolution, which declared Zionism to be a form of racism and racial discrimination, was based on ideas that had gained widespread popularity owing to *The Protocols*. Islamic countries where *The Protocols* had come to form part of the official ideology initiated this resolution. The states of the socialist camp, where *The Protocols* had entered official propaganda "through the back door," so to speak, actively supported the declaration.

The Protocols IN THE LATE TWENTIETH CENTURY. The political crisis that led to the collapse of the communist system prompted a wave of antisemitism in Eastern Europe. Already in the 1970s V. Yemelyanov's book *De-Zionization*, published in Paris, had circulated in antisemitic circles in the Soviet Union; it quoted generously from *The Protocols* and spread mystical terror of the Jews. From the beginning of 1980s lecturers at the "patriotic societies" Pamyat (Memory) and Otechestvo (Fatherland) read selected passages from *The Protocols* in Moscow, Leningrad, Novosibirsk, Sverdlovsk, and Minsk, provokingly comparing the horrific realities of Russian history after the October Revolution with the predictions of the "Elders." A new forgery entitled *The Catechism of the Soviet Jew* portrayed a traditional image of the Jew as an evil enemy of the Russian people and emerged as part of antisemitic samizdat.[5] The newly reprinted *Protocols* have been distributed freely in post-perestroika[6] Russia, Belarus, and other former Soviet republics. Some periodicals also utilize reprints of *The Protocols*, accompanied by antisemitic caricatures. Even the "respectable" right-wing mass media (such as the *Molodaya gvardia* and *Nash sovremennik* magazines) have fueled interest in *The Protocols* by opening new debates on the question of their authenticity, even though this question was resolved long ago; they also hint that the execution of the tsar's family in 1918 and the genocide of the peasantry in the 1930s constituted "ritual murders" carried out in accordance with the plans outlined in *The Protocols*.

---

[5] **Samizdat** ("self-publishing") consisted in copying dissident and forbidden works by hand and passing them from reader to reader.

[6] **Perestroika** ("restructuring") was a new economic and political program initiated by Mikhail Gorbachev in the mid-1980s.

In East European countries, translations of *The Protocols* circulate widely. New publications in Hungary and Romania have caused serious concern in Jewish democratic circles. The forgery is also still reprinted in Islamic countries and around the world. The statement by Iraqi President Saddam Hussein that "All Western leaders are puppets in the hands of the Zionists" (October 1991) indisputably represents a reflection of the myth outlined in *The Protocols*. Even in democratic countries *The Protocols* remain in use. In the US, for example, some leaders of the Black Muslims and other movements still cite them.

Translated by Yeshaya Gruber and Yulia Mestechkin

The Evil Storyteller N. P. Wagner

Outbursts of anti-Semitism at one time or another in some way have been always tied to historical events: Jews were blamed for a country's economic or political failures and for starting wars and revolutions.

Thus, in the Crimean war, which ended in Russia's defeat, some saw signs of a Yiddo-masonic conspiracy. We are talking about Nikolai Wagner's novel *Dark Path*.

The Crimean war did not seem to affect Jews, since the battles happened in places where Jewish population (Krymchaks and Karaites) was sparse. This time it was Tatars who were accused of collaboration with the occupational forces: during the allies' landing in Yevpatoria in 1854 several Tatar villages rebelled. The punishment immediately followed: a mass deportation of Tatars from Crimea began. [1]

Freemasonry that had been banned by Alexander I in 1822, went fully underground after the defeat of the Decembrist rebellion. Up to the revolution of 1905, hardly anything was known about Russian freemasonry. But the state police machine never forgot the masons. In his *Sevastopol Sketches* Leo Tolstoy describes the fate of an officer who volunteered for the war and had to answer the question about his belonging to a masonic lodge. In the same *Sevastopol Sketches* are mentioned soldiers "of Yid appearance." Indeed, during the reign of Nicholas I there were proportionally more Jewish soldiers in the military than Christians: ten Jews were recruited per thousand men, whereas Christians provided only seven. Mark Aldanov writes that Jewish participation in the wars with Persia (1826–1828), Turkey (1828–1829), and the Eastern war (1853–1856) was very noticeable. [2] It is less known that on the other side of the front lines an Israeli regiment was created and there was an attempt to create a Jewish legion by Adam Mickiewicz, Armand Levy, and Sadyk Pasha (Michal Czajkowski). This was Mickiewicz's dream come true, to see Israel revived and armed.

The regiment recruited prisoner Jews who had volunteered to serve in a regiment of Ottoman Cossacks; the latter were shunned in Turkey as much as Jews were in Russia.

Addendum. The Evil Storyteller N. P. Wagner

That is why the accusations of treason should be addressed to Nekrasov Cossacks as well as to the conglomerate of Polish, German, and Hebrew families. [3] The great states met this idea quite coldly and did not wish to make any promises to Jews; in the same way, the Sublime Porte, while agreeing to the creation of the legion, never issued an official decree. Apparently, this case did not interest Baron Rothchild, either, although his representative was negotiating a loan with Turkey. In any case, the possible anti-Semitic trump card was not, as far as I know, used in Russian journalistic genre or literature of the time (the issue of a "warrior Jew" could not be considered seriously).

Nikolai Petrovich Wagner belongs to a group of well forgotten writers whose revival is unlikely even in the post-perestroika times. But the name of Wagner the scientist is well-known and any Soviet encyclopedia mentions his scientific work. He was born in 1829 into a family of a medical professor of Kazan University. The Wagner family were Jewish converts. Their ancestor, Vassily Alexeyevich, was an estate manager to Count Alexey Kirillovich Razumovsky, he converted to Christianity in 1744 and was given his Godfather's first name as a patronymic. A personal decree of the Empress of 19 March 1745 granted him a hereditary nobility. Later he became Razumovsky's aide-de-camp. [4]

His descendant, N. P. Wagner, became a professor of Zoology at Kazan University (1860) and later at Petersburg University (1871), and was the founder and director of the Solovetskaya biology station, as well as a prominent researcher of the White Sea fauna. In 1877–1879 he edited and published a popular science magazine "Svet" ("Light"), and in 1891 was elected President of the Russian Society for Experimental Psychology. The summit of Wagner's scientific work is his paper of 1862 that became a scientific sensation: "Spontaneous reproduction of insect larvae." This paper was the first in the world to establish the phenomenon of paedogenesis, or neoteny (the sexual maturity of an animal while it is still in a mainly larval state).

In 1869 the French Academy of Science awarded Wagner the *Prix Bordin*. This, however, did not stop Wagner from being an adept of spiritism and polemizing with Dmitri Mendeleyev on the subject.

We should especially mention his relationship with F. M. Do_ stoyevsky: a significant amount of correspondence between the two remains, mostly concerning spiritual seances and the possible participation of Dostoyevsky in Wagner's magazine "Svet" (there is a total of seven letters from Dostoyevsky to Wagner dating back to 1875–1877, and eleven Wagner's letters from the same period).

There is no doubt that Dostoyevsky's views, reflected in *A Writer's Diary,* influenced Wagner. His scientific and author biography is told in sufficient detail by V. I. Mildon in the new biographical dictionary "Russian Writers of 1800–1917" (M, 1989. Vol.1). There is one important mistake in the article, and the tragedy in the family of the famous professor is not mentioned, either. I am talking about his son, the author Vladimir Nikolayevich, who shot and killed his own wife.

In court, a curious circumstance surfaced: it was the parents, with their cruel abuse, who drove their son to degradation. A witness wrote: "Vladimir is a product of a strange, inexplicable cruelty and thoughtlessness, a neglected and unloved child. For mischief and poor grades, he would be locked in a closet all day and, eventually, he was kicked out of the house. Abused, embittered, and, perhaps, mentally ill, he ended up committing the crime." Later, an explanation for the Cat Purr's treatment of his son was found: the old Wagner was insane and ended up with paralytic dementia. [5] It all happened in the '90s (*I wonder what Fyodor Dostoyevsky would have said to this...*). [6]

As far as the literary path of our hero, it began in the 1850s with editing the magazine of the Moscow Society for Agriculture.

However, real popularity was brought to him by the collection of philosophical tales and fables *The Tales of Cat Purr* (first printed in 1872 and last, the 10th edition, published in the Soviet times, in 1923).

Most contemporary critics agreed that in its depth, colorfulness, original plot, and artistic simplicity of narration, these *Tales* had to be counted among the classics of children's literature.

He succeeded little in other popular books for youth, however. Thus, Samuel Marshak wrote on Wagner's *Pictures from the Lives of Animals* that they were heavy on the "conjunction of scientific information, anecdotal detail, and stylistic frills." [7]

Wagner's novel *Dark Path* (*Tyomny Put*) stands alone. Its history is as follows: its first part was published in a "mysterious" and "fantastical" magazine "Rebus," in 1881.

The novel continued in the magazine until 1884, but only its first three parts were published. The fourth, and the last, part was included into a separate copy of the book (SPb.,1890). In "Rebus" the novel was called *Tyomnoe Delo* (*Dark Deed*) and later received its title *Tyomny Put* due to the changes in the plot that unexpectedly switched from a criminal (ritual) act to a subject that had nothing to do with the story's outset.

The timeline of Wagner's novel encompasses the early 1850s through the famous Spirit's Day of 1862, 26 May (Old Style), when fires erupted in Petersburg.

If the end date can be easily verified and is clear, the beginning presents a problem that is primarily related to the inaccuracy by the author himself, who realized that only by the middle of the novel and had to come up with an explanation: "...in the first and last chapters of my tale I noticed inaccuracies in the dates. I do not know how this happened, but the whole incident got moved ten years back and many things became a complete anachronism. My mother was murdered in 1851..." [8]

It is noteworthy that the novel has no straight storyline; the author failed. It consists of separate and barely connected chapters. Some of those (although very few) possess certain literary merits and can be viewed as inserted novellas.

The story begins with a mysterious murder at an abandoned mill. The victim is the protagonist's mother and the murder itself has some features of a ritual. The protagonist visits the mill and learns that it is a place of sectarian worship. [9] Sacrifices for these Russian "nights in Athens" were taken from surrounding villages.

The protagonist, from whose point of view the story is told (by the way, we learn his last name, Olinsky, only in Chapter 40 of Part 1, and his first name, Vladimir, only in Part 2), attempts to find his mother's murderers, but unexpectedly for the reader who thought that murder mystery would be the plot of the novel, engages in investigating the global Jewish conspiracy.

The protagonist's friend understandably disapproves:

"And you are just sitting here?! You do not denounce murderers and debauchees!..." [10]

No, the hero does not denounce the wicked, but instead falls in love with a beautiful Jewess, Sarra, a circus performer who had been brilliantly educated at a women's institution in Brussels where she took classes in history and philosophy with Dr. Schoepfel and classes in political economy and jurisprudence with Dr. Mittermer. Besides, she was an agent of the global "qahal." The hero at first believes that his beloved is an immoral adventurist, but soon realizes that "a vast, disciplined freedom was hidden behind this false adventurism." Sarra is a greatly gifted, brilliant, and even genius actress, a talented piano player, but she gave her beauty and talent to the service of Jewry.

To this end (*Jewish world domination*) Sarra gets involved with a Grand Duke (his name is never mentioned, but, apparently, in this episode the reader is supposed to recognize the love affair of the Grand Duke Nikolai Konstantinovich and the American adventurist Fanny Lear).

However, the outstanding qahal spy, as well as the rest of the Jewish characters, is extremely garrulous. With touching frankness, she explains to the hero:

"I hate, I despise your entire people of despots and persecutors of the poor tribe of the great Jehovah. If I could trick all of your despicable people, ruin you, drown you, slowly burn you... I... I...," and she put her face, distorted by spite, very close to mine. 'I, Sarra, would do this with my own hands.'" [11]

At the same time, we see a completely wild and ridiculous description by Wagner of a provincial show, in which Sarra's wanton 12-year-old sister also takes part, and where a secret meeting of "global conspirators" takes place. Naturally, the hero finds the simplest way to learn the qahal's secrets: he eavesdrops when he finds himself backstage. The similarities between this and the anti-Semitic chapters of Goedsche's (Retcliffe) novel *After Sedan* are obvious: in *After Sedan* the main characters listen to the talks of the Council of conspirators at an old Jewish cemetery; in Wagner's novel, the protagonist eavesdrops in the wings of a theater and circus show. The meeting opens with an address in German (possibly, Yiddish is what the author means when he calls it "a Jewish jargon"): "'I greet the meeting of the leaders of the abused people of Jehovah!' the rabbi began. 'I greet the east and the west, the north and the south. Let us thank the Almighty who allowed us to gather here and discuss the Lord's cause.'" [12]

"Then the rabbi continues: 'Brothers of God's family! Suffering, persecution, and exile is our fate, but some day the Almighty will lead His people out of slavery and to the Promised Land. Our enemy rose against us with a sword, but we laid gold upon the Lord's cup of wrath to appease Him! The enemy is strong in his hosts, but we can buy them all. He leeches our blood and blood of our children. We suck out his gold. He made our children into cantonists. But these are little lion cubs who, once grown, will sow discord in his troops and devour his insides. He has power, we have cunning. We are Samson's foxes and we shall burn the Philistines' pastures with our tails. They shall drink a full cup of famine and ruin. Their mothers and wives shall curse their fertility when they see their children starve at their feet. We, lean cows, shall devour fat cows, but first we shall milk their udders. Death to Philistines! death to the enemies of the God's people.'" [13]

Undoubtedly, this philippic deserves close attention. Some of its fragments are reminiscent of *The Protocols of the Elders of Zion*: on the power and strength of gold, on cunning, etc. We should specifically mention the passage about cantonists. It is difficult to say what Wagner means. Let us mark one circumstance: in 29 years the total number of Jewish cantonists, according to "The Concise Jewish Encyclopedia" was about 50,000. Most of them were baptized and assimilated into the Russian people and made up a significant part of the educated city population of the Empire outside of the Pale of Settlement.

How "young lion cubs" could rip out the "insides" of the enemy, remains Wagner's secret. [14]

Further, the secret council of "global conspirators," according to a tradition that goes back to the novel by Dumas Sr. *Memoirs of a Physician,* begins analyzing the situation in the countries they represent.

The renowned leader of the East, i.e., the representative of Russia, recounts the successes (the growing number of members of the society, although, unclear what society exactly; establishing of the Qahal in Astrakhan; agents' penetration into Sarepta; successful competition in Kazan; trade in Orenburg, etc.) and complains of the carelessness of Brother Ben Itzik whose overzealousness in killing of "two infidel infants" in Saratov in 1852 already cost 50,000.

Finally, the "leader of the East" makes public a financial report that is approved by those present.

"'The renowned leader of the West' insists that they have found a key to an entire country and that key is gold. Every ministry has a button that can be pushed, if necessary, and a center in Paris is 'woven' (created). Further, the leader of the West talks about the unlimited power of Jewry and gives the following example: 'Recently, they (The Russian powers – *Transl.*) tried to take his manor from a voluntary emigrant H. (there he named a famous person), but Samuel von Rothschild threatened to deny them a simple loan and the manor was returned.' [15] They mean of course Herzen, but due to censorship Wagner could not spell out his name. And this is what Alexander Ivanovich Herzen himself has to say in *My Past and Thoughts* on how James (not Samuel) made Nicholas I obey financial law that was the same for the Tsar and for a mortal man: 'The letter was fabulous, sharp, insistent, as it should be when power talks to power... Rothschild... demanded payment... in case of refusal he would pass the matter to lawyers and would advise to consider thoroughly the consequences of such a refusal, which would be especially strange at the time when the Russian government wished to receive a new loan from him. Rothschild concluded that in case of further delays he would have to publicize the story through magazines to warn capitalists.' Herzen, without sarcasm, calls Rothchild an emperor, because 'In a month or a month and a half the stingy 1st Class Petersburg merchant Nikolai Romanov, in fear of competition and a publication in 'Vedomosti,' at Rothchild's high order, paid the unlawfully held monies with interest and excused himself with having been ignorant of the law... Since then, Rothchild and I were best pals; he loved in me the battlefield where he defeated Nicholas, I was something of a Marengo or an Austerlitz for him, and he would narrate the details of the affair in my presence several times...'

"Then, however, the leader of the West moves on to the most important thing: 'We are starting a war in the East, a big war, in which three states will take part: Turkey, England, and France, and, possibly, Austria and Italy will join. Everyone shall rise to break the northern Colossus that oppresses the sons of Jehovah.'" [16]

This passage is the climax of the novel. The Russian government should have been forewarned, but... There are several "buts." The hero makes a deal with the beautiful Sarra and agrees, in exchange for 20,000 rubles, to give his nobleman's word to "keep quiet" about "Yid schemes." [17]

The second "but" is more important and, undoubtedly, the following tirade was written under the influence of Dostoyevsky (which is easy to prove). Olinsky reasons: "... why wouldn't you report this?! You are Russian! Against your homeland, Russia, the Yid qahal is arming. The secret society is scheming... And you, you, a Russian, sold your silence for a woman's beauty and 20,000 rubles. Shame on you, a Russian noble! But how would I report?.. report! This is the business of the cops, the police, and, if they overlook it that means they have been well paid. Besides, it is very dangerous to mingle in any political affair at this time. Especially in an affair Jewish or Yid (what difference he sees between a Jew and a Yid is unclear — S.D.). They will report you twenty times before you report once. No, it is better and more prudent to keep quiet! And, after all, which one of us nobles, of our society, would do differently? I considered our landowners one after another and repeated with satisfaction: nobody! nobody! nobody!." [18]

A. S. Suvorin's "Diary" opens with a piece of a memoir about F. M. Dostoyevsky, whom Suvorin saw on the day of the attempted assassination of Loris-Melikov by Mlodetsky. Dostoyevsky was talking about a strange attitude of the society towards political crime and as an example brought up the idea that if he should overhear a conversation about an explosive device being set up in the Winter Palace, he could not go to the police with a warning.

Suvorin, too, replied negatively to the question put by Dostoevsky. Dostoyevsky says:

"And I would not go, either. Why? This is terrible. This is a crime. We could prevent it, perhaps... I went over every reason that could make me do so. Those were reasons strong and solid. Then I considered the reasons that would not let me do this. Those were insignificant. It was just the fear of being known as a snitch. I imagined how I would come to the police, how they would look at me, how they would question me, make me take part in confrontations, how they would probably offer me a reward, or maybe even suspect me of being an accomplice. They would print: Dostoyevsky pointed out the criminals. Is this any of my business? This is the police's business... Is this normal? Everything with us is abnormal; that is why things like this happen, and nobody knows what to do... I'd write about it. I could say many things good and bad for society and for the government, but this is not allowed. We are not allowed to talk about the most important matters." [19]

The hero's first encounter with the qahal ends in court and it is clear that Nicholas I's policing organs did not sleep and were aware of "Yid schemes."

Vladimir Olinsky's case interested the Tsar himself, but a scene in the spirit of *Captain's Daughter* ended with the hero's exile to the Caucasus. The entire second part of the novel is dedicated to Olinsky the conscript's dwelling in a small border fortress. We know of the war in the Caucasus from the descriptions by Bestuzhev-Marlinsky, Lermontov, Leo Tolstoy, and Mordovtsev.

It should be noted that Wagner's depiction of the war is very different from those of his predecessors. Think of Pechorin in *A Hero of Our Time:* he is involved in love affairs, duels, card play, etc., and never even gives a thought to why he is in the Caucasus in the first place. He, like other characters of "colonial novels," from those of Bestuzhev to N. N. Karamzin, does not seek the reason.

Only in the remote future the reason for acceding those "wild outskirts" would be declared, one the one hand, voluntary, and on the other, *kulturtrager* in nature. Wagner, unlike his predecessors, poses this question; forty years of social studies were not wasted on him.

The garrison of the fortress nicknamed "Oblomovka," very similar to Captain Mironov's team of invalids, dwelled in a state of carefree "Oblomov" doze. [20] Every now and then they would fight off a highlander raid that always ended in a slaughter. Sometimes, as entertainment, they would "pacify" non-combatant highland population: "We devastated entire auls... Took their livestock." [21] And why? "We, the "great Russians" ... shall go forth and plant... the power of a bribe at the top of the Caucasus. We shall corrupt these peaceful children of the highlands with our greed, and them now living patriarchally and with no notion of bribery. And again, I imagined "*batalyk*." Piles of bodies in a peaceful God's church!.. Blood!.. A broken iconostasis... And the disfigured face of He who banished from the church corrupt merchants who had defiled Him with their trading!.. What a great and terrible price is being paid for this disgusting right to steal, corrupt, and loot!" [22] Olinsky participated in raids and "observed in horror my comrades slaughtering the highlanders mercilessly and taking away their sheep and horses. And that was not enough. They began to loot." The protagonist tried to stop the looting, but got only this profound response: "We have to loot them... If we don't loot them, they'll loot us." [23]

This dialogue is akin to a dialogue between a missionary and a Hottentot, who tried to explain to each other that robbery was bad when "my livestock and wives are taken," and good "when I take from them."

The hero's stay in the Caucasus was interrupted by the start of the Eastern (Crimean) war when Olinsky got transferred to Sevastopol. Vladimir's conclusion is curious from a psychological point of view: the Caucasian war was not a war, since now Russia found itself in the position of the highlanders before a more powerful adversary:

"The Caucasian war. Can it even be called a war? Compared to that real European war that stands at the door and threatens our Russia? This is, so to speak, our domestic war, in which we try and take a necessary chunk away from small peoples, and over there is a powerful enemy that has risen against us and threatens Russia." [24]

Wagner did not forget Jews. In the last pages of Chapter 2 there appears a new character, one Seraphima Lvovna. She, in the modern terms, is a medium. Besides, this seer is crazy with hatred of Jews. Her hatred, however, is quite practical: Jews interfered in one of her schemes and snatched a large sum in the process. [25]

This modern Deborah predicts Russia's defeat, liberation of serfs, and the coming bloody revolution: "Free the serfs... They will devour one another... First, they will devour us the landowners and then start devouring one another. A cloud, a bloody cloud hangs over Russia and perpetrates a terrible and dark deed... And there is no way out for us...

none!." [26] Seraphima Lvovna insists that Russia is "A poor and noble country! It must go through a long and bloody trial, a beautiful page in people's martyrology." [27] She also insists that the Eastern war did not begin by accident. The goal of a war (current or future) is to topple the "idol that weighs upon Tsardoms" and cast it into the abyss. Jews, in her words, are "Alpha and Omega of the entire world" and the only nation the future belongs to, for they know "where they go and why." (Upon hearing these words Vladimir Pavlovich recalls having heard some such once before.) Jews are omnipresent and they have agents everywhere:

"They invisibly hold the fates of the entire world." They arrange wars in Europe and get rich from them. Not a half century would pass and all the commerce would be in their hands. They would own literature, science, and art. "Everyone says: this is an "oppressed people" ... Nonsense! Illusion! It is they who own us, not we them! And we shall be fully in their hands once they multiply." [28]

Part 2 ends with Olinsky's mystical dream in which he appears to attend a funeral wake that alternates between the size of a small party and a grand feast. He sees the Tsar (Nicholas I), and Benkendorf, scared and pale, and hears talk about breaking some fetters.

In the middle of the hall, on a tall pedestal stood the "renowned leader of the East." Everyone gathered there was entangled with thin chains coming up from underneath. Under the surface, ugly dwarves who used to be giants, dug the dirt, moved rocks, and built a huge burial vault. All of them were connected with chains that went up to the "renowned leader of the east" and the entire Yid Qahal. The dwarves, pale and famished, died, and up above "stronger and louder glittered and jingled the gold of the Yid Qahal." [29]

And so, the prophecy began to come true. First, Sevastopol was besieged and soon fell. Wagner speaks in detail about the fight for the city and brings in new characters who, undoubtedly, had historical prototypes.

Rather bravely, he brings in Count Leo Tolstoy (Count Tonkiy in the novel), whose soldier songs were passed from person to person and were sung at every battery. Count Tonkiy's reasoning is very similar to Tolstoy's, but, of course, the Tolstoy of 1860s-1870s, not the 1850s (the anachronism does not bother the author). The main topic of the count's thinking is this: the slaughter that is going on is senseless.

Russia's situation is hopeless: "...we have been cornered... we cannot fight off the enemy... Where we drop a million missiles, "he" drops two or three million... And why, allow me to ask? Because his treasury is bigger... On his side are the Rothchilds, the Mendelsohns, the Stephensons, and all other -sons." [30] In the fire of the defense of Sevastopol, where "the greatness of Russia was buried," Olinsky had an idea to create a circle of like-minded people to fight the "dark deed." In essence, he talks about a masonic lodge, although, due to censorship, Wagner never says it directly. The first order of business would be abolishing serfdom and then, fighting bribery and any and all injustice. Obviously, the second part of the plan was much harder to realize, since it had to do with human nature. Further, they had to try and keep "militant men" away from power and try to avoid domination of egotists. By egotists the author means people who care about themselves and their families. [31]

Chapter 3 ends in philippic against the tribe of Judah that "we" had nurtured and raised, for whom greed and larceny is natural, and who eighteen centuries before killed "the love of the human race." Vladimir Pavlovich addresses the reader with a passionate call to join the fight against the "dark deed" of the global Qahal.

Chapter 4 was included in the stand-alone edition of the book and dedicated to the hero's fight against the dark powers. The timeline is from the end of the Crimean war to the summer of 1862. Olinsky's father, speaking of the death of Nicholas I, mentions a persistent rumor that Dr. Mandt could not disobey the Tsar and gave him poison (nearly 40 years later this rumor referred to Alexander III who, allegedly, was poisoned by his Jewish doctor Zakharyin at the order of Yiddo-Masons).

Meanwhile, in 1855 the ground was laid for the myth of a Tsar Knight who was broken by the war and could not bear Russia's humiliation. The Gentry Assembly openly spoke about diplomatic isolation of Russia. (Wagner remains true to himself and all the talking is done while drinking vodka; in this the author casts an accusation at the society that refuses to concentrate on an important matter.) The new reign, greeted with joy, led to the liberation of 20 million slaves. The entire Russia turned into one huge chatterbox. Liberal rhetoric encompassed every circle of the society. In a lecture on China's lagging in development that was given, apparently, by Chernyshevsky, everyone saw an overt hint at their homeland. Vladimir Pavlovich himself decided to recreate a masonic lodge. His senior colleague was one Pavel Mikhailovich Sambunov, possibly a freemason of the 1820s, for he tried to reestablish connections with his former comrades, of whom he had "plenty in every corner of Russia. [32] Olinsky himself recruited adherents among his acquaintances, and the membership of the lodge reached 25 in three years.

Such a small number of "brethren" is explained by the fact that the club's activity was peaceful and the majority of freethinkers joined radical organizations. To join Olinsky's society one had to take a "brotherly" oath to live not for oneself, but for others, to place a "brother's" need above one's own and to stand up for that "brother" as for oneself.

Everything greedy, selfish, corruptive for the soul was banished. This was a sober society where wine, vodka and gambling were prohibited.

The members of the club employed secrecy and, in their correspondence, used exclusively nicknames (the "brethren" themselves explained that their names could not be known neither to the populace nor to the government). In the 1860s they "practiced the principle that now is defended by Tolstoy and his followers. We did not oppose evil with evil." The members of the club opposed themselves to Slavophiles, since the ideas of Slavophilia were secondary for the brethren: "We were for all humans." Finally, Wagner utters the forbidden word: "Our club partially revived freemasonry, but without its mysticism." Obviously, such a society could not exist long; it was too perfect; after five or six years the club disbanded. Through some circumstances Olinsky faces Jewry again. It happens against the background of the "people of the sixties" fight against the government. [33] Under obvious pseudonyms, Wagner brings in many public figures of the time, including the members of the famous Sleptsov's commune. He finds some sharp words to describe the experimenters.

All in all, by the time Wagner's novel came out, the anti-nihilist topic had already been well developed in Leskov's *Nowhere,* Markevich's *Abyss,* and Krestovsky's *Moutons de Panurge.* The main difference between Wagner's book and the above-mentioned novels is in the fact that there is no protagonist fighting against nihilism in his work. Nihilists, in fact, have no opponent. Sarcastic words addressed to Chernychevsky's novel ("unnatural Utopia") and free love ("dog love") are not balanced by calls to ultimate personal improvement, because the author himself admits the failure of the "club's purpose."

At one of the meetings Olinsky meets the "late Sarra's" doppelganger, the pretty Hesya. (Clearly the author did not pick the name at random; it was meant to point to Hesya Helfman). At the meeting, a representative of the Central Revolutionary Committee of Geneva, a Jew by the name of Cardin, calling for rebellion, suggests that to avoid failure they should create groups of five: "...the fives will not know what the leader knows. The leaders will not know what the bosses know, and only the bosses will know the will of the Central Committee. The secret will be kept and fruit will be borne. Here, gentlemen, is... the will, the ruling, and the program of the Central Revolutionary Committee." The authorship of the program is ascribed to one Tokunov (a nod to Tkachev, Nechayev, and Bakunin).

Olinsky the protagonist joins Hesya in a "civil union." She herself is a secret agent of the Central Committee and is quite familiar with Vladimir Pavlovich's club activity. By the way, she mocks the hero's ideal to love the entire human race: "Here, you and I can love each other... but how can you love the entire humanity? What side of it do you hug and kiss?" Hesya's love for Vladimir, or, rather, their affair, is very earthly in nature. Hesya sucks money out of her well-to-do lover and gives him Central Committee receipts in exchange. She demands monies for an "evil" deed that is supposed, in the end, to bring about the "good." Curious is the naivete of the hero who refuses to drink Jewish beer before the pretty Hesya tries it; his old experience, his relationship with Sarra, was not wasted on him. In the end it turns out that Hesya is not only an agent of a secret organization, but a daughter of the banker Bergenblatt, who owns a luxurious two-story stone manor. The banker is also the head of a secret qahal. Mr. Bergenblatt wishes to bring Olinsky to the Jewish side and for this reason lets slip (Jews in Wagner's novel are very loose-tongued in general) some closely guarded secrets: "We, in part, belong to the sect of Ebionites, but, in any case, our beliefs are the direct legacy of the sect of the Essenes, the sect whose beliefs were so clearly, definitely, and sincerely presented by the Great Prophet of Christianity." Further he declares: "We who stand at the head of the aspirations of entire Jewry... we look at everyone from the point of view of unity of spirit and freedom of thought and feeling." In response to Olinsky's accusation that Jews are a self-proclaimed exclusive race hostile to the rest of mankind, Bergenblatt says: "We have no class, ethnic, or ritual boundaries... Our unity is for every nation, but it only penetrates into the higher circles." Of course, Bergenblatt is not responsible for every one of his tribesmen, and love of gold has the flipside; just consider Montefiori's philanthropy. But other nations are also known for their greed. In any case, "riches are the only earthly power that is above other powers, and whenever you expect to fight... it is necessary to accumulate and store this power." (Attention should be paid to the similarity of this passage to some of the items of *The Protocols of the Elders of Zion*.")

Olinsky learns that the next day, Jews would set on fire the shops of minor merchants at Apraxin and Shchukin markets. It is still unknown who was guilty of these instances of arson.

But Wagner knows. What was arson necessary for? Jews explain to Olinsky that it was important to devastate Russia merchants and put "our traders" in their place. And our hero sees again: "What is this? It is some kind of Jews' conspiracy against Russians. What will they achieve with this unity? Will they promote their huckster people?! Oppress our trade, already weak, suppress the power of our capital… To hell with you," he raged, "with your freedom and unity! This is no unity but a fight to suppress Christian nations, the nations full of love for the Great Son of man and all humans… even for you, "the mangy cut ones." At the same time the hero learns that pretty Hesya is the new Judith of the Jewish people, for her lot was to serve Israel with her body. The "secrets" of freemasonry and Jewry fill many pages of the novel. Here is one of the character's thoughts on the Decembrists: the dream of the Decembrists is a dream of oligarchy and hegemony of the nobility. Modern reformers hate the nobility and dream of the oligarchy of intelligentsia. We should compare this passage, for instance, to *The Protocols* Item 1, where it literally says the following: "On the ruins of natural and hereditary aristocracy we placed the aristocracy of our intelligentsia." It is logical to suppose that the creators of *The Protocols* studied the "treatises" of their predecessors well.

The revealing of secret plans continues: "Now, two great questions are being raised and are brewing in the whole wide world: on the one hand… the underground serpent is the fifth, working class, on the other it is Jewry… We are coming back around… We may not be in the position of Greek helots or Egyptian slaves yet, but we certainly will be, yes, we will… We will work for Israel… in reparation for them having worked for Egyptians… history zealously guards its global circle of retribution… Eye for an eye! Tooth for a tooth! The lords of Assyria and Babylon! These are Gogs and Magogs! Who shall prevail, workers or Jews! Only the shortsighted cannot see it… — You forget the bourgeoisie… — But that is Jewry! Yids! They have the same goals: to suppress, to devour, to profit!"

At the order of the "leader and teacher" Bergenblatt, Olinsky is informed that his masonic club can join eastern clubs with western ones. To his puzzled question whether there are any such clubs in Western Europe, he receives the following response: yes, there are, Jewish only, and well-organized according to the twelve tribes of Israel. Apparently, Olinsky considered those clubs proselytic organizations: "At the time I did not yet know that there existed a sect of "Judaizers" and that it… raged in our southern lands."

Jews converting to Christianity, though, were only pretending, as Olinsky had a chance to make sure. Thus, a merchant he knew, Moisei Yochimovich Haber turned into an Orthodox merchant Mikhei Yakimovich Havrov, who frequented the Naval Church of St. Nicholas and at the same time sat in the Jewish qahal. The author again brings Vladimir Pavlovich to the meeting of the global conspirators, meaning that the hero gets a chance to eavesdrop on the conversations at one of the meetings of the global Qahal, with Bergenblatt at its head. Receiving a report from one of his colleagues, Bergenblatt launches into a speech that makes it clear that almost every European government is in Jewish hands. The foreign courts own Jewish bankers millions and billions. At the top of the debtors' list is Austria, and in the third place is Russia. Establishing a *Union Israelite* in Russian should wait, but "the future is in our hands... we shall take much in our hands, and pull them into debt they cannot repay... and then we shall set our beneficent France against the Slavs, the English against the Turks, and the Turks against the Slavs. And believe me, at the end of this enterprise we will have pulled Russia into a sizable war." As far as internal affairs, the plan involved resettling of Jews in capital cities:

"We move slowly but surely... Local stock markets are in our hands... Hopefully, also the press... will soon be ours... You understand that most effectively we can influence family...

There, in the heart of the home, we must spread and promote... Besides, we are taking steps to print a paper, or even two, in the Hebrew language and Hebrew-oriented." As far as the propaganda among the people, the plan is simple: "This is labor stock which we shall conquer with the help of vodka and slow, systematic devastation." Yet again, we find similarities to *The Protocols*: where they speak about the possibility of corrupting society with propaganda and spirits, the abolition of serfdom gave Jews the opportunity to take over timber and bread trades.

I wonder if the reality matched Bergenblatt's plans? According to the data in the well-known article by I. M. Dijour "Jews in the economic life of Russia," Bergenblatt's tribesmen, despite insurmountable barriers set by the government, managed to open Russian bread and timber export to the world market. Jews also played an important role in banking.

In two banks only, the Moscow Merchant Bank and the Volga-Kama Bank, Jews were not represented in the board of directors or among clerks and customers. In the rest of the banks, Jews played a significant role. Jews were successful not only in light industry (sugar processing, flour milling, leatherworks, etc.), but also became the founders of large-scale gold and platinum mining, and were engaged in railroad industry, machinery building, etc. As far as the bar of attorneys, they were represented by such brilliant names as Gruzenberg, Vinaver, Passover. In publishing, Jews found renown not only in printing and publication, but also as talented journalists. All in all, a wide field for consideration was opened for anti-Semitists.

Let us, however, return to our hero. Having suffered defeat in the fight against "global evil," he, at the author's will, leaves Russia for as long as 18 years. The last thing he sees when leaving his friend, the mason Sambunov's village is: "...on the knoll stood the same bloodsuckers and Jewlings, the victors in post-reformation Russia."

V. I. Mildon, the author of the article about Nikolai Wagner in the biographical dictionary "Russian Authors," writes: "The author's thoughts are expressed less artistically and organically in his most voluminous work *Dark Path*... that claims to depict the events in the lives of Russian and European societies of 1850s-1870s and presents, in itself, a sort of anti-nihilistic novel (one of its topics being a global conspiracy of Zionists)." In essence, this is correct, with some exceptions: the expression "conspiracy of Zionists" sounds too modern; besides, Jews in the novel do not try to repatriate to their ancient homeland. The second mistake concerns the words "depiction of Russian and European social life," since there is no description of European life in *Dark Path*, and that is completely obvious to anyone who read the novel.

The novel can be counted among anti-nihilistic as well as anti-Semitic, which was instantly noted by Jewish press when it came out as separate edition in 1890. Its publication in "Rebus" must not have attracted their attention. The Jewish critic "Accidental Feuilletonist" (the famous poet Simon Frug) was astounded: The Yid-hating narration did not come off the quill of a pulp press representative of the sort of Suvorin or Okreyts, but off that of a reputable scientist and well-known writer. Simon Frug pointed out various absurdities that fill the novel, but he never analyzed more than one chapter in detail; I believe, this reader/reviewer got tired.

The conclusion of the "Accidental Feuilletonist" is as follows: the novel *Dark Path* is a book clearly weak, laborious, and mediocre. Even the critics of "Novoye Vremya" were bewildered. One of them wrote: "Mr. Cat Purr should have employed the entire material he possessed to uncover all the horrors that Jews performed to ruin the poor defenseless Russia, while he only used part of it, and that unskillfully, and thus turned the factual material he possessed into something theatrical, fictional, and exultant," and ruined the scenes that "could have been sketched by the author based on documented data." [34]

The charming part of the "Novoye Vremya" review is the mention of "documented data"! Could that be the future *Protocols of the Elders of Zion* the author is talking about?

We should note that Wagner had spoken out on the Jewish question much earlier. In the same "Novoye Vremya" he published a lengthy article *in memoriam* of Charles Darwin. Having listed the scientific merits of the late scientist and mentioned the importance of the theory of evolution, Wagner adapted it to the needs of the organ that published him. History, he said, indisputably proved the truth of Darwin's teaching about the species' fight for survival.

Applying the laws of evolution to human society, or, more precisely, the Russian society, Wagner writes: "Victory comes to the wandering, nomadic people that have no homeland and whose grasping and enduring vitality has developed over centuries of oppression and persecution. These are the strongest and most experienced fighters for life, for survival. Their ability to adapt to life's conditions has developed over a long line of generations. They are cunning, clever, smart, resourceful, and talented. They are capable of anything and can achieve anything with their resourcefulness, patience, trickstery, unabashed impudence, and plain insolence. They are strong alone, but are even stronger and more frightening for all other nations in their unity and their corporate and ethnic togetherness. They have long understood that power is not in altruism, but in economic principle. They have long learned the hard way that the most convenient valuable substance, mobile and easily concealed, is precious metal. They have long realized that money is the only power that can conquer the world, and now they dominate at least half the globe, if not more. These are the fighters that brilliantly prove Darwin's theory. Over many centuries under the influence of persecution this nation has developed a selection of sires more cunning and resourceful, who can hide in time, and dodge or pay off any persecution. The progeny of these sires a long line of generations, have existed in the same situation of struggle that penetrated the flesh and blood of these people and became a crucial feature of their bodies, and now only brutal physical force can stop them from their further aspirations to exploit other ethnicities." [35]

Shelgunov sarcastically noted on the subject that "the man of science" honored Darwin's memory in his peculiar way by narrowing the theory of evolution to genocide of Jews. Of course, sarcasm is not out of place here. Still, Wagner's suggestion of employing "brutal physical force" found its adherents, and not only in Russia. It is not accidental that we find the honorable professor among the correspondents of K. P. Pobedonostsev.

The shock experienced by the Jewish reader was quite powerful. In the obituary by A. G. Gornfeld, we find these bitter words: "Death brought Cat Purr back to me. The dear old friend of my long-ago early childhood, he was dead to me a while back... when, as a college student, I read his *Dark Path* and, in horror, backed away from this familiar kindly face that was disfigured by a frightening and malicious grimace." [36] Then Gornfeld remembers a heavy and painful blow that he received upon reading his mentor's new works: "In their wild, raging, slandering anti-Semitism was something nightmarish and insane." Speaking of those pages of the novel that describe how Jewry plans their crimes with the purpose of destroying the Aryan world, Gornfeld uses new "post-*Protocols*" semantics: "...Jewish elders discuss the most certain and evil ways to destroy the entire Aryan world." [37] To Gornfeld, it is immensely painful to see the creator of Cat Purr pile up nightmares and ugly libel. Still, the respectable critic noted that Wagner's anti-Semitism fell on infertile ground. His anti-Semitism was too absurd, burlesque, and reeked of mental disorder too much to play any part outside the circles that did not really need it in the first place: those circles devoured Jews without the help of any ideology. Gornfeld's nobility of character was revealed in his last words:

"We drifted too far apart to love each other, but we shall not throw a stone at his grave." [38]

In the article "Russkaya Laska" Wagner the Cat Purr was mentioned with unkind words by Jabotinsky. [39]

Most scholars of anti-Semitic literature — Kunitz, Zaslavsky, Lvov-Rogachevsky, and Sobol — never even mentioned Cat Purr.

Right-wing activists never used his name, either; one can re-publish Wagner, but hardly read him. He does not offer any positive plan to fight global evil anyway. His hero is not the hero of Markevich, Leskov, or Krestovsky: a true Russian patriot prepared to sacrifice his life in the fight against the "global qahal." Security agents cannot be greatly impressed by denunciations of the Caucasian war or depiction of a Russian countryside, permanently drunk, lecherous, suffering from syphilis [40], and trading in ten-year-old girls.

Years went by. Wagner was never mentioned. Should his name surface in the emigrant press, it was always in connection to the famous tales of Cat Purr. [41] And then memory connected the famous zoologist and the writer of children's books. Such is the nature of memory of an emigrant that it assigned to Wagner kindness and wisdom. Boris Panteleimonov wrote:

"Wagner was a zoology professor at Petersburg University. He is known also as a fairytale writer through his Cat Purr. He was a poet and a mystic. He had a white mouse and never parted from it... Professor Wagner, a zoologist and a poet, was a fascinating conversationalist. His whole life he studied living things and joined positive knowledge with mysticism; he had a mysterious mouse friend and formed his notion of an animal's soul. Undoubtedly, this bearded eccentric achieved some kind of special wisdom." [42]

The reader may argue with this opinion. But Cat Purr experienced much stranger transformations. Who would believe that such tales as "Max" and "Volchok" were used by members of Narodnaya Volya (People's Will) as material for propaganda? Yet, Makar-Sinegub recalls just that. [43]

In the collection dedicated to the memory of Father Alexander Men there is an article by V. N. Toporov where he speaks of Wagner as a defender of Jews. This is a misunderstanding.

As for the collective petition of 55 Russian authors in defense of two Jewish journalists, Chatskin and Horwitz, who were defamed in the magazine "Illustration," Professor Ettinger was right in believing that this petition, published in Katkov's "Russkiy Vestnik," was meant to defend not the Jews but freedom of speech. It is sufficient to remember that decades later Vlfdimir Solovyov could not raise such an impressive group to sign his petition against pogroms.

NOTES AND LITERATURE

INTRODUCTION

[1] Quoted from: Burtsev, V.L. 1938. "Protokoly Sionskih mudretsov — dokazannyi podlog" [The Protocols of the Elders of Zion — A Proven Forgery]. Ed. Oreste Zeluk. Paris: 132. From the interrogation of P. N. Milyukov: "Not only a historian... cannot... believe in *The Protocols*'s authenticity, especially after everything that became known about its origin. Up to 40% of *The Protocols* is directly copied from the French book by Joly." Also see: Milyukov, P.N. 1922. "Predisloviye" [Foreword]. In: "Pravda o Sionskih Protokolakh" [Truth About *the Protocols of Zion*]. Paris: 7–14.

[2] —— Compare to: Bernstein, H. 1928. The History of a Lie. N.Y.; Bernstein, H. 1971. The Truth about *The Protocols of Zion*. Introduction by Norman Cohn. N.Y.

[3] Delevsky, Yu. 1923. "Protokoly Sionskih mudretsov (Istoriya odnogo podloga)" [*The Protocols of the Elders of Zion*: A History of a Forgery]. Berlin: Izdatelstvo "Epokha."

[4] Rollin, H. 1939. L'apocalypse de notre temps. Paris: Gallimard.

[5] Cohn, N. 1970. Warrant for Genocide: The Myth of the Jewish World-Conspiracy and *The Protocols of the Elders of Zion*. London.

[6] Poliakov, L. 1986. L'Histoire de l'Antisemitisme. Vol. 4. La Emancipación y la Reacción Racista. Barcelona; 1987. Les totalitarismes du XXe siècle: Un phénomène historique dépassé? Paris.

[7] Rozov, N.N. 1977. "Kniga v Drevnei Rusi" [Book in Ancient Russia]. Moscow: 73–75.

[8] Although Nestor mentioned in *Life of Theodosius* the arguments of the "holy father" with Jews of Kiev, the colony of Hebrews of Khazaria was hardly as populous as D.V. Ainalov believed (1941. "Istoriya Russkoy literatury. Literatura XI — nachala XIII v. Istoricheskiy obzor" [History of Russian Literature. Literature of the 11th-early 13th century. A Historical Review.]. Moscow, Leningrad: Vol. 1: 15). Unfortunately, we have no data on the size of the Jewish diaspora in Kiev.

[9] 1978. "Povest vremennykh let// Pamyatniki literatury Drevnei Rusi" [Primary Chronicle: Artifacts of the Literature of Ancient Russia] Moscow: XI — early XII c.: 100.

[10] ———: P. 166.
[11] Istrin, V.M. 1920. "Knigy vremennyya i obraznyya Georgiya Mnikha. Khronika Georgiya Amartola v drevnem slavyano-russkom perevode" [Books of Chronicles and Images by George the Monk: The Chronicle of George Hamartolos in an Ancient Slavic Russian Translation]. Petrograd: Vol. 1: 337–338.
[12] "Khronika Georgiya Amartola" [The Chronicle of George Hamartolos]: 426–427.
[13] Istrin, V.M. 1923. "Ocherk Istorii drevnerusskoi literatury domoskovskogo perioda" [An Essay on the History of Ancient Russian Literature of Pre-Moscow Period]. Petrograd: 214.
[14] Schwarzband, S.M. 1989. "K voprosu ob istochnikakh 'Skazaniya o kreshchenii Rusi'" [On the Issue of the Origin of *The Tale of Baptism of Russia*]. Jerusalem: Russian Literature and History: 132–146. I thank S. Schwarzband for the opportunity to use his materials on the history of Ancient Russian literature.
[15] Rozov, N.N. 1963. "Sinodalnyi spisok sochineniy Ilariona — russkogo pisatelya XI v. [Synodal List of Works by Ilarion, a Russian Writer of the 11th Century]. *Slavia*: Roč. XXXI 1: 141–175.
[16] Istrin, V.M. Op. cit.: 218..
[17] ———: 218.
[18] Porfiryev, I. Ya. 1887. "Apokrificheskiye skazaniya o vetkhozavetnykh litsakh i sobytiyakh po rukopisyam Solovetskoi biblioteki" [Apocryphal Tales of Old Testament Characters and Events According to the Manuscripts from Solovetskaya Library]. St. Petersburg: 6–12.
[19] Istrin, V.M. Op.cit.: 219. I. Ya. Porfiryev provides a number of examples of "slandering of Hebrews" from the most ancient parts of *The Palea*, which most likely came to Russia from Byzanthian and Bulgarian sources: "I ask thee, Yid..., listen, Yid..., for you are cursed Yids and foul infidels as you behold the miracles and grace of the Lord..., and shut your eyes... as you hear the Prophets and the Holy Scriptures... and plug your ears... in every way you are like an earthly dog, that hears not with ears nor sees with eyes, but only exists and is as angry." (Porfiryev, I. Ya. Op. cit.: 10).
[20] Porfiryev, I. Ya. Op. cit.: 11–14.
[21] ———: 161–166.
[22] Istrin, V.M. Op. cit.: 130–131.
[23] ———: 218. Compare to: Peretz, V. 1926–1927. "K voprosu o evreysko-russkom literaturnom obshchenii" [On the Issue of Jewish/Russian Literary Communication]. Prague: *Slavia*: No. 5.
[24] "Paleya Tolkovaya. Po spisku, sdelannomu v g. Kolomne v 1406 g." [The Explanatory Palaea: According to the Copy Made in Kolomna in 1406]. Moscow: 54–56.

[25] ———: 2.
[26] Helena Watrobska. 1986. "Polata knigopisnaya. Izbornik XIII veka" [Полата кънигописьная: The Digest of the 13th Century] (God. Leningrad, GPB, Q.p. 1.18). Switzerland: 194.
[27] ———:196.
[28] Rumyantsev, V.S. 1986. "Narodnoye antitserkovnoye dvizheniye v Rossii v XVII v." [People's Anti-Church Movement in Russia in the 17th Century]: Moscow: 220–224. It should be noted that the 14th-16th centuries saw the largest spread of the surviving copies of *The Palaea* in Russia; it was the time when the heresy of the Judaizers originated as well as the fight against it. Ref: Porfiryev, I. Ya. Op. cit.: 11–12, Note 1.
[29] Zabelin, I. 1905. "Istoriya goroda Moskvy, napisannaya po porucheniyu Moskovskoi gorodskoi Dumy" [A History of the City of Moscow Written at the Order of the Moscow City Council]. Moscow: 1:24.
[30] ———: 25–26.
[31] Ilyinsky, F. 1895. "Dyak Fyodor Kuritsyn" [Dyak Fyodor Kuritsyn]. *Russkiy Arkhiv*: 2: 5–16. See also: Edited by Ya. S. Lurie. 1970. "Istoki russkoi belletristiki. Vozniknoveniye zhanrov syuzhetno-go povestvovaniya v drevnerusskoi literature" [Origins of Russian Popular Fiction: The Birth of Genres of Storytelling in Ancient Russian Literature]. Leningrad: 362. Here is an interesting review of the novella as given by Ya. S. Lurie: "*The Novella About Dracula* stood even further apart from the standards of didactic literature. The author of the novella, seemingly intentionally, tried to pose a riddle to the reader by presenting the protagonist who did not fit into any single category. In the beginning of the novel, he informed the reader that the name "Dracula" meant "devil" and that Dracula's life fit his name. There seems to be a traditional villain in front of us. However, further on it became clear that Dracula fought the Turks, heroically and, undoubtedly, deserving the reader's approval; that he hated "evil" and to battle it, he established in his country a just and unprejudiced court that no rich or famous person could bribe. At the same time, Dracula performed innumerable evil deeds: he burned the destitute, executed monks, and dined among stakes that held rotting "corpses of dead people." Talking about the treacherous murder of trademasters who helped Dracula to hide his treasure, the author could not but condemn his protagonist and again remind the reader of the protagonist's similarities to his namesake, the devil" (Lurie, Ya. S. Op. cit.: 378.)
[32] Golitsyn, I.N. 1886. "Istoriya russkogo zakonodatelstva o evreyakh (1649–1825)" [The History of Russian Law Concerning Jews]. St. Petersburg: Vol.1:642. Modern Soviet scholars "dissected" the

essence of the heresy and replaced, first of all, its historical name with the euphemism "Moscow-Novgorod heresy." Regardless of the issue of Judaism's place in the ideology of this religious and mystical movement, it should be noted that in the modern times all the members of the sect who had survived the Great Terror and escaped to the West, without exception, converted to Judaism.

[33] Edited by Dmitrij E. Kožančikov. 1863. "Stoglav" [Book of One Hundred Chapters]. St. Petersburg: 27.

[34] One of the most consistent anti-Westerners of the time, an ethnic Croat Juraj Križanić wrote: "The Russian Tsardom... accepts anyone and will even convince, beg, and force many... to take baptism, and those who get baptized for their body's profit and not for their soul's salvation, it accepts into its people and gives them high seats. Some [of them] make our most important decisions, others make peace treaties and trade agreements with other nations... Should the Russian Tsardom ever perish, it will perish by these converts or their descendants. Or, perhaps, they will conquer our Tsardom to the shame of our entire kin. They will mix [with us] in blood, but will never join [with us] in [their] goals. The children and grandchildren of converts have different thoughts than the original people born [in this country]." (Križanić, J. 1965. Moscow: Politika: 501–502). This was written during the reign of Alexei Mikhailovich. But who did Juraj Križanić mean? Who are these converts that occupied top positions in Alexei Mikhailovich's government? Undoubtedly, one of them was a Duma clerk Almaz Ivanovich. We know neither his date of birth nor his real last name, but only a few nicknames. Almaz (Yerofey) Ivanovich Ivanov (d. 1669) came from a *posad* (settlement) in Vologda. As a young man, he visited the East,— Turkey and Persia,— where he studied Eastern languages and, according to Adam Olearius, could negotiate without an interpreter. In 1640, he was appointed a clerk of the Treasury, and in 1649 transferred to the Ambassadorial department. As a member of the Russian embassy, he visited Stockholm in 1649 and was present at the signing of an agreement. In 1652–1653, he was a member of an ambassadorial delegation to the King of Poland John II Casimir Vasa. In 1653, he was appointed a clerk of the Duma and the head of the Ambassadorial department, where he remained until 1667. At the same time (from 1653) he headed the Seal department and in 1667 was awarded the title of "the Seal Keeper." Almaz Ivanovich participated in negotiations with visiting foreigners in Moscow and often conducted those negotiations himself. During the Russo-Polish war of 1654–1667 he always participated in ambassadorial meetings with the Poles (Vilna, 1658; Borisov, 1660; near Smolensk, 1662–1663; Smolensk, 1664). Under his leadership,

the new Customs Order was created that unified trade dues. Finally, Almaz Ivanovich played a significant part in the case of Patriarch Nikon. The Holstein Ambassador Adam Olearius wrote that in Russia he met "people quite talented, gifted with good mind and memory" and as an example named the state chancellor, "the Seal Keeper" of the Great Seal of the Tsar, Almaz Ivanovich. Many notations by Almaz Ivanovich that testify to the sharpness of his mind and his brilliant knowledge of the law are preserved in the cases of the Novgorod Chapter and the Ambassadorial department. (See: 1955. "Ocherki istorii SSSR. Period feodalisma" [Essays on the History of the USSR: The Period of Feudalism]. Moscow: 380–381). The Jewish origin of "Alexei Mikhailovich's favorite" is beyond doubt (See: Zagoskin, I.P. 1876. "Ocherki organizatsii i proiskhozhdeniya sluzhilogo sosloviya v dopetrovskoi Rusi" [Essays on the Organization and Origin of the Service Class in pre-Peter's Rus]. Kazan: 198). Curiously, a convert was entrusted with such a subtle assignment as to press the Poles into abolishing the Treaty of Zboriv. (See: "Ocherki istorii SSSR" [Essays on the History of the USSR]: 381. However, Juraj Križanić did not mean only the state chancellor. Apparently, there were other Jewish converts serving in the Ambassadorial department, for, according to S. K. Bogoyavlensky, "noble origins lost its significance for service appointments at the Ambassadorial department before all others: the importance of the service demanded primarily talent, education, and steadfastness in defending the interests of the state." (See: Bogoyavlensky, S.K. 1937. "Prikaznye dyaki v XVII v." [The Department Clerks in the 17th Century]// *Istoricheskiye Zapiski*. Moscow: Vol. 1: 223). Thus, the Russian ambassador to Kakheti was V. S. Zhidovin, and the department clerk was Vassily Yudin of "visitors," i.e., merchants. Finally, the leader of the Moscow Streltsy (in modern terms, a position higher than that of the Commander of the Moscow Military Region) was Ivan Vasilyevich Zhidovin. Therefore, in the opinion of Juraj Križanić, Jewish "domination" (even though these Jews were converts) in Alexey Mikhailovich's court was becoming "dangerous." At the same time, foreign settlers in Russia, with their *Kulturtrager* activity, and the benefits of the Muscovites' familiarization with the Western civilization received a significantly different appraisal from the historical perspective. V. O. Klyuchevsky justifiably noted: "Many of these newcomers were people educated and renowned... and they did not wish to cut the ties of their new homeland with Western Europe; their education and merits stuck out like a sore thumb among the ignorant and idle majority of the Russian nobility" (Klyuchevsky, V.O. 1918. "Kurs russkoi istorii" [A Course in Russian History]. Petrograd:

Part 4: 300–301). The situation reached its climax during the reign of Peter I. The foreign entourage of the Russian reformer, and his rare for the times religious tolerance, provoked anger in the camp of his opponents, and his church reforms and abolishing of the Patriarchy gave birth to a legend among the Old Believers, which was shaped into the tale *Of the Antichrist Who is Peter the First.* (See: 1882. "O raskolnikakh pri imperatore Nikolaye I i Aleksandre II (popolneno zapiskoyu Melnikova-Pecherskogo)" [On the Old Believers at the time of Nicholas I and Alexander II: Amended with the Note by Melnikov-Pechersky]. Berlin/Leipzig: 73). The idea of a "changeling" in place of the pious Russian Tsar and the "reign" of the Antichrist "of the tribe of Dan" (i.e., a Jew) in the Russian Tsardom, as well as the "peopling" of Russia with foreigners, regardless of its legendary and mythical basis, later greatly furthered the search for "scapegoats" in the troubles of Russia. Remarkably, the very precise and accurate Jesuit reports of 1698–1720 stressed that one of the reasons for the failure of the union between "Muscovites" and the Catholic church was the following: "The tenth problem is the power of the Jews. There are here very many Jewish families that came from neighboring Poland. Although they have been baptized, they observe Sabbath in secret or even openly, as they did before. And such people occupy the top positions. One of them heads the Chancellery of His Brightness the Tsar (*N.M. Zotov before 1718; A.V. Makarov, after — S.D.*), another leads several most important departments (*Baron Shafirov — S.D.*), the third is the top manager for Duke Menshikov (*Fyodor Solovyov, the founder of the noble family of the Solovyovs; his sister was married to the first Policemeister General of St. Petersburg, a Dutch-Portugese Jew Anton de Vieira — S.D.*), the fourth serves as a Voivode in Vologda (*before 1708, the Voivode of Vologda was the Centurion Pyotr Yakovlevich Veselovsky — S.D.*) They are the primary and, compared to others, the staunchest enemies of the Holy Church... And now they protect with all their might the Lutheran and Calvinist heresies; and whenever they get a chance to do us harm, they are never without support from their allies." (1904. "Pisma i doneseniya iezuitov o Rossii kontsa XVII nachala XVIII vv." [Jesuit Letters and Reports on Russia in the late 17th-early 18th centuries]. St. Petersburg: 195–196). Indeed, according to the testimony of their contemporaries, the Shafirov family observed *kashrut* at home. Shafirov's son, who was sent as an apprentice to the Danish ambassador, refused to eat pork and said that it was not consumed in his home:... to my question why he didn't eat it, he responded that neither his parents nor his siblings ate it, since it was considered a sin" (Juel, Just. 1899. "Zapiski Yusta Yulya, datskogo poslannika pri Petre Velikom. Izvlek iz Kopengagenskogo gosarkhiva i perevel s datsk. Yu. L. Shcherbachev" [Journal of Just Juel, the Danish Ambassador to Peter the Great. Retrieved from the State Archives in Copenhagenand and translated from Danish by Yu. L. Shcherbachev] // "Chteniya v Imp. o-ve istorii i drevnostei rossiyskikh pri Mosk. un-te" [Readings at the Emperor's department of History and Artifacts of Russia at Moscow University]. Moscow: 224).

[35] Semeka, A.V. "Russkoye masonstvo v XVII v." [Russian Freemasonry in the 17th century]. In: 1914–1915. "Masonstvo v ego proshlom i nastoyashchem" [Freemasonry: Its Past and Present]. Moscow: Vol.1: 124.

[36] Ravrebe, I. 1928. "Puteshestvennik kontsa XVII v. — Avraam Kunki" [The Traveler of the late 17th century: Abraham Kunki] // *Evreiskaya Starina*. Moscow: Vol. 13: 208–212.

[37] Quoted from: 1913. "Russkiy biograficheskiy slovar (Kulman Kvirin)" [Russian Biographical Dictionary: Quirinus Kuhlmann]. St. Petersburg: 546.

[38] ———: 547.

[39] Berlin, I. 1885. "Sozhzheniye lyudei v Rossii v XIII–XVIII vv." [Burning of People in Russia in the 13th-18th centuries] // *Russkaya Starina*: January: 187–192.

[40] Vernadsky, G.V. 1917. "Russkoye masonstvo v tsarstvovaniye Ekateriny II" [Russian Freemasonry During the Reign of Catherine II] Petrograd: 2.

[41] ———: 2.

[42] Ivanin, I.S. 1882. "K istoriyi russkogo masonstva v Rossii" [On the History of Russian Freemasonry in Russia]. *Russkaya Starina*: September: 534.

[43] Bashilov, B. 1955. "Robespierre na trone. Pyotr I i istoricheskiye resultaty sovershennoi im revolutsii" [Robespierre on the Throne: Peter I and the Results of His Revolution]. Buenos Aires: 20.

[44] Ivanin, I. S. Op. cit.: 533–534.

[45] ———: 534.

[46] Pypin, A.N. 1916. "Issledovaniya i materialy po epokhe Ekateriny II i Aleksandra I" [Studies and Materials on the Reign of Catherine II and Alexander I]. St. Petersburg: 88.

[47] Semeka, A. Op. cit.: 126. Vernadsky, G. V. Op. cit.: 4. Pypin, A. N. Op. cit.: 89.

[48] See: 1897. "Russkiy biograficheskiy slovar. (Keit)" [Russian Biographical Dictionary: Keith]. St. Petersburg: 605–607.

[49] ———: 607.

[50] Pypin, A. N. Op. cit.: 89–90.

[51] See: Sokolovskaya, T. 1907. "O masonstve v prezhnem russkom flote" [On Freemasonry in Older Russian Navy] //*More*: No. 8: 216–236.
[52] Pypin, A. N. Op. cit.: 91.
[53] Vernadsky, G. V. Op. cit.: 6.
[54] Bashilov, B. Op. cit.: 49–53.
[55] Pypin, A. N. Op. cit.: 92–93.
[56] ———: 92.
[57] ———: 96.
[58] Derzhavin, G.R. 1871. "Sochinenya (Izdaniye Ya. K. Grota)" [Writings. Edited by Ya. K. Grot]. St. Petersburg: Vol. 6: 437–438.
[59] 1914. "Russkiy biographicheskiy slovar" [Russian Biographical Dictionary]. St. Petersburg: 324–326. Archimandrite of the Holy Trinity-St. Sergius Lavra Hedeon Krinovsky was born in 1726. On February 8, 1753, he became the court preacher; on February 2, 1757, he was appointed the Archimandrite of the Savvino-Storozhevsky monastery; on March 4, 1758, he became a member of the Synod; and on April 17 of the same year, he became the Archimandrite of the Holy Trinity-St. Sergius Lavra. He passed away on his trip to Pskov where he was invited to the coronation of Catherine II, and was interred in the Pskov Holy Trinity monastery. There is the following epitaph on his tombstone:

> *Here is buried Hedeon, Hedeon the Glorious,*
> *The Orthodox priest of the Pskov Diocese,*
> *A pillar of the Russian Church, an adherent of Faith,*
> *A preacher, of God's word a teacher.*
> *A priest of good image, of honor, and a theologian,*
> *He left to the Church his wise speeches,*
> *And at the age of 37 he went to the Lord,*
> *Leaving behind his flock in many tears and sorrow.*

Most likely, A. N. Pypin was mistaken in his reference to "Letopis russkoi literatury i drevnosti" [The Chronicle of Russian Literature and Antiquity] published by N. S. Tikhomirov; Volume 2 ("Propovedi 1741–1749 gg." [Preachings of 1741–1749]) mentions Hedeon Antonsky, not Hedeon Krinovsky whose anti-masonic preachings were not included in this edition.

[60] Brockhaus and Efron. 1893. "Entsiklopedicheskiy slovar" [The Encyclopedic Dictionary]: Matsiyevich: St. Petersburg: 172–173.
[61] ———: 173.
[62] 1947. "Istoriya russkoi literatury. V 9 t. Literatura XVIII v." [The History of Russian Literature in Nine Volumes: Literature of the 18th Century]. Moscow/Leningrad: Vol. 4: Part 2: 52.

[63] Semeka, A. 1902. "Russkiye rozencreitsery i socineniya imperatritsy Ekateriny II protiv masonstva" [The Russian Rosicrucians and the Writings of Catherine II Against Freemasonry]. See: *Zhurnal Ministerstva narodnogo prosveshcheniya*: Vol. II: 344.

[64] Goethe's play *The Grand Kofta* was repeatedly interpreted in anti-masonic circles as a "prophecy of the great poet." See, e.g., Bostunitsch, G. 1921. "Masonstvo" [Freemasonry]: Yugoslavia: 71.

[65] Quoted from: 1893. "Sochineniya imperatritsy Ekateriny II. Proizvedeniya literaturnyye. A. Vvedensky. Vstupitelnaya statya" [Writings by the Empress Catherine II: Fictional Works: Introduction by A. Vvedensky]: St. Petersburg: 11.

[66] All quotes from Catherine II's plays are from the following publication: "Sochinenya imperatritsy Ekateriny II..." [Writings of the Empress Catherine II...]: Pages not specified.

[67] It is known that Catherine II herself hired a librarian who was required to know Hebrew. Freemasons' interest in the Hebrew teachings about God and various worlds that are laid out in the books *Zohar* and *Sefer Yetzirah*, encouraged their study of the Hebrew language. Russian freemasons were not the only ones in this respect, therefore Catherine II's mocking of freemasons' natural philosophy was aimed at their meddling in mysticism.

[68] Semeka, A. Op. cit.: 384.

[69] Catherine's warning to Novikov and the "imported" Professor I. Schwarz about possible persecution was obvious. However, this was precisely what revealed the Empress's impotence.

[70] Zotov, V. 1875. "Kaliostro. Ego zhizn i prebyvaniye v Rossii" [Cagliostro: His Life and Sojourn in Russia]. *Russkaya Starina*; January: 67.

[71] ———: 70–71.

[72] Semennikov, V.P. 1921. Knigoizdatelskaya deyatelnost N.I. Novikova i Tipograficheskoi kompanii" [Publishing Activity of N.I. Novikov and the Printing Company]. Petrograd: 89.

[73] 1907. "Zapiski imperatritsy Ekateriny Vtoroi" [Journal of the Empress Catherine II]. St. Petersburg: 585.

[74] Orshansky, I.L. 1872. "Iz noveishei istorii evreyev v Rossii. V 2 t." [From the Modern History of Jews in Russia in Two Volumes]. St. Petersburg.

Shugurov, M.F. 1895. "Istoriya evreyev v Rossii" [History of Jews in Russia]. *Russkiy Arkhiv*: No. 3.

Hessen, Yu. 1916. "Istoriya evreiskogo naroda v Rossii. V 2 t." [The History of the Jewish People in Russia. In 2 Volumes]. Petrograd: Vol. 1: 186–187.

[75] Shugurov, M. F. Op. cit.: 78.
[76] 1916. "Russkiy Biograficheskiy slovar (Glebov A. I.)" [The Russian Biographical Dictionary: Glebov, A.I.]. Petrograd: 346.
[77] Golitsyn, N. N. Op. cit.: 61.
[78] Chechulin, I. 1889. "Russkoye provintsialnoye obshchestvo vo vtoroy polovine XVIII v." [The Russian Provincial Society in the Second Half of the 18th Century]. St. Petersburg: 28.
[79] Firsova, N.N. quoted from: Kozlova, N.V. 1969. "Nekotoryye aspekty kulturno-istoricheskoi kharakteristiki russkogo kupechestva" [Some Aspects of Cultural and Historical Characteristic of Russian Merchantry]. *Vestnik Moskovskogo Universiteta (History)*: No. 4: 33.
[80] Gordon, L. 1881. "K istorii poseleniya evreyev v Peterburge" [On the History of Jewish Settlement in Petersburg]. *Voskhod*: No. 1–2.
[81] Golitsyn, N. Ya. Op. cit.: 299–313.
[82] Epstein, M.B. 1923. "K istorii evreiskoi kolonii v Peterburge" [On the History of the Jewish Colony in Petersburg]. *Evreyskaya Letopis*: Petrograd/Moscow: Issue 2: 104.
[83] Golitsyn, N. N. Op. cit.: 311.
[84] Ioffe, I. "Iz zhizni pervoi evreyskoi obshchiny v Rige" [From the Life of the First Jewish Diaspora in Riga]. *Perezhitoye*: Issue 2; 190.
[85] Bakounine T. 1967. Répertoire Biographique des franc-maçons russes. Paris: 330.
[86] Polonskaya-Vasilenko, N.D. 1945. "Iz istorii Yuzhnoi Ukrainy v XVIII v." [From the History of Southern Ukraine in the 18th Century]. *Istoricheskiye Zapiski*: Moscow; Vol. 14; 162–163.
[87] 1876. "Besedy Ekateriny II s Dalem' [Conversations of Catherine II with Dal]. *Russkaya Starina*: Vol. 17: 12.
[88] Golitsyn, N. N. Op. cit.: 83–84.
[89] Hessen, Yu.M. "Istoriya evreyskogo naroda v Rossii..." [The History of the Jewish People in Russia...]: 145.
[90] Golitsyn, N. N. Op. cit.: 153.
[91] The naturalist Carl-Ludwig Ivanovich Hablitz (1752–1821) came to Russia from Germany in 1758. In 1783, Potemkin appointed him the Vice-Governor of the Crimea. Since 1802, Hablitz was the chief director of state forests. Thanks to him, the first forest schools opened in Russia. Stieglitz is a Russian Baron family name of Jewish origin. The Stieglitzes moved to Russia in the late 17th century. Nikolai Stieglitz, a merchant from Kherson, ran a trade office in Odessa. The Stieglitzes were converted in 1812. Nikolai's nephew Alexander Stieglitz was the founder of an Art School in Petersburg (now the V. Mukhina College of Art).
[92] According to N. A. Engelgardt, the year of founding of the regiment, 1786, was calculated based on the fact that the writer portrays an

English philosopher and economist Jeremiah Bentam (1748–1832) as Zachariah Kleischbotam. Bentham traveled Russia in 1786 and visited the borough of Krichev at Mstislav uezd of Mogilev Province in Belarus, which at the time was owned by Potemkin.

[93] Engelgardt, N.A. 1908. "Ekaterininskiy koloss" [The Colossus of Catherine]. *Istoricheskiy Vestnik*: April: 55–57.
[94] Berko Yoselevich himself perished in 1809.
[95] 1924. Der Fürst von Ligne.— New Briefe Wien: 192; Schulsinger J., 1936. Annales Prince de Ligne: Un précurseur du sionisme au XVIII-e siècle: le Prince de Ligne. Paris.
[96] Paléologue, M. 1922. "Imperatorskaya Rossiya v epokhu Velikoi Voiny" [The Imperial Russia at the Time of the Great War]. In: "Istoriya i sovremennost" [History and Modern Day]. Berlin: Vol.3: 70–89.

CHAPTER 1
THE WAR OF 1812 AND DENOUNCIATION "OF ALL RUSSIA"

[1] Przecławski, O.A. 1883. "Vospominaniya" [A Memoir]. *Russkaya Starina*: No. 14: 488–489.
[2] Tsvibak, M. 1931. "Platonov i ego shkola" [Platonov and His School]. In: "Klassovyi vrag na istoricheskom fronte" [Class Enemy on the Historical Front]. Moscow/Leningrad: 94–95.
[3] In detail: Sliozberg, G.B. 1934. "Dela davno minuvshikh dnei" [The Matters of the Days Long Past]. Paris: Vol.3: 19–25. Dubnov, S.M. 1935. "Kniga zhizni" [Book of Life]. Riga: Vol. 2; 64–65.
[4] Voronkov, I.A. "Polskiye tainyye obshchestva v Litve i Belorussii v kontse XVIII v. i pervom tridtsatiletii XIX v." [Polish Secret Societies in Lithuania and Belarus in the late 18th and the first third of the 19th century]. *Istoricheskiye zapiski*: Vol. 60: 285.
[5] Joseph Przecławski complained that Poles did not seize upon their opportunities for promotion in service, unlike "foreign aborigines of one of the outskirts of the Empire." Przecławski, O.A. 1875. "Vospominaniya" [A Memoir]. *Russkaya Starina*: September: 135.
[6] ———: 1875. December: 713–714.
[7] Examples from the book by Sh. Ashkenazi taken from: Voronkov, I.A. Op. cit.: 272–281.
[8] Hessen, Yu.I. 1916. "Istoriya evreiskogo naroda v Rossii. V 2 t." [The History of the Jewish people in Russia in Two Volumes]. Petrograd: Vol. 1: 142.
[9] Krebs, V. 1879. "Umanskaya Reznya" [The Uman Massacre]. Kiev. Translated by I.M. Rev.

[10] Edited by Sh. Ettinger. 1979. "Istoriya evreiskogo naroda. V 2 t." [The History of the Jewish People in Two Volumes] Jerusalem: Vol. 2: 452–453.
[11] ———: 453–461.
[12] ———: 447.
[13] ———: 446.
[14] Dubnov, S.M. 1923. "Noveishaya istoriya evreiskogo naroda" [Modern History of the Jewish people]. Berlin: Vol. 1: 241–243.
[15] 1910. "Perezhitoye" [The Lived Through] St. Petersburg: 279.
[16] On the Argument in Jewish Circles Concerning Napoleon see: 1930. "Stranitsy proshlogo. Messianskiye nastroeniya v 1813 g." [Pages of the Past: Messianic Tendencies in 1813]. *Rassvet*: Moscow: No. 42: 7–8.
[17] Hessen, Yu. I. Op. cit.: Vol. 1: 361. On Alexander I's attitude towards Jews see: 1931. "Aleksandr I v roli... Balfura" [Alexander I as... Balfour]. *Rassvet*: Vol. 1: 10–11.
[18] Schilder, I.K. 1903. "Imperator Nikolai I, ego zhizn i tsarstvovaniye" [The Emperor Nicholas I: His Life and Reign]. St. Petersburg: 68.
[19] Yermolov. 1865. "Zapiski Alekseya Petrovicha Yermolova" [Journal of Alexei Petrovich Yermolov]. Moscow: Part 1: 258, 270.
[20] Volkonsky. 1912. "Zapiski Sergeya Grigorievicha Volkonskogo" [Journal of Sergey Grigorievich Volkonsky]. St. Petersburg: 174–175.
[21] Davydov, D.V. 1962. "Sochineniya" [Writings]. Moscow: 364. Jewish participants in the War of 1812 later received permission to reside in the capital. See: Mironova, M.V., Menaker, A.S. 1984. "V svoyom repertuare" [As They Would]. Moscow: 9.
[22] *Syn Otechestva*. 1816: No. 26: 289–291.
[23] Berlin, P. 1911. "Otechestvennaya voina i evreyi" [The Patriotic War and the Jews]. *Novyi Voskhod*: No. 29: 23–24.
[24] Saint-Glin, J. I. 1883. "Zapiski" [Journal]. *Russkaya Starina*: March: 543–544.
[25] Ginsburg, S.M. 1912. "Otechestvennaya voina 1812 g. i russkiye evreyi" [The Patriotic War of 1812 and the Russian Jews]. St. Petersburg: 93–96.
[26] Orshansky, I.L. 1872. "Iz noveishei istorii evreyev v Rossii. (Evreiskaya biblioteka. T.2)" [From the Modern History of Jews in Russia: Jewish Library. Vol.2]. St. Petersburg: 253.
[27] Romanovsky, A.M. 1877. "Frantsuzy v Chausakh v 1812 godu" [The French in Chavusy in 1812]. *Russkaya Starina*: December: 688–696.
[28] Lavrinovich, M. 1897. "Vilna v 1812 g." [Vilna in 1812]. *Istoricheskiy Vestnik*: Vol. 10–12: 873.

NOTES AND LITERATURE

[29] Przecławski, O.A. 1878. "Knyaz Ksaveriy Drutskiy-Lubetskiy" [Prince Ksawery Drucki-Lubecki]. *Russkaya Starina*: Vol. 21: 630–631.
[30] "Russkiy biograficheskiy slovar (Chartoryiskiy, A.)" [Russian Biographical Dictionary: Czartoryski, Adam]: 49–50.
[31] Schilder, N.K. "Imperator Nikolai Pervyi..." [The Emperor Nicholas I...]: 68.
[32] Schilder, N.K. 1905. "Imperator Aleksandr Pervyi. V 4 t." [The Emperor Alexander I. In Four Volumes]. St. Petersburg: Vol. 1: 140.
[33] ———: 141–142.
[34] Romanov. 1914. "Vel. kn. Nikolai Mikhailovich. Imperator Aleksandr I. Opyt istoricheskogo issledovanya" [Grand Prince Nicholas Mikhailovich. The Emperor Alexander I: A Historical Study]. Petrograd: 137.
[35] Shick, A. 1951. "Denis Davydov" [Denis Davydov]. Paris: 76.
[36] Przecławski, O.A. 1872. "Kaleidoskop vospominaniy' [Various Memories]. *Russkiy Arkhiv*: Vol. 12: 2300–2301. See also: Shatskin, Ya. 1914. "Novyye materialy ob uchastii evreyev v voine 1812 g." [New Materials on Jewish Participation in the War of 1812]. *Evreiskaya Starina*: 496–497.
[37] Davydov, D.V. Op. cit.: 358–360; 397–402; 447.
[38] 1912. 'Ritualnye protsessy 1816 goda" [Ritual Trials of 1816]. *Evreiskaya Starina*: Issue 1: 145.
[39] ———: 144.
[40] Dubnov, S.M. "Noveyshaya istoriya evreiskogo naroda..." [Modern History of the Jewish people...]. Vol. 2: 200.
[41] Przecławski, O.A. 1882. "Vospominaniya" [A Memoir]. *Russkaya Starina*: Vol. 14: 487–488.
[42] Dubnov, S.M. Op. cit. Vol. 2: 185.
[43] ———: 186.
[44] ———: 187.
[45] ———: 188.
[46] ———: 189.
[47] ———: 189–191.
[48] "Velizhskoye Delo" [The Velizh Affair]. In: Brockhaus and Efron. 1911–1916. "Evreiskaya Entsiklopedia. V 16 t." [The Jewish Encyclopedia in 16 Volumes]. St. Petersburg: Vol. 5.
[49] Ryvin, M.D. 1912. "Navet" [The Libel]. St. Petersburg: 73.
[50] ———: 85.
[51] Grossman, L. 1941. "Lermontov i kultura Vostoka" [Lermontov and the Culture of the East]. *Literaturnoye Nasledstvo*: Moscow: Vol. 43–44: 723. See also on Lermontov's outline of the tragedy *Spaniards*, inspired, in the scholar's opinion, by the Velizh affair.

[52] Przecławski, O.A. 1883. "Vospominaniya' [A Memoir]. *Russkaya Starina*: Vol. 39: 490–491.
[53] Przecławski, O.A. 1872. "Kaleidoskop vospominaniy" [Various Memories]. *Russkiy arkhiv*: Vol. 12: 2301–2302.
[54] ———: 2302.
[55] Afanasyev, V.V. 1982. "Ryleyev" [Ryleev]. Moscow: 232–233. See: Galant, I. 1903. "Arendovaly li evreyi tserkvi na Ukraine?" [Did Jews Lease Churches in Ukraine?]. Kiev.
[56] On the superstitions of the local Belarus population see: 1903. "Kosti evreya kak predokhraneniye ot padezha skota. Raport Pravitelsvennomu Sinodu Volynsko-Zhitomirskogo Episkopa Daniila ot 18 fevralya 1810 g." [Bones of a Jew as a Preventive for Loss of Livestock: A Report to the State Synod from Daniel, Bishop of Volyn and Zhytomyr]. *Russkaya Starina*: Vol. 10: 204.
[57] Przecławski, O.A. "Kaleidoskop Vospominaniy" [Various Memories]. *Russkiy Arkhiv*: Vol. 12: 2301–2302.
[58] 1959. "Khrestomatiya po istorii Ukrainy" [Reading-book in the History of Ukraine]. Kiev: Vol. 1: 641–642.
[59] Hessen, Yu.I. "Rokovoy Purim" [The Fatal Purim]. In: 1928. "Evreiskiy vestnik" [The Jewish Messenger]. Leningrad.
[60] Ginzburg, S.M. Op. cit.: 94–95.
[61] Florovsky, A.V. 1913. "Otechestvennaya voina i Novorossiyskiy krai" [The Patriotic War and Novorossiysk Region]. *"Zapiski Imperatorskogo Odesskogo obshchestva istorii i drevnosti" [Journal of the Odessa Imperial Society for History and Antiquity]*. Odessa: Vol. 31: 33,38,48.
[62] Semevsky, V. 1902. "Dekabristy-masony" [The Decembrists Freemasons]. *Minuvshiye Gody*: St. Petersburg: Vol. 2: 4–5.
[63] Pigalev, V.A. 1980. "Bazhenov (ZhZL)" [Bazhenov (Lives of Distinguished People)]. Moscow: 157–175.
[64] Mikhailov, O.N. 1977. "Derzhavin (ZhZL)" [Derzhavin (Lives of Distinguished People)]. Moscow: 216–219.
[65] Melnikov-Pechersky, A. 1958. "Na gorakh. V 2 t." [In the Mountains. In Two Volumes]. Leningrad: Vol.1: 338–340.
[66] Bostunitsch, G. 1928. "Masonstvo v svoyey sushchnosti i proyavleniyakh" [Freemasonry in Its Essence and Manifestations]. Yugoslavia: 35–36: "In his last novel *Freemasons*, excellent in structure but very improbable in ideology, A.F. Pisemsky describes to us the extinction of freemasonry in Russia... That is why the reader who knows freemasonry only from this novel does not see anything anti-Christian or criminal in this dangerous phenomenon, but, on the contrary, often starts arguing with those who take upon themselves the fruitless labor of opening his eyes..."

NOTES AND LITERATURE

[67] Kotelnikov, E.N. was born in 1774 or 1775 to a family of a village scribe in Verkne-Kurmoyarskaya Stanitsa. He began his military service in 1789, and by 1800 became a Yesaul. He was sent to serve at customs at the Austrian border, but on December 24, 1804, was demoted to Private for letting smuggled goods through. On April 18, 1815, after attracting the attention of Barclay de Tolly during the Patriotic War of 1812, he was restored to the grade of Yesaul. He spoke Polish, French, and German languages.

[68] Pypin, A. 1871. "Bibleyskaya sekta dvadtsatykh godov." [A Biblical Sect of the '20s]. *Vestnik Evropy*: March: 252.

[69] ———: 254–259.

[70] On certain similarity between masonic and sectarian initiation, see: Bonch-Bruyevich, V.D. 1959. "Sektantstvo i staroobryadchestvo v pervoy polovine XIX v. Izbrannyye sochineniya v 2 t." [Sectarianism and Old Believers in the First Half of the 19th Century. Selected Works in Two Volumes]. Moscow: Vol. 1: 279–280.

[71] 1907. "K istorii masonstva v Rossii" [On the History of Freemasonry in Russia]. *Russkaya Starina*: April: 113–114.

[72] ———: 216.

[73] ———: 219.

[74] ———: 221.

[75] ———: 1907: May: 413.

[76] ———: 414–415.

[77] ———: 423.

[78] ———: 426–427.

[79] See: Edited by A. K. Borozdin. 1906. "Iz bumag grafa Mamonova. Iz pisem i pokazaniy dekabristov. Kritika sovremennogo sostoyaniya Rossii i plany budushchego ustroistva" [From the papers of Count Mamonov: From Letters and Testimonies of Decemberists: Criticism of the Modern State of Affairs in Russia and Plans for Its Future Development]. St. Petersburg: 145–149.

[80] Schilder, N.K. 1898. "Dva donosa v 1831 g." [Two Reports in 1831]. *Russkaya Starina*: December: 522.

[81] Ch-v. 1875. "Mikhail Leontievich Magnitsky. Novye dannye k ego kharakteristike" [Mikhail Leontievich Magnitsky: New Information to His Characterization]. *Russkaya Starina*: November: 485.

[82] Schilder, N.K. 1899. "Dva donosa v 1831 g." [Two Reports in 1931]. *Russkaya Starina*: January: 69.

[83] ———: 75–76.

[84] ———: 80.

[85] ———: 87.

[86] ———: 1899. February: 296.

[87] ———: 1899. March: 623.

[88] ———: 625. Magnitsky should not have worried. Nicholas's censors kept a watchful eye on the publication of Jewish books. Around that time, the Shapiro brothers attempted to print Kabbalah books censorship-free, for which they were sentenced to punishment by rod; one of the brothers died as a result. See: Zeltser. Lipman. 1907. "Iz semeinykh vospominaniy" [From Family Memories]. *Evreiskaya Starina*: 23–43.

[89] Schilder, N.K. 1899. 'Dva donosa v 1831 godu" [Two Reports in 1831]. *Russkaya Starina*: March: 629.

[90] Magnitsky, M.L. 1883. "Duma pri grobe gr. Speranskogo" [Thoughts next to the Coffin of Speransky]. *Russkaya Starina*: November: 329.

CHAPTER 2
THE GREAT SECRET OF FREEMASONS

[1] 1984. "Istoriya vsemirnoy literatury. V 9 t." [History of World Literature in 9 Volumes]. Moscow: Vol. 2: 216–219: "The Quran is a collection of the preachings of Mohammed... didactic tales, canonic rules, prayers, etc. ... Any compositional unity is absent in the Quran... The Quran's pathos is aimed at paganism... The Quran contains no consistent narration of the stories of the Old and New Testaments..." The absence of a "Gospel story" of Mohammed's life in the Quran is the reason why Hebrews and Christians, as those who believe in One God (Allah), are equally recognized as "God-bearers": "Truly those who believe and those who converted to Judaism, and Christians, and Sabians who believe in Allah... they shall receive their reward from the Lord and there shall be no fear among them and they shall not know sorrow" (The Quran: Al-Baqarah: 59).

[2] Levitina, V. 1988. "Russkiy teatr i evreyi. V 2 kn." [Russian Theater and the Jews. In 2 Books]. Jerusalem: Book 1: 30.

[3] ———: 30.

[4] Compare the line "like a Yid about Jerusalem" in Pushkin's poem with the ending of the foreword to Part III of Adam Mickiewicz's *Dziady*: "As far as sympathetic European people who cried over Poland like once did the wives of Jerusalem..." (Mickiewicz, A. 1968. "Stikhotvoreniya. Poemy. Biblioteka Vsemirnoy Literatury' [Verses. Poems. Library of World Literature]. Moscow: Vol. 96: 289).

[5] Pushkin, A.S. 1962–1965. "Polnoye sobranyye sochineniy. V 10 t." [Full Collection of Works in 10 Volumes]. Moscow: Vol. 3: 421.

[6] Galant, I. 1903. "Arendovali li evreyi tserkvi na Ukraine?" [Did Jews Lease Churches in Ukraine?]. Kiev: 72–74.

[7] Gogol, N.V. 1948–1951. "Sobranye sochineniy v 6 t." [Collection of Works in Six Volumes]. Moscow: Vol. 2: 30–147. Further, the novella *Taras Bulba* is quoted from this edition.

[8] Kushner, B. 1989. "Otkrytoye pismo akademiku I. Shafarevichu" [A Public Letter to Academician Shafarevich]. *"22"*: Jerusalem: No. 64: 164. ("*Taras Bulba*, with its apologia of national arrogance and hatred, and romanticizing of a bloody riot!"). Most likely, to an attentive reader, the author's word is a bit different from the thoughts and deeds of his characters.

[9] In this respect, Haim Nahman Bialik is no better or worse than Fyodor Dostoyevsky or Alexander Pushkin, who, for example, said: "The Poles must be strangled." Compare to: Shafarevich, I. 1989. "Rusofobia" [Russophobia]. *"22"*: Jerusalem: No. 63: 140–142.

[10] See, e.g.: Kuzmin, A. 1989. "K kakomu khramu ishchem my dorogu?" [To Which Temple Are We Searching for a Path?]. Moscow: 129. ("Another correction is necessary: In old Russia the divide lay not between ethnicities, but between religious denominations...").

10a. Stepanov, N. Foreword to: Narezhnyi, V.T. 1938. "Rossiyskiy Zhilblaz" [Russian Gil Blas]. Moscow: IV.

[11] See: "Russkiye pisateli XI–XX vv. A. F. Veltman" [Russian Writers of 11–20th centuries. Alexander Veltman]. Moscow: Vol. 1: 405.

[12] Veltman, A.F. 1977. "Strannik. (Literaturnye pamyatniki" [The Wanderer. (Literary Artifacts)]. Moscow: 125.

[13] ———: 132.

[14] ———: 133.

[15] ———: 133–135. Compare to the sermon by Rabbi Shmuel ben Nahman, in which he tells how Abraham calls on the Torah and the letters of the Hebrew alphabet as witnesses to God in defense of Israel: "Alef stood and testified that Israel broke the commandments of the Torah. Abraham responded to him: 'You, Alef, are the first letter and you testify against Israel in the days of its trouble! Remember the day when the Holy Lord, let Him be blessed, revealed Himself on Mount Sinai and began with you — I am the LORD your God (Exodus 20:2), and no people accepted you, except for my sons, and now you testify against them!' And then Alef stepped aside and did not testify against them. Bet, shamed through Bereishith: "In the beginning God created," and Gimel, shamed through *gedilim*: "You shall make yourself tassels" (Deuteronomy 22:12), did the same." Quoted from: Roskes, D. 1919. "Vopreki Apokalipsisu" [Despite the Apocalypse]. Jerusalem: 38.

[16] Belinsky, V.G. 1961–1965. "Poln. sobr. soch. V 13 t." [Full Collection of Works in 13 Volumes]. Moscow: Vol. 9: 231.
[17] "Russkiye pisateli XI–XX vv." [Russian Writers of the 11th-20th Centuries]: 406.
[18] Pushkarev, S.G. 1956. "Rossiya v XIX v." [Russia in the 19th Century]. New York: 180.
[19] Oksman, Yu.G. "Kommentarii" [Commentary]. In: Pushkin, A.S. 1961–1963. "Sobr. soch. V 10 t." [Collection of Works in 10 Volumes]. Moscow: Vol. 6: 484.
[20] Okreyts, S.S. 1916. "Vospominaniya" [A Memoir]. *Istoricheskiy Vestnik*: Vol. 145: 616.
[21] Oksman, Yu. G. Op. cit.: 484.
[22] Pushkin, A.S. 1962–1964. "Poln. sobr. soch. V 10 t." [Full Collection of Works in 10 Volumes]. Moscow: Vol. 7: 251.
[23] ———: Vol. 10: 393.
[24] ———: 324.
[25] See: *Vestnik Rizhskikh Evreyev*: 1872: No.24: 746.
[26] Bulgarin, F.V. 1830. "Ivan Vyzhygin" [Ivan Vyzhygin]. St. Petersburg: 82.
[27] Przecławski, O.A. 1872. "Kaleidoskop vospominaniy" [Various Memories]. *Russkiy Arkhiv*: Vol. 10: 1949.
[28] See: Ryabinin, I. "Polskoye masonstvo" [Polish Freemasons]. In: Edited by Melgunov, S.P. and Sidorov, N.P. 1915. "Masonstvo v ego proshlom i nastoyashchem. V 2 t." [Freemasonry: Its Past and Present. In 2 Volumes]. St. Petersburg: Vol. 2.
[29] Afanasyev, V. 1982. "Ryleyev (ZhZL)" [Ryleyev. Lives of Distinguished People]. Moscow: 182–186.
[30] *Russkaya Starina*: 1876: Vol. 16: 559.
[31] Aksakov, S.T. 1955. "Sobr. soch. V 5 t." [Collection of Works. In 5 Volumes]. Moscow: Vol. 2: 308–309.
[32] ———: 312.
[33] Przecławski, O.A. 1874. "Vospominaniya" [A Memoir]. *Russkaya Starina*: November: 474.
[34] A special significance for Przecławski was held by his study of the works of "the thrice great" Hermes Trismegistus (a fictional author of early Christian theosophy).
[35] Heinrich Cornelius Agrippa von Nettesheim (1486–1535) was a philosopher and a mystic whom Rabelais mocked in his novel *Gargantua and Pantagruel* under the name of Herr Trippa. Cornelius Agrippa's work *De Occulta Philosophia* (1533) was a special favorite of Przecławski.
[36] Przecławski, O.A. 1874. "Vospominaniya" [A Memoir]. *Russkaya Starina*: November: 474.
[37] ———: 481.

[38] Przecławski, O.A. 1872. "Kaleidoskop vospominaniy" [Various Memories]. *Russkiy Arkhiv*: Vol. 10: 1887–1954.

[39] Przecławski promoted transliteration of personal names using Latin pronunciation, that is why it is "Tsiprian" and not "Kiprian" (Cypriani citatio angelorum, Dimisso Cypriani, etc.).

[40] Przecławski, O.A. 1875. "Vospominaniya" [A Memoir]. *Russkaya Starina*: September: 136.

[41] ———: 145–146.

[42] ———: 154.

[43] Nikitenko, A.V. 1955. "Dnevnik. V 3 t." [A Journal. In Three Volumes]. Moscow: Vol. 2: 108.

[44] ———: 110.

[45] ———: 112–113.

[46] ———: 113.

[47] Muravyov, M.N. 1884. "Zapiski grafa M.N. Muravyova Vilenskogo" [A Journal of Count M.N. Muravyov of Vilna]. *Russkaya Starina*: 1.1: 35–36.

[48] Buchbinder, N.A. 1928. "O.A. Przecławski o romane N.G. Chernyshevskogo *Chto Delat?*" [Josef Przecławski On Chernyshevsky's novel *What Is to Be Done?*] *Katorga i Ssylka*: No. 44: 32–48.

[49] Przecławski, O.A. 1875. "Vospominaniya" [A Memoir]. *Russkaya Starina*: September: 156.

[50] Przecławski, O.A. 1870. "Kaleidoskop vospominaniy" [Various Memories]. *Russkiy Arkhiv*: 1031–1055.

[51] Koni, A.F. 1957. "Sobr. soch. V 5 t." {Collection of Works. In 5 Volumes]. Moscow: Vol. 3: 286.

[52] "Russkiy biograficheskiy slovar" [Russian Biographical Dictionary]: 432.

[53] ———.

[54] Przecławski, O.A. 1872. "Kaleidoskop vospominaniy" [Various Memories]. *Russkiy Arkhiv*: Vol. 10: 1825–1926.

[55] Schilder, N.K. 1897–1898. "Imperator Aleksandr I. Ego zhizn i tsarstvovaniye. V 4 kn." [The Emperor Alexander I: His Life and His Reign. In 4 Books]. St. Petersburg: Book 1: 43.

[56] Mickiewicz, A. 1968. "Stikhotvorenya. Poemy. V "Biblioteka vsemirnoy literatury" [Verses. Poems. In: Library of World Literature]. Moscow: Vol. 96: 287–288.

[57] Przecławski, O.A. 1872. "Kaleidoskop vospominaniy" [Various Memories]. *Russkiy Arkhiv*: Vol. 10: 1929–1931.

[58] Kukolnik, P.V. 1873. "Anti-Tsiprinus. Vospominaniya o N.N. Novosiltseve" [Anti-Cyprinus: A Memoir About N.N. Novosiltsev]. *Russkiy Arkhiv*: Vol. 15: 204–224; 0193–0200.

[59] See: Pushkarev, S.G. Op. cit.: 28–29.

[60] ———: 30.
[61] ———: 30: Note 7.
[62] See: Hessen, Yu.I. 1928. "Rokovoy Purim" [The Fatal Purim]. *Evreiskiy Vestnik*: Leningrad.
[63] See: Dubnov, S.D. 1909. "Kak byla vvedena rekrutskaya povinnost dlya evreyev v 1827 godu" [How Conscription of Jews Was Intruduced in 1827]. *Evreiskaya Starina*: Vol. 2: 265. Compare to: Hessen, Yu.I. 1827. "Istoriya evreiskogo naroda v Rossii. V 2 t." [History of Jewish People in Russia. In 2 Volumes]. Leningrad: Vol. 2: 26–34; Ashkenazi, Sh. 1910. "Pervyi polskiy "sionist" [The First Polish "Zionist"]. *Perezhitoye*: Issue 2: 87; Yuditsky, A.D. 1935. "Evrei v tekstilnoi promyshlennosti XIX veka" [Jews in the Textile Industry of the 19th Century]. *Istoricheskiy Sbornik*: Moscow/Leningrad: Vol. 4: 129–132.
[64] Przecławski, O.A. 1883. "Vospominaniya" [A Memoir]. *Russkaya Starina*: August/September.
[65] Przecławski, O.A. 1883. "Vospominaniya" [A Memoir]. *Russkaya Starina*: September: 482–483.
[66] Mann, Yu. "Fakultety N.I. Nadezhdina" [Studies of N.I. Nadezhdin]. In: N.I. Nadezhdin. 1972. "Literaturnaya Kritika" [Literary Criticism]. Moscow.
[67] Przecławski, O.A. 1883. "Vospominaniya" [A Memoir]. *Russkaya Starina*: September: 485.
[68] V.I. Dal was a friend of N.I. Pirogov, who was a militant philo-Semitist. This fact alone makes one doubt his part in compiling "Rozyskaniya..."
[69] Porudominsky, V.I. 1971. "Dal (ZhZL)" [Dal. Lives of Distinguished People]. Moscow: 247.
[70] Hessen, Yu.I. 1914. "Pisal li Dal o krovavom navete?" [Did Dal Write About the Blood Libel?]. *Golos Minuvshego*: Issue 3; 331.
[71] ———.
[72] Przecławski, O.A. 1875. "Vospominaniya" [A Memoir]. *Russkaya Starina*: December: 712.
[73] Tolstoy-Znamenski, D.M. 1876. "Otvet Tsiprinusu" [A Response to Cyprinus]. *Russkiy Arkhiv*.
[74] Grigoriev, V.V. 1846. "Evreiskiye religioznye sekty v Rossii" [Jewish Religious Sects in Russia]. St. Petersburg: 4.
[75] Hessen, Yu.I. 1914. "Zapiska o ritualnykh ubiystvakh (pripisyvayemaya V.I. Dalyu) i yeyo istochniki" [The Note on Ritual Murders, ascribed to V.I. Dal, and Its Origins]. St. Petersburg: 31.
[76] Grigoriev, V.V. Op. cit.: 4–5.
[77] Przecławski, O.A. 1883. "Vospominaniya" [A Memoir]. *Russkaya Starina*: Vol. 14: 484.
[78] ———: 483.

[79] Porudominsky, V.I. Op. cit.: 238–239.
[80] "Evreiskaya entsiklopediya" [The Jewish Encyclopedia]: Vol. 4: 449: Entry "Besht": "He who laughs at these strange body movements is akin to a man who would laugh at the seizures and desperate cries of a drowning man. He who performs these movements while praying fights off the waves of earthly bustle that will not let him concentrate on his thoughts of God."
[81] 1914. "Zapiska o ritualnikh ubiystvakh" [The Note on Ritual Murders]. St. Petersburg: 13.
[82] Przecławski, O.A. 1883. "Vospominaniya" [A Memoir]. *Russkaya Starina*: Vol. 14: 487.
[83] ———: 487.
[84] Przecławski, O.A. 1875. "Ignatiy Turkul — ministr Tsarstva Polskogo" [Ignatiy Turkul, A Minister of the Kingdom of Poland]. *Russkaya Starina*: December.
[85] "Zapiska o ritualnykh ubiystvakh" [The Note on Ritual Murders]: 3–7.
[86] Przecławski, O.A. 1883. "Vospominaniya" [A Memoir]. *Russkaya Starina*: Vol. 14: 490.
[87] Grigoriev, V.V. Op. cit.: 14.
[88] Przecławski, O.A. 1883. "Vospominaniya" [A Memoir]. *Russkaya Starina*: Vol. 14: 495–496. See the lists of Frankist families: Mieses, M. 1938. Polacy-Chrześcijanie pochodzenia żydowskiego. Warszawa: Vol. I–IV.
[89] Korneyev, L. 1982. "Klassovaya sushchnost sionizma" [The Class Essense of Zionism]. Kiev: 206. Compare to: Gumilev, L. 1989. "Drevnyaya Rus i Velikaya step" [Ancient Russia and the Great Steppe]. Moscow: 131–133: "Having failed in the business of war, the Khazar Jews made up for it with love... Every Eurasian tribe considered a child a member of his father's family... Jews equaled ethnic origins with belonging to a community. The right to be a member of a community and, therefore, a Jew, was defined by being born to a Jewish mother... So it was that a son of a Khazarian man and a Jewish woman had all the rights of his father and opportunities of his mother... And a son of a Jewish man and a Khazar woman was an alien..."
[90] Przecławski, O.A. 1883. "Vospominaniya" [A Memoir]. *Russkaya Starina*: Vol. 14: 531–532.
[91] See: Mieses, M. Op. cit.: Vol. 3: 145–153.
[92] See: S.P. 1910. "Evrey na evropeiskoy stsene" [A Jew on European Stage]. *Evreiskaya Nedelya*: No. 9.
[93] Przecławski, O.A. 1883. "Vospominaniya" [A Memoir]. *Russkaya Starina*: Vol. 14: 533.
[94] ———: 534.

[95] ———: 535.
[96] ———: 492.
[97] ———: 493. Compare to: 1909. "Razoblacheniye velikoi tainy frankmasonstva" [Exposing the Great Secret of Freemasons]. Moscow: 86: Note by the editor A. O. Przecławski: "One of the simplest reasons for Jews' advantage over our common people is that these people are fond of hard liquor, while a drunk Yid is a great rarity. Is it at all surprising then that a sober man reigns almost without a limit among drunks?"
[98] Przecławski, O.A. 1883. "Vospominaniya" [A Memoir]. *Russkaya Starina*: Vol. 14: 494.
[99] ———: 493.
[100] ———: 493. Compare to: A. O. Przecławski's foreword to the manuscript: "The author of the manuscript... proves that this order is nothing but camouflaged activity of a malicious Jewish sect of the Sadducees" ("Razoblacheniye...": 5).
[101] Przecławski, O.A. 1883. "Vospominaniya" [A Memoir]. *Russkaya Starina*: Vol. 14: 493–494. Compare to: Katsnelson, L. "Fariseyi i Saddukeyi" [The Pharisees and the Sadducees]. In: "Evreyskaya Entsiklopediya" [Jewish Encyclopedia]. Vol. 15: 172–191.
[102] Przecławski, O.A. 1883. "Vospominaniya" [A Memoir]. *Russkaya Starina*: Vol. 14: 494.

CHAPTER 3
ZEALOTS

[1] Samarin, Yu.F. 1868. "Iezuity i ikh otnosheniye k Rossii" [Jesuits and Their View of Russia]. Moscow: 461.
[2] Bitsyn, N. 1973. "Zametka na statyu Sankt-Peterburgskikh Vedomostei o polskom katekhizise" [A Note on the Article in *St. Petersburg Vedomosti* About the Polish Catechism]. *Russkiy Arkhiv*: 1: 200–203. ("The notorious Polish catechism, this *katechizm rycerski*, undoubtedly exists... The Poles themselves do not deny the existence of its copies in the Polish language... Since... it is quite probable that at this moment we could find only a few of the copies of this *katechizm rycerski*. But, in the same area another brochure was popular, also in Polish, not copied, but printed and... published in Paris. This other, printed Polish brochure is almost word for word a response to that *katechizm rycerski*... Whoever its author may be, this Polish brochure exists open to the entire Europe, although it does not enjoy European popularity. It is titled *Katechizm nierycerski*.) The "logic" of the opponent is remarkable:

NOTES AND LITERATURE

most importantly, the other, printed brochure exists, and, being a "response" to the articles of the first copied one, proves its existence.

[3] Quoted from: Samarin, Yu. F. Op. cit.: 462.
[4] ———: 462–469.
[5] Golitsyn, N.N. "O neobkhodimosti i vozmozhnosti evreiskoy reformy v Rossii" [On the Necessity and Possibility of a Jewish Reform in Russia]. *Grazhdanin*: 32–34: 597–598. For example, N. N. Golitsyn's definition of the essence of "Jewish evil": "I believe that Jewish evil in Russia mostly affects the three areas of moral existence... On the whole, the existence of this patented anti-Christian teaching in an Orthodox Christian society is quite odd... Here the convictions, goals, and loyalties of Jews and those who rejected the Gospel come together... (compare to the Opinion on Catholicism of Poles and malignancy of Jesuits — *S.D.*). If you add the deep perversion of thinking due to the Talmudian upbringing (*substitute 'szlachcic'* — *S.D.*), everyday evil activity in forgery, trickery, and the entire way of life (compare to: "steal from the Russian treasury" — *S.D.*), the blatant rules of the popular and living "Jewish catechism" that allows for any trickstery and any lie (*"any measure is not only permissible, but necessary... all means are good... do not hesitate to have two faces...," etc* — *S.D.*) and legalizes a cruel, arrogant, and tyrannical view of a non-Jew...," etc.
[6] Volkov, V.K. "Osnovnye etapy razvitiya slavyano-germanskikh otnosheniy v XIX–XX vv. v svete germanskoi imperialisticheskoi politiki "Drang nach Osten" (problemy i zadachi issledovaniya)" [The Main Steps in Development of Slavo-German Relations in the 19th-20th Centuries in the Light of the German Imperialist Policy *Drang nach Osten*: The Issues and Tasks of the Study]. In: 1971. "Issledovaniya po slavyano-germanskim otnosheniyam" [Studies of Slavo-German Relations]. Moscow: 9.
[7] Kuzmin, A. 1989. "K Kakomu khramu ishchem my dorogu?" [To What Temple Are We Searching for a Path?]. Moscow: 220.
[8] ———: 221.
[9] Compare to the categorical statement by A. G. Kuzmin (———: 221): "Contrary to the opinion supported in the West, pan-Slavism in general was hostile to Russian autocracy."
[10] Chernukha, V.G. 1989. "Pravitelstvennaya politika v otnoshenii pechati v 60–70-e gody XIX veka" [Government Policy Regarding the Press in the 1860s-1870s]. Leningrad: 29–31.
[11] Quoted from: Chernukha, V. G. Op. cit.: 59.
[12] ———: 160–161.

[13] Strakhov, N. "Zhizn i trudy N. Ya. Danilevskogo" [Life and Works of N. Ya. Danilevsky]. In: Danilevsky, N. Ya. 1895. "Rossiya i Evropa" [Russia and Europe]. St. Petersburg: XXIII–XXIV.
[14] ———: XXVI.
[15] ———: XXIX.
[16] See: Kuzmin, A. Op. cit.: 220. The scholar, while quoting V. K. Volkov, purposefully mixes the notions of "Austro-Slavism" and "pan-Germanism," by which he pushes the date of birth of ideological trend of German nationalistic thought forward, to the reign of Nicholas I. At the same time, the author of the book whose chapters were earlier published in the magazines *Molodaya Gvardiya* and *Nash Sovremennik* involves A. N. Radishchev, the Decembrists, and the members of the "Brotherhood of Cyril and Methodius" in his "defense" of the idea of anti-autocratic concept of "pan-Slavism."
[17] Manfred, A. Z. 1975. "Obrazovaniye russko-frantsuzskogo soyuza" [Formation of Russo-French Alliance]. Moscow: 220–225.
[18] See, for example: Kuzmin, A. G. Op. cit.: 228–299, with reference to V. K. Volkov: "The war that began in 1914 was viewed by the German government as a battle between Gemanism and Slavism."
[19] This is how the early "exposers" Yu. Delevsky and V. Burtsev built their proof of "forgery," "fake," and "plagiarism" by S. A. Nilus.
[20] As shown by historical events, both ideological trends, "pan-Slavism" and "pan-Germanism," were most receptive to the myth of a "global Yiddo-masonic conspiracy," which resulted in such a wide distribution of *The Protocols of the Elders of Zion* in Germany after the Russian Revolution of 1917.
[21] "Russkiy biograficheskiy slovar (Ya. Brafman)" [Russian Biographical Dictionary: Ya. Brafman].
[22] ———.
[23] Dudakov, S. Yu. 1989. "K. P. Kaufman i evreistvo" [K. P. Kaufman and Jewry]. *Vozrozhdeniye*: Jerusalem: No. 11: 184.
[24] Bostunitsch, G. 1928. "Masonstvo v svoei sushchnosti i proyavleniyakh" [Freemasonry in Its Essence and Manifestations]. Belgrade: 82: "That such a secret international government exists was foreseen and sensed in the soul of our genius prophet F. M. Dostoyevsky, who wrote (see his "Dnevnik Pisatelya" [Writer's Journal] of March 1877, Book 2) that the existence of such unified nationality was impossible without secret inner self-governing, and who came directly to the conclusion that 'The Yid and his Qahal is the same as a conspiracy against Russians'."
[25] Bostunitsch, G. Op. cit.: 82.
[26] Brafman, Ya. A. 1882. "Kniga Kagala. V 2 ch." [The Book of Qahal in 2 Parts]. St. Petersburg: Book 2: 348.

[27] ———: 351.
[28] ———: Book 1: 61–62.
[29] ———: 63.
[30] ———: 64–65.
[31] ———: 129.
[32] Przecławski, O.A. 1883. "Vospominaniya" [A Memoir]. *Russkaya Starina*: Vol. 14: 493–494.
[33] "M. A. Filippov (1828–1886), pisatel i redaktor zhurnala "Vek" [M. A. Filippov, a Writer and the Editor of the Magazine *Vek*]. See: 1959. "Russkaya periodcheskaya pechat (1702–1894)" [Russian Periodicals of 1702–1894]. Moscow.
[34] Anonymous. 1883. "Velikaya taina frankmasonov" [The Great Secret of Freemasons]. *Vek*: Book 2. See the editor's disclaimer on P. 127: "From the late O. Przecławski's papers. Although we do not share many of the author's opinions, the notes are quite interesting. M. Filippov."
[35] 1909. "Razoblacheniye velikoi tainy frankmasonov (Iz bumag pokoinogo O. A. Przheslavskogo)" [Exposing the Great Secret of Freemasons: From the Papers of the Late O. A. Przecławski]. Moscow: 3. On the Filosofovs family, including the "author" A. D. Filosofov, see: Benois, A.N. 1980. "Moi vospominaniya" [My Memoir]. Moscow: Vol. 1: 499–508.
[36] "Razoblacheniye..." [Exposing...]. Title page.
[37] A. R. Drenteln became P. I. Rachkovsky's "godfather": he employed Rachkovsky as an informer and later promoted his career as the Chief of Foreign agents at the Department of Police.
[38] Filippov, T.I. (1825–1899) was a Slavophile writer. He served as State controller from 1889. See: Bogdanovich, A.L. 1924. "Dnevnik" [Journal]. Moscow/Leningrad: 156. ("T. I. Filippov, of whom even the Bishop says that he is quite a bastard... changes his opinions as one would gloves. Today he holds on to one view and tomorrow, to another. There is nothing sacred to him. He loves adulation and does not tolerate objections. He is a friend of *Grazhdanin*, where he is undermining Pobedonostsev to take his place and there do his deeds with the assistance of the Old Believers whom he has always secretly patronized, and not because of his faith (he has none) but because they are rich.").
[39] "Razoblacheniye..." [Exposing...]: 7.
[40] ———: 3.
[41] See: Nikitenko, A.V. 1955. "Dnevnik. V 3 t." [Journal in 3 Volumes]. Moscow: Vol. 2: 112.
[42] "Razoblacheniye..." [Exposing...]: 9.
[43] 1905. "Koren' nashikh bed" [The Root of Our Troubles]. Moscow.
[44] "Razoblacheniye..." [Exposing...]: 4–5.

[45] ———: 6.
[46] ———: 121.
[47] ———: 9.
[48] ———. The "anonymous" work is quoted from this edition, with page numbers in parentheses.
[49] Kuzmin, A. Op. cit.: 163–174. Compare to: Markish, D. 1990. "Nakanune" [The Eve]. *Sputnik*: No. 305: August: 3: "The songs of the Western Slavs trouble the minds of the Russian people, and there in the borders of Russia appear societies of Perun worshippers who are convinced that only pre-Christian polytheism is the salvation of the Russian people, and Christianity is Yid heresy, and Vladimir the Great was bribed by the Khazars, and he himself was a half-blood Jew, and rejected Yiddo-Masonry..."
[50] Bostunitsch, G. "Masonstvo v svoyei sushchnosti..." [Freemasonry in Its Essence...]: 267–270. ("... now comes revenge not for shadows, but for the execution of historical criminals").
[51] Nilus, S.A. 1920. "Velikoye v malom" [The Great within the Small]. *Luch Sveta*: Berlin: Issue 3: 301–312.
[52] Bostunitsch, G. "Masonstvo v svoyei sushchnosti..." [Freemasonry in Its Essence...]: 250: Note 5; 251: Note 12.
[53] ———: 254–255.
[54] ———: 255.
[55] ———: 256.
[56] ———: 260–263.
[57] See: "Razoblachenye..." [Exposing...}]: 119–120: "This professor was, in our opinion, A. Smirnov, the author of the article "Messianskiye ozhidaniya i verovaniya iudeyev okolo vremen Iisusa Khrista (*ot makkaveiskikh voin, do razrusheniya Ierusalima rimlyanami*)" [Messianic expectations and beliefs of Hebrews around the time of Jesus Christ (*From Maccabean Revolt to the Siege of Jerusalem by Romans*)." (*Uchenye zapiski Kazanskogo Universiteta. January, 1900*).
[58] Skabichevsky, A.M. 1909. "Istoriya noveishei russkoi literatury. 1848–1908." [History of Modern Russian Literature: 1848–1908] St. Petersburg: 56–92. (The anti-nihilistic novel is quoted from: Markevich, B. 1885. "Polnoye sobraniye sochineniy. V 10 t." [Full Collection of Works in 10 Volumes]. St. Petersburg: *Bezdna*: Vol. 8,9,10.)
[59] Markevich, B. Op. cit.: Vol. 9: 254–257.
[60] ———: Vol. 10: 95.
[61] ———: 93.
[62] ———: 98.
[63] ———: 163.
[64] ———: 123–124.

[65] ———: 256.
[66] Krestovsky, Vs. 1935. "Peterburgskiye trushchoby. V 2 t." [The Slums of Petersburg. In 2 Volumes]. Moscow/Leningrad: Vol. 1: 72.
[67] ———: 141-143.
[68] ———: Vol. 2: 89-91.
[69] Krestovsky, Vs. 1870. "Panurgovo stado" [The Flock of Panurge]. Leipzig: 44.
[70] Krestovsky, Vs. 1899-1905. "Sobranye sochineniy. V 9 t." [Collected Works. In 9 Volumes]. St. Petersburg: Vol. 7: 52.
[71] ———: 71-72.
[72] Zayonchkovsky, P.A. 1964. "Krisis samoderzhaviya na rubezhe 1870-1880 godov" [The Crisis of Autocracy in the Late 1870s-Early 1880s]. Moscow: 338.
[73] Zayonchkovsky, P. A. Op. cit.: 339-340.
[74] Krestovsky, Vs. "Sobranye sochineniy" [Collected Works]. Vol. 8: 205-206.
[75] ———: 284-285.
[76] ———: 288-289.
[77] Yakimov, V. 1902. "Krestovsky v Nakhichevani" [Krestovsky in Nakhichevan]. *Istoricheskiy Vestnik*: No.3: 952-953. Vs. Krestovky's personal attitude towards Jews was quite liberal. The writer possibly knew Yiddish. At least, he enjoyed singing Jewish songs and telling jokes about Jews, although his oral tales about the residents of Westland were always restrained and fairly objective.
[78] See: Anonymous. 1880. "Eshche po povodu zhidovskogo nashestviya" [More on the Yid Invasion]. *Kievlyanin*: Kiev: 106.
[79] Likhachevsky, a cleric. 1881. "Kak my, russkiye, pritesnyaem evreyev" [The Ways We Russians Oppress Jews]. *Rus*: No. 40.
[80] Anonymous. 1880. "Plach evreyev na beregakh Dnepra" [Jews Weeping on the Banks of the Dnieper]. *Novorossiyskiy Telegraf*: No. 1665.
[81] See: Anonymous. 1880. "Sumbur idyot" [Confusion Coming]. *Rassvet*: No. 13.
[82] Krestovsky, Vs. "Sobraniye sochineniy" [Collected Works]. Vol. 8: 286.
[83] The first part of the novel was published in the magazine *Russkiy Vestnik*, No. 1-2, 1881. The first stand-alone publication: Krestovsky, Vs. 1889. "T'ma Egipetskaya" [Egyptian Darkness]. St. Petersburg.
[84] See: Krestovsky, Vs. "Sobraniye sochineniy" [Collected Works]. Vol. 9: 488.
[85] Germanophobia of Vs. Krestovsky is an extremely important historical phenomenon. Compare to: Manfred, A. Z. Op. cit.: 22-23: "During the war of 1870-1871 the official position of the Russian government was, as we know, overtly friendly towards Prussia...

Gabriac... defines the peculiarity of Russia's neutrality as follows: "The Emperor... remained neutral until the end... when most of Russia held on to the neutrality friendly towards France..." "Never before has our government found itself in such disagreement with public opinion...," wrote Feoktistov. Even Meshchersky, the editor of *Grazhdanin* and "the Tsar's servant," noted in his memoir the divergence between the government and public opinion... Similar sentiment is expressed in the testimonies by Count Valuyev, F. I. Tyutchev, Nikitenko, et al." Anti-German mood only strengthened after the Congress of Berlin of 1878.

[86] Krestovsky, Vs. "Sobraniye sochineniy" [Collected Works]. Vol. 8. Further, the pages of the novel are in parentheses.
[87] Elets, Yu. "Poslesloviye" [Afterword]. In: Krestovsky, Vs. "Sobraniye sochineniy" [Collected Works]. Vol. 9: 489.
[88] ———: Vol. 8: 207.
[89] ———: 489.
[90] ———: 248.
[91] ———: 290–291.
[92] ———: 289.

CHAPTER 4
ENIMIES OF THE HUMAN RACE

[1] Zaretsky, L.M. 1873. "Evreiskiye tainy' [Jewish Secrets]. Odessa; Mordvinov, V. 1880. "Tainy Talmuda i evreyi v otnoshenii k khristianskomu miru" [Secrets of the Talmud and Jews in Relation to the Christian World]. Moscow; Osman-Bei (Major). 1880. "Zavoyevaniye mira evreyami" [Jewish Conquest of the World]. Warsaw; Volsky, K. 1887. "Evreyi v Rossii. Ikh byt, tseli i sredstva" [Jews in Russia: Their Everyday Life, Goals, and Means]. St. Petersburg; Skalkovsky, K. 1889. "Sovremennaya Rossiya. Ocherki nashei gosudarstvennoi i obshchestvennoi zhizni" [Modern Russia: Essays on Our State and Social Life]. St. Petersburg; Anonymous. "Taina evreistva. Zapiska iz arkhiva departamenta politsii" [The Secret of Jewry: A Note from the Archives of the Department of Police]. In: Delevsky, Yu. 1923. "Protokoly Sionskikh mudretsov (Istoriya odnogo podloga)" [*The Protocols of the Elders of Zion*: A History of a Forgery]. Berlin: 137–158.

[2] Antonius, Bishop. "F. M. Dostoyevskiy kak propovednik Vozrozhdeniya" [F. M. Dostoyevsky as a Preacher of Renaissance]. North American Diocese of Canada: 244.

[3] Gilyarov-Platonov, N.P. (1834–1887) was a professor of the Moscow Spiritual Academy, an opinion writer, a publisher, a historian of the Old Believers, a censor, the editor of *Sovremennye Izvestiya* and *Raduga*. It is to him that the theory of "two poles of Jewry" belongs: the cosmopolitan wealth of Rothchild and the cosmopolitan union of Marx. See: 1906. "Evreiskiy vopros v Rossii" [Jewish Question in Russia]. St. Petersburg.

[4] Antonius, Bishop. Op. cit.: 257.

[5] Litvin, S. 1897. "Ocherki "Kolymazhnogo dvora" [Tales of the Coach House]. *Istoricheskiy Vestnik*: Vol. 69: 752.

[6] Kugel, A. 1926. "Listya s dereva" [Leaves of a Tree]. Leningrad: 60.

[7] 1889. "Rasskazy iz byta zhenevskikh buntarei" [Everyday Tales of Geneva Rebels]. *Russkiy Vestnik*: No. 7–8.

[8] Ginzburg, S. 1897. "Literatura rynochnogo sprosa" [Literature of Market Demand]. *Voskhod*: No. 10; Hessen, Yu.M. 1899. "Kleveta v forme dramaticheskogo proizvedeniya" [A Lie in the Form of a Drama]. *Voskhod*: No. 3; Hessen, Yu.M. 1900. "Syny Israelya v Peterburge' [Sons of Israel in Petersburg]. *Budushchnost*: No. 46–47.

[9] Tutkevich, D.V. 1906. "Chto takoye evrei" [What Jews Are]. Kiev: 22.

[10] Rozanov, V. 1899. "Religiya i kultura' [Religion and Culture]. St. Petersburg: 259–260.

[11] Litvin, S. 1895. "Zamuzhestvo Revekki' [Rebecca's Marriage]. St. Petersburg; Litvin, S. 1897. "Zhertvoprinosheniye" [Sacrifice]. *Istoricheskiy Vestnik*: October/November: 391–392.

[12] Litvin, S. 1896. "Sredi evreyev' [Among Jews]. *Istoricheskiy Vestnik*: No. 10–12; Litvin, S. 1897. "Sredi evreyev. Sbornik" [Among Jews: A Collection]. Moscow. All quotes are from this edition. Pages are in parentheses.

[13] The heroine's conflicting feelings are shown in the following impression: "Studying with rebe Boruch, I was amazed by his energy, memory, and mind. To write letters he dictated was a real pleasure; he was brief and clear in explaining the most complicated situations and in formulating his thoughts... He could easily grasp the point of any matter and read between the lines and, when needed, especially in the beginning, expressed his thoughts in a way that only an initiated man could understand, and the letters remained a mystery for a stranger. This was a kind of a code, very clever and, at the very least, hard to break" (84).

[14] Schwarz-Bostunitsch, G. (?) 1943. "Sovremennye rezultaty issledovaniya voprosa o proiskhozhdenii "Protokolov Sionskikh mudretsov" [Modern Results of the Study of the Origin of *The Protocols of the Elders of Zion*] *Welt Dienst*: Frankfurt: No. 1/2 (47): 11.

[15] Snetkovsky, P. 1921. "Sankt-Peterburgskoye otdeleniye v 1896–1901 gg." [The St. Petersburg Department in 1896–1901]. *Byloye*: No. 16: 132.

[16] Kugel, A.R. 1926. "Listya s dereva" [Leaves of a Tree]. Leningrad: 60.

[17] A copy of the play with a dedication by S. K. Efron-Litvin is kept in the archives of the National Library of Israel in Jerusalem.

[18] Litvin, S. 1906. "Vospominaniya" [A Memoir]. *Istoricheskiy Vestnik*: 252.

[19] Mezhetsky. 1899. "Vospominaniya Mitrofana Porfiryevicha Mezhetskogo" [A Memoir of Mitrofan Porfiryevich Mezhetsky]. *Istoricheskiy Vestnik*: August.

[20] See, e.g Dymov's article reprinted in the magazine *Rassvet* from American newspapers (1926, No. 4).

[21] 1927. "Tainye akty iudaisma" [Secret Actions of Judaism]. *Dvukhglavy Oryol*: No. 11: August 15.

[22] Cohn, N. 1990. "Blagosloveniye na genotsid: mif o vsemirnom zagovore evreiev i "Protokolakh Sionskikh mudretsov" [Warrant for Genocide: The Myth of the Jewish World-Conspiracy and *The Protocols of the Elders of Zion*.]. See also: Cohn, N. 1970. Warrant for Genocide: The Myth of the Jewish World-Conspiracy and the Protocols of the Elders of Zion. London. (With some corrections in the Russian edition).

[23] Nilus, S.A. 1920. "Velikoye v malom" [The Great within the Small]. *Luch Sveta*: Issue 3: 101. All further quotes are taken from this edition, with pages in parentheses.

[24] Cohn, N. Op. cit. P. 12. Nilus borrowed his book's title from the Gospel of Mark: "Even so, when you see these things happening, you know that it is near, right at the door." (Mark 13:29). In Old Slavic translation: "близъ есть при дверехъ."

[25] Osman-Bei. 1873. "Zavoyevaniye mira evreyami" [Jewish Conquest of the World]. Basel (in German); In Russian: 1874. Odessa. Quoted from: 1880. Warsaw: 13–39. Pointing out that the goal of Jewry is conquering the world, the author insisted that Jews' dispersion was "voluntary" and served as a militant advance on "the entire humankind." "Jewish crowds flooded colleges, flowed into literature, medicine, law, and journalism." Osman-Bei tells the plan of conquering the world according to John Retcliffe, although he mentioned a "Jewish council" in Krakow, and not Prague: "Since then began the hellish work, the true work of Satan, and the press... began to obey the lying, malicious orders and became a slave to the interests of the Jewish people and a weapon to strike everything that dared to oppose the financial and political domination of Jews." Critical analysis of the book

can be found at: Lerner, O.M. 1874. "Maior Osman-Bei pered sudom zdravogo smysla" [Major Osman-Bei in front of the Court of Common Sense]. Odessa.

[26] Volsky, K. 1887. "Evreyi v Rossii. Ikh byt, tseli i sredstva" [Jews in Russia: Their Everyday Life, Goals, and Means]. St. Petersburg. Explaining that Napoleon's defeat and the Congress of Vienna allowed Jews to gather to perform the total ruin of states (P. 5), the author quotes John Retcliffe, who, in his opinion, "unveils to us the persistence and perseverance with which the Jewish people pursues its goal since times immemorial and by any means available, the goal of establishing their reign on Earth" (P. 10), and then quotes the rabbi's speech at the Prague cemetery verbatim.

[27] Kaluzhsky, A. (A.M. Lavrov). Censor's permission of January 17, 1906. "Druzheskiy sovet evreiam" [Friendly Advice to Jews]. Place of publication unknown. While expressing negative attitude towards the "Zionist program" (whose goals, in an anti-Semitist's opinion, are instigating ethnic hostilities, encouraging isolationism and closedness of Jews, teaching intolerance of Christianity, etc.), the author of this brochure offers Jews "friendly advice": to leave Russia as soon as possible or face wide extermination. Insisting that the ultimate goal of Jewry is world domination, the author brings up as proof the speech of Rabbi Eiger ("a Jesuit-Yid catechism") in... one of the masonic lodges of Prague where "all the tribes of Israel" gather.

[28] Demchenko, Ya. 1906. "Evreiskoye ravnopraviye ili russkoye poraboshcheniye? S izlozheniyem printsipov evreiskoy nauki o dvukh pravdakh: odnoi — istovoi dlya evreyev, i drugoi falshivoi — dlya goyev, i razyasneniem tainykh evreiskikh planov i programm" [Jewish Equality or Enslaving of Russians? Including the Principles of Jewish Teaching of Two Truths: One Real, for Jews, and Another, False, for Goyim, and Explaining the Secret Jewish Plans and Programs]. Kiev. In the author's opinion, *The Protocols of the Elders of Zion* are a variation on "the Englishman John Retcliffe," who, having obtained them, did not have time to include *The Protocols* in his work, because he was poisoned by Jews.

[29] Rossov, S. "Evreyskiy vopros" [Jewish Question]. S. l., S. a. The author insists, like A. Kaluzhsky (Lavrov), that "the rabbi's speech" was given at a masonic lodge... in a cemetery, where once in a century the representatives of the twelve "tribes of Israel" gather: "This speech by Rabbi Eiger is a compendium of Jewish wishes, goals, and means. There is everything: Israel must enslave Christians, humiliate their faith, seize their gold, occupy their lands, push them out of governments and take over the entire states by weakening them through various disasters and revolutions" (P. 79). The con-

clusion of the book is curious: According to S. Rossov, Jews are doomed to disappear, for "there was a million and a half of them in the exodus out of Egypt" and 3,500 years later there was only 11 million and "not more than the Chinese, of whom there are several hundred million, and, where are they?.. Extinct, or, rather, have been eradicated as a dangerous element" (Pp. 106–107).

[30] Protopopov, V. 1908. "V poiskakh zemli obetovannoi" [In Search of the Promised Land]. St. Petersburg. To analyze the Zionist movement and its prospects the author liberally utilizes the book by G. Butmi de Katzman *Enemies of the Human Race*. While repeatedly quoting *The Protocols of the Elders of Zion*, V. Protopopov stresses that G. Butmi, allegedly, quoted a "precisely" dated speech of a Jewish rabbi that coincides with the above-mentioned protocols in its main point. Then he states that this speech was given in 1869 in Hebrew, in Paris, and later translated by John Retcliffe into English and published in his political review (Pp. 27–29).

[31] Butmi, G. 1906. "Oblichitelnye rechi. Vragi roda chelovecheskogo" [Denunciation Speeches: The Enemies of the Human Race]. St. Petersburg: 94.

[32] 1909. "Razoblacheniye velikoi tainy frankmasonov (Iz bumag pokoinogo O. A. Przheslavskogo)" [Exposing the Great Secret of Freemasons: From the Papers of the Late O. A. Przecławski]. Moscow: 115.

[33] Pushkin, A.S. "Polnoye sobranyye sochineniy. V 10 t." [Full Collection of Works in 10 Volumes]. Vol. 6: 325.

[34] Cohn, N. Op. cit.

[35] Burtsev, V.L. 1938. "Protokoly Sionskih mudretsov — dokazannyi podlog" [The Protocols of the Elders of Zion — A Proven Forgery]. Paris; Delevsky, Yu. 1921. "Etapy plagiata" [Steps of Plagiarism]. *Evreiskaya Tribuna*: October 7; Delevsky, Yu. 1922. "Zagadka" podloga i plagiata (Stolypin o "Sionskikh protokolakh" [The Mystery of Forgery and Plagiarism: Stolypin on *The Protocols of the Elders of Zion*]. *Evreiskaya Tribuna*: December 28.

[36] Shafarevich, I. 1989. "Rusofobia" [Russophobia]. *"22"*: No. 63: 102. "The concept of "Moscow as the Third Rome" was formulated in the early 16th century by a Pskov monk Philotheus and reflected the historical situation of the time... This theory had no political aspect and did not push Russia to any kind of expansion or Orthodox missionary work. It did not reflect at all in people's consciousness, i.e., in folklore.

[37] There are millions of you. Of us there are myriads.
Try and fight us!
Yes, we are Scythians! Yes, we are Asians,
With slanted and greedy eyes!

> *To you it's centuries, to us it's only an hour.*
> *We, like obedient slaves,*
> *Held the shield between the two hostile races —*
> *The Mongols and Europe!*

Compare to the well-known verses of A. Bely:
> *Russia, Russia, Russia —*
> *The Messiah of the coming days!*

[38] Pushkin, A.S. "Polnoye sobranyye sochineniy. V 10 t." [Full Collection of Works in 10 Volumes]. Vol. 6: 408.

[39] Kuzmin, A. 1989. "K kakomu khramu ishchem my dorogu?" [To Which Temple Are We Searching for a Path?]. Moscow: 244–245. Noting that L. N. Gumilev defined the period of burning of an "energy basis" as 1,200 years and suggested that "Slavic ethnogenesis began in the 2nd century... a new explosion happened in the 14th century," the critic fairly points out that the period of ethnogenesis was "made up" (Compare to: Gumilev, L.N. 1974. "Etnognez i biosfera: Avtoreferat dissertatsii na soiskaniye uchenoi stepeni doktora geograficheskikh nauk" [Ethnogenesis and Biosphere: The Author's Summary of His Doctorate Thesis in Geography]. Leningrad: 3–8).

[40] Posnov, M.E. 1964. "Istoriya khristianskoy tserkvi" [A History of Christian Church]. Brussels: 230.

[41] To Russian messianic ideas the concept of "holy Russia" is undoubtedly related to the tale of the Apostle Andrew the First-Called: "The Dnieper enters the Sea of Pont: this sea is known as Russian. On its shores, they say, St. Andre, brother of Peter, taught... Andrew taught in Sinope and arrived in Korsun..." Quoted from the text of *The Primary Chronicle*: 1969. Izbornik. Library of World Literature. Moscow: 31.

[42] The image of Saul (Paul) of the New Testament, a former zealous persecutor of Christ's followers who became an equally zealous keeper of "the Holy Spirit" (see: Acts 9:1–11; 13:9; etc.), was chosen by Nilus on purpose, despite the fact that it was Saul (Paul) who first among the Apostles began to preach Christianity to Gentiles. Apparently, shaming Paul for "secretly" being a follower of Judaism, Nilus, in one way or another, was proceeding from the Apostle's words: "For I am not ashamed of the gospel, because it is the power of God that brings salvation to everyone who believes: first to the Jew, then to the Gentile" (Romans 1:16) or "We who are Jews by birth and not sinful Gentiles" (Galatians 2:15). Compare to the following statement of an anonymous author: "The blatant audacity of Jews which, indeed, is often supported by non-Jews, is

in their insistence that all culture came from the East: Ex Oriente lux!" (Introduction to the German translation of Nilus's book. *Luch Sveta*: 1920: Issue 3: 113).

[43] Dudakov, S. "Vladimir Solovyov i Sergei Nilus" [Vladimir Solovyov and Sergei Nilus]. In: 1989. Russian Literature and History. Jerusalem: 165.

[44] Compare to: Orlova-Smirnova, M.V. "Pamyati Sergeya Aleksandrovicha i Eleny Aleksandrovny Nilus" [In memory of Sergei and Elena Nilus]. In: 1986. "Pravoslavny Put" [Orthodox Path]. Jordanville, NY: 54–69.

[45] Dudakov, S. Op. cit.: 169: Note 15.

[46] The source of the plot of Vl. Solovyov's novella about the Antichrist was some apocrypha that had reached Russia in the 17th century. The best-known version was included in a large theological work by Simeon of Polotsk *The Crown of Catholic Faith* (1670). See the retelling of the legend of the Antichrist by N. I. Kostomarov in *Historical Portraits* (Epiphany Slavinets, Simeon of Polotsk, and their heirs).

[47] S.A. (S. I. Umanets). 1912. "Mozaika (Iz starykh zapisnykh knizhek)" [Mosaic: From Old Notebooks]. *Istoricheskiy Vestnik*: No. 12: 1032–1034. Compare to: Dudakov, S. Op. cit.: 167: Note 1.

[48] "Evreiskaya entsiclopediya. V 16 t." [Jewish Encyclopedia in 16 Volumes]. Vol. 14: 445.

[49] Solovyov, V. 1907. "Pisma. V 2 t." [Letters: In 2 Volumes]. St. Petersburg: Vol. 2:144.

[50] Velichko, V.L. 1902. "Vladimir Solovyov. Zhizn i tvoreniya" [Vladimir Solovyov: His Life and Works]. St. Petersburg: 89–90; Solovyov, S.M. 1977. "Zhizn i tvorcheskaya evolutsiya V. Solovyova" [Life and Creative Evolution of V. Solovyov]. Brussels: 238–246; Mochulsky, K. 1951. "Vladimir Solovyov. Zhizn i ucheniye" [Vladimir Solovyov: His Life and Teaching]: Paris: 148–150.

[51] Dubnov, S.M. 1918. "Furor judophobicus v posledniye gody tsarstvovaniya Aleksandra III" [Furor Judophobicus in the Later Years of the Reign of Alexander III]. *Evreiskaya Starina*: Petrograd: 32–34.

[52] The Summary of a lecture by V. Solovyov in the magazine *Russkiy Evrei*. 1882: No. 9: 344–345.

[53] S. M. Dubnov points to Professor D. I. Ilovaisky (1832–1920) as the author of the "anonymous letter" (See: Dubnov, S.M. Op. cit.: 34).

[54] Quoted from: Maor, I. 1985. "Russkiy filosof Vladimir Solovyov" [Russian Philosopher Vladimir Solovyov]. *Panorama Izrailya*: No. 175: 11.

[55] See: Stroyev, V. 1925. "Vladimir Solovyov i evreistvo' [Vladimir Solovyov and Jewry]. *Rassvet*: Paris: No. 49.

[56] See: Speransky, V. 1929. "Vladimir Solovyov o evreiskom voprose" [Vladimir Solovyov on Jewish Question]. *Rassvet*: Paris: No. 6: 12.

[57] See: Sliozberg, G.B. 1933. "Baron Ginzburg. Ego zhizn i deyatelnost" [Baron Ginsburg: His Life and Work] Paris: 64.
[58] Quoted from: Kaufman, A.E. 1908. "Druzya i vragi evreiev. V 3 t." [Friends and Enemies of Jews. In 3 Volumes]. St. Petersburg: Vol. 3: 57–58.
[59] Quoted from: *Budushchnost*: St. Petersburg: 1990: No. 46: 929.
[60] Bostunitsch, G. 1928. "Masonstvo v svoyey sushchnosti i proyavleniyakh" [Freemasonry in Its Essence and Manifestations]. Belgrade: 114.
[61] Solovyov, V. 1954. "Tri Razgovora" [Three Conversations]. New York: 207.
[62] ———: 230–231.
[63] Bostunitsch, G. 1928. "Masonstvo v svoyey sushchnosti i proyavleniyakh" [Freemasonry in Its Essence and Manifestations]. Belgrade: 114.
[64] Editions R.I.S.S., 8 av. Portalis, Paris, 1931.
[65] Zhevakhov, N.D. 1936. "Sergei Aleksandrovich Nilus. Kratkiy Ocherk zhizni i tvorchestva" [Sergei Nilus: A Summary of Life and Work]. Yugoslavia: 23–24.
[66] Vinberg, F.V. 1922. "Vsemirny tainy zagovor" [Secret World Conspiracy]. Berlin: 10.
[67] On the police origins of *The Protocols* see: Burtsev, V.L. 1938. "Protokoly Sionskih mudretsov — dokazannyi podlog" [The Protocols of the Elders of Zion — A Proven Forgery]. Paris; Delevsky, Yu. 1923. "Protokoly Sionskih mudretsov (Istoriya odnogo podloga)" [*The Protocols of the Elders of Zion*: A History of a Forgery]. Berlin; Cohn, N. 1970. Warrant for Genocide: The Myth of the Jewish World-Conspiracy and *The Protocols of the Elders of Zion*. London; et al. The most interesting in relation to this issue, in our opinion, is a mention by F.P. Stepanov and by Nilus himself of a woman who gave *The Protocols* to Nilus. In fact, this was probably one Justina Glinka, an adventurist and a secret agent of the Tsar's security service, who for many years ran errands in political investigation in France. B.I. Nikolayevsky remarked that "her connections to the police were known since 1882–1883" (see: Burtsev, V.L. Op. cit.: 129). In Biarritz, France, Nilus met Glinka in the early 1890s, and in 1900 they returned together to Russia. By the time she met the author of the book about "the coming Antichrist," Glinka was an experienced agent of the Chief of Russian Secret Service, P.I. Rachkovsky (1853–1911), who in those years managed the foreign agents net (1885–1902) and later, as a "service obligation," became one of the founders of the Union of the Russian People. Nilus, in his conversation with du Chayla, mentioned that the agent had received the manuscript

of *The Protocols* from the hands of General Rachkovsky who, in turn, obtained it in "Masonic archives." Du Chayla recalled the character review of the General by Nilus: "C'est le General Ratchkovsky, a good active man, who in his time did much to pull out the sting of the enemies of Christ" (See: Du Chayla, A. 1922. "Vospominaniya o S. A. Niluse i o Sionskikh protokolakh' [A Memoir of Sergei Nilus and the Protocols of Zion]. *Evreiskaya Tribuna*: Moscow: 72).

[68] Zhevakhov, N. D. Op. cit. Notes on Pp. 39–40. The Department of Police's part in the "forgery of the century" can be estimated by the "contribution" of the Chief of Foreign agents, P. I. Rachkovsky, to the "secret history" of the acquiring of *The Protocols of the Elders of Zion*. Rachkovsky's career is unusual and is directly related to the "backstage" of the process of creation of *The Protocols*. He began his service in 1867 as a junior mail sorter at the Kiev Postal Office and was quickly promoted in the offices of governors of Odessa, Kiev, Warsaw, and Kalicz. In 1877 he already held the position of the court investigator in Archangel Province. Suddenly, Rachkovsky's career as a government official came to a stop and he found himself a manager at the office of a newly created magazine *Russkiy Evrei*. Soon, however, Rachkovsky was arrested because of his reputation as an "outstanding revolutionary" in the student circles of the capital. Rachkovsky expresses his willingness to cooperate with the investigation and becomes a provocateur. His "godfather" in this field was the Chief of Police himself, Adjutant General A. V. Drenteln. Soon the provocateur was exposed by Kletochnikov. However, thanks to his acquaintances in the "Holy Druzhina," in the spring of 1884 Rachkovsky became the head of the Russian political investigation net abroad. At this post he earned a hereditary noble title and the rank of an Active Secret Advisor (see: 1918. "Karyera P. I. Rachkovskogo" [Career of P. I. Rachkovsky]. *Byloye*: No. 2(30): February). At the same time, we should remember that Rachkovsky's "godfather," General Drenteln, was interested in the "Jewish question" and was very familiar with *Exposing the Great Secret of Freemasons* (either "from the papers of O. A. Przecławski" or from the manuscript of Cyprinus himself). During Jewish pogroms of 1881–1882, Drenteln was the Governor General of Kiev, Podolsk and Volyn. In response to "dozens of telegrams from all the boroughs (their name is legion!) of the Southwestern area from Jews" about sending troops to protect them, the future Chief of Police wrote: "There are many lies about this mess in the papers... It's all either nonsense or unimportant. The main cause is hatred of Jews" (see: 1905. "Russkiy biograficheskiy slovar (Drenteln)" [Russian Biographical Dictionary: Drenteln]. St. Petersburg: 696).

Thus, the ways of this "police fabrication" seem to be fully revealed. Not without participation of the Chief of Police Drenteln who knew well the anti-Semitic and anti-Masonic literature of 1860–1880 in Russia, the head of Russian political investigation abroad Rachkovsky passed the manuscript of *The Protocols* to his secret agent (Justina Glinka) and this lady, in turn, handed this "work" over to the mystic Sergei Nilus.

[69] Cohn, N. Op. cit.: 63.
[70] ———: 61.
[71] Bostunitsch, G. "Masonstvo..." [Freemasonry...]: 104. "It would be, of course, foolish to accuse all freemasons of that which even all Yids cannot be accused of as a group."
[72] Rozov, N.N. 1963. "Sinodalny spisok sochineniy Ilariona — pisatelya XI v." [A Synodal Copy of Works by Ilarion, an 11th Century Writer}. *Slavia*: XXXII: 141–175. Compare to: Rozov, N.N. 1977. "Kniga Drevnei Rusi" [The Book of Ancient Russia]. Moscow: 50–51.
[73] Quoted from: Posnov, M.E. "Istoriya khristianskoi tserkvi" [A History of Christian Church]: 436: Note 324.
[74] ———: 48.
[75] Zhevakhov, N.D. Op. cit.: 41. In another place Nilus's biographer was even more sincere: "Strictly speaking, the negative attitude towards the book among clerics predetermined the same attitude by everyone else." (Ibid: 42).
[76] The history and character of Christian heresies is told in the following work: Ivantsov-Platonov, A.M. 1878. "Eresy i raskoly pervykh tryokh vekov" [Heresies and Schisms of the First Three Centuries]. Moscow.
[77] Danilevsky, N. Ya. Op. cit.: 398–431.
[78] Posnov, M.E. Op.cit.: 141.
[79] ———: 147–148.
[80] ———: 149.
[81] ———: 153.
[82] See the analysis of the legend: Bostutitsch, G. "Masonstvo..." [Freemasonry...]: 241–271.
[83] Shifrin, I. Sh. 1967. "K kharakteristike tsarskikh povinnostei v Palestine v pervoi polovine I tys. do n.e. po dannym bibleiskoi traditsii" [On the Characterization of King's Levies in Palestine in the First Half of the 1st Century B.C. Based on the data of Biblical Tradition]. *Vestnik Drevnei Istorii*: Moscow: No.1(99): 47.
[84] Posnov, M.E. Op. cit.: 154–155.
[85] See the review of the biographer of *The Protocols* (and, indirectly, the entire book): "It was seen, at best, as a fantasy with no solid basis, and at worst, as a pamphlet... even now the editor of

Vozrozhdeniye Mr. Semyonov says that "writings of Mr. Nilus are inept and colorless" ... and Mr. Bostunitsch in his foreword... goes further still and calls them "hysteria" (Zhevakhov, N. D. Op. cit.: 41–42).

[86] Sholem, G. 1984. "Osnovnye techeniya v evreiskoi mistike. V 2 t." [The Main Trends in Jewish Mysticism. In 2 Volumes}. Jerusalem: Vol. 2: 49.
[87] ———: 201.
[88] Bosman A. 1916. *The Mysteries of the Qabalah*: 31–32.

CHAPTER 5
TWENTIETH-CENTURY SATANISTS

[1] Cohn, N. 1970. Warrant for genocide: The Myth of the Jewish World-Conspiracy and the Protocols of the Elders of Zion. London: 42–54.
[2] Ibid: 53.
[3] Shmakov, A.S. 1912. 'Mezhdunarodnoye tainoye pravitelstvo" [Secret Global Government]. Moscow. A. S. Shmakov (1852–1916) was a committed pogrom maker and judeophobe who dedicated his entire life to fighting against Jews not out of career ambitions but out of belief in the truth of his views. After graduating from the Law School of the University of Novorossiysk, he worked for five years as a court investigator in Kherson. Then he joined the Board of Attorneys, moved to Moscow and became an assistant of one of best-known and most liberal legal defenders, F. N. Plevako. After leaving his patron, he moved to the camp of pogrom makers and security agents. He defended members of the Black Hundred in Starodub, Kishinev, Gomel, and Kiev. He was a civil plaintiff (with G. G. Zamyslovsky) in the Beilis case. He repeatedly ran for the State Duma from Moscow and repeatedly was not elected. He authored the book "Sudebnyye oratory vo Frantsii" [Court Speakers in France] (Moscow, 1887) that received high praise in scholarly circles and then, in the name of his idée fixe, abandoned scholarly work and published "Evreiskiye rechi" [Jewish Speeches] (Moscow, 1897), "Minsky Protsess" [The Minsk Trial] (Moscow, 1899), "Gomelskoye delo" [The Gomel Case] (Moscow, 1905), "Svoboda i evrei" [Freedom and The Jew] (Moscow, 1906), "Delo o pogrome evreiev v Vyazme 19/20 oktyabrya 1905 g." [The Case of the Jewish Pogrom of October 19–20, 1905 in Vyazma] (Moscow, 1907), "Pogrom evreiev v Kieve" [Jewish Pogrom in Kiev] (Moscow, 1906), "Delo "Soyedinennogo banka"" [The Case

of the "United Bank"] (Moscow, 1909), and "Evreiskiy vopros na stsene vsemirnoi istorii" [Jewish Question on the Stage of World History] (Moscow, 1912).

[4] Shugurov, M.F. 1891. "Istoriya evreyev v Rossii" [History of Jews in Russia]. *Russkiy Arkhiv*: No. 1-5. M. F. Shugurov (1829-1891) was born to a noble family. He grew up in Bendery and Khotino. Orphaned early, he moved to Kishinev and entered the Kishinev Gymnasium to graduate with high honors. He entered the Department of History and Philology of Moscow University and graduated with a Ph D. For the next six years he taught Russian at the Kishinev Gymnasium. He knew English, French, Italian, and German. With the assistance of a great Russian surgeon and philosemite N. I. Pirogov who at the time was a member of the Board of Odessa School District, in 1858 Shugurov began teaching Russian in the 2nd Odessa Gymnasium for Boys and History in the Odessa Institute for Noble Young Ladies. In 1868, he took up the position of the Inspector of the Institute. For thirty years, Shugurov published articles on topics of history in *Russkiy Arkhiv*, including some on the Jewish question (e.g., "The Report to the Emperor Alexander Pavlovich on Jews"). In 1873, Shugurov was accused of nihilism. Instead of leaving for Warsaw University where he was offered a tenure with the Department of Russian History, he resigned, but a year later was appointed the director of the newly founded Teacher Institute of Feodosia. In 1879, he finally resigned and settled in Odessa but later moved abroad and from 1890 until his death, lived in Switzerland.

[5] Tikhomirov, L.A. 1912. "K reforme obnovlennoi Rossii (Statyi 1909-1911 gg.) [On the Reform of the New Russia: Articles of 1909-1911]. Moscow.

[6] Benz, A.I. 1906. "Masony" [Masons]. Moscow.

[7] Bostunitsch, G. 1928. "Masonstvo v svoyey sushchnosti i proyavleniyakh" [Freemasonry in Its Essence and Manifestations]. Belgrade: 68.

[8] Rochester-Kryzhanovskaya, V.I. 1906. "Pautina" [Spiderweb]. Revel.

[9] Ibid: 417.

[10] Bostunitsch, G. "Masony..." [Masons...]: 143.

[11] Rochester-Kryzhanovskaya, V. I. Op. cit.: 451.

[12] Bostunitsch, G. "Masony..." [Masons...]: 89.

[13] Suvorin, A.S. 1923. "Dnevnik" [Journal]. Moscow/Petrograd.

[14] Ibid: 82-96.

[15] Ibid.

[16] Gumbel, E. 1925. "Zagovorshchiki" [Conspirators]. Leningrad: 42-45.

[17] Meshchersky, V.P. 1912. "Moi Vospominaniya. V 3 ch." [My Memoir. In Three Parts]. St. Petersburg: 390.
[18] Witte, S. Yu. 1960. "Vospominaniya. V 3 t." [A Memoir. In Three Volumes]. Moscow: Vol. 2: 78.
[19] Suvorin, A. S. Op. cit.: 233.
[20] Ibid: 298.
[21] Compiled by Chernovsky, A. 1929. "Soyuz Russkogo naroda. Po materialam Chrezvychainoi sledstvennoi komissii Vremennogo pravitelstva 1917 g." [The Union of the Russian People: Based on the Materials of the Emergency Investigative Committee of the Provisional Government, 1917]. Moscow/Leningrad: 441.
[22] Kugel, A.R. 1926. "Listya s dereva" [Leaves of a Tree]. Leningrad: 47.
[23] The trilogy by E. A. Shabelskaya includes the following novels: "Satanisty XX v." [Satanists of the 20th Century]. Riga, 1934 (Part 1); "Pyatnadtsat let spustya" [Fifteen Years Later]. Riga, 1934 (Part 2); "Taina Martiniki" [The Secret of Martinique]. Riga, 1936 (Part 3). All quotes are from this edition of the trilogy; the Part and Page are indicated in parentheses.
[24] Introducing historical persons as characters of fictional works is a well-known phenomenon. This is particularly typical for accusatory pulp fiction. See, for example, the novel by Alexandre Dumas *The Memoirs of a Physician (Joseph Balsamo)*: among masonic leaders in Dumas' "depictions" are the Swedish philosopher Emanuel Swedenborg (1688–1772), the admiral P. Jones, et al.
[25] On his mother's "Russian side" (Princess Dolgorukaya was a daughter of Peter's Vice-Chancellor Baron Shafirov) Witte could be considered a Jew, as well as on his father's side: his paternal grandmother was a Kramer. Possible sources of information about Witte for Shabelskaya could be Kovalevsky and I. F. Manasevich-Manuilov (1869–1918), one of the main characters of the novel by a Soviet writer V. Pikul "U poslednei cherty" [At the Last Frontier]. I. F. Manuilov was a court advisor, an official of the Department of Police, a journalist, and a conman. As a theater critic he wrote under the pen name "Mask." He knew E. A. Shabelskaya well (possibly also from his service in the Department of Police). Together with M. V. Golovinsky (an associate at the newspaper *Figaro* and a secret Russian agent) he participated in compiling *The Protocols of the Elders of Zion* under the supervision of P. I. Rachkovsky. I. F. Manasevich-Manuilov (*his mother's maiden name was Khotimskaya*) was a nephew of Witte's wife. For some time, he worked at the office of the Prime Minister and negotiated with Gapon. Manuilov was aware of the telegram Witte sent to A. S. Suvorin: "In my veins flows the blood of a Russian super-

patriot, General Fadeyev" (Quoted from: Kaufman, A.E. 1915. "Cherty iz zhizni gr. S. Yu. Witte" [Sketches of Life of Count S. Yu. Witte]. *Istoricheskiy Vestnik*: April: 227).

[26] Vinaver, M.M. 1915. "Besedy s grafom S. Yu. Witte" [Conversations with Count Witte]. *Novy Voskhod*: 6.
[27] Rauch, G.O. 1926. "Dnevnik" [Journal]. *Krasny Arkhiv*: Issue 19: 90.
[28] Efron, S.K. 1916. "Vospominaniya o S. F. Sharapove' [A Memoir of S. F. Sharapov]. *Istoricheskiy Vestnik*: Vol. 143: 519.
[29] Kugel, A. R. Op. cit.: 56.
[30] Ibid: 56.
[31] Vishnyak, M. 1954. "Dan' proshlomu" [To the Past Its Due]. New York: 333.
[32] Korchmiy, L. Note to Page 65. In: Shabelskaya, E.A. 1934. "Satanisty XX v." [Satanists of the 20th Century]. Riga.
[33] Vinberg, F.V. 1921. "Korni Zla" [Roots of Evil]. Munich: 304–307.
[34] Pikul, V. 1979. "U poslednei cherty. Roman-khronika" [At the last Frontier: A Chronicle]. *Nash Sovremennik*: No. 9–12: 9: 100.
[35] Bostunitsch, G. "Masony..." [Masons...]: 89.
[36] Abramowicz, L., Feinerman, E. 1980. Les juifs du Défi. Paris: 66–74.
[37] See: Rosenblum, S.A. 1982. Etre juif en U.R.S.S. Paris: 149–154.
[38] See: Weinryb, B. D. Anti-Semitism in Soviet Russia. In: 1970. The Jews in Soviet Russia since 1917. London: 288–290.
[39] Laqueur, W. 1965. Russia and Germany: A Century of Conflict. Boston.
[40] Cohn, N. Op. cit.: 42–54.
[41] Ettinger, Sh. חמו ביתית ומאבק היהודים// ש.אטינגר שרשי האנטישמיות
[42] Brant, E. 1929. "Ritualnoye ubiystvo u evreiev. V 3 t." [Ritual Murder and the Jews. In Three Volumes]. Belgrad.
[43] Akhmatov, V. 1927. "Evreyi i budushcheye mira" [Jews and the Future of the World]. Belgrad.
[44] Rosenblum S. A. Op. cit.: 43–46.
[45] Bostunitsch, G. 1922. "Masonstvo i russkaya revolyutsiya. Pravda misticheskaya i pravda realnaya" [Freemasonry and the Russian Revolution: The Truth Mystical and Real]. Yugoslavia.
[46] Breshko-Breshkovsky, N.N. 1908. "V mire atletov" [In the World of Athletes]. St. Petersburg; 1910. "Chukhonsky Bog" [The Chukhna God]. Kiev.
[47] Breshko-Breshkovsky, N.N. 1909. "Zapiski Naturshchitsy' [Diary of a Model]. St. Petersburg; 1914. "V potyomkakh zhizni" [In the Dark of Life]. Petrograd/Moscow.
[48] Breshko-Breshkovsky, N.N. 1914. "Gadiny tyla" [Bastards of the Rear]. Petrograd; 1916. "V setyakh predatelstva" [In the Web of Treachery]. Petrograd.

[49] Lyubimov, L. 1953. "Na chuzhbine" [In a Strange Land]. Moscow: 335.

[50] Breshko-Breshkovky, N.N. 1923. "Pod zvezdoi dyavola" [Under the Star of Devil]. Yugoslavia. The novel is quoted from this edition. Page numbers are in parentheses.

[51] The conclusion that "it's always Jews' own fault" is as traditional for anti-Semitism as blaming Jews for hating Christians. Remember that V. M. Istrin believed that The Explanatory Palaea was a reaction to some messianic hopes that sprung from the sermons of Yehuda Hasid, and he blamed the anti-Judaism of the artifact of the 13th century on Jews as well. (See: Istrin, V.M. 1923. "Ocherk istorii drevnerusskoi literatury domoskovskogo perioda" [An Essay on the History of Ancient Russian Literature of Pre-Moscow Period]. Petrograd: 214.)

[52] Compare to the remark on Jews' cowardice in 1812 by O. A. Przecławski (See: Przecławski, J. 1844. Śmierć e odrodzenie. Wilno: 73–74).

[53] Ivanov, Yu. 1971. "Ostorozhno, sionizm!" [Beware of Zionism!]. Moscow; Bolshakov, V. 1972. "Sionizm na sluzhbe antikommunizma" [Zionism in Service of Anti-Communism]. Moscow; 1978. "Ideologiya i praktika mezhdunarodnogo sionizma" [Ideology and Practice of International Zionism]. Moscow; Semenyuk, V. 1981. "Natsionalisticheskoye bezumiye" [Nationalistic Madness]. Minsk; et al. The figure "80%" is present in all these books that expose the "reactionary essence" of Zionism.

[54] Shafarevich, I. 1989. "Rusofobia" [Russophobia]. 22: Jerusalem: No. 63: 132–133.

[55] "Short-sighted, having learned nothing, thinking of stopping the wheel of history, they dream of, upon restoration of Russia, to herd Poland into the borders of the ten provinces adjacent to the Vistula, the former general-governorate (the Nazis borrowed the name "general governorate" for destroyed Poland from the Russian authorities—S.D.). Nonsense, rubbish! Poland that proved its survival abilities is a fact! A forever and undisputed fact" (229). The sententia of the "Russian prince" in a "Polish novel" by Breshko-Breshkovsky in 1923 is juxtaposed to the "genuine Russian" (*Slavophilic, imperialist, chauvinistic*) sententia: "Poles demand for themselves Belorussia, Volyn, Podolia, Galich, and even Kiev and Smolensk... All these crowns of the Stephanians, the Jagiellonians, the Palaiologos... These historical dead... Should they conceive to wander... and confuse... bringing up their long-gone rights to that which has passed into the ownership of the living, there's nothing else left to pacify them than, according to a Slavic tradition, to put them on a stake... The stake is the only right left to the crowns of the Palaiologos, the

Jagiellonians, and St. Stephans..." (Danilevsky, N. Ya. 1895. "Rossiya i Evropa" [Russia and Europe]. St. Petersburg: 402–403.

[56] Brant, E. Op. cit.: Book 2: 6. "As the reader will notice, in this book the incorrect terms "anti-Semitism" and "anti-Semite" are replaced by "Yid-fighting" and "Yid-fighter" ... It is desirable that the reader would learn and practice these terms..."

[57] Przecławski, A.O. "Predisloviye" [Foreword]. In: 1909. "Razoblacheniye velikoi tainy frankmasonov" [Exposing the Great Secret of Freemasons]. Moscow: 9.

[58] Schwarz, G. 1915. "Iz vrazheskogo plena. Istoriya mytarstv russkogo literatora v nemetskom plenu" [Out of Enemy Prison: A Story of a Russian Writer's Suffering in German Captivity]. St. Petersburg.

[59] Bostunitsch, G. 1922. "Masonstvo i russkaya revolyutsiya" [Freemasonry and the Russian Revolution]. Yugoslavia: 6–7.

[60] Bostunitsch, G. 1928. "Masonstvo v svoyey sushchnosti i proyavleniyakh" [Freemasonry in Its Essence and Manifestations]. Belgrade: 78.

[61] Brant, E. Op. cit.: Book 1: 13.

[62] Shafarevich, I. Op. cit.: 149.

[63] Krestovsky, Vs. 1889. "T'ma egipetskaya" [Egyptian Darkness]. St. Petersburg: 21, 31, 37.

[64] Litvin, S.K. 1897. "Sredi evreyev" [Among Jews]. Moscow: 33, 81–85.

[65] Breshko-Breshkovky, N.N. 1923. "Pod zvezdoi dyavola" [Under the Star of Devil]. Yugoslavia: 45, 47, 192, 200.

[66] Rodionov, I.A. 1932. "Syny dyavola" [Sons of the Devil]. Belgrade: 4–6.

[67] Ibid: 46.

[68] Bostunitsch, G. 1922. "Masonstvo i russkaya revolyutsiya" [Freemasonry and the Russian Revolution]: 6–7.

[69] Brant, E. Op. cit.: 13.

[70] Rodionov, I.A. 1909. "Nashe prestupleniye (Ne bred, a byl). Iz sovremennoi narodnoi zhizni" [Our Crime: Not Fiction, But Real: From Modern Common People Life]. St. Petersburg. The author (?-1943) was an Army Sergeant Major, scandalously connected to Rasputin and Hermogenes (see: 1988 "Gorky i russkaya zhurnalistika nachala XX v. Neizdannaya perepiska. (Literaturnoye nasledstvo)" [Gorky and Russian Journalism of the Early 20th Century: Unpublished Correspondence (Literary Legacy)]. Moscow: Vol. 95: 983). During the Civil War, he published *The Protocols of the Elders of Zion* in Novocherkassk. See: Bostunitsch, G. 1921. "Pravda o sionskikh protokolakh" [The Truth About the Protocols of Zion]. Yugoslavia: Mitrovica: 16.

[71] Rodionov, I.A. "Syny dyavola" [Sons of the Devil}: 32.

[72] Compare the following items of the "protocols" to some documents of the Nazi Party: "Politics has nothing to do with morality... Our right is in power" (218), "our laws shall be brief, clear, solid, without any interpretation... Their main feature shall be obedience to one's superiors on a grand scale" (258), "Death is the inevitable end for everyone. We should bring this end closer to those who stands in our way" (258), "We must sacrifice individuals without hesitation... for in the exemplary punishment of evil lies the great reforming goal" (261), "In our program, a third of our subjects shall watch the rest" (265), "A true power does not forgo any right, even the Divine" (278). Pages indicated by: Nilus, S.A. 1920. "Velikoye v malom" [The Great within the Small]. *Luch Sveta*: Berlin: Issue 3.

CHAPTER 6
THE SOVIET VERSION OF ANTI-SEMITISM

[1] Pinkus B. 1988. The Jews of the Soviet Union. Cambridge.
[2] Brushlinskaya, O., Mikheleva, S. 1973. "Rytsarskiy maskarad pri dvore Pavla I" [Knights Masquerading at the Court of Paul I]. *Nauka i Religiya*: No. 9; Mikheleva, S.B. 1974. "Naivnye vremena masonskikh lozh..." [The Naive Times of Masonic Lodges...]. *Nauka i Religiya*; Nekrasov, S. 1974. "Obryady i simvoly volnykh kamenshchikov" [Rituals and Symbols of Freemasons]. *Nauka i Religiya*: No. 10.
[3] Lozinsky, S.G. 1923. "Srednevekovye rostovshchiki" [Medieval Usurers]. Petrograd.
[4] Levandovsky, A.L. 1975. "Protsess rytsarei khrama" [The Process of Knights Templar]. *Chelovek i Zakon*: No. 11.
[5] Yakovlev, N.N. 1974. "1 avgusta 1914" [August 1, 1914]. Moscow.
[6] Ivanov, E. 1977. "Negromkiy vystrel" [A Quiet Gunshot]. Moscow. Four years after the publication of "Ivanov's" book, extracts from it appeared in the newspaper *Golos Rodiny* (1981, No. 32, August), apparently, to "educate" the foreign reader that he was still kicking.
[7] Pikul, V. 1979. "U poslednei cherty. Roman-khronika" [At the last Frontier: A Chronicle]. *Nash Sovremennik*: No. 4-7. Further on, the issue and page number are in parentheses.
[8] Mikhailov, O.N. 1977. "Derzhavin" [Derzhavin]. Moscow. Earlier, O. N. Mikhailov, while describing the Battle of Kulikovo, "recognized" Jews... in the camp of the Tatars (*Dmitry Donskoy*, Moscow, 1975) and "established" connections of the Russian writer A.I. Kuprin with... rabbi Meir Kahane (*Kuprin*. Moscow, 1978). In his book about Derzhavin, the writer made no sensational discoveries, although, of course, he, as much as he could, tried to com-

municate to the reader the "correctness" of the great poet's and minor senator's views of Jews. Derzhavin's report and epigram on his "colleague" A. N. Radishchev — a freemason, therefore, according to Mikhailov, a foreign agent, and a revolutionary, therefore, a nihilist who rejects patriotic values — the biographer declared a petty slander that diminished the ideal image of Derzhavin the anti-Semitist.

[9] Pigalev, V. 1980. "Bazhenov" [Bazhenov]. Moscow. The author honorably carried out the difficult task of a biographer of a great architect and... indeed a mason: in the chapter "The Schemes of the Order" he told the reader how the "innocent lambs" Novikov and Bazhenov got caught in the net of an experienced schemer Schwarz.

[10] Kuzmin, A. 1981. "Tatishchev" [Tatishchev]. Moscow.

[11] Ibid.

[12] Butmi, G. 1906. "Vragi roda chelovecheskogo" [The Enemies of the Human Race]. St. Petersburg: 109.

[13] Losev, S., Petrusenko, V. 1981. "Mest' po-amerikanski" [American Revenge]. *Ogonyok*: No. 15: 29.

[14] Pigalev, V. 1982. "Tyomnye tropy reaktsii" [Dark Paths of Reactionism]. *Sovetsky Voin*: No. 3: 46–47.

[15] *Sovetskaya Kultura*: 1979, September, 25.

[16] Bostunitsch, G. 1943. "Sovremennye rezultaty issledovaniya voprosa o proiskhozhdenii "Protokolov Sionskikh mudretsov" [Modern Results of the Study of the Origin of *The Protocols of the Elders of Zion*] *Welt Dienst*: The first week of August.

[17] Korneyev, L. 1982. "Klassovaya sushchnost sionisma" [Class Essence of Zionism]. Kiev: 75.

[18] Ibid.

[19] Mashovets, N. 1980. "Trevozhnost ochevidnogo: ideologicheskiye zametki" [The Disturbing Obvious: Ideological Notes]. *Nash Sovremennik*: No. 69: 166–167. The reviewer declared that freemasonry "at this historical stage became a most dangerous secret alliance between monopolistic financial capital that promotes openly anticommunist and antidemocratic policy and does not hide its historical and practical connection to dogmas of Judaism"; Aleksandrovsky, B.N. 1969. "Iz perezhitogo v chuzhikh krayakh. Vospominaniya i dumy byvshego emigranta" [What I Lived Through in a Strange Land: A Memoir and Contemplations of a Former Emigrant]. Moscow. In the chapter "Freemasons" (he put the name into quotation marks to stress that freemasons were neither "free" nor "masons") the author denied the masons the right to "engage in moral embetterment of humankind" based on the fact that their goal was "domination of the world." This goal attracted nearly all Jewish emigrants to lodges. Because of masons and Jews,

I. Bunin, for example, received the Nobel Prize that bypassed the more deserving, in Aleksandrovsky's opinion, like Kuprin or even Shmelyov.

[20] Stashkevich, N. 1983. "Proci plyni historyi" [Going Through the Flow of History]. *Polymya*: No. 10.

[21] Zhevakhov, N.D. 1936. "Sergei Aleksandrovich Nilus. Kratkiy Ocherk zhizni i tvorchestva" [Sergei Nilus: A Summary of Life and Work]. Yugoslavia: 22.

[22] V. Pikul, apparently, learned from the recent works by Soviet historians that one of the most probable participants in creating the "factory for producing"— not gods, but *The Protocols of the Elders of Zion*, P. I. Rachkovsky, had been recruited by General Drenteln and even worked for Jewish press. However, not wishing for the "Jewish past" of the provocateur General to cast a "Jewish" shadow on *The Protocols*, the author only mentioned the part of the chief of the agents abroad in the case of exposing Nizier Philippe.

[23] Shafarevich, I. 1989. "Rusofobia" [Russophobia]. *22*: Jerusalem: No. 63–64. Further quotes are taken from this edition. The issue and page numbers are in parentheses.

[24] Danilevsky, N. Ya. 1895. "Rossiya i Evropa" [Russia and Europe]. St. Petersburg: 283–325.

[25] Since the editorial team of the magazine *22* warned the reader that Shafarevich's manuscript "came through *Samizdat* channels," we shall consider the spelling "Cauchin" a mistake by the magazine, and not by the author of *Russophobia*, for whom "Cauchy" was connected to the theories of the great French mathematician. It should be noted that the credit for creating a new, social, trend in study of historical events presented in the Bible belongs to Max Weber. His book *Das Antike Judentum* was published posthumously in 1921. However, many of the scholar's premises are now outdated and some reasonings and layouts based on secondary material and lacking sufficient testing have long been criticized.

[26] Bostunitsch, G. 1922. "Masonstvo i russkaya revolyutsiya" [Freemasonry and the Russian Revolution]. Yugoslavia. Bostunitsch, G. 1928. "Masonstvo v svoyey sushchnosti i proyavleniyakh" [Freemasonry in Its Essence and Manifestations]. Belgrade. Further, while quoting G. Bostunitsch, the year of publication and page numbers are in parentheses.

[27] Shafarevich, I. R. Op. cit.

[28] 1978. "Povest vremennykh let" [Primary Chronicle]. In: "Pamyatniki literatury Drevnei Rusi" [Artifacts of the Literature of Ancient Russia] Moscow: XI — early XII c.: 69.

[29] Klimov, G. 1980. "Knyaz mira sego" [Prince of This World]. San Francisco.

ADDENDUM

[1] Wolfson, B.M. 1940. "Emigratsiya Krymskikh tatar v 1860 g." [Emigration of Crimean Tatars in 1860]. *Istoricheskiye Zapiski*: No. 9: 186–197.
[2] Aldanov, M.A. 1960. "Russkiye evreyi v 70–80-kh godakh. Istoricheskiy etyud. [Russian Jews in 1870s-1880s: A Historical Sketch]. In: "Kniga o russkom evreistve" [A Book of Russian Jewry]. New York: 45.
[3] Jastrun, M. 1963. Mickiewicz. Moscow: 566–575.
[4] Golitsyn I.N. 1886. "Istoriya russkogo zakonodatelstva o evreyakh (1649–1825)" [The History of Russian Law Concerning Jews]. St. Petersburg: Vol. 1: 51.
[5] Altayev, Al. 1959. "Pamyatnye vstrechi" [Memorable Meetings]. Moscow: 300–304.
[6] We cannot neglect the details of the writer's biography, for they help better to understand his books. General issues of relations between a person and creative work are brilliantly discussed in the following work: Lichtenstein, E.L. 1974. "Posobiye po meditsinskoi deontologii" [Deontological Ethics in Medicine]. Kiev.
[7] Marshak, S. Ya. 1961. "Vospitaniye slovom" [Teaching Through the Word]. Moscow: 291.
[8] *Rebus*. 1882. No. 48: 499.
[9] Those studying the notorious Saratov Affair suggest that the reason for the blood libel was the struggle between sects in the towns in the Volga region. Thus, in the neighboring Samara, half of its 80,000 population were constantly competing sectants.
[10] *Rebus*. 1881. No. 9: 80.
[11] *Rebus*. 1882. No. 37: 306.
[12] Ibid: 307.
[13] Ibid: 307.
[14] Many years later, after the Revolution and Nicholas II's abdication, right-wing emigrants accused Russian General Staff of a conspiracy against the Tsar. It was pointed out that neither the Chief of Staff, General M.V. Alekseyev, nor a single one of outstanding generals (*including the famous A.A. Brusilov*) supported the Tsar, and they even conspired against him. Back in 1910, General A.A. Polivanov mentioned in his journal that generals A.L. Kuropatkin, Ya. G. Zhilinsky, and D.I Subbotin were connected to freemasons, and that Jews aimed at penetrating the military and the General Staff where they were already present under Russian names. In the latter case, we see an obvious hint at General M.V. Grulev (see: Polivanov, A.A. 1924. "Iz dnevnikov i vospminaniy po dolzhnosti voennogo ministra i ego pomoshchnika. 1907–1916" [From

Journals and Memoirs in the Position of the Military Minister and His Assistant, 1907–1916]. Moscow: Vol. 1: 94). It is difficult to tell who of the mentioned and non-mentioned generals came from a Cantonist family, but there were several persons of undoubtedly Cantonist birth: Nikolai Iudovich Ivanov, Adjutant General and Commander of the Southwestern front; General Vassily Fyodorovich Novitsky; General Alexander Pamfamilovich Nikolayev. The latter two defected to the Soviet side. Moreover, General Nikolayev, captured by Yudenich, "refused to repent" and was executed by the Whtite Guard. His last words were: "Long live the Third International and World revolution!" There is information that General M. V. Alekseyev came from a Cantonist family. As for the Military Minister A. F. Roediger (1905–1909), he had long been accused by the right wing (*"a Swedish name and a masonic heart,"* said E. A. Shabelskaya). The above-mentioned General M. V. Grulev, a provisional Military Minister in 1909, was a converted Jew. General Brusilov was married to Zhelikhovskaya, a niece of Blavatskaya, and meddled in mysticism. His defection to the Soviet side was unanimously condemned by the Whites (who, by the way, executed the only son of this outstanding military leader). The author of the memoir, the Military Minister A. A. Polivanov himself also defected to the Reds. Neither Brusilov, nor Polivanov, nor Zayonchkovsky could be forgiven by the Whites. General P. N. Krasnov pictured them under false names in his anti-Semitic and anti-Masonic novels. As far as penetrating the General Staff, A. I. Denikin in his memoir wrote about seven of his comrades, converted Jews, who had attended the Academy of General Staff with him, and six of whom were generals by the beginning of World War I (see: Denikin, A.I. 1953. "Put' russkogo ofitsera" [The Path of a Russian Officer]. New York: 283). To top it off, let us add that during World War II the leader of the White movement, A. I. Denikin, was accused by the Nazis of defecting to the "Yiddo-masonic camp" (Ibid: 250).

[15] *Rebus*. 1882. No. 37: 307.
[16] Ibid: 308.
[17] *Rebus*. 1882. No. 38: 314.
[18] Ibid: 315.
[19] 1923. "Dnevnik A. S. Suvorina" [Journal of A. S. Suvorin]. Moscow/Petrograd: 15–16.
[20] *Rebus*. 1882. No. 40: Part 2: 432–433.
[21] *Rebus*. 1882. No. 45: 472.
[22] Ibid: 471.
[23] *Rebus*. 1882. No. 49: 508.
[24] *Rebus*. 1882. No. 50: 519.

[25] *Rebus.* 1883. No. 4: 38.
[26] *Rebus.* 1883. No.5: 51.
[27] Ibid: 30.
[28] *Rebus.* 1883. No. 7: 70–71.
[29] *Rebus.* 1883. No. 8: 78.
[30] *Rebus.* 1883. No. 42: 381.
[31] *Rebus.* 1883. No.37: 347.
[32] Wagner, N.P. 1890. "Tyomny Put'" [The Dark Path]. St. Petersburg.
[33] We should mention the "sixtiers" attitude towards Jews. One would think, for instance, that A. I. Herzen would be grateful to "world Jewry" for rescuing his fortune. Not at all. In a letter to a friend with whom he could be honest, the great democrat resolves to garden variety anti-Semitism: "How does reading Chernyshevsky affect you? For a year and a day, I have begged you to read "Chto Delat?" You have read everything, Dostoyevsky, Yergunov, but you never opened "Chto Delat?" There is a reason for this. I think you are afraid to be disappointed." Further talking about "sixtiers," he rails: "How can we not destroy this conning gang that shames the young generation. Find me one nation from Iceland to Abyssinia where such hobos and with such behavior can be out and about *en plein du jour*? Turgenev was just messing around with them. They ought to be tied to the pillory naked, in all their groveling and impudence, their ignorance and cowardice, their thieving and snitching. And perhaps, if I am still strong enough, I will be their executioner and brand their foreheads with foolishness. Only the antechamber, the barracks, the prison cell and clerks could put this Spanish collar on Russia's neck. Here's everyone: Bakst, who denied his own words; sweet-speaking Semitic Veneri; and brain-farting Elpidin; Vorms the snot and Serno-Solovyevich the pus; Yidlings, ducklings, and wagabonds." Herzen, A.I. "Polnoye sobraniye sochineniy" [Complete Collection of Works]. Vol. 28: 326. It should be added that there is information about Jewish origin of Herzen himself—see: 1915. *Evreiskaya Starina*: Petrograd: 366.
[34] *Nedelnaya Khronika Voskhoda*: 1890, No. 6: 157.
[35] Shelgunov, N.V. 1907. "Iskopayemye lyudi. Sbornik statei po evreiskomu voprosu" [Cavemen: A Collection of Essays on Jewish Question]. St. Petersburg: 32–33.
[36] Gornfeld, A.G. 1908. "Knigi i lyudi" [Books and People]. St. Petersburg: 228.
[37] Ibid: 233.
[38] Ibid: 234.
[39] Jabotinsky, V. 1990. "Izbrannoye" [Selected Works]. Jerusalem: 89.
[40] This is supported by Russian medical statistics of the past century. V.N. Nikitin presents interesting data of the time of the Crimean

war. His regiment was lodged near the town of Borovichi and almost to a man contracted syphilis that was raging in the area (Nikitin, V.N. 1906. "Vospominaniya" [A Memoir]. *Russkaya Starina*: No. 9: 611–612.

[41] However, there are anti-Semitic passages even in the *Tales of Cat Purr*. For example, in a Christmas tale *Mirra,* under the transparent pseudonym "Prince Pavel Antonovich Sgaborsky" is presented Count Pavel Stroganov who was lured into the "dastardly Jews" net and robbed with the help of a beautiful Jewess who claimed there was in her veins the blood of ancient Pharaohs, Nineveh, Ashur, Midians, Persians, Canaan, Chaldeans, and Khazars. She claimed to be a direct descendant of the tribe of Judah. In Mirra, according to her claim, was embodied the best part of the blood of Jehovah's chosen people. There are anti-Semitic attacks in other tales of *Cat Purr*: *New Year's Eve,* and *Pebbles.* An attentive contemporary noted that Cat Purr, in his old age, was sowing the seeds of hostility and discord with his gift and quill. (Frug, S.G. 1888. "Sluchainyi felyetonist" [An Accidental Feuilleton Writer]. *Nedelnaya Khronika Voskhoda*: No. 18: 422–430).

[42] Panteleimonov, B. 1950. "My zhili s Wagnerom" [We Lived with Wagner]. *Novoselye*: Paris/New York: No. 42–44: 54.

[43] Tikhomirov, L. 1930. "Zagovorshchiki i politsiya" [Conspirators and Police]. Moscow: 159.

BIBLIOGRAPHY

Abramowicz, L., Feinerman, E. *Les juifs du Défi*. Paris, 1980.
Afanasyev, V.V. "Ryleyev (ZhZL)" [Ryleyev: Lives of Distinguished People]. Moscow, 1982.
Akhmatov, V. "Evreyi i budushcheye mira" [Jews and the Future of the World]. Belgrade, 1927.
Aksakov, S.T. "Sobr. soch. V 5 t." [Collected Works. In 5 Vol.]. Moscow, 1955: Vol. 2
"Aleksandr I v roli Balfura" [Alexander I as Balfour]. *Rassvet*: 1931: No.1: 10-11.
Aleksandrovsky, B.N. "Iz perezhitogo v chuzhikh kraiakh. Vospominaniya i dumy byvshego emigranta" [What I Have Lived Through in a Strange Land: A Memoir and Contemplations of a Former Emigrant]. Moscow, 1969.
Anonymous. "Eshchyo po povodu zhidovskogo nashestviya" [More on the Subject of Yid Invasion]. *Kievlyanin*: 1880: No. 106.
Anonymous. "Plach evreyev na beregakh Dnepra" [Jews Weeping on the Banks of the Dnieper]. *Novorossiyskiy Telegraf*: 1880: No. 1665.
Anonymous. "Sumbur idyot" [Confusion Coming]. *Rassvet*: 1880: No. 13.
Anonymous. "Taina evreistva. Zapiska iz arkhiva departamenta politsii" [The Secret of Jewry: A Note from the Archives of the Department of Police]. S.n., S.a., S.l.
Anonymous. "Velikaya taina frankmasonov" [The Great Secret of Freemasons]. *Vek*: 1883: B. 2.
Antonius, Bishop. "F.M. Dostoyevsky kak propovednik Vozrozhdeniya" [F.M. Dostoyevsky as a Preacher of Renaissance]. North American Diocese of Canada, 1965.
Askenazi, Sh. "Pervyi polskiy "sionist" [The First Polish "Zionist"]. *Perezhitoye*: 1910: Issue 2.
Bakounine, T. *Répertoire biographique des franc-maçons russes*. Paris, 1967.
Bashilov, B. "Robespierre na trone. Pyotr I i istoricheskiye resultaty sovershennoi im revolyutsii" [Robespierre on the Throne. Peter I and Historical Results of His Revolution]. Buenos Aires, 1955 (?).
Belinsky, V.G. "Poln. sobr. Soch. V 13 t." [Complete Collection of Works. In 13 Vol.]. Moscow, 1961-1965: Vol. 9.

Benois, A.L. "Moi vospominaniya" [My Memoir] Moscow, 1980: Vol. 1: 499–508.

Benz, A.I. "Masony" [Masons]. Moscow, 1906.

Berkhin, I. "Sozhzheniye lyudei v Rossii v XIII–XVIII vv." [Burning People in Russia in the 13th-18th Centuries]. *Russkaya Starina*: 1885.

Berlin, P. "Otechesvennaya voina i evreyi' [PatrioticWar and Jews]. *Novy Voskhod*: 1911: No. 29.

Bernstein, H. The History of a Lie. New York, 1928.

Bernstein, H. The Truth about *The Protocols of Zion*. Introduction by N. Cohn. New York, 1971.

"Besedy Ekateriny II s Dalem" [Catherine II's Conversations with Dal]. *Russkaya Starina:* 1876: Vol. 17.

Bitsyn, N. "Zametka na statyu Sankt-Peterburgskikh vedomostei o polskom katekhizise" [A Note to the Article about the Polish Catechism in *St. Petersburg Vedomosti*]. *Russkiy Arkhiv:* 1873: 1.

Bogdanovich, A.L. "Dnevnik" [Journal]. Moscow/Leningrad, 1924.

Bogoyavlensky, S.K. "Prikaznye dyaki v XVII v." [*Prikaz* Clerks in the 17th Century]. *Istoricheskiye Zapiski:* Moscow, 1937: Vol. 1.

Bolshakov, V. "Sionizm na sluzhbe antikommunizma" [Zionism in the Service of Anti-Communism]. Moscow, 1972.

Bonch-Bruyevich, V.D. "Sektantstvo i staroobryadchestvo v pervoi polovine XIX v. Izbrannye sochineniya. V 2 t." [Sectarianism and Old Believers in the First Half of the 19th Century. Selected Works. In 2 Vol.]. Moscow, 1959: Vol. 1.

Bosman, A. *The Mysteries of the Qabalah.* 1916.

Bostunitsch, G. (?) "Sovremennye resultaty issledovaniya voprosa o proiskhozhdenii "Protokolov sionskikh mudretsov' [Modern Outcomes of the Study of the Question of the Origin of *The Protocols of the Elders of Zion*]. *Welt Dienst:* 1943: The first week of August.

Bostunitsch, G. "Masonstvo v svoyey sushchnosti i proyavleniyakh" [Freemasonry in Its Essence and Manifestations]. Belgrade, 1922.

Bostunitsch, G. "Pravda o sionskikh protokolakh" [The Truth about the Zion Protocols]. Yugoslavia: Mitrovica, 1921.

Bostunitsch. G. "Masonstvo i russkaya revolutsia. Pravda misticheskaya i pravda realnaya" [Freemasonry and Russian Revolution: Truth Mystical and Real]. Yugoslavia, 1922.

Brafman, Ya. A. "Kniga Kagala. V 2 ch." [The Book of Qahal in 2 Parts]. St. Petersburg, 1882.

Brant, B. "Ritualnoye ubiystvo u evreiev. V 3 t." [Rirual Murder and Jews. In Three Volumes]. Belgrade, 1929.

Breshko-Breshkovky, N.N. "Pod zvezdoi dyavola" [Under the Star of Devil]. Yugoslavia, 1923.

Breshko-Breshkovsky, N.N. "Chukhonsky Bog" [The Chukhna God]. Kiev, 1910.

Breshko-Breshkovsky, N.N. "Gadiny tyla" [Bastards of the Rear]. Petrograd, 1914.
Breshko-Breshkovsky, N.N. "V mire atletov" [In the World of Athletes]. St. Petersburg, 1908.
Breshko-Breshkovsky, N.N. "V potyomkakh zhizni" [In the Dark of Life]. Petrograd/Moscow., 1914.
Breshko-Breshkovsky, N.N. "V setyakh predatelstva" [In the Web of Treachery]. Petrograd, 1916.
Breshko-Breshkovsky, N.N. "Zapiski Naturshchitsy' [Diary of a Model]. St. Petersburg, 1909.
Brockhaus and Efron. "Entsiklopedicheskiy slovar" [The Encyclopedic Dictionary]: Matsiyevich: St. Petersburg, 1893.
Brushlinskaya, O., Mikheleva, S. "Rytsarskiy maskarad pri dvore Pavla I" [Knights Masquerading at the Court of Paul I]. *Nauka i Religiya*: No. 9, 1973.
Buchbinder, N.A. "O. A. Przecławski o romane N. G. Chernyshevskogo *Chto Delat?*" [Josef Przecławski On Chernyshevsky's novel *What Is to Be Done?*] *Katorga i Ssylka*: No. 44, 1928.
Budushchnost: St. Petersburg: 1900: No. 46.
Bulgarin, F.V. "Ivan Vyzhygin" [Ivan Vyzhygin]. St. Petersburg, 1830: 82.
Burtsev, V.L. "Protokoly Sionskih mudretsov — dokazannyi podlog" [The Protocols of the Elders of Zion — A Proven Forgery]. Paris, 1938.
Ch-v. "Mikhail Leontievich Magnitsky. Novye dannye k ego kharakteristike" [Mikhail Leontievich Magnitsky: New Information to His Characterization]. *Russkaya Starina*: November, 1875.
Chechulin, N. "Russkoye provintsialnoye obshchestvo vo vtoroy polovine XVIII v." [The Russian Provincial Society in the Second Half of the 18th Century]. St. Petersburg, 1889.
Chernukha, V.G. "Pravitelstvennaya politika v otnoshenii pechati v 60–70-e gody XIX veka" [Government Policy Regarding the Press in the 1860s-1870s]. Leningrad, 1989.
Cohn, N. *Warrant for Genocide: The Myth of the Jewish World-Conspiracy and the Protocols of the Elders of Zion.* London, 1970.
Cohn, N. "Blagosloveniye na genotsid: mif o vsemirnom zagovore evreiev i "Protokolakh Sionskikh mudretsov" [Warrant for Genocide: The Myth of the Jewish World-Conspiracy and *The Protocols of the Elders of Zion*]. Moscow, 1990.
Danilevsky, N. Ya. "Rossiya i Evropa" [Russia and Europe]. St. Petersburg, 1895.: XXIII–XXIV.
Davydov, D.V. "Sochineniya" [Writings]. Moscow, 1962.
Davydov, Yu. "Temna voda vo oblatsekh" [Dark Is the Water from the Clouds]. *Prometei*: Moscow, 1977: Issue 11.
Delevsky, Yu. "Etapy plagiata" [Steps of Plagiarism]. *Evreiskaya Tribuna*: October 7, 1921.

Delevsky, Yu. "Protokoly Sionskih mudretsov (Istoriya odnogo podloga)" [*The Protocols of the Elders of Zion*: A History of a Forgery]. Berlin, 1923.

Delevsky, Yu. "Zagadka" podloga i plagiata (Stolypin o "Sionskikh protokolakh") [The "Mystery" of Forgery and Plagiarism: Stolypin on *The Protocols of the Elders of Zion*]. *Evreiskaya Tribuna*: December 28, 1922.

Demchenko, Ya. "Evreiskoye ravnopraviye ili russkoye poraboshcheniye? S izlozheniyem printsipov evreiskoy nauki o dvukh pravdakh: odnoi — istovoi dlya evreyev, i drugoi falshivoi — dlya goyev, i razyasneniem tainykh evreiskikh planov i programm" [Jewish Equality or Enslaving of Russians? Including the Principles of Jewish Teaching of Two Truths: One Real, for Jews, and Another, False, for Goyim, and Explaining the Secret Jewish Plans and Programs]. Kiev, 1906.

Der Fürst von Ligne. — *Neue Briefe*: Wien, 1924.

Derzhavin, G.R. "Polnoye sobraniye sochineniy. V 9 t." [Complete Collection of Works. In 9 Vol.]. St. Petersburg, 1887: Vol. 6.

Dubnov, S.M. "Furor judophobicus v posledniye gody tsarstvovaniya Aleksandra III" [Furor Judophobicus in the Later Years of the Reign of Alexander III]. *Evreiskaya Starina*: Petrograd, 1918.

Dubnov, S.M. "Kniga zhizni. V 2 t." [Book of Life. In 2 Vol.]. Riga, 1935: Vol. 2.

Dubnov, S.M. "Noveishaya istoriya evreiskogo naroda" [Modern History of the Jewish people]. Berlin, 1923: Vol. 1.

Dubnov, S. "Kak byla vvedena rekrutskaya povinnost dlya evreyev v 1827 godu" [How Conscription of Jews Was Introduced in 1827]. *Evreiskaya Starina*: Vol. 2, 1909.

Du Chayla, A. "Vospominaniya o S. A. Niluse i o Sionskikh protokolakh' [A Memoir of Sergei Nilus and the Protocols of Zion]. *Evreiskaya Tribuna*: Moscow, 1922.

Dudakov, S. Yu. "K. P. Kaufman i evreistvo" [K. P. Kaufman and Jewry]. *Vozrozhdeniye*: Jerusalem: No. 11, 1989.

Dudakov, S. Yu. "Vladimir Solovyov i Sergei Nilus" [Vladimir Solovyov and Sergei Nilus]. In: Russian Literature and History. Jerusalem, 1989.

Dymov, O. "Efron-Litvin. Nekrolog" [Efron-Litvin. An Obituary]. *Rassvet*: 1926: 4.

Efron, S.K. "Vospominaniya o S. F. Sharapove' [A Memoir of S. F. Sharapov]. *Istoricheskiy Vestnik*: Vol. 143, 1916.

Elets, Yu. 1885–1905 "Poslesloviye" [Afterword]. In: Krestovsky, Vs. "Sobraniye sochineniy" v 9 t [Collected Works in 9 v]. Spp Vol. 9.

Engelgardt, N.A. "Ekaterininskiy koloss" [The Colossus of Catherine]. *Istoricheskiy Vestnik*: April, 1908.

Epstein, M.B. "K istorii evreiskoi kolonii v Peterburge" [On the History of the Jewish Colony in Petersburg]. *Evreyskaya Letopis*: Petrograd/Moscow, 1923: Issue 2.

Ettinger, Sh. מח ו תיב תי אמו קב היה ידו ס// ש.א ט ני רג רש יש אה טנ מ שי מי ו ת

Florovsky, A.V. "Otechestvennaya voina i Novorossiyskiy krai" [The Patriotic War and Novorossiysk Region]. *"Zapiski Imperatorskogo Odesskogo obshchestva istorii i drevnosti" [Journal of the Odessa Imperial Society for History and Antiquity].* Odessa: Vol. 31, 1913.

Frankel, J. *Prophecy and Politics: Socialism, Nationalism and the Russian Jews.* 1862–1917. Cambridge, 1981.

Galant, I. "Arendovali li evreyi tserkvi na Ukraine?" [Did Jews Lease Churches in Ukraine?]. Kiev, 1903.

Galberstadt, S. "Literaturno-yuridicheskaya zametka (Po povodu knizhki "Evreiskiye tainy" Ludviga Maryana Zaretskogo)" [A Legal and Literary Note on the Book by Ludwig Marian Zarecki *Jewish Secrets*]. *Vestnik Russkogo Evreia*: 1873: No. 17.

Gervais, V. "Drenteln" [Drenteln]. In: "Russkiy biograficheskiy slovar" [Russian Biographical Dictionary]. St. Petersburg, 1905.

Gilyarov-Platonov, N.P. "Evreiskiy vopros v Rossii" [Jewish Question in Russia]. St. Petersburg, 1906.

Ginsburg, S.M. "Otechestvennaya voina 1812 g. i russkiye evreyi" [The Patriotic War of 1812 and Russian Jews]. St. Petersburg, 1912.

Ginzburg, S. "Literatura rynochnogo sprosa" [Literature of Market Demand]. *Voskhod*: No. 10, 1897.

Glebov, A.M. "Russkiy Biograficheskiy slovar" [The Russian Biographical Dictionary]. St. Petersburg, 1916.

Gogol, N.V. "Sobranye sochineniy v 6 t." [Collection of Works in Six Volumes]. Moscow, 1948–1951: Vol. 2.

Golitsyn, N.I. "O neobkhodimosti i vozmozhnosti evreiskoy reformy v Rossii" [On the Necessity and Possibility of a Jewish Reform in Russia]. *Grazhdanin*: 32–34.

Golitsyn I. N. "Istoriya russkogo zakonodatelstva o evreyakh (1649–1825). V 2 t." [The History of Russian Law Concerning Jews. In 2 Vol.]. St. Petersburg, 1886: Vol. 1

Gordon, L. "K istorii poseleniya evreyev v Peterburge" [On the History of Jewish Settlement in Petersburg]. *Voskhod*: No. 1-2, 1881.

"Gorky i russkaya zhurnalistika nachala XX v. Neizdannaya perepiska. (Literaturnoye nasledstvo)" [Gorky and Russian Journalism of the Early 20th Century: Unpublished Correspondence (Literary Legacy)]. Moscow, 1988: Vol. 95.

Grigoriev, V.V. "Evreiskiye religioznye sekty v Rossii" [Jewish Religious Sects in Russia]. St. Petersburg, 1846.

Grossman, L. "Lermontov i kultura Vostoka" [Lermontov and the Culture of the East]. *Literaturnoye Nasledstvo*: Moscow, 1941.: Vol. 43–44.

Gumbel, E. "Zagovorshchiki" [Conspirators]. Leningrad, 1925: 42–45.
Gumilev, L. N. "Drevnyaya Rus i Velikaya step" [Ancient Russia and the Great Steppe]. Moscow, 1989.
Gumilev, L.N. "Etnogenez i biosfera: Avtoreferat dissertatsii na soiskaniye uchenoi stepeni doktora geograficheskikh nauk" [Ethnogenesis and Biosphere: The Author's Summary of His Doctorate Thesis in Geography]. Leningrad, 1974.
Helena Watrobska. "Polata knigopisnaya. Izbornik XIII veka" [Полата кънигописьная: The Izbornik of the 13th Century] (God. Leningrad, GPB, Q.p. 1.18). Switzerland, 1989.
Hessen, Yu.I. "Istoriya evreiskogo naroda v Rossii. V 2 t." [The History of the Jewish People in Russia: In Two Volumes]. Petrograd, 1916: Vol. 1.
Hessen, Yu.I. "Kleveta v forme dramaticheskogo proizvedeniya" [A Lie in the Form of a Drama]. *Voskhod*: No. 3, 1899.
Hessen, Yu.I. "Pisal li Dal o krovavom navete?" [Did Dal Write About the Blood Libel?]. *Golos Minuvshego*: Issue 3, 1914.
Hessen, Yu.I. "Rokovoy Purim" [The Fatal Purim]. *Evreiskiy vestnik*: Leningrad, 1928.
Hessen, Yu.I. "Syny Israelya v Peterburge' [Sons of Israel in Petersburg]. *Budushchnost*: No. 46–47, 1900.
Hessen, Yu.I. "Zapiska o ritualnykh ubiystvakh (pripisyvayemaya V. I. Dalyu) i yeyo istochniki" [The Note on Ritual Murders, ascribed to V. I. Dal, and Its Origins]. St. Petersburg, 1914.
Ideologiya i praktika mezhdunarodnogo sionizma" [Ideology and Practice of International Zionism]. Moscow, 1978.
Ilyinsky, F. "Dyak Fyodor Kuritsyn" [Dyak Fyodor Kuritsyn]. *Russkiy Arkhiv*: 2, 1895.
Introduction to the German translation of S. A. Nilus's book. *Luch Sveta*: 1920: Issue 3.
Ioffe, I. "Iz zhizni pervoi evreyskoi obshchiny v Rige" [From the Life of the First Jewish Diaspora in Riga]. *Perezhitoye*: Issue 2.
"Istoki russkoi belletristiki. Vozniknoveniye zhanrov syuzhetnogo povestvovaniya v drevnerusskoi literature" [Origins of Russian Popular Fiction: The Birth of Genres of Storytelling in Ancient Russian Literature]. Leningrad, 1970.
"Istoriya evreiskogo naroda. V 2 t." [The History of the Jewish People in Two Volumes] Jerusalem, 1979: Vol. 2.
"Istoriya russkoi literatury. V 9 t." [The History of Russian Literature in Nine Volumes]. Moscow/Leningrad, 1941–1947.
"Istoriya vsemirnoy literatury. V 9 t." [History of World Literature in 9 Volumes]. Moscow, 1984: Vol. 2.
Istrin, V.M. "Knigy vremennyya i obraznyya Georgiya Mnikha. Khronika Georgiya Amartola v drevnem slavyano-russkom perevode. V 2 t."

[Books of Chronicles and Images by George the Monk: The Chronicle of George Hamartolos in an Ancient Slavic Russian Translation. In 2 Vol]. Petrograd, 1920.

Istrin, V.M. "Ocherk Istorii drevnerusskoi literatury domoskovskogo perioda" [An Essay on the History of Ancient Russian Literature of Pre-Moscow Period]. Petrograd, 1923.

Ivanin, I.S. "K istoriyi russkogo masonstva v Rossii" [On the History of Russian Freemasonry in Russia]. *Russkaya Starina*: September, 1882.

Ivanov, Yu. "Ostorozhno, sionizm!" [Beware of Zionism!]. Moscow, 1971.

Ivantsov-Platonov, A.M. "Eresy i raskoly pervykh tryokh vekov" [Heresies and Schisms of the First Three Centuries]. Moscow, 1878.

"Izbornik. Biblioteka Vsemirnoi Literatury" [Izbornik. Library of World Literature]. Moscow,1969: Vol. 15.

"Iz bumag grafa Mamonova. Iz pisem i pokazaniy dekabristov. Kritika sovremennogo sostoyaniya Rossii i plany budushchego ustroistva" [From the papers of Count Mamonov: From Letters and Testimonies of Decembrists: Criticism of the Modern State of Affairs in Russia and Plans for Its Future Development]. St. Petersburg, 1906.

Jost, W. *Geschichte der Israeliten*. 1846.

Juel, Just. "Zapiski Yusta Yulya, datskogo poslannika pri Petre Velikom. Izvlek iz Kopengagenskogo gosarkhiva i perevel s datsk. Yu. L. Shcherbachev" [Journal of Just Juel, the Danish Ambassador to Peter the Great. Retrieved from the State Archives in Copenhagen and translated from Danish by Yu. L. Shcherbachev]// "Chteniya v Imp. o-ve istorii i drevnostei rossiyskikh pri Mosk. un-te" [Readings at the Emperor's department of History and Artifacts of Russia at Moscow University]. Moscow, 1899.

Kaluzhsky, A. (A.M. Lavrov). *Censor's permission of January 17, 1906.* "Druzheskiy sovet evreiam" [Friendly Advice to Jews]. S.l.

"Karyera P. I. Rachkovskogo" [Career of P. I. Rachkovsky]. *Byloye*: 1918. No. 2.

Kaufman, A.E. "Cherty iz zhizni gr. S. Yu. Witte" [Sketches of Life of Count S. Yu. Witte]. *Istoricheskiy Vestnik*: April, 1915.

Kaufman, A.E. "Druzya i vragi evreiev. V 3 t." [Friends and Enemies of Jews. In 3 Volumes]. St. Petersburg, 1908: Vol. 3.

"Khrestomatiya po istorii Ukrainy" [Reading-book in the History of Ukraine]. Kiev: Vol. 1, 1959.

Klimov, G. "Knyaz mira sego" [Prince of This World]. San Francisco, 1980.

Klyuchevsky, V.O. "Kurs russkoi istorii" [A Course in Russian History]. Petrograd, 1918: Part 4.

Koni, A.F. "Sobr. soch. V 5 t." {Collection of Works. In 5 Volumes]. Moscow, 1957.

Korneyev, L. "Klassovaya sushchnost sionizma" [The Class Essense of Zionism]. Kiev, 1982.

"Kosti evreya kak predokhraneniye ot padezha skota. Raport Pravitelsvennomu Sinodu Volynsko-Zhitomirskogo Episkopa Daniila ot 18 fevralya 1810 g." [Bones of a Jew as a Preventive for Loss of Livestock: A Report to the State Synod from Daniel, Bishop of Volyn and Zhytomyr]. *Russkaya Starina*: Vol. 10, 1903.

Kozlova, N.V. "Nekotoryye aspekty kulturno-istoricheskoi kharakteristiki russkogo kupechestva" [Some Aspects of Cultural and Historical Characteristics of Russian Merchantry]. *Vestnik Moskovskogo Universiteta (History)*: No. 4, 1969.

Krebs, V. "Umanskaya Reznya" [The Uman Massacre]. Kiev, 1879.

Krestovsky, Vs. "Panurgovo stado" [The Flock of Panurge]. Leipzig, 1870.

Krestovsky, Vs. "Peterburgskiye trushchoby. V 2 t." [The Slums of Petersburg in Two Volumes]. Moscow/Leningrad, 1935.

Krestovsky, Vs. "Sobranye sochineniy. V 9 t." [Collected Works. In 9 Volumes]. St. Petersburg, 1899–1905.

Krestovsky, Vs. "Tma egipetskaya" [Egyptian Darkness]. St. Petersburg, 1889.

Križanić, J. Moscow: Politika, 1965.

Kugel, A. "Listya s dereva" [Leaves of a Tree]. Leningrad, 1926.

Kukolnik, P.V. "Anti-Tsiprinus. Vospominaniya o N. N. Novosiltseve" [Anti-Cyprinus: A Memoir About N. N. Novosiltsev]. *Russkiy Arkhiv*: Vol. 15, 1873.

Kushner, B. "Otkrytoye pismo akademiku I. Shafarevichu" [A Public Letter to Academician Shafarevich]. *"22"*: Jerusalem: No. 64, 1989.

Kuzmin, A. "K kakomu khramu ishchem my dorogu?" [To Which Temple Are We Searching for a Path?]. Moscow, 1989.

Kuzmin, A. "Tatishchev" [Tatishchev]. Moscow, 1981.

Laqueur, W. *Russia and Germany: A Century of Conflict.* Boston, 1965.

Lavrinovich, M. "Vilna v 1812 g." [Vilna in 1812]. *Istoricheskiy Vestnik*: Vol. 10–12, 1897.

Lerner, O.M. "Maior Osman-Bei pered sudom zdravogo smysla" [Major Osman-Bei in front of the Court of Common Sense]. Odessa, 1874.

Levandovsky, A.L. "Protsess rytsarei khrama" [The Trial of Knights Templar]. *Chelovek i Zakon*: No. 1, 1975.

Levitina, V. "Russkiy teatr i evreyi. V 2 kn." [Russian Theater and Jews. In 2 Books]. Jerusalem, 1988.

Likhachevsky, cleric. "Kak my, russkiye, pritesnyaem evreyev" [The Ways We Russians Oppress Jews]. *Rus*: No. 40, 1881.

Lipman, Z. "Iz semeinykh vospominaniy" [From Family Memories]. *Evreiskaya Starina*, 1907.

Litvin, S. "Ocherki "Kolymazhnogo dvora" [Tales of the Coach House]. *Istoricheskiy Vestnik*: Vol. 69: September, 1897.

Litvin, S. "Sredi evreyev' [Among Jews]. *Istoricheskiy Vestnik*: No. 10–12, 1896.

Litvin, S. "Sredi evreyev" [Among Jews]. Moscow, 1897.
Litvin, S. "Vospominaniya" [A Memoir]. *Istoricheskiy Vestnik,* 1906.
Litvin, S. "Zamuzhestvo Revekki' [Rebecca's Marriage]. St. Petersburg, 1895.
Litvin, S. "Zhertvoprinosheniye" [Sacrifice]. *Istoricheskiy Vestnik*: October/November, 1897.
Losev, S., Petrusenko, V. "Mest po-amerikanski" [American Revenge]. *Ogonyok*: No. 15, 1981.
Lozinsky, S.G. "Srednevekovye rostovshchiki" [Medieval Usurers]. Petrograd, 1923.
Lyubimov, L. "Na chuzhbine" [In a Strange Land]. Moscow, 1963.
Magnitsky, M.L. "Duma pri grobe gr. Speranskogo" [Thoughts at the Coffin of Speransky]. *Russkaya Starina*: November, 1883.
Maikova, T. "Pyotr I i pravoslavnaya tserkov" [Peter I and Orthodox Church]. *Nauka i Religiya:* No. 2, 1979.
Manfred, A.Z. "Obrazovaniye russko-frantsuzskogo soyuza" [Formation of Russo-French Alliance]. Moscow, 1975.
Mann, Yu. "Fakultety N.I. Nadezhdina" [Studies of N.I. Nadezhdin]. In: N.I. Nadezhdin. "Literaturnaya Kritika" [Literary Criticism]. Moscow, 1972.
Maor, I. "Russkiy filosof Vladimir Solovyov" [Russian Philosopher Vladimir Solovyov]. *Panorama Izrailya*: No. 175, 1985.
Markevich, B. "Bezdna" [Abyss]. In: "Polnoye sobraniye sochineniy. V 10 t." [Full Collection of Works in 10 Volumes]. St. Petersburg, 1885: Vol. 8,9,10.
Markish, D. "Nakanune" [The Eve]. *Sputnik*: No. 305, 1990.
Mashovets, N. "Trevozhnost ochevidnogo: ideologicheskiye zametki" [The Disturbing Obvious: Ideological Notes]. *Nash Sovremennik*: No. 69, 1980.
Masonov, I.F. "Slovar psevdonimov. V 4 t." [Dictionary of Pseudonyms. In 4 Vol.]. Moscow, 1960: Vol. 4.
"Masonstvo v ego proshlom i nastoyashchem" [Freemasonry: Its Past and Present]. Moscow, 1914–1915: Vol.1.
Melnikov-Pechersky, A. "Na gorakh. V 2 t." [In the Mountains. In Two Volumes]. Leningrad, 1958.
Meshchersky, V.P. "Moi Vospominaniya. V 3 ch." [My Memoir. In Three Parts]. St. Petersburg, 1912.
Mezhetsky. "Vospominaniya Mitrofana Porfiryevicha Mezhetskogo" [A Memoir of Mitrofan Porfiryevich Mezhetsky]. *Istoricheskiy Vestnik*: August, 1899.
Mickiewicz, A. "Stikhotvorenya. Poemy. V "Biblioteka vsemirnoy literatury" [Verses. Poems. In: Library of World Literature]. Moscow, 1968: Vol. 96.

Mieses, M. *Polacy-Chrześcijanie pochodzenia żydowskiego*. Warszawa, 1938: Vol. I–IV.
Mikhailov, O.M. "Dmitriy Donskoy" [Dmitri of the Don]. Moscow, 1975.
Mikhailov, O.M. "Kuprin" [Kuprin]. Moscow, 1978.
Mikhailov, O.M. "Derzhavin (ZhZL)" [Derzhavin (Lives of Distinguished People)]. Moscow, 1977: 216–219.
Mikhailov, O.M. "Derzhavin" [Derzhavin]. Moscow, 1977.
Mikheleva, S.B. "Naivnye vremena masonskikh lozh..." [The Naive Times of Masonic Lodges...]. *Nauka i Religiya*, 1974.
Milyukov, P.N. "Predisloviye" [Foreword]. In: "Pravda o Sionskih Protokolakh." [Truth About *the Protocols of Zion*. A Literary Forgery.] Paris, 1922.
Mints, I. I. "Metamorfozy masonskoi legendy" [Metamorphoses of the Masonic Legend.] Istoria SSSR. M44, 1980.
Mironova, M.V., Menaker, A.S. "V svoyom repertuare" [As They Would]. Moscow, 1984.
Mochulsky, K. "Vladimir Solovyov. Zhizn i ucheniye" [Vladimir Solovyov: Life and Teaching]: Paris, 1951.
Mordvinov, V. "Tainy Talmuda i evreyi v otnoshenii k khristianskomu miru" [Secrets of the Talmud and Jews in Relation to the Christian World]. Moscow, 1880.
Muravyov, M.N. "Zapiski grafa M. N. Muravyova Vilenskogo" [A Journal of Count M. N. Muravyov of Vilna]. *Russkaya Starina*: Vol. 1, 1884.
N. "K istorii masonstva v Rossii" [On the History of Freemasonry in Russia]. *Russkaya Starina*: April, 1907.
Nekrasov, S. "Obryady i simvoly volnykh kamenshchikov" [Rituals and Symbols of Freemasons]. *Nauka i Religiya*: No. 10, 1974.
Nikitenko, A.V. "Dnevnik. V 3 t." [Journal in 3 Volumes]. Moscow, 1955.
Nilus, S.A. "Velikoye v malom" [The Great within the Small]. *Luch Sveta*: Berlin: Issue 3, 1920.
"Ocherki istorii SSSR. Period feodalisma" [Essays on the History of the USSR: The Period of Feudalism]. Moscow, 1955.
Okreyts, S.S. "Vospominaniya" [A Memoir]. *Istoricheskiy Vestnik*: Vol. 145, 1916.
Oksman, Yu.G. "Kommentarii" [Commentary]. In: Pushkin, A.S. 1961–1963. "Sobr. soch. V 10 t." [Collection of Works in 10 Volumes]. Moscow: Vol. 6.
"O raskolnikakh pri imperatore Nikolaye I i Aleksandre II (popolneno zapiskoyu Melnikova-Pecherskogo)" [On the Old Believers at the time of Nicholas I and Alexander II: Amended with the Note by Melnikov-Pechersky]. Berlin/Leipzig, 1882.
Orlova-Smirnova, M.V. "Pamyati Sergeya Aleksandrovicha i Eleny Aleksandrovny Nilus" [In memory of Sergei and Elena Nilus]. In: 1986. "Pravoslavny Put" [Orthodox Path]. Jordanville, NY.

Orshansky, I.L. "Iz noveishei istorii evreyev v Rossii. V 2 t." [From the Modern History of Jews in Russia in Two Volumes]. St. Petersburg, 1872.

Osman-Bei, V.A. "Zavoyevaniye mira evreyami" [Jewish Conquest of the World]. Basel (in German), 1873.

Osman-Bei, V.A. "Zavoyevaniye mira evreyami" [Jewish Conquest of the World]. Warsaw, 1880.

"Paleya Tolkovaya. Po spisku, sdelannomu v g. Kolomne v 1406 g." [The Explanatory Palaea: According to the Copy Made in Kolomna in 1406]. Moscow.

Paléologue, M. "Imperatorskaya Rossiya v epokhu Velikoi Voiny" [The Imperial Russia at the Time of the Great War]. In: "Istoriya i sovremennost" [History and Modern Day]. Berlin, 1922: Vol.3.

Peretz, V. "K voprosu o evreysko-russkom literaturnom obshchenii" [On the Issue of Jewish/Russian Literary Communication]. Prague: *Slavia*: No. 5, 1926–1927.

"Perezhitoye" [The Lived Through]. St. Petersburg, 1910.

Pigalev, V.A. "Bazhenov (ZhZL)" [Bazhenov (Lives of Distinguished People)]. Moscow, 1980: 157–175.

Pigalev, V. "Tyomnye tropy reaktsii" [Dark Paths of Reactionism]. *Sovetsky Voin*: No. 3, 1982.

(Pikul, V.) Ivanov, E. "Negromkiy vystrel" [A Quiet Gunshot]. Moscow, 1977.

Pikul, V. "U poslednei cherty. Roman-khronika" [At the last Frontier: A Chronicle]. *Nash Sovremennik*: No. 4–7, 1979.

"Pisma i doneseniya iezuitov o Rossii kontsa XVII nachala XVIII vv." [Jesuit Letters and Reports on Russia in the late 17th-early 18th centuries]. St. Petersburg, 1904.

Poliakov, L. *Histoire de L'antisemitisme*. Vol. 4. La Emancipación y la Reacción Racista. Barcelona, 1986.

Poliakov, L. *Les totalitarismes du XXe siècle: Un phénomène historique dépassé?* Paris, 1987.

Polonskaya-Vasilenko, N.D. "Iz istorii Yuzhnoi Ukrainy v XVIII v." [From the History of Southern Ukraine in the 18th Century]. *Istoricheskiye Zapiski*: Moscow: Vol. 14, 1945.

"Polskiy katekhizis" [Polish Catechism]. In: Samarin, Yu.F. 1868. "Iezuity i ikh otnosheniye k Rossii" [Jesuits and Their View of Russia]. Moscow.

Porfiryev, I. Ya. "Apokrificheskiye skazaniya o vetkhozavetnykh litsakh i sobytiyakh po rukopisyam Solovetskoi biblioteki" [Apocryphal Tales of Old Testament Characters and Events According to the Manuscripts from Solovetskaya Library]. St. Petersburg, 1887.

Porudominsky, V.I. "Dal (ZhZL)" [Dal. Lives of Distinguished People]. Moscow, 1971: 247.

Posnov, M.E. "Istoriya khristianskoy tserkvi" [A History of Christian Church]. Brussels, 1964.

"Povest vremennykh let." V 2 ch. (Literaturnye pamyatniki) [The Primary Chronicle. In 2 Parts. Literary Artifacts]. Moscow/Leningrad, 1950.

Protopopov, V. "V poiskakh zemli obetovannoi" [In Search of the Promised Land]. St. Petersburg, 1908.

Przecławski, J. *Pamiętniki rozumowanie*. Wilno, 1844.

Przecławski, J. *Śmierć i odrodzenie*. Wilno, 1844.

Przecławski, O.A. "Ignatiy Turkul — ministr Tsarstva Polskogo" [Ignatiy Turkul, A Minister of the Kingdom of Poland]. *Russkaya Starina*: December, 1875.

Przecławski, O.A. "Kaleidoskop vospominaniy' [Various Memories]. *Russkiy Arkhiv*: Vol. 10, 1872.

Przecławski, O.A. "Kaleidoskop vospominaniy' [Various Memories]. *Russkiy Arkhiv*: Vol. 12, 1872.

Przecławski, O.A. "Knyaz Ksaveriy Drutskiy-Lubetskiy" [Prince Ksawery Drucki-Lubecki]. *Russkaya Starina*: Vol. 21, 1878.

Przecławski, O.A. "Vospominaniya" [A Memoir]. *Russkaya Starina*: No. 14, 1883.

Przecławski, O.A. "Vospominaniya" [A Memoir]. *Russkaya Starina*: Vol. 14, 1883.

Przecławski, O.A. "Vospominaniya" [A Memoir]. *Russkiy Arkhiv*: Vol. 10., 1872.

Pushkarev, S.G. "Rossiya v XIX v." [Russia in the 19th Century]. New York, 1956.

Pushkin, A.S. "Poln. sobr. soch. V 10 t." [Complete Collection of Works in 10 Vol.]. Moscow/Leningrad, 1954–1956: Vol. 6.

Pypin, A. N. "Bibleyskaya sekta dvadtsatykh godov." [A Biblical Sect of the '20s]. *Vestnik Evropy*: March, 1871.

Pypin, A.N. "Issledovaniya i materialy po epokhe Ekateriny II i Aleksandra I" [Studies and Materials on the Reign of Catherine II and Alexander I]. St. Petersburg, 1916.

Rauch, G.O. "Dnevnik" [Journal]. *Krasny Arkhiv*: Issue 19, 1926.

Ravrebe, I. "Puteshestvennik kontsa XVII v. — Avraam Kunki" [The Traveler of the late 17th century: Abraham Kunki]// *Evreiskaya Starina*. Moscow: Vol. 13, 1928.

"Razoblacheniye velikoi tainy frankmasonov (Iz bumag pokoinogo O. A. Przheslavskogo)" [Exposing the Great Secret of Freemasons: From the Papers of the Late O. A. Przecławski]. Moscow, 1909.

"Ritualnye protsessy 1816 goda" [Ritual Trials of 1816]. *Evreiskaya Starina*: Issue 1, 1912.

Rochester-Kryzhanovskaya, V.I. "Pautina" [Spiderweb]. Revel, 1906.

Rodionov, I.A. "Nashe prestupleniye (Ne bred, a byl). Iz sovremennoi narodnoi zhizni" [Our Crime: Not Fiction, But Real: From Modern Common People Life]. St. Petersburg, 1909.
Rodionov, I.A. "Syny dyavola" [Sons of the Devil]. Belgrade: 4-6, 1932.
(Romanov). "Vel. kn. Nikolai Mikhailovoch. Imperator Aleksandr I. Opyt istoricheskogo issledovaniya" [Grand Prince Nicholas Mikhailovich. The Emperor Alexander I: A Historical Study]. Petrograd, 1914.
Romanovsky, A.M. "Frantsuzy v Chausakh v 1812 godu" [The French in Chavusy in 1812]. *Russkaya Starina*: December, 1877.
Rosenblum, S. A. *Être juif en U.R.S.S.* Paris, 1982.
Roskes, D. "Vopreki Apokalipsisu" [Despite the Apocalypse]. Jerusalem, 1919.
Rossov, S. "Evreyskiy vopros" [Jewish Question]. S. l., S. a.
Rozanov, V. "Religiya i kultura' [Religion and Culture]. St. Petersburg, 1899.
Rozov, N.N. "Kniga v Drevnei Rusi" [Book in Ancient Russia]. Moscow, 1977.
Rozov, N.N. "Sinodalny spisok sochineniy Ilariona — pisatelya XI v." [A Synodal Copy of Works by Ilarion, an 11th Century Writer}. *Slavia*: Roch: XXXII, 1963.
Rumyantseva, V.S. "Narodnoye antitserkovnoye dvizheniye v Rossii v XVII v." [People's Anti-Church Movement in Russia in the 17th Century]: Moscow, 1986.
"Russkaya periodicheskaya pechat (1702-1894)" [Russian Periodicals of 1702-1894]. Moscow, 1959.
Russkaya Starina: Vol. 16, 1876.
"Russkiy biograficheskiy slovar" [Russian Biographical Dictionary]: St. Petersburg, 1897-1914.
"Russkiye Izbranniki" [The Russian Chosen]: Berlin, 1907.
"Russkiye lyudi o evreyakh" [Russian People Talk About Jews]. St. Petersburg, 1891.
"Russkiye pisateli XI-XX vv. A. F. Veltman" [Russian Writers of 11-20th centuries. Alexander Veltman]. Moscow: Vol. 1, 1989.
"Russko-turetskaya voina 1877-1878 gg." [Russo-Turkish war of 1877-1878]. Moscow, 1977.
Ryabinin, I. "Polskoye masonstvo" [Polish Freemasons]. In: Edited by Melgunov, S.P. and Sidorov, N.P. 1915. "Masonstvo v ego proshlom i nastoyashchem. V 2 t." [Freemasonry: Its Past and Present. In 2 Volumes]. St. Petersburg: Vol. 2.
Ryvin, M.D. "Navet" [The Libel]. St. Petersburg, 1912.
S.P. "Evrey na evropeiskoy stsene" [A Jew on European Stage]. *Evreiskaya Nedelya*: No. 9, 1910.
Saint-Glin, J. I. "Zapiski" [Journal]. *Russkaya Starina*: March, 1883.
Samarin, Yu.F. "Iezuity i ikh otnosheniye k Rossii" [Jesuits and Their View of Russia]. Moscow, 1868.

Schilder, N.K. "Dva donosa v 1831 g." [Two Reports in 1831]. *Russkaya Starina*: December, 1898.

Schilder, N.K. "Imperator Aleksandr I. Ego zhizn i tsarstvovaniye. V 4 t." [The Emperor Alexander I: His Life and Reign. In 4 Vol.]. St. Petersburg, 1905.

Schilder, N.K. "Imperator Nikolai I, ego zhizn i tsarstvovaniye" [The Emperor Nicholas I: His Life and Reign]. St. Petersburg, 1903.

Schulsinger J., *Annales du Prince de Ligne; Un précurseur du sionisme au XVIII-e siècle*: le Prince de Ligne. Paris, 1936.

Schwarz, G. (Bostunitsch, G.). "Iz vrazheskogo plena. Istoriya mytarstv russkogo literatora v nemetskom plenu" [Out of Enemy's Prison: The Story of Suffering of a Russian Writer in German Captivity]. St. Petersburg, 1915.

Schwarzband, S.M. "K voprosu ob istochnikakh 'Skazaniya o kreshchenii Rusi'" [On the Origin of *The Tale of Baptism of Russia*]. Jerusalem: Russian Literature and History, 1989.

Semeka, A.V. "Russkiye rozencreitsery i socineniya imperatritsy Ekateriny II protiv masonstva" [The Russian Rosicrucians and the Writings of Catherine II Against Freemasonry]. See: *Zhurnal Ministerstva narodnogo prosveshcheniya*: Vol. II, 1902.

Semeka, A.V. "Russkoye masonstvo v XVII v." [Russian Freemasonry in the 17th century]. In: 1914–1915. "Masonstvo v ego proshlom i nastoyashchem" [Freemasonry: Its Past and Present]. Moscow: Vol.1.

Semennikov, V. P. Knigoizdatelskaya deyatelnost N. I. Novikova i Tipograficheskoi kompanii" [Publishing Activity of N. I. Novikov and the Printing Company]. Petrograd, 1921.

Semenyuk, V. "Natsionalisticheskoye bezumiye" [Nationalistic Madness]. Minsk, 1981.

Semevsky, V. "Dekabristy-masony" [The Decembrists Freemasons]. *Minuvshiye Gody*: St. Petersburg: Vol. 2, 1902.

Shabelskaya, E.A. "Satanisty XX v." [Satanists of the 20th Century]. Riga, 1934: Part 1.

Shabelskaya, E.A. "Pyatnadtsat let spustya" [Fifteen Years Later]. Riga, 1934: Part 2.

Shabelskaya, E.A. "Taina Martiniki" [The Secret of Martinique]. Riga, 1936: Part 3.

Shafarevich, I. "Rusofobia" [Russophobia]. "22." Jerusalem: No. 63–64, 1989.

Shatskin, Ya. "Novyye materialy ob uchastii evreyev v voine 1812 g." [New Materials on Jewish Participation in the War of 1812]. *Evreiskaya Starina*, 1914.

Shick, A. "Denis Davydov" [Denis Davydov]. Paris, 1951.

Shifrin, N. Sh. "K kharakteristike tsarskikh povinnostei v Palestine v pervoi polovine I tys. do n.e. po dannym bibleiskoi traditsii" [On the

Characterization of King's Levies in Palestine in the First Half of the 1st Century B. C. Based on the Biblical Tradition]. *Vestnik Drevnei Istorii*: Moscow: No.1(99), 1967.

Shmakov, A.S. "Delo o pogrome evreiev v Vyazme 19/20 oktyabrya 1905 g." [The Case of the Jewish Pogrom of October 19-20, 1905 in Vyazma]. Moscow, 1907.

Shmakov, A.S. "Delo "Soyedinennogo banka"" [The Case of the "United Bank"]. Moscow, 1909.

Shmakov, A.S. "Evreiskiye rechi" [Jewish Speeches]. Moscow, 1897.

Shmakov, A.S. "Evreiskiy vopros na stsene vsemirnoi istorii" [Jewish Question on the Stage of World History]. Moscow, 1912.

Shmakov, A.S. "Gomelskoye delo" [The Gomel Case]. Moscow, 1905.

Shmakov, A.S. "Mezhdunarodnoye tainoye pravitelstvo" [Secret Global Government]. Moscow, 1912.

Shmakov, A.S. "Minskiy protsess" [The Minsk Trial]: Moscow, 1899.

Shmakov, A.S. "Pogrom evreiev v Kieve" [Jewish Pogrom in Kiev]. Moscow, 1906.

Shmakov. A.S. "Svoboda i evrei" [Freedom and the Jew]: Moscow, 1906.

Sholem, G. "Osnovnye techeniya v evreiskoi mistike. V 2 t." [The Main Trends in Jewish Mysticism. In 2 Volumes}. Jerusalem,1984: Vol. 2.

Shugurov, M.F. "Istoriya evreyev v Rossii" [History of Jews in Russia]. *Russkiy Arkhiv*: No. 1-5, 1891.

Shugurov, M.F. "Istoriya evreyev v Rossii" [History of Jews in Russia]. *Russkiy Arkhiv*: No. 3, 1895.

Skabichevsky, A.M. "Isroriya noveishei russkoi literatury. 1848-1908." [History of Modern Russian Literature: 1848-1908] St. Petersburg, 1909.

Skalkovsky, K. "Sovremennaya Rossiya. Ocherki nashei gosudarstvennoi i obshchestvennoi zhizni" [Modern Russia: Essays on Our State and Social Life]. St. Petersburg, 1889.

Sliozberg, G.B. "Baron Ginzburg. Ego zhizn i deyatelnost" [Baron Ginsburg: His Life and Activities]. Paris, 1933.

Sliozberg, G.B. "Dela davno minuvshikh dnei" [The Matters of the Days Long Past]. Paris: Vol.3, 1934.

Smirnov, A. "Messianskiye ozhidaniya i verovaniya iudeyev okolo vremen Iisusa Khrista (ot makkaveiskikh voin, do razrusheniya Ierusalima rimlyanami)" [Messianic expectations and beliefs of Hebrews around the time of Jesus Christ (from Maccabean Revolt to the Siege of Jerusalem by Romans)]. *Uchenye zapiski Kazanskogo Universiteta*: January, 1900.

Snetkovsky, P. "Sankt-Peterburgskoye otdeleniye v 1896-1901 gg." [The St. Petersburg Department in 1896-1901]. *Byloye*: No. 16, 1921.

"Sochineniya imperatritsy Ekateriny II. Proizvedeniya literaturnyye. A. Vvedensky. Vstupitelnaya statya" [Writings by the Empress

Catherine II: Fictional Works: Introduction by A. Vvedensky]: St. Petersburg, 1893.

Sokolovskaya, T. "O masonstve v prezhnem russkom flote" [On Freemasonry in Older Russian Navy] //*More*: No. 8, 1907.

Soloukhin, V.A. "Kameshki na ladoni" [Pebbles in My Hand]. *Novy Mir*: No. 8, 1986.

Solovyov, S.M. "Zhizn i tvorcheskaya evolutsiya V. Solovyova" [Life and Creative Evolution of V. Solovyov]. Brussels, 1977.

Solovyov, V. S. "Pisma. V 2 t." [Letters: In 2 Volumes]. St. Petersburg: Vol. 2, 1907.

Solovyov, V. S. "Tri Razgovora" [Three Conversations]. New York, 1954.

"Soyuz Russkogo naroda. Po materialam Chrezvychainoi sledstvennoi komissii Vremennogo pravitelstva 1917 g." [The Union of the Russian People: Based on the Materials of the Emergency Investigative Committee of the Provisional Government, 1917]. Moscow/Leningrad, 1929.

Speransky, V. "Vladimir Solovyov o evreiskom voprose" [Vladimir Solovyov on Jewish Question]. *Rassvet*: Paris: No. 6, 1929.

Stanislawski, M. *Tsar Nicholas I and the Jews: The Transformation of Jewish Society in Russia*. 1825–1855. Philadelphia, 1983.

Stashkevich, N. "Proci plyni historyi" [Going Through the Flow of History]. *Polymya*: No. 10, 1983.

"Stoglav" [Book of One Hundred Chapters]. St. Petersburg, 1863.

Strakhov, N. "Zhizn i trudy N. Ya. Danilevskogo" [Life and Works of N. Ya. Danilevsky]. St. Petersburg, 1996.

"Stranitsy proshlogo. Messianskiye nastroeniya v 1813 g." [Pages of the Past: Messianic Tendencies in 1813]. *Rassvet*: Moscow, 1930: No. 42.

Stroyev, V. "Vladimir Solovyov i evreistvo" [Vladimir Solovyov and The Jewry]. *Rassvet*: Paris: No. 49, 1925.

Suvorin, A.S. "Dnevnik" [Journal]. Moscow/Petrograd, 1923.

Syn Otechestva. 1816: No. 26.

"Tainye akty iudaisma" [Secret Acts of Judaism]. *Dvukhglavy Oryol*: No. 11, 1927.

The Summary of a lecture by V. Solovyov in the magazine *Russkiy Evrei*. 1882: No. 9.

Tikhomirov, L.A. "K reforme obnovlennoi Rossii (Statyi 1909–1911 gg.) [Towards the Reform of the New Russia: Articles of 1909–1911]. Moscow, 1912.

Tolstoy-Znamenski, D.M. "Otvet Tsiprinusu" [A Response to Cyprinus]. *Russkiy Arkhiv*, 1876.

Tsvibak, M. "Platonov i ego shkola" [Platonov and His School]. In: "Klassovyi vrag na istoricheskom fronte" [Class Enemy on the Historical Front]. Moscow/Leningrad, 1931.

Tutkevich, D.V. "Chto takoye evrei" [What Jews Are]. Kiev, 1906.

(Umanets, S.I.) S.A. "Mozaika (Iz starykh zapisnykh knizhek)" [Mosaic: From Old Notebooks]. *Istoricheskiy Vestnik*: No. 12, 1912.
Velichko, V.L. "Vladimir Solovyov. Zhizn i tvoreniya" [Vladimir Solovyov: His Life and Works]. St. Petersburg, 1902.
"Velizhskoye Delo" [The Velizh Affair]. In: Brockhaus and Efron. 1911–1916. "Evreiskaya Entsiklopedia. V 16 t." [The Jewish Encyclopedia in 16 Volumes]. St. Petersburg.
Veltman, A.F. "Strannik. (Literaturnye pamyatniki)" [The Wanderer. (Literary Artifacts)]. Moscow, 1977.
Vernadsky, G.V. "Russkoye masonstvo v tsarstvovaniye Ekateriny II" [Russian Freemasonry During the Reign of Catherine II] Petrograd, 1917.
Vinaver, M.M. "Besedy s grafom S. Yu. Witte" [Conversations with Count Witte]. *Novy Voskhod*, 1915.
Vinberg, F.V. "Korni Zla" [Roots of Evil]. Munich, 1921.
Vinberg, F.V. "Vsemirny tainy zagovor" [Secret World Conspiracy]. Berlin., 1922.
Vishnyak, M. "Dan proshlomu" [To the Past Its Due]. New York. 1954.
Volkonsky. "Zapiski Sergeya Grigorievicha Volkonskogo" [Journal of Sergey Grigorievich Volkonsky]. St. Petersburg, 1912.
Volkov, V.K. "Osnovnye etapy razvitiya slavyano-germanskikh otnosheniy v XIX–XX vv. v svete germanskoi imperialisticheskoi politiki "Drang nach Osten" (problemy i zadachi issledovaniya)" [The Main Steps in Development of Slavo-German Relations in the 19th-20th Centuries in the Light of the German Imperialist Policy *Drang nach Osten*: The Issues and Tasks of the Study]. In: 1971. "Issledovaniya po slavyano-germanskim otnosheniyam" [Studies of Slavo-German Relations]. Moscow.
Volsky, K. "Evreyi v Rossii. Ikh byt, tseli i sredstva" [Jews in Russia: Their Everyday Life, Goals, and Means]. St. Petersburg, 1887.
Voronkov, I.A. "Polskiye tainyye obshchestva v Litve i Belorussii v kontse XVIII v. i pervom tridtsatiletii XIX v." [Polish Secret Societies in Lithuania and Belarus in the late 18th and the first third of the 19th century]. *Istoricheskiye zapiski*: Vol. 60.
Weber, M. *Ancient Judaism*. Glencoe, IL, 1952.
Weinryb, B.D. *Anti-Semitism in Soviet Russia*. In: 1970. The Jews in Soviet Russia since 1917. London.
Witte, S. Yu. "Vospominaniya. V 3 t." [A Memoir. In Three Volumes]. Moscow, 1960.
Yakimov, V. "Krestovsky v Nakhichevani" [Krestovsky in Nakhichevan]. *Istoricheskiy Vestnik*: No.3, 1902.
Yakovlev, N.N. "1 avgusta 1914" [August 1, 1914]. Moscow, 1974.
Yermolov. "Zapiski Alekseya Petrovicha Yermolova" [Journal of Alexei Petrovich Yermolov]. Moscow, 1865: Part 1.

Yuditsky, A.D. "Evreyi v tekstilnoi promyshlennosti XIX veka" [Jews in the Textile Industry of the 19th Century]. *Istoricheskiy Sbornik*: Moscow/Leningrad: Vol. 4, 1935.

Zabelin, I. "Istoriya goroda Moskvy, napisannaya po porucheniyu Moskovskoi gorodskoi Dumy" [A History of the City of Moscow Written at the Order of the Moscow City Council]. Moscow, 1905: Part 1.

Zagoskin, N.P. "Ocherki organizatsii i proiskhozhdeniya sluzhilogo sosloviya v dopetrovskoi Rusi" [Essays on the Organization and Origin of the Service Class in pre-Peter's Rus]. Kazan, 1876.

"Zapiska o ritualnykh ubiystvakh" [The Note on Ritual Murders]. St. Petersburg, 1914.

Zaretsky, L.M. "Evreiskiye tainy' [Jewish Secrets]. Odessa, 1873.

Zaslavsky, D.I. "Evrei v russkoi literature" [Jews in Russian Literature]. *Evreiskaya Letopis*: 1923: Issue 1.

Zayonchkovsky, P.A. "Krisis samoderzhaviya na rubezhe 1870–1880 godov" [The Crisis of Autocracy in the Late 1870s-Early 1880s]. Moscow, 1964.

Zhevakhov, N.D. "Sergei Aleksandrovich Nilus. Kratkiy Ocherk zhizni i tvorchestva" [Sergei Nilus: A Summary of Life and Work]. Yugoslavia, 1936.

Zotov, V. "Kaliostro. Ego zhizn i prebyvaniye v Rossii" [Cagliostro: His Life and Sojourn in Russia]. *Russkaya Starina*; January, 1875.

PRINCIPAL WORKS BY SAVELY DUDAKOV

BOOKS

1. "Pyotr Shafirov." Jerusalem, 1989, Pp. 117. The series: *Jews in World Culture.*
2. "Istoriya odnogo mifa. Ocherki russkoi literatury XIX–XX vv." [A History of a Myth: Essays on Russian Literature of the Nineteenth and Twentieth Centuries]. Moscow: Nauka. 1993. Pp. 282.
3. "Paradoksy i prichudy filosemitizma i antisemitizma v Rossii. Ocherki" [Paradoxes and Peculiarities of Philo-Semitism and Anti-Semitism in Russia: Essays]. Moscow: Russian State University of Humanities. 2000. Pp. 640.
4. "Etyudy lyubvi i nenavisti. Ocherki" [Sketches of Love and Hate: Essays]. Moscow: Russian State University of Humanities. 2003. Pp. 542.
5. "Lenin kak Messiya" [Lenin as the Messiah]. Jerusalem/Moscow. 2007. Pp. 164.
6. "Lenin kak Messiya" [Lenin as the Messiah]. Jerusalem/Moscow. 2008. Pp. 164. 2nd edition.
7. "Kaissa i Votan" [Caïssa and Wotan]. Jerusalem/Moscow. 2009. Pp. 420.
8. "Pyotr Shafirov i drugiye" [Pyotr Shafirov and Others]. Jerusalem/Moscow. 2011. Pp. 432.
9. "Kniga very i beznadyozhnosty" [The Book of Faith and Hopelessness}. Jerusalem/Moscow. 2012. Pp. 408.
10. "Iz lichnogo arkhiva" [From Personal Archives]. Jerusalem/Moscow. 2014. Pp. 500.
11. "Lenin kak Messiya" [Lenin as the Messiah]. Jerusalem/Moscow. 2016. Pp. 184. 3rd edition.
12. "Istoriya odnogo mifa. Ocherki russkoi literatury XIX–XX vv." [A History of a Myth: Essays on Russian Literature of the Nineteenth and Twentieth Centuries]. Evgarm. 2018. Pp. 368. Re-printing.

Festschrift Dr. Saveliy Dudakov. The Hebrew University of Jerusalem. Center for Slavic Languages and Literature. Edited by W. Moskovich and S. Schwazband. — Was published In 2004 and dedicated to the author's 65th birthday.

SELECTED ARTICLES

1. "Russkiye predtechi "Protokolov sionskikh mudretsov." [Russian Predessors of *The Protocols of the Elders of Zion*]. Jewish cultural magazine *Narod i zemlya [People and Land]*.
2. "Vladimir Solovyov i Sergei Nilus" [Vladimir Solovyov and Sergei Nilus]. In: Russian Literature and History. Jerusalem, 1989.
3. "Russkaya partiya" [Russian Party]. Jewish cultural magazine *Narod i zemlya [People and Land]*.
4. "K. P. Kaufman i evreistvo" [K. P. Kaufman and Jewry]. *Vozrozhdeniye*.
5. "Geniy i zlodeistvo" [Genius and Evil]. *"22"*: 2002.
6. "Voina 1812 goda i ritualnye protsessy v Rossii" [The War of 1812 and Ritual Processes in Russia]. Almanach of Jewish culture *Kovcheg [The Ark]*: 1990.
7. "Grigory Rasputin i Yerusalim" [Grigory Rasputin and Jerusalem]. *Jews and Slavs*: 2003: No. 10: 251–270.
8. E.A. Shabelskaya. In Honor of Professor Victor Levin. *Russian Philology and History*: 392–410. The Hebrew University of Jerusalem. Department of Russian and Slavic Studies. Center for Slavic Languages and Literature.
9. "Zloi skazochnik" [The Evil Storyteller]. Quarterly magazine *Stranitsy filosofii, kultury, nauki v Izraile [Pages of Philosophy, Culture, and Science in Israel]*: 1993: No. 2.
10. "Shafirov i ego potomki" [Shafirov and His Descendants]. *Tarbut*: 1983: No. 2.
11. "Zametki po istorii filosemitizma v Rossii" [Notes on the History of Philo-Semitism in Russia]. Jerusalem: *Jews and Slavs*: 1995: No. 4.
12. "Evrei v kulture russkogo zarubezhya. Ob "ariyskikh" i "neariyskikh" shakhmatakh: Sbornik statei, publicatsyi, memuarov i esse" [Jews in the Culture of Russian Diaspora: On "Aryan" and "non-Aryan" chess. A Collection of articles, publications, memoirs, and essays]. Jerusalem: 1995: Issue 1.
13. "Russkiye evrei na frontakh pervoi mirovoi voiny" [Russian Jews on the Battlefields of World War I]. Jerusalem: *Nota Bene*: 2004: 345–352.
14. "Oh, Jerusalem! "Ierusalimskiye zametki" [Oh, Jerusalem! Jerusalem Notes]. *Pica-Jerusalem*: 1999: 279–288.
15. "Evreiskaya tema v tvorchestve Vereshchagina" [Jewish Theme in Vereshchagin's Creative Work]. Almanach of Jewish Culture *Kovcheg [The Ark]*: *Tarbut*: 1992: Issue 3.
16. "Evrei v kulture russkogo zarubezhya. "On uvidel Ierusalim iznutri." Slovo o khudozhnike Aleksandre Kopeloviche" [Jews in the Culture

of Russian Diaspora: "He saw Jerusalen from the Inside." A Word About the Artist Alexander Kopelovich]. 1994: Vol. 3: 350–365.
17. "Ulyanov-Lenin. Shtrikhi k portretu" [Lenin: Sketching the Image]. *Rossiya i sovremennyi mir [Russia and Modern World]*: 2017: No. 1(94): 35–45.
18. "Ierusalimskiye zametki" [Jerusalem Notes]. *Vestnik*: 1999: No. 21(228): October 12.

INDEX

Abramovich 36
Abramowicz, L. 305, 315
Adamovich, M. 51
Afanasyev, V. V. 54, 80, 278, 282, 315
Agrippa, Cornelius 81, 282
Agursky M. S. 231
Ahad Ha'am 243
Ainalov, D. V. 265
Akhmatov, V. 187, 305, 315
Aksakov, S. T. 81, 99, 282, 315
Aldanov, M. A. 246, 311
Aleksandrovsky, B. N. 309–310, 315
Alekseyev, M. V. 311–312
Alexander I 34, 43–45, 47–48, 50, 56, 62, 74, 86–87, 111, 246, 271, 276–277, 283, 315, 326–328
Alexander II 99, 102, 105, 111–112, 114, 117, 119, 121–122, 129, 135, 238, 270, 324
Alexander III 124, 151, 178, 256, 298, 318
Alexandra Fyodorovna 6, 149
Alexey Mikhailovich 27, 269
Altayev, Al. 311
Amalrik, A. 213
Ambrose, of Optina 163
Amfiteatrov, A. F. 174
Ancelot 76
Andrei Bogolyubsky 20
Anthony (Bochkov) 163
Arakcheyev, A. A. 57, 61, 80
Arndt 33
Ashkenazi, Sh. 43, 275, 284
Augereau 46

Baggovut 47
Bagritsky, E. G. 223
Bakounine, T. 274, 315
Bakst, N. I. 152, 313
Bakunin, M. A. 216, 258
Balashov, A. D. 47
Balfour, Arthur James 276, 315
Bamberger, David and Leo 36
Barclay de Tolly, M. B. 47, 58, 279
Bartenev, P. I. 56, 96
Bartenev, Yu. N. 56, 96
Bashilov, B. 29, 271–272, 315
Bazhenov, V. 201–202, 278, 309, 325
Beaconsfield, see: Disraeli, Benjamin 94
Beilis, M. 41–42, 219–220, 240, 302
Belinsky, V. G. 72, 74, 282, 315
Bely, A. (Bugayev, B. N.) 297
Beneš, Edvard 175
Benois, A. N. 289, 316
Bentham, Jeremy 275
Benz, A. I. 174, 303, 316
Berdyaev, N. A. 242
Bergelsohn, David 202
Berkhin, I. 316
Berlin, N. B. 6, 52–53, 126, 128, 132, 137–138, 152, 177, 188, 194, 211–212, 236, 265, 270–271, 275–276, 290, 292, 299, 308, 316, 318, 324–325, 327, 331
Berlin, P. 6, 52–53, 126, 128, 132, 137–138, 152, 177, 188, 194, 211–212, 236, 265, 270–271, 275–276, 290, 292, 299, 308, 316, 318, 324–325, 327, 331

INDEX

Berlin, S. 6, 52–53, 126, 128, 132, 137–138, 152, 177, 188, 194, 211–212, 236, 265, 270–271, 275–276, 290, 292, 299, 308, 316, 318, 324–325, 327, 331
Bernstein, H. 7–8, 242, 265, 316
Besht, Israel (Baal Shem Tov) 285
Bestuzhev, N.A. 80, 253
Bestuzhev-Marlinsky, A.A. 253
Betsky I.I. 31
Bezobrazov 54
Bezymensky, A. 218
Bismark, Otto 177–178, 192, 204
Bitsyn, N. 96, 286, 316
Blavatskaya, E.L. 171, 312
Bleichroeder 126
Blinov, I.A. 41–42
Blok, A.A. 146, 205
Bludov, D.N. 75
Boehme, Jakob 26–27, 57, 170
Boetticher, P. 146
Bogachev 46
Bogdanovich, A.L. 289, 316
Bogoyavlensky, S.K. 269, 316
Bogrov, G.I. 128, 136
Bolshakov, V. 306, 316
Boltin, I.N. 30
Bonch-Bruyevich, V.D. 279, 316
Bork, A.N. 179, 184, 240
Borozdin, A.K. 279
Borzymowski, F. 80
Bostunitsch, G. (Schwarz) 106, 139, 217–221, 223–228, 273, 278, 288, 290, 293, 299, 301–303, 305, 307, 309–310, 316, 328
Brafman, A. 1, 10, 104–109, 128, 174, 235, 288, 316
Brafman, Jacob 1, 10, 104–109, 128, 174, 235, 288, 316
Brant, E. 195, 198, 227, 305, 307, 316
Breshko-Breshkovsky, N.N. 174, 187–199, 204, 305–306, 316–317

Brodsky, I.A. 219
Bronsky 79
Brushlinskaya, O. 308, 317
Brusilov, A.A. 311–312
Buchbinder, N.A. 283, 317
Bulgarin, F.V. 9–10, 66, 71, 74–78, 88, 282, 317
Bunin, I.A. 9, 310
Burtsev, V.L. 8, 16, 187, 237, 242, 265, 288, 296, 299, 317
Butmi, G.V. (de Katzman) 4–6, 142–144, 156–159, 173, 195, 198, 201, 220, 231, 233, 239, 296, 309
Byalik, Hayim Nahman 217
Byron, George 65

C. Theophania Stanislavovna 80
Cagliostro 32–33, 273, 332
Catherine II 31, 34, 37, 39, 43, 111, 271–274, 316, 326, 328, 330–331
Cauchy, Augustin-Louis 213, 217, 220, 310
Chaadayev, P.A. 11, 89
Chaikovsky, N.V. 184
Chamberlain, H.S. 117, 146, 149, 154
Chateaubriand, F.-R. 93
Chatskin 264
Chaucer, Geoffrey 65
Chayla, A. du 149, 238, 299–300, 318
Chechulin, N. 274, 317
Chekhonin 181
Chernukha, V.T. 287, 317
Chernyaev, M.G. 122
Chernyshev, I.G. 29
Chernyshev, Z.G. 29
Chernyshevsky, N.G. 84, 256, 283, 313, 317
Chiari, P. 174
Chichagov, P.V. 47
Chopin, F. 93

Cohn, N, 4, 8, 141–142, 265, 294, 296, 299, 301–302, 305, 316–317
Corey, D. 228
Couteulx De Canteleu, J.H.E Le 116
Cromwell, O. 217–218
Crémieux 203, 236, 241
Cyon, Elias von 5–6, 238
Czaplicki 54
Czartoryski, A. 43, 48–50, 81, 86, 277

Dal, I.M. 37, 89–90, 195, 274, 284, 316, 320, 325
Dal, V.I. 37, 89–90, 195, 274, 284, 316, 320, 325
Danilevsky, N.Ya. 1, 100–102, 104, 174, 183, 204, 216, 288, 301, 307, 310, 317, 330
Dante 65
Darwin, Charles 262
Dashkov, D.V. 75
David 27, 36, 121, 127–128, 151, 161, 165, 169, 223, 233
Davydov, D.V. 46, 49–50, 276–277, 317, 328
Delevsky, Yu. 6, 16, 64, 187, 225, 236–237, 242, 265, 288, 292, 296, 299, 317–318
Delyanov, I.D. 83, 105
Demchenko, Ya.G. 143, 295, 318
Denikin, A.I. 7, 312
Denisov, A. 27
Derzhavin, G.R. 29–30, 201, 272, 278, 308–309, 318, 324
Dibich, I.I. 58–59, 202
Dibich, V.I. 58–59, 202
Diderot, Denis 35, 39
Dijour, I.M. 260
Dikiy, A.I. 203
Dillon 49
Diminsky 195
Disraeli, Benjamin 94
Dmitriev-Mamonov, M.A. 59–60

Dmitry Donskoy 308
Dobronin, A. 156
Dobrovolsky, V. 54
Dobuzhinsky, M.V. 181
Dolgoruky 183
Dombrovski 55
Donnelly, I. 174
Dostoyevsky, F.M. 9, 106, 176, 217, 247–248, 252–253, 281, 288, 292, 313, 315
Drabkin, A.N. 152
Drenteln, A.V. 110, 236, 289, 300–301, 310, 319
Dreyfus, A. 219, 235
Drucki-Lubecki, F.K. 42–43, 48, 50–52, 55, 80, 87, 277, 326
Drucki-Sokolski 179
Drumont, E. 15, 235
Druzhinin, V.D. 41
Dubelt, L.V. 75
Dubnov, S.M. 35, 41, 51, 275–277, 284, 298, 318
Dubrovin, A.I. 173, 181, 206, 225
Dumas, A. 176, 251, 304
Dunin-Skrzynno, W. 52
Dymov, O. 294, 318
Dühring, E. 235
d'Alembert 39

Efron-Litvin, S.K. 1, 134, 136, 139–140, 182, 294, 318
Elagin, I.P. 32, 61
Elets, Yu. 129, 131, 292, 318
Elizabeth 29, 34–35
Engelgardt, N.A. 274–275, 318
Epstein, M.B. 274, 319
Ertell 46
Ettinger, Sh. 13, 264, 276, 305, 319
Eulenburg, Philipp 178
Evseyev, E.S. 202–203

Fedotov 176
Feigin 94
Feinerman, E. 305, 315

INDEX

Ferdinand, Duke 38, 80
Fessler, I. L. 58–60, 62
Figner, A. S. 46, 132
Filippov, M. M. 109–110, 135, 289
Filippov, T. I. 109–110, 135, 289
Filosofov, A. D. 109–111, 116, 289
Firsova, N. N. 274
Flavius, Josephus 18, 24–25
Florensky, P. A. 240
Florinsky, K. 31
Florovsky, A. V. 278, 319
Ford, Henry 7, 242
Fosch 189
Fourier, Charles 217
Frank, I. 88, 92–93
Frankel, J. 319
Frederick the Great 204
Freud, S. 219, 229
Fritsch, T. 241
Fritzsche 207
Frug, S. 261, 314
Fry, L. 154

Gagarin 43, 190, 193
Galant, I 278, 281, 319
Gapon, G. A. 304
Garden, M. (Witkowsky) 10, 38, 64, 103, 179, 203, 222, 313
Goebbels, J. 9, 147, 207
Genin 27
Gerres 91
Gershuni, G. A. 180
Gervais, V. 319
Gessen, Yu. I. 89, 91
Getz, F. 150
Gilyarov-Platonov, N. P. 135, 293, 319
Ginzburg, S. M. 136, 278, 293, 299, 319, 329
Glama-Meshcherskaya 177
Glaubicz 78, 82
Glebov, A. I. 35, 274, 319
Glinka, Yu. 65, 149, 238–239, 299, 301

Gobineau, J. A. de 146
Goedsche, H. 8, 15, 143, 235, 250
Goethe, Johann Wolfgang von 31, 33, 65, 273
Gogol, N. V. 2, 67–70, 72, 281, 319
Golitsyn, A. N. 25, 30–31, 35, 50–51, 56–57, 60, 62, 71, 267, 274, 287, 311, 319
Golitsyn, D. M. 25, 30–31, 35, 50–51, 56–57, 60, 62, 71, 267, 274, 287, 311, 319
Golitsyn, N. N. 25, 30–31, 35, 50–51, 56–57, 60, 62, 71, 267, 274, 287, 311, 319
Golitsyna, V. F. 155
Golovin, N. A. 29
Golovinsky, M. B. 5, 304
Goncharov, I. A. 83
Gonta, I. 44
Gordon, I. 28, 106, 274, 319
Gordon, L. 28, 106, 274, 319
Gorky, M. 307, 319
Gornfeld, A. G. 263, 313
Graves, F. 7–8, 162, 189, 242
Grech, N. I. 75, 77
Greig, S. K. 29
Griboyedov, A. S. 75
Grigoriev, V. V. 90, 92, 94, 284–285, 319
Grimm 32
Grossman, L. P. 277, 319
Grulev, M. B. 311–312
Gruzenberg, O. O. 261
Guberman, I. V. 223
Gumbel, E. 303, 320
Gumilev, L. N. 285, 297, 320
Gummer, R. 46–47

Hablitz, Carl Ludwig 37, 274
Hamartolos, George , 18–19, 266, 321
Hecht, K. 170
Heine, H. 120, 217
Helfman, H. 257

Henry VIII 216
Herblet, H. 237, 242
Herzen, A. I. 123, 216, 224, 251–252, 313
Herzl, T. 142, 151, 202–203, 239, 243
Hesse 208
Hilarion 20
Hitler, A. 8–9, 200, 203, 227–228, 241
Hobbes, T. 217
Horace 120
Horwitz 264
Ignatiev, N. P. 124
Ilovaisky, V. I. 298
Ilyin, N. 208
Ilyinsky, F. 267, 320

Ioffe, I. 274, 320
Istrin, V. M. 19–21, 266, 306, 320–321
Ivan the Terrible, 25, 214, 216
Ivanin, I. S. 271, 321
Ivanov, A. I. 201, 243, 268, 306, 308, 312, 321, 325
Ivanov, E. 201, 243, 268, 306, 308, 312, 321, 325
Ivanov, N. I. 201, 243, 268, 306, 308, 312, 321, 325
Ivanov, Yu. 201, 243, 268, 306, 308, 312, 321, 325
Ivantsov-Platonov, A. M. 301, 321
Ivan III 25, 215
Izvolsky, A. P. 211

Jabotinsky, W. E. (Ze'ev) 263, 313
Jastrun, M. 311
Jodl, A. 207
John II Casimir 268
Joly, M. 7–8, 15–16, 237–242, 265
Jost, W. 321
Juel, J. 270–271, 321
Jung-Stilling 57
Kafka, F. 219

Kahane, M. 308
Kamenev, L. B. 185, 202
Kamenevich-Rvovsky, T. 24
Kantemir, A. D. 29–30
Karamzin, N. N. 253
Karmelyuk, U. 54
Karsavin, T. P. 41
Kartashev, A. 242
Kashpirev, V. V. 100
Katkov, M. N. 117, 129, 135, 264
Katsnelson, L. 286
Kaufman, A. E. 105–106, 288, 299, 305, 318, 321, 334
Kaufman, K. P. 105–106, 288, 299, 305, 318, 321, 334
Keith, James 29, 271
Keith, John 29, 271
Kelepovsky, A. I. 155
Kennedy, J. 202
Khmelnytsky, Bohdan 43
Khotimskaya, M. A. 180, 304
Khovansky, N. N. 52
Khrapovitsky 33
Kierkegaard, S. 229
Kinsey, A. 228
Kletochnikov, A. V. 300
Klimov, G. 224–229, 310, 321
Klimovich 212
Klyuchevsky, V. O. 269, 321
Kochetov, V. A. 213, 227
Kolchak, A. V. 240–241
Koni, A. F. 283, 321
Konopka, I. 54
Konstantinovsky, M. A. 163
Korchmiy, D. 184, 305
Korneyev, L. 93, 285, 309, 321
Kornilov, I. N. 105
Korsh 177
Kostomarov, N. I. 298
Kotelnikov, E. N. 57, 279
Kovalevsky, V. I. 178–179, 304
Kozlova, N. V. 274, 322
Kramář, K. 175
Krasnov, N. P. 312

INDEX

Krasny-Admoni, G. Ya. 41
Kraszewski, J. 82
Krebs, V. 275, 322
Krestovsky, V. V. 1, 4, 10, 16, 77, 106, 117, 119–133, 136, 140, 144, 159, 174–176, 182–184, 192–194, 195–197, 204, 236, 257, 263, 291–292, 307, 318, 322, 331
Krinovsky, G. 30, 272
Križanić, J. 268–269, 322
Krupp 207
Krushevan, P. A. 5–6, 141–142, 159, 231, 239
Krylov, V. A. 139
Kuechelbecker, W. 65, 75
Kugel, S. R. 135, 140, 179, 182–183, 293–294, 304–305, 322
Kuhlmann, Q. 26–27, 271
Kukolnik, N. V. 87, 283, 322
Kukolnik, P. V. 87, 283, 322
Kulisher, M. I. 152
Kulun, I. 108
Kunitz 263
Kunki, A. 27, 271, 326
Kuprin, A. I. 308, 310, 324
Kuritsyn, F. V. 25, 267, 320
Kuritsyn-Volk 25
Kuropatkin, A. N. 311
Kushner, B. 221, 281, 322
Kutler, N. N. 184
Kutuzov, M. I. 45, 50
Kuzmin, A. G. 227, 281, 287–288, 290, 297, 309, 322

Labzin, A. F. 56
Landau 126
Lanskoy, V. S. 56, 82
Lapin, Sh. 51
Laqueur, W. 305, 322
Lavrinovich, M. 276, 322
Lavrov, A. M. 143, 295, 321
Lefort, F. J. 28
Leisbovich, M. 88

Lenin, V. I. 205, 209, 228–229, 333, 335
Lermontov, M. Yu. 9, 65, 253, 277, 319
Lerner, O. M. 295, 322
Leskov, N. S. 176, 257, 263
Lesovsky, G. 122
Lessing, G. 31, 33, 139
Levandovsky, A. P. 201, 308, 322
Levitina, V. 280, 322
Levy, A. 168, 246
Liberg 126
Lichtenstein, E. I. 311
Ligne, Charles-Joseph de 39, 275, 318, 328
Likhachevsky, A. 291, 322
Lilienthal, M. 47
Lindau, P. 177
Lipman, Z. 198–199, 280, 322
Litvin, S. I. see Efron-Litvin 1, 134, 136, 139–140, 175, 182–184, 196, 238, 293–294, 307, 318, 322–323
Llull, R. 27
Lombroso, Cesare 229
Loris-Melikov, M. T. 252
Losev, S. 202, 309, 323
Lovell 29
Lozinsky, S. G. 201, 308, 323
Lurie, S. A. 220, 267
Lvov-Rogachevsky 263
Lyubarzhevskaya, Yu. O. see Narbut, Yu. O.
Lyubimov, L. 188, 306, 323
Lyutostansky, I. 195

Machiavelli, N. 7–8, 202, 237–238
Magnitsky, M. L. 60–64, 71, 279–280, 317, 323
Maikova, T. 323
Makarov, A. V. 270
Makov, L. S. 119
Malalas, John 18
Malevsky, F. 82

341

Malinovsky, N. 82
Malishevsky 55
Manasevich-Manuilov, I. F. 5, 211, 304
Manfred, A. 288, 291, 323
Mann, Yu. 177, 284, 323
Maor, I. 298, 323
Markevich, B. M. 1–2, 4, 10, 16, 106, 117–120, 137, 182, 257, 263, 290, 323
Markish, D. 202, 223, 290, 323
Markish, P. 202, 223, 290, 323
Markov 173
Marsden, W. 241
Marshak, S. Ya. 248, 311
Marshall, L. L. 7, 189, 242
Martov, Yu. O. 184, 217
Marx, Karl 228, 293
Mashovets, N. 309, 323
Meinecke 27
Melgunov, A. I. 37, 282, 327
Melnikov-Pechersky, P. I. 56, 270, 278, 323–324
Menaker, A. S. 276, 324
Mendel, Leo 36
Mendeleyev, D. I. 247
Mendelsohn 63, 209
Mendelsohns 256
Menshikov, A. D. 151, 239, 270
Menshikov, M. O. 151, 239, 270
Meshchersky, S. 30, 178, 292, 304, 323
Meshchersky, V. P. 30, 178, 292, 304, 323
Mezhetsky, M. P. 140, 294, 323
Mickiewicz, A. 66, 76–79, 82–86, 93–94, 246, 280, 283, 311, 323
Mieses, M. 285, 324
Mikhailo Olelkovich 24
Mikhailov, M. K. 82, 244, 278, 308–309, 324
Mikhailov, O. N. 82, 244, 278, 308–309, 324
Mikheleva, S. B. 308, 317, 324

Mikhoels, S. M. 202
Mildon, V. I. 248, 261
Miller 30
Miloradovich, M. A. 47
Milyukov, P. N. 15–16, 183–184, 237, 242, 265, 324
Minor, Z. 9, 43, 82, 132, 136, 196, 213, 217, 219–220, 223–224, 228–229, 233, 258, 309
Mironova, M. V. 276, 324
Mladanovitch 44
Mlodetsky 132, 252
Mochulsky, K. 298, 324
Molière 65
Monk, George 44, 54, 57, 140, 215, 266, 296, 321
Monomakh, Vladimir 18
Montesquieu, Charles-Louis 7, 29, 202, 237
Mordovtsev, D. L. 253
Mordvinov, N. S. 53, 91, 292, 324
Mordvinov, V. 53, 91, 292, 324
Morgulis 108
Motovilov, N. A. 161
Murat, J. 79
Muravyov, M. N. 84, 96, 123, 283, 324
Myasoyedov 212
Mérimée, P. 67
Müller von Hausen 241

Nabokov, V. D. 183–184
Nadezhdin, N. I. 89–90, 284, 323
Napoleon 7–8, 43–45, 47–49, 54–55, 74, 79–80, 87, 111, 202, 235, 238, 276, 295
Napoleon III 7, 202, 238
Narbut, Yu. Yu. 81
Narezhny, V. T. 71–72
Natanson, M. A. 184
Nechayev, S. G. 258
Nekrasov, S. 247, 308, 324
Nemetti 179
Nestor 265

INDEX

Nicholas I 42, 48, 52–53, 57, 60, 75, 92, 111, 114, 246, 251, 253, 255–256, 270, 276–277, 288, 324, 328, 330
Nicholas II 173, 201, 208, 240, 311
Nikitenko, A. V. 83–84, 283, 289, 292, 324
Nikitin, V. N. 313–314
Nikolai 33, 63, 119, 188, 208, 236, 240, 242, 244, 246–247, 250, 252, 261, 274, 276–277, 312, 327–328
Nikolayev, A. P. 312
Nikon 195, 240, 269
Nilus, D. A. 1, 4–7, 15, 106, 116, 142–145, 148–150, 152–159, 161–173, 183, 187, 194–195, 198–199, 203, 206–207, 220, 226–228, 231, 233–234, 237–240, 288, 290, 294, 297–302, 308, 310, 318, 320, 324, 332, 334
Nilus, S. A. 1, 4–7, 15, 106, 116, 142–145, 148–150, 152–159, 161–173, 183, 187, 194–195, 198–199, 203, 206–207, 220, 226–228, 231, 233–234, 237–240, 288, 290, 294, 297–302, 308, 310, 318, 320, 324, 332, 334
Noah 11, 24, 36
Nordau, M. 229, 243
Nordermann, C. 27
Norwich, William of 92
Notovitch, N. 237
Novikov, N. I. 26, 32–33, 61, 225–228, 273, 309, 328
Novikov, S. P. 26, 32–33, 61, 225–228, 273, 309, 328
Novitsky, V. F. 312
Novosiltsev, N. N. 50–51, 62, 80, 85–88, 283, 322

Odoyevsky 34
Oetinger, F. 170
Offenbach, J. 176
Ohryzko, J. P. 84–85, 94
Okreyts, S. S. 77, 261, 282, 324
Oksman, Yu.G. 282, 324
Olearius, A. 268–269
Olga, the Princess 221–222
Olsufyev, M. 30
Orlenev, P. N. 140
Orlova-Smirnova, M. V. 298, 324
Orlovski, A. O. 51–52
Orshansky, I. L. 35, 273, 276, 325
Osman-Bei, V. A. (Millingen, F.) 292, 294–295, 322, 325
Ostrovsky, A. N. 177, 218
Oudinot 47, 74
Ovsyaniko-Kulikovsky, D. N. 118
Ozerov, D. A. 149
Ozerova, E. A. 149

Paléologue, M. 275, 325
Panin, V. M. 53, 91, 93
Panteleimonov, B. 264, 314
Papus 208
Parchevsky, A. 82
Paskevich, I. F. 87
Paul the Apostle 148
Paul I 43–44, 121, 308, 317
Peretz, A. 36, 266, 325
Peretz, V. 36, 266, 325
Perovsky, L. A. 42, 88, 92
Peshekhonov, A. V. 184
Petazzi-Bordeaux 79
Peter I 26–29, 59, 111, 149, 214, 216, 270–271, 315, 323
Petrusenko, V. 202, 309, 323
Philippe, Nizier 208, 310
Philips, John 29
Philotheus 23, 215, 296
Photios 57
Picasso, P. 219, 229
Pigalev, V. A. 244, 278, 309, 325
Pikul, V. S. 184–185, 201–213, 227, 244, 304–310, 325
Pikulsky 44
Pinkus, B. 308

Pinsky, L. E. 213
Pipes, R. 223
Piramidov 139
Pirogov, N. I. 284, 303
Pisarev, D. I. 120
Pisemsky, A. F. 56, 116, 278
Plater-Sieberg 43
Platonov, S. F. 41–42, 135, 275, 293, 301, 319, 321, 330
Platov, M. I. 45
Plehve, V. K. 5, 224
Plevako, F. N. 302
Pobedonostsev, K. P. 135, 151, 263, 289
Poliakov, L. 1, 265, 325
Polikarpov, N. 47
Polivanov, A. A. 311–312
Polonskaya-Vasilenko, N. D. 274, 325
Polovtsev, L. A. 119
Pomerants, G. 213
Popov, B. M. 62
Porfiryev, I. Ya. 266–267, 325
Porudominsky, V. P. 89, 284–285, 325
Posnov, M. E. 297, 301, 326
Possart, Ernst von 177
Potapov, A. L. 105
Potyomkin, G. A.
Pranaitis, J. B. 42
Protopopov, V. I. 143, 296, 326
Przecławski, A. O. 16, 64, 143–144, 167, 236
Przecławski, J. E. 1, 10, 42, 51–54, 77–90, 96, 109–111
Purishkevich, V. M. 141, 206, 241
Pushkarev, S. G. 87, 282–283, 326
Pushkin, A. S. 2, 9–10, 35, 43, 65–67, 70, 74–78, 82, 85, 144, 146, 280–282, 296–297, 324, 326
Puslovsky, V. 82
Pypin, A. N. 28–29, 271–279, 326

Rabelais, F. 282

Rachkovsky, P. I. 5, 9, 149, 208, 237–238, 289, 299–304, 310, 321
Radek, K. 194
Radishchev, A. N. 33, 288, 309
Radziwiłł 237, 242
Rappoport, Sh. 224
Rasputin, G. 184–185, 201, 206, 208–212, 307, 334
Rathenau, W. 178, 241
Rauch, G. O. 181, 305, 326
Ravrebe, I. 271, 326
Razumovsky, A. K. 247
Reinach, Th. 242
Repnin, R. V. 61
Retcliffe 8, 143–144, 159, 235, 250, 294–296
Retcliffe, J. see Goedsche, H. 8, 143–144, 159, 235, 250, 294–296
Robespierre, M. 271, 315
Rochester-Kryzhanovskaya, V. I. 174–175, 184, 303, 326
Rodionov, I. A. 174, 187, 196–199, 307, 327
Roediger, A. F. 312
Rollin, H. 16, 265
Romanovsky, A. M. 48, 276, 327
Roosevelt, Theodore 7, 242
Rosenberg, A. 147, 203, 207, 241
Rosenblum, S. A. 305, 327
Roskes, D. 281, 327
Rossolimo, G. I. 210
Rossov, S. 143, 295–296, 327
Rothschilds 10, 139
Rozanov, V. V. 136, 293, 327
Rozov, N. N. 265–266, 301, 327
Rubinstein, N. G. 119, 212
Ruge 217, 224
Rumyantseva, V. S. 327
Ryabchinskaya 177
Ryabinin, I. 282, 327
Ryleyev, K. F. 54, 75, 80, 278, 282, 315
Ryvin, D. M. 277, 327
Rzewuski, A. 81–82

INDEX

S. P. 285, 327
Sadyk Pasha (Czajkowski) 246
Saint-Glin, J. de 60, 276, 327
Saint-Simon, C. H. de 217
Sakharov, B. V. 227–229
Saltykov-Shchedrin, M. E. 2, 217
Samarin, Yu.F. 96, 226, 286–287, 325, 327
Schabtai, Berel 36
Schiff 224
Schilder, N. K. 48, 276–277, 279–280, 283, 328
Schneersohn, Zalman 45
Schoenberg, A. 219
Scholem, G. 170
Schulsinger, J. 275, 328
Schwarz, I. E. 26, 106, 139, 273, 293, 307, 309, 328
Schwarz-Bostunitsch, G. 106, 139, 293
Schwarzband, S. M. 266, 328
Scott, Walter 67
Selyaninov 195, 203
Semeka, A. 31, 271, 273, 328
Semennikov, V. P. 273, 328
Semenyuk, V. 306, 328
Semevsky, V. I. 278, 328
Semyonov, S. V. 174, 302
Seraphim of Sarov 150, 161, 166, 207
Seraphim, Bishop 57, 150, 161, 166, 207
Seslavin, A. N. 46
Seyss-Inquart 207
Shabelskaya, E. A. 10, 174–185, 195–196, 198, 228, 240, 304–305, 312, 328, 334
Shabelskaya, M. A. 10, 174–185, 195–196, 198, 228, 240, 304–305, 312, 328, 334
Shabelsky-Bork, P. N. 184
Shafarevich, I. R. 193, 196, 204, 213–229, 281, 296, 306–310, 322, 328

Shafirov, P. P. 270, 304, 333–334
Shakespeare, William 16, 65
Sharapov, S. F. 135, 182, 305, 318
Shatskin, Ya. 277, 328
Shcheglovitov, I. G. 42
Shcherbachev, Yu.N. 271, 321
Shelgunov, N. V. 262, 313
Shick, A. 277, 328
Shifrin, N. Sh. 301, 328
Shishkov, A. S. 29, 49, 81
Shmakov, A. S. 106, 173–174, 195, 302, 329
Shmelyov, I. S. 310
Shragin, B. N. 213, 216, 223
Shtraletsky, I. Ya. 124
Shugurov, M. F. 35, 174, 273–274, 303, 329
Shuvalov, A. I. 29–30, 62
Simanovich, A. 212
Simeon of Polotsk 298
Sinyavsky, A. D. 213, 223
Sipyagin 208
Sirhan 202
Sirin, E. 158
Skabichevsky, A. M. 118, 290, 329
Skalkovsky, K. 292, 329
Skripitsyn, V. V. 89–90
Skvortsov 179
Sliozberg, G. B. 41, 236, 242, 275, 299, 329
Smirnov, A. 290, 329
Snetkovsky, P. 294, 329
Sobol 263
Sokolovskaya, T. 29, 272, 330
Sollogub, G. R. 43
Solomon, King 25, 66, 115, 123, 129, 148, 161, 167–169, 234
Soloukhin 330
Solovyov, V. S. 150–154, 166, 217, 264, 270, 298–299, 318, 323–324, 330–331, 334
Soltan, A. 79
Sonnenberg, Z. 49, 51, 54, 88

Speransky, M. M. 58, 60–63, 80, 112, 151, 280, 298, 323, 330
Speransky, V. 58, 60–63, 80, 112, 151, 280, 298, 323, 330
Stalin, J. V. 192, 200, 227–228, 231
Stanislawski, M. 330
Stashkevich, M. 310, 330
Staszic, A. 50–51
Stepanov, F. P. 154–155, 239, 281, 299
Stepanov, N. 154–155, 239, 281, 299
Sternberg, L. Ya. 41
Stieglitz, N. and A. 37, 274
Stoecker, A. 235
Stolypin, P. A. 173, 209–210, 231, 240, 296, 318
Strakhov, N. N. 100, 288, 330
Stribon 177
Stroganov, P. A. 86–87, 314
Stroyev 298, 330
Stryjkowski, M. 24
Subbotin, D. I. 311
Sue, E. 121
Sukhotin, A. N. 154–155, 239
Sulistrowski 43
Sumarokov, A. P. 30
Suvorin, A. S. 38, 127, 136, 140, 176, 178–179, 212, 252–253, 261, 303–304, 312, 330
Suvorov, A. V. 39, 60
Svatikov, S. 237
Sverdlov, Ya.M. 185
Sviridov, A. G. 29
Swedenborg, E. 304

Tatishchev, D. P. 54, 201, 309, 322
Taxil, L. 237
Tikhomirov, L. A. 136, 174, 195, 213, 217, 272, 303, 314, 330
Tikhomirov, N. S. 136, 174, 195, 213, 217, 272, 303, 314, 330
Timashev 83, 119
Tkachev, P. N. 258

Tolstoy, A. K. 2, 9, 57, 72, 118, 152, 163, 176, 240, 246, 253, 255, 257, 284, 330
Tolstoy, A. P. 2, 9, 57, 72, 118, 152, 163, 176, 240, 246, 253, 255, 257, 284, 330
Tolstoy, Leo N. 2, 9, 57, 72, 118, 152, 163, 176, 240, 246, 253, 255, 257, 284, 330
Tolstoy-Znamensky, D. N.
Tompakov 179
Toporov, V. N. 264
Tormasov 46
Toussenel, Alphonse 235
Tovbich, M. O. 120
Trotsky, Leon D. 185, 192, 202, 228
Tsetlin 52
Tsvibak, M 275, 330
Tur, K. I. 144
Turgenev, I. S. 2, 9, 313
Turkul, I. L. 42, 83, 92–93, 285, 326
Tutkevich, D. V. 136, 293, 330
Tyutchev, F. I. 83, 292

Umanets, S. I. 298, 331
Utkin, N. I. 57

Valuyev, P. A. 99–100, 292
Varlaam 48
Velichko, V. L. 150, 153, 298, 331
Veltman, A. F. 281, 327, 331
Vernadsky, G. V. 271–272, 331
Veselovsky, P. Ya. 270
Vilkin, E. 209
Vinaver, M. M. 181, 184, 261, 305, 331
Vinberg, F. V. 184–185, 195, 299, 305, 331
Vishnyak, M. A. 184, 305, 331
Vlasov, A. A. 243
Vodovozov, V. I. 120
Volkonsky, S. G. 45, 276, 331
Volkov, F. G. 30, 287–288, 331

INDEX

Volkov, V. K. 30, 287–288, 331
Volodimirova, N. A. 149
Volsky, K. 143, 292, 295, 331
Voltaire 29, 39, 219
Voronel, N. 223
Voronkov, I. A. 275, 331
Vorontsov, R. I. 30
Vrel, A. 31

Wagecir 27
Wagner, N. P. 4, 16, 236, 246–251, 253–259, 261–264, 313–314
Wagner, V. A. 4, 16, 236, 246–251, 253–259, 261–264, 313–314
Wagner, V. N. 4, 16, 236, 246–251, 253–259, 261–264, 313–314
Warner 170
Watrobska, H. 267, 320
Weber, M. 213, 217, 220, 310, 331
Weinryb, B. D. 305, 331
Weishaupt 63
Weizmann, Ch. 240
Wilson, V. 7, 242
Witte, S. Yu. 5, 151, 153, 178–183, 209–210, 224, 238, 240, 304–305, 321, 331
Wittgenstein, P. C. 45
Wolf, L. 25, 36, 120, 135, 137, 242
Wolf, Levi 25, 36, 120, 135, 137, 242
Wolfson, B. M. 311
Wrangel, P. N. 156
Wren, C. 28

Yagoda, G. 229
Yakimov, V. 291, 331
Yakovlev, N. N. 201, 244, 308, 331
Yanov, A, 213, 223
Yaroslav Vladimirovich 18
Yemelyanov, F. 52, 244
Yemelyanov, V. 52, 244
Yenukidze, A. S. 228
Yermolov, A. P. 45, 276, 331
Yoselevich, B. 39, 275
Yudenich, N. N. 312
Yudin, V. 269
Yuditsky, A. D. 284, 332
Yushchinsky, A. 42

Zabelin, I. E. 267, 332
Zagoskin, N. P. 269, 332
Zakharyin, G. A. 256
Zaluski 81
Zambry 19
Zamyslovsky, G. G. 302
Zaretsky, L. M. 292, 332
Zaslavsky 263, 332
Zayonchenok 50
Zayonchkovsky, P. A. 291, 312, 332
Zhelikhovskaya 312
Zhelyabov, A. I. 120, 137
Zhevakhov, N. D. 154–156, 159, 165, 187, 299–300, 301–302, 310, 332
Zhidovin, V. S. 269
Zhilinsky, Ya. G. 311
Zhukovsky 44
Zhuravlev, I. V. 80
Zimmerman 33
Zinovyev, G. E. 190
Zotov, N. M. 270
Zotov, V. 273, 332

www.ingramcontent.com/pod-product-compliance
Lightning Source LLC
Chambersburg PA
CBHW050123170426
43197CB00011B/1693